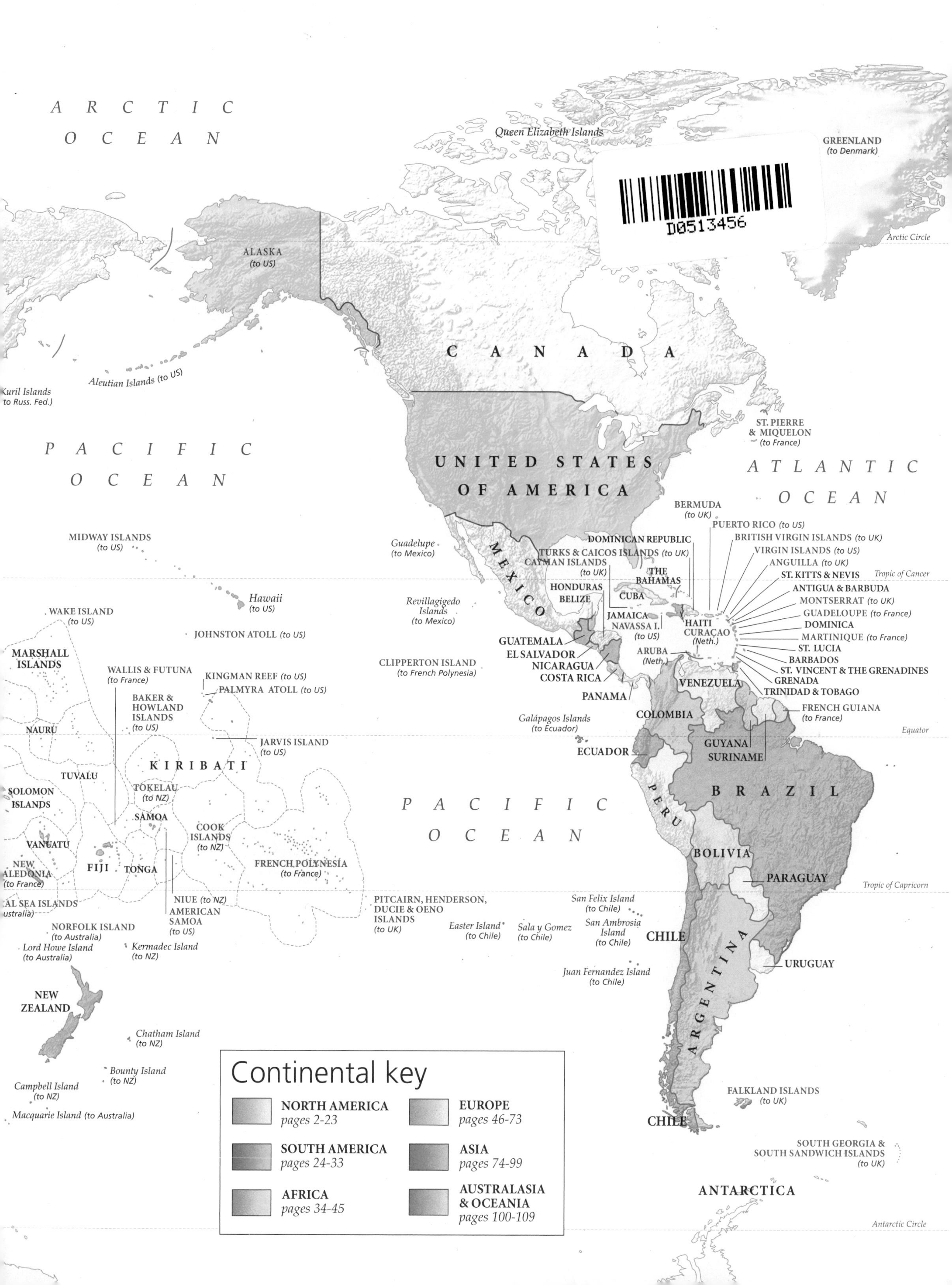

ARCTIC OCEAN
Queen Elizabeth Islands
GREENLAND (to Denmark)
Arctic Circle
ALASKA (to US)
CANADA
Aleutian Islands (to US)
Kuril Islands (to Russ. Fed.)
ST. PIERRE & MIQUELON (to France)
PACIFIC OCEAN
UNITED STATES OF AMERICA
ATLANTIC OCEAN
BERMUDA (to UK)
PUERTO RICO (to US)
BRITISH VIRGIN ISLANDS (to UK)
VIRGIN ISLANDS (to US)
ANGUILLA (to UK)
ST. KITTS & NEVIS
Tropic of Cancer
ANTIGUA & BARBUDA
MONTSERRAT (to UK)
GUADELOUPE (to France)
DOMINICA
MARTINIQUE (to France)
ST. LUCIA
BARBADOS
ST. VINCENT & THE GRENADINES
GRENADA
TRINIDAD & TOBAGO
DOMINICAN REPUBLIC
TURKS & CAICOS ISLANDS (to UK)
CAYMAN ISLANDS (to UK)
THE BAHAMAS
CUBA
HONDURAS
BELIZE
JAMAICA
NAVASSA I. (to US)
HAITI
CURAÇAO (Neth.)
ARUBA (Neth.)
MIDWAY ISLANDS (to US)
Guadelupe (to Mexico)
MEXICO
Hawaii (to US)
Revillagigedo Islands (to Mexico)
WAKE ISLAND (to US)
JOHNSTON ATOLL (to US)
GUATEMALA
EL SALVADOR
NICARAGUA
COSTA RICA
PANAMA
VENEZUELA
MARSHALL ISLANDS
WALLIS & FUTUNA (to France)
KINGMAN REEF (to US)
PALMYRA ATOLL (to US)
CLIPPERTON ISLAND (to French Polynesia)
BAKER & HOWLAND ISLANDS (to US)
FRENCH GUIANA (to France)
COLOMBIA
NAURU
Galápagos Islands (to Ecuador)
Equator
JARVIS ISLAND (to US)
ECUADOR
GUYANA
SURINAME
KIRIBATI
TUVALU
SOLOMON ISLANDS
TOKELAU (to NZ)
PERU
BRAZIL
SAMOA
COOK ISLANDS (to NZ)
VANUATU
FIJI
TONGA
NEW CALEDONIA (to France)
FRENCH POLYNESIA (to France)
BOLIVIA
PARAGUAY
Tropic of Capricorn
CORAL SEA ISLANDS (to Australia)
NIUE (to NZ)
AMERICAN SAMOA (to US)
PITCAIRN, HENDERSON, DUCIE & OENO ISLANDS (to UK)
San Felix Island (to Chile)
Easter Island (to Chile)
Sala y Gomez (to Chile)
San Ambrosia Island (to Chile)
NORFOLK ISLAND (to Australia)
Lord Howe Island (to Australia)
Kermadec Island (to NZ)
CHILE
ARGENTINA
URUGUAY
Juan Fernandez Island (to Chile)
NEW ZEALAND
Chatham Island (to NZ)
Bounty Island (to NZ)
Campbell Island (to NZ)
Macquarie Island (to Australia)
FALKLAND ISLANDS (to UK)
CHILE
SOUTH GEORGIA & SOUTH SANDWICH ISLANDS (to UK)
ANTARCTICA
Antarctic Circle
Continental key
NORTH AMERICA pages 2-23
EUROPE pages 46-73
SOUTH AMERICA pages 24-33
ASIA pages 74-99
AFRICA pages 34-45
AUSTRALASIA & OCEANIA pages 100-109

Children's Illustrated World Atlas

Consultant
Dr Kathleen Baker
Senior Lecturer in Geography, King's College London (retired)
Senior Visiting Fellow, London South Bank University

Written by
Simon Adams • Mary Atkinson • Sarah Phillips • John Woodward

A Dorling Kindersley Book

DK | Penguin Random House

THIS EDITION

DK DELHI
Senior editor Rupa Rao
Editor Neha Ruth Samuel
Jacket designer Dhirendra Singh
Jackets editorial coordinator Priyanka Sharma
Senior DTP designer Harish Aggarwal
DTP designer Jaypal Chauhan
Managing jackets editor Sreshtha Bhattacharya
Pre-production manager Balwant Singh
Production manager Pankaj Sharma
Managing editor Kingshuk Ghoshal
Managing art editor Govind Mittal

DK LONDON
Senior editor Anna Streiffert Limerick
Senior art editor Spencer Holbrook
Senior cartographic editor Simon Mumford
Senior jacket designer Mark Cavanagh
Jacket editor Claire Gell
Jacket design development manager Sophia MTT
Producer, pre-production Andy Hilliard
Producer Gary Batchelor
Managing editor Francesca Baines
Managing art editor Philip Letsu
Publisher Andrew Macintyre
Associate publishing director Liz Wheeler
Art director Karen Self
Design director Philip Ormerod
Publishing director Jonathan Metcalf

FIRST EDITION

Project editors Lucy Hurst, Sadie Smith, Shaila Awan, Amber Tokeley
Art editors Joe Conneally, Sheila Collins, Rebecca Johns, Simon Oon, Andrew Nash
Senior editor Fran Jones
Senior art editor Floyd Sayers
Managing editor Andrew Macintyre
Managing art editor Jane Thomas
Picture research Carolyn Clerkin, Brenda Clynch
DK Pictures Sarah Mills
Production Jenny Jacoby
DTP designer Siu Yin Ho
Senior cartographic editor Simon Mumford
Cartographer Ed Merritt
Digital Cartography Encompass Graphics Limited
Satellite images Rob Stokes
3D globes Planetary Visions Ltd., London

This edition published in 2017
First published in Great Britain in 2003 by
Dorling Kindersley Limited
80 Strand, London WC2R 0RL

10 9 8 7 6 5 4 3 2 1
001 – 305057 – July/2017

A CIP catalogue record for this book is available from the British Library.

ISBN: 978-0-2412-9691-2

Printed and bound in Hong Kong

Contents

Active Planet

EARTH IS A DYNAMIC PLANET that is always changing its form. Heat generated by nuclear reactions deep below the surface creates hugely powerful currents that keep Earth's rocks on the move, triggering earthquakes and volcanic eruptions. Meanwhile, solar energy striking the planet in different ways creates currents in the air, driving the atmospheric turmoil of the weather. This changes with the seasons and from place to place, creating an enormous range of climates and habitats for the most dynamic element of all – life.

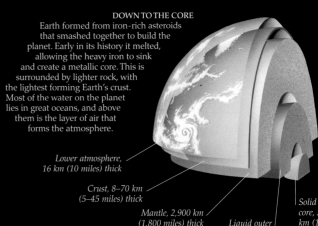

DOWN TO THE CORE
Earth formed from iron-rich asteroids that smashed together to build the planet. Early in its history it melted, allowing the heavy iron to sink and create a metallic core. This is surrounded by lighter rock, with the lightest forming Earth's crust. Most of the water on the planet lies in great oceans, and above them is the layer of air that forms the atmosphere.

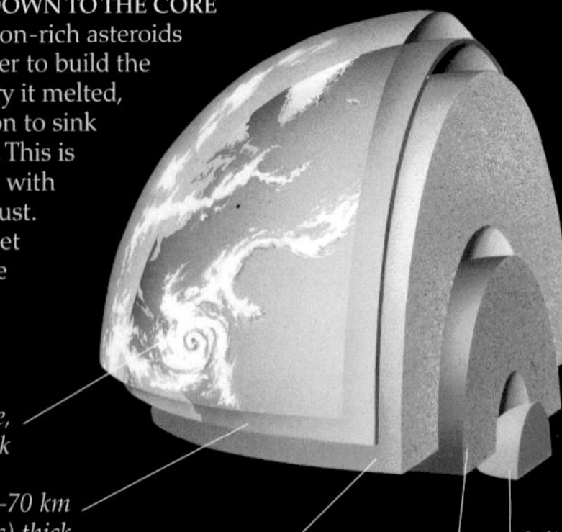
Lower atmosphere, 16 km (10 miles) thick
Crust, 8–70 km (5–45 miles) thick
Mantle, 2,900 km (1,800 miles) thick
Liquid outer core, 2,250 km (1,400 miles) thick
Solid inner core, 2,440 km (1,515 miles) across

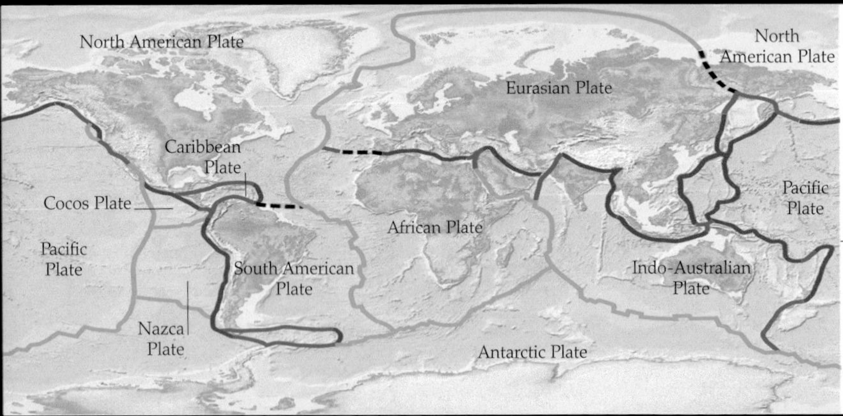
North American Plate
North American Plate
Eurasian Plate
Caribbean Plate
Cocos Plate
Pacific Plate
African Plate
Pacific Plate
South American Plate
Indo-Australian Plate
Nazca Plate
Antarctic Plate

THE PLATES OF EARTH'S CRUST
Heat generated deep within the planet creates currents in the mobile mantle rock beneath the crust. These currents drag some sections of the cool, brittle crust apart while pushing other parts together, fracturing the crust into separate plates. The biggest of these span oceans and continents, but there are many smaller plates. At their boundaries the plates may be diverging (pulling apart), converging (pushing together), or sliding past each other at transform faults.

Key to map
- Transform fault
- Divergent boundary
- Uncertain boundary
- Convergent boundary

WHERE MOVING PLATES MEET
The boundaries between the plates are volcanic earthquake zones. The plates move very slowly, pulling apart at divergent boundaries. This allows hot rock below to melt, erupt, and cool to form new crust – especially at the spreading rifts that form mid-ocean ridges. Meanwhile at convergent boundaries, one plate slides beneath another, pushing up mountain ranges and making volcanoes erupt. Other volcanoes erupt over hot spots in the mantle below the crust.

1. Continental crust, much thicker than oceanic crust
2. Broad basin formed near uplifted area
3. Ancient converging boundary, now inactive
4. Mountains created when plate boundary was active
5. Oceanic crust formed from heavy basalt rock
6. Upper mantle, mainly solid but very hot
7. Mantle, solid but mobile owing to heat currents
8. Spreading rift forming a mid-ocean ridge
9. Hot-spot volcano erupting over mantle plume
10. Ocean trench marking convergent plate boundary
11. Volcano erupting over convergent boundary
12. Earthquake zone – one plate grinding under another
13. Plates pulling apart, creating a rift valley

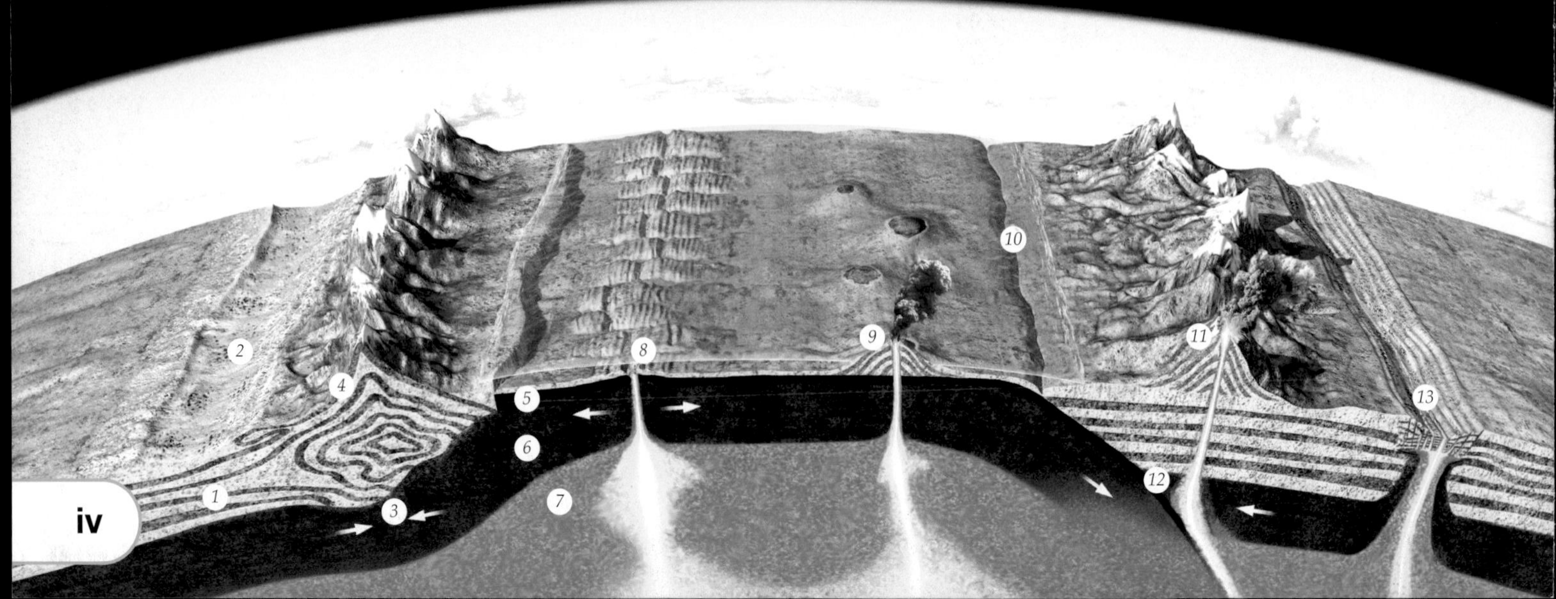
1
2
3
4
5
6
7
8
9
10
11
12
13

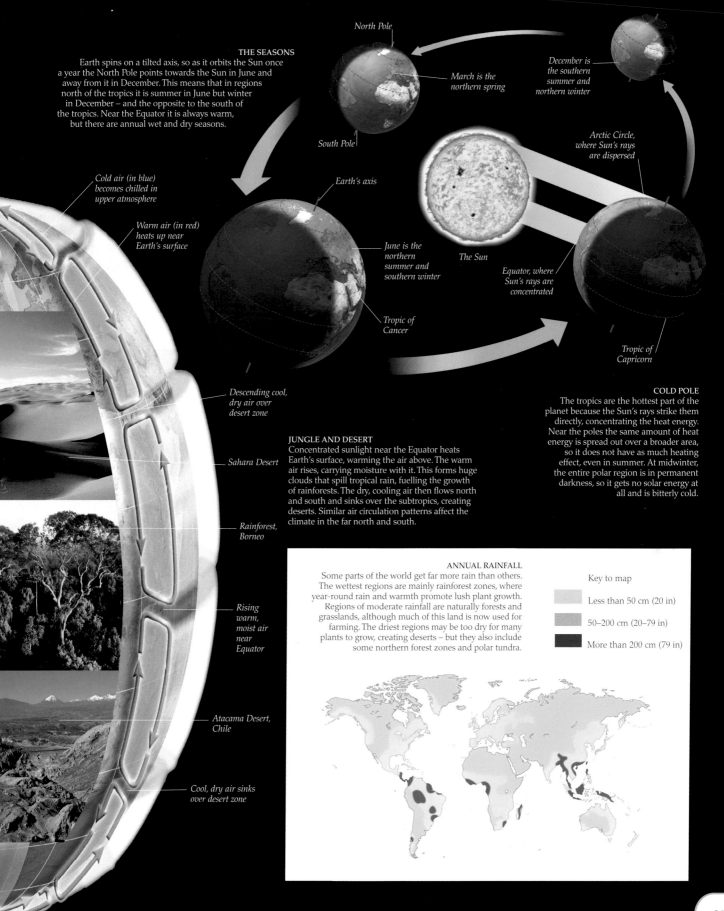

THE SEASONS

Earth spins on a tilted axis, so as it orbits the Sun once a year the North Pole points towards the Sun in June and away from it in December. This means that in regions north of the tropics it is summer in June but winter in December – and the opposite to the south of the tropics. Near the Equator it is always warm, but there are annual wet and dry seasons.

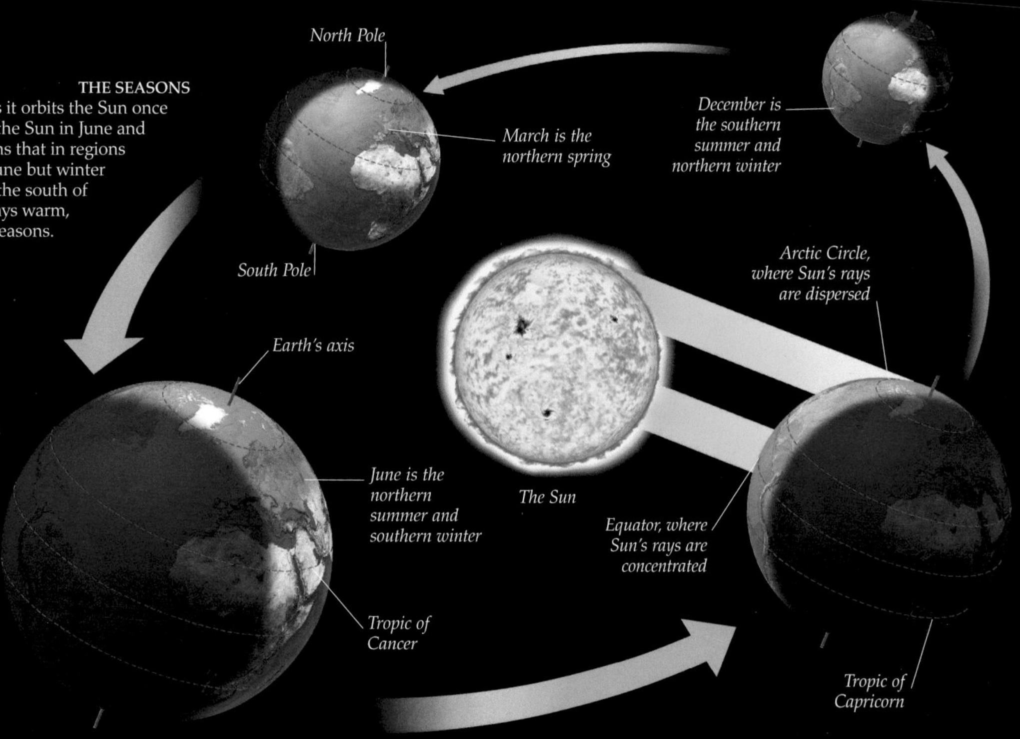
North Pole
March is the northern spring
South Pole
December is the southern summer and northern winter
Arctic Circle, where Sun's rays are dispersed
Earth's axis
June is the northern summer and southern winter
The Sun
Equator, where Sun's rays are concentrated
Tropic of Cancer
Tropic of Capricorn

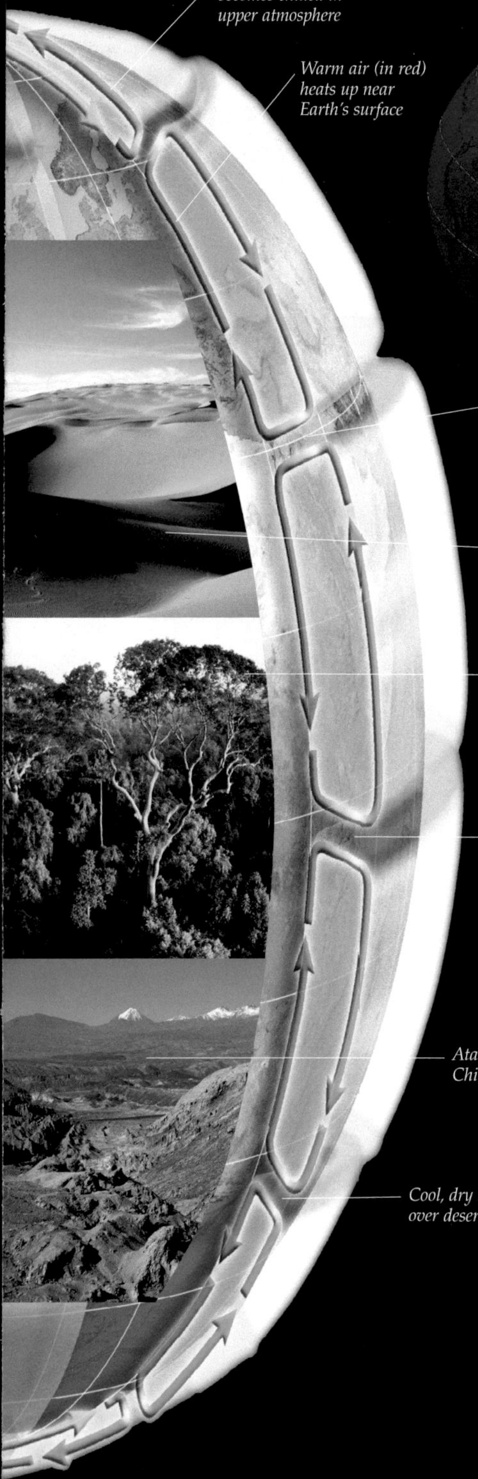
Cold air (in blue) becomes chilled in upper atmosphere
Warm air (in red) heats up near Earth's surface
Descending cool, dry air over desert zone
Sahara Desert
Rainforest, Borneo
Rising warm, moist air near Equator
Atacama Desert, Chile
Cool, dry air sinks over desert zone

JUNGLE AND DESERT

Concentrated sunlight near the Equator heats Earth's surface, warming the air above. The warm air rises, carrying moisture with it. This forms huge clouds that spill tropical rain, fuelling the growth of rainforests. The dry, cooling air then flows north and south and sinks over the subtropics, creating deserts. Similar air circulation patterns affect the climate in the far north and south.

COLD POLE

The tropics are the hottest part of the planet because the Sun's rays strike them directly, concentrating the heat energy. Near the poles the same amount of heat energy is spread out over a broader area, so it does not have as much heating effect, even in summer. At midwinter, the entire polar region is in permanent darkness, so it gets no solar energy at all and is bitterly cold.

ANNUAL RAINFALL

Some parts of the world get far more rain than others. The wettest regions are mainly rainforest zones, where year-round rain and warmth promote lush plant growth. Regions of moderate rainfall are naturally forests and grasslands, although much of this land is now used for farming. The driest regions may be too dry for many plants to grow, creating deserts – but they also include some northern forest zones and polar tundra.

Key to map

- Less than 50 cm (20 in)
- 50–200 cm (20–79 in)
- More than 200 cm (79 in)

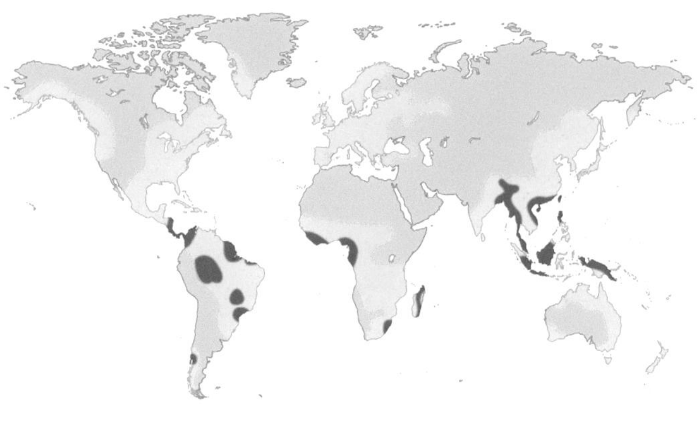

Planet People

THE NUMBER OF PEOPLE ON THE PLANET has quadrupled since 1900. Much of this growth has taken place in the developing world, which is now home to more than 80 per cent of the population. Many of these people are very poor and do not experience the living conditions that most citizens of the developed world take for granted. This is changing, however, especially in nations such as China, India, and Brazil. Here, new technology and international trade are fuelling rapid economic growth that is transforming how people live. But as more of the planet's people demand more of its scarce resources, there may be some difficult challenges ahead.

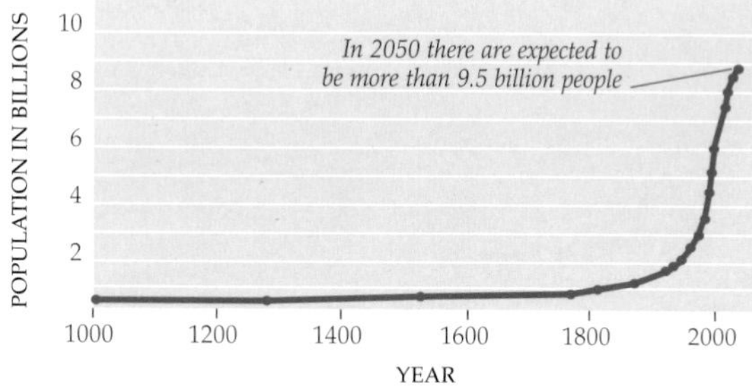
POPULATION IN BILLIONS
10
8
6
4
2
1000
1200
1400
1600
1800
2000
YEAR
In 2050 there are expected to be more than 9.5 billion people

POPULATION INCREASE
For centuries, the number of people on the planet stayed the same, at roughly 300 million. But since the 1750s, better living conditions and healthcare have allowed more babies to survive, causing a population explosion. Since 1950, the population has soared from 2.5 billion to nearly 7.5 billion today. It will keep growing, but probably not quite so fast.

POPULATION DENSITY
On this map the area of each part of the world is adjusted to reflect the number of people who live there. For example, Japan's population of 127 million is far bigger than that of Australia, with 23 million, so it is shown much larger here despite being a smaller country. More people live in Nigeria – 186 million – than in the whole of Russia. But the nations with the biggest populations by far are India and China, each with far more than 1 billion citizens.

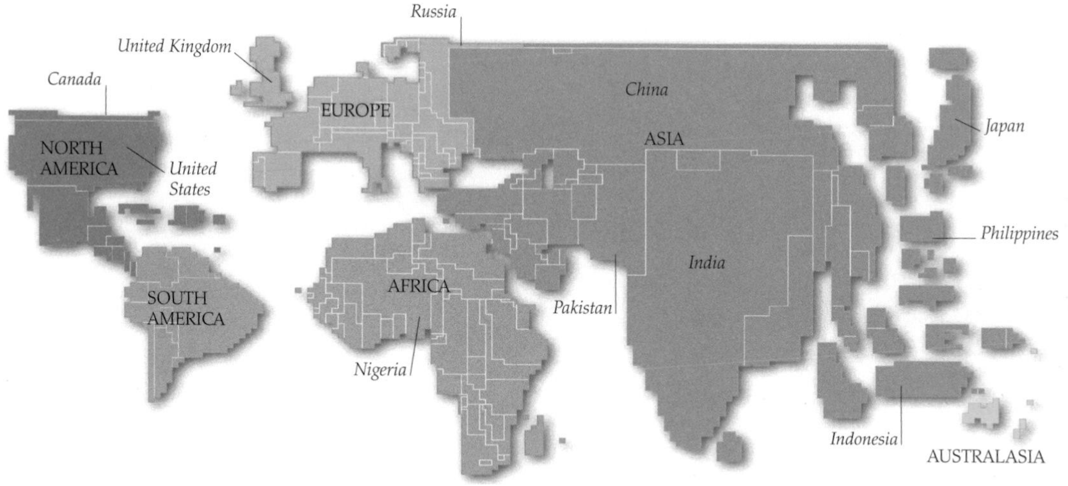
Russia
United Kingdom
Canada
EUROPE
China
ASIA
Japan
NORTH AMERICA
United States
Philippines
India
AFRICA
Pakistan
SOUTH AMERICA
Nigeria
Indonesia
AUSTRALASIA

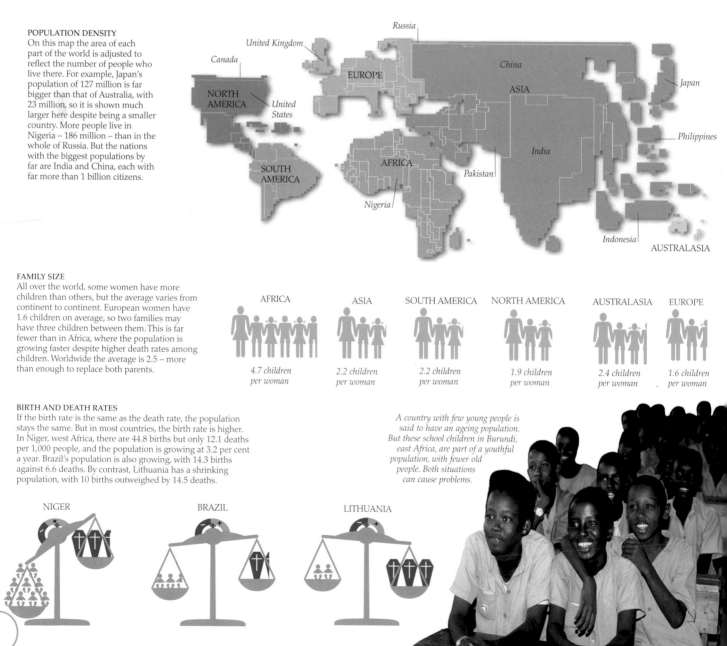

FAMILY SIZE
All over the world, some women have more children than others, but the average varies from continent to continent. European women have 1.6 children on average, so two families may have three children between them. This is far fewer than in Africa, where the population is growing faster despite higher death rates among children. Worldwide the average is 2.5 – more than enough to replace both parents.

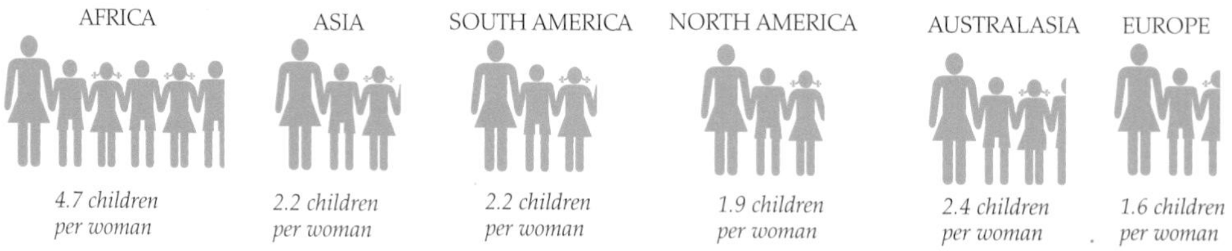
AFRICA
4.7 children per woman
ASIA
2.2 children per woman
SOUTH AMERICA
2.2 children per woman
NORTH AMERICA
1.9 children per woman
AUSTRALASIA
2.4 children per woman
EUROPE
1.6 children per woman

BIRTH AND DEATH RATES
If the birth rate is the same as the death rate, the population stays the same. But in most countries, the birth rate is higher. In Niger, west Africa, there are 44.8 births but only 12.1 deaths per 1,000 people, and the population is growing at 3.2 per cent a year. Brazil's population is also growing, with 14.3 births against 6.6 deaths. By contrast, Lithuania has a shrinking population, with 10 births outweighed by 14.5 deaths.

NIGER
BRAZIL
LITHUANIA

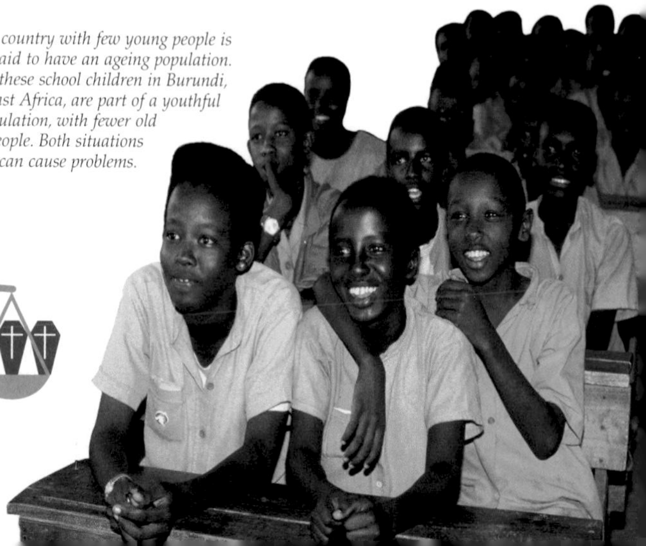

A country with few young people is said to have an ageing population. But these school children in Burundi, east Africa, are part of a youthful population, with fewer old people. Both situations can cause problems.

CITY POPULATIONS

As populations grow, people tend to move from the country to a city to find work. Today, one-third of the world's people live in cities, which grow bigger every year. Some are colossal, like Tokyo – the largest city in Asia. The other cities shown here are the most populous on each continent. They are vibrant centres of civilization, but some cities are fringed by sprawling shantytowns, where poor people live in makeshift shacks with no proper services such as clean water.

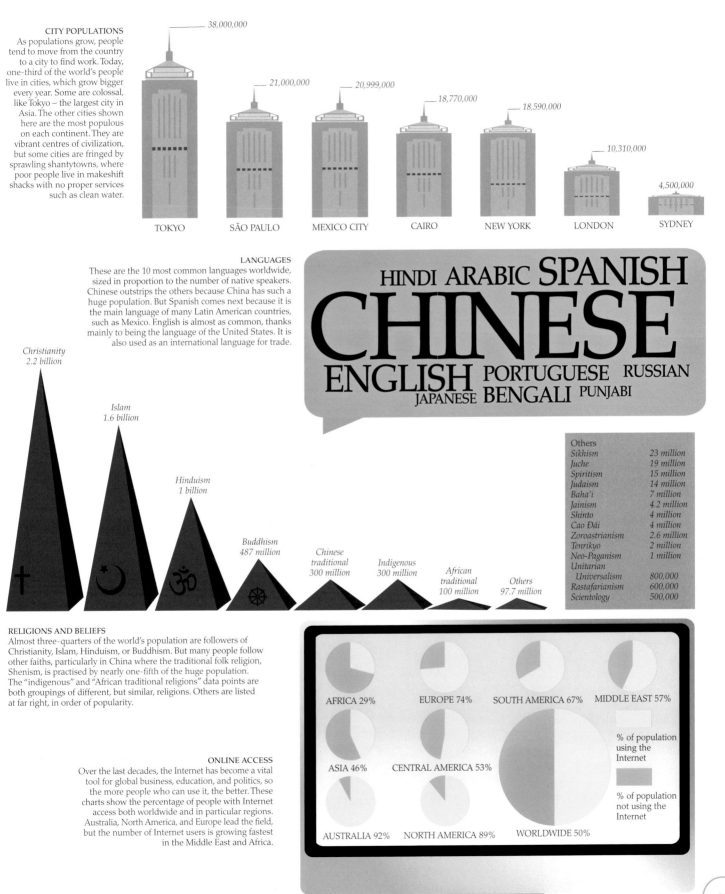

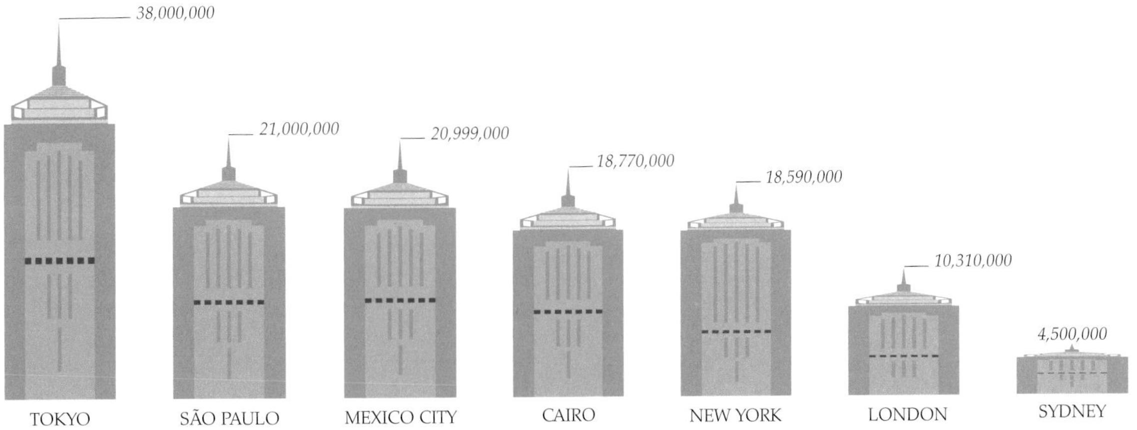
38,000,000
21,000,000
20,999,000
18,770,000
18,590,000
10,310,000
4,500,000
TOKYO
SÃO PAULO
MEXICO CITY
CAIRO
NEW YORK
LONDON
SYDNEY

LANGUAGES

These are the 10 most common languages worldwide, sized in proportion to the number of native speakers. Chinese outstrips the others because China has such a huge population. But Spanish comes next because it is the main language of many Latin American countries, such as Mexico. English is almost as common, thanks mainly to being the language of the United States. It is also used as an international language for trade.

HINDI ARABIC SPANISH
CHINESE
ENGLISH PORTUGUESE RUSSIAN
JAPANESE BENGALI PUNJABI

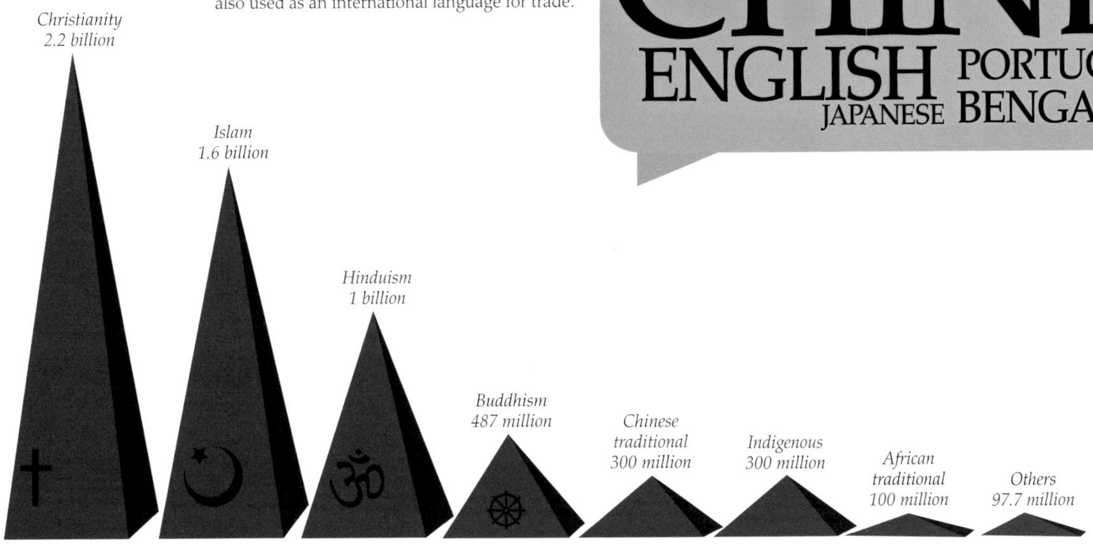
Christianity
2.2 billion
Islam
1.6 billion
Hinduism
1 billion
Buddhism
487 million
Chinese
traditional
300 million
Indigenous
300 million
African
traditional
100 million
Others
97.7 million

Others	
Sikhism	*23 million*
Juche	*19 million*
Spiritism	*15 million*
Judaism	*14 million*
Baha'i	*7 million*
Jainism	*4.2 million*
Shinto	*4 million*
Cao Đài	*4 million*
Zoroastrianism	*2.6 million*
Tenrikyo	*2 million*
Neo-Paganism	*1 million*
Unitarian Universalism	*800,000*
Rastafarianism	*600,000*
Scientology	*500,000*

RELIGIONS AND BELIEFS

Almost three-quarters of the world's population are followers of Christianity, Islam, Hinduism, or Buddhism. But many people follow other faiths, particularly in China where the traditional folk religion, Shenism, is practised by nearly one-fifth of the huge population. The "indigenous" and "African traditional religions" data points are both groupings of different, but similar, religions. Others are listed at far right, in order of popularity.

ONLINE ACCESS

Over the last decades, the Internet has become a vital tool for global business, education, and politics, so the more people who can use it, the better. These charts show the percentage of people with Internet access both worldwide and in particular regions. Australia, North America, and Europe lead the field, but the number of Internet users is growing fastest in the Middle East and Africa.

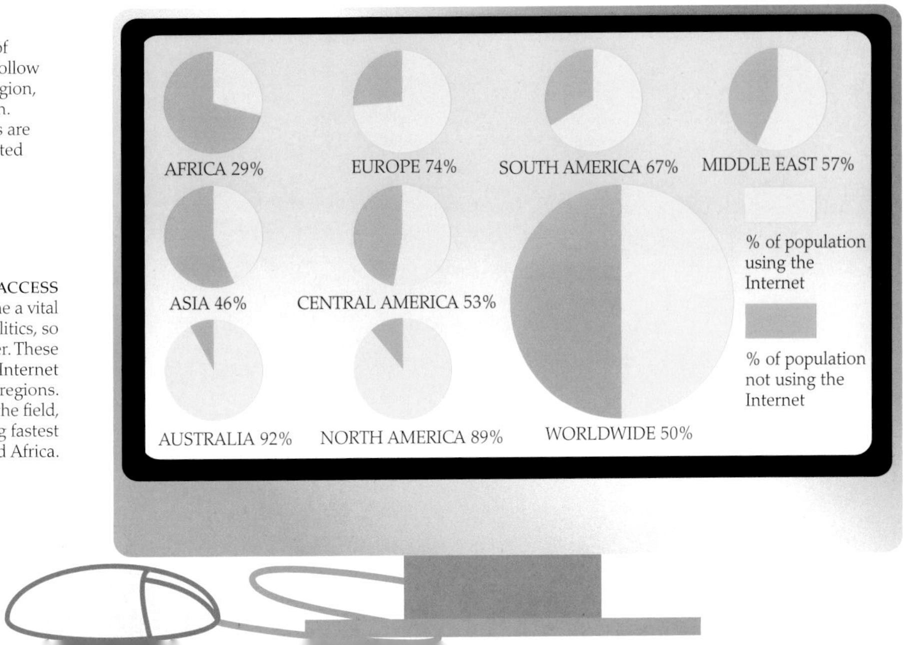
AFRICA 29%
EUROPE 74%
SOUTH AMERICA 67%
MIDDLE EAST 57%
ASIA 46%
CENTRAL AMERICA 53%
AUSTRALIA 92%
NORTH AMERICA 89%
WORLDWIDE 50%
% of population using the Internet
% of population not using the Internet

» Planet People

WEALTH
A country's wealth is often measured in terms of the money it earns in a year divided by its number of inhabitants. This is called its Gross Domestic Product (GDP) per capita. Both Norway and Qatar make lots of money from exporting oil and gas, and since they have small populations their GDP per capita are very high. Burundi in east Africa has only one-twentyfifth of the income of Qatar divided between five times as many people, so its GDP per capita is very low.

Burundi $277
Bolivia $3,076
Lithuania $14,147
Japan $32,477
Canada $43,248
Qatar $73,653
Norway $74,400

BUSIEST AIRPORTS
Air travel has expanded hugely since the 1950s, when international air travel was a luxury enjoyed by a few wealthy people known as the "jet set". Today, flying is often the most economical way to travel, as well as the quickest. This is reflected in the vast number of passengers who pass through the world's airports as they travel for business or pleasure. The world's busiest airport is Hartsfield-Jackson International Airport in Atlanta, USA, with more than 100 million people arriving and departing each year. The graphics below show the busiest airport in each continent, and number of passengers.

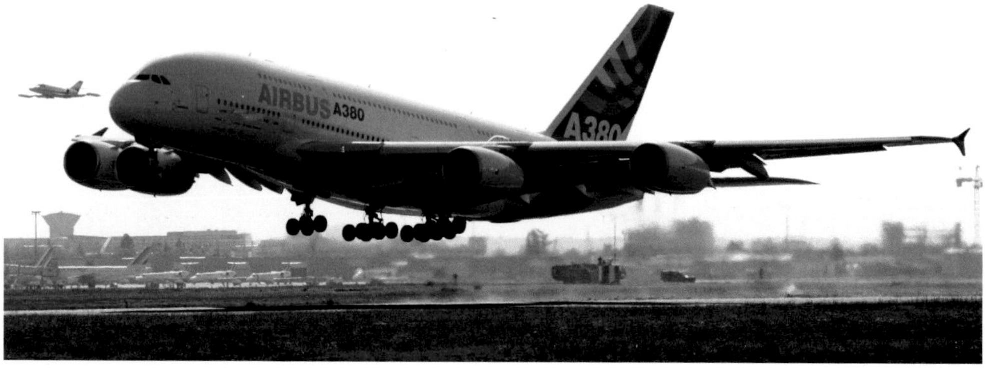
AIRBUS A380
A380

AIRBUS A380
The growth in air travel has led to the development of giant airliners such as the Airbus A380. When it entered service in 2007, this was the world's largest passenger plane, capable of carrying up to 853 people.

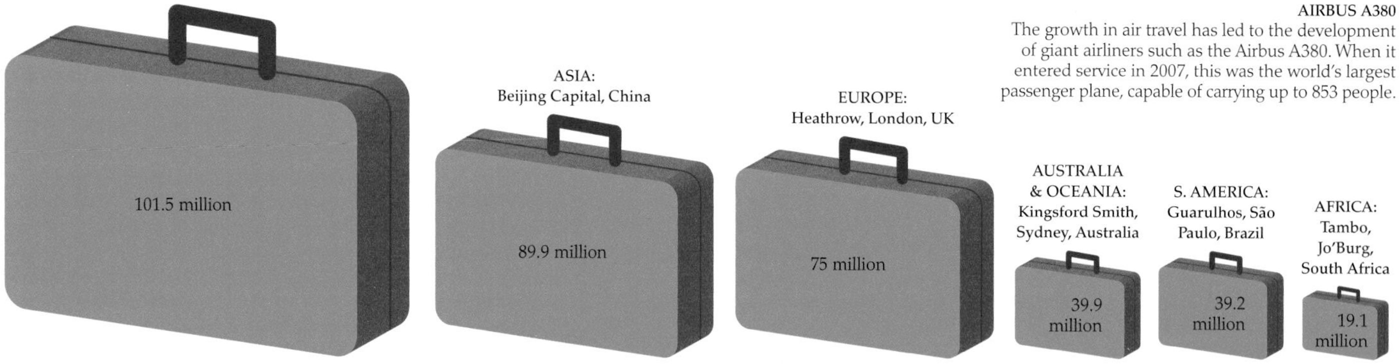
N. AMERICA: Hartsfield-Jackson, Atlanta, USA
101.5 million
ASIA: Beijing Capital, China
89.9 million
EUROPE: Heathrow, London, UK
75 million
AUSTRALIA & OCEANIA: Kingsford Smith, Sydney, Australia
39.9 million
S. AMERICA: Guarulhos, São Paulo, Brazil
39.2 million
AFRICA: Tambo, Jo'Burg, South Africa
19.1 million

TRADE
Although air freight is an important element of international trade, about 90 per cent of cargo by weight is transported by sea. Altogether, this adds up to around 10 billion tonnes of freight. Much of this is transported in containers, carried by more than 5,000 container ships. The busiest shipping routes link Europe and North America with the Middle East and Far East, with ports such as Singapore, Shanghai, Dubai, and Rotterdam handling most of the trade.

Traffic in millions of tonnes

- 400+
- 300–400
- 200–300
- 100–200
- 20–100
- 10–20
- 5–10

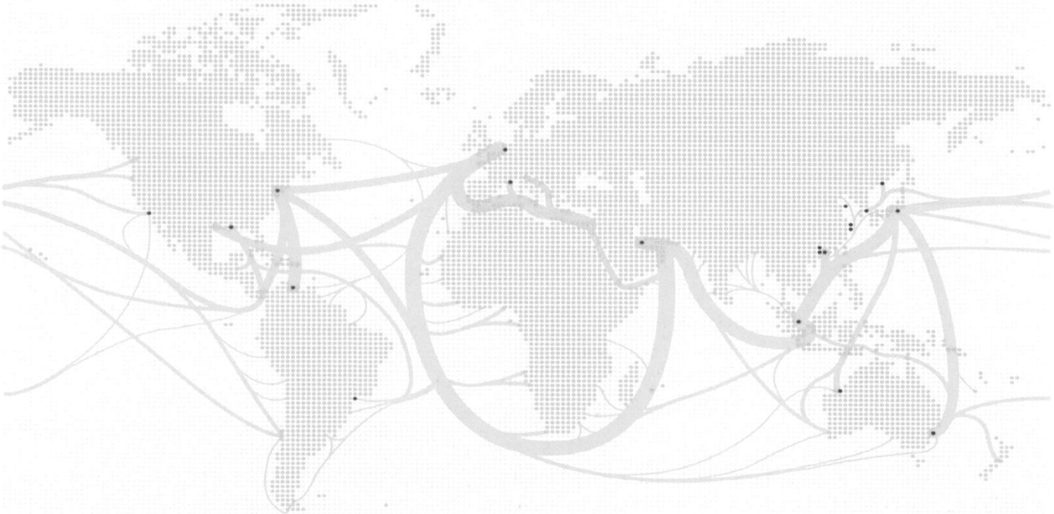

Mapping the World

ABOUT THE ATLAS
This atlas is divided into six continental sections – North America, South America, Africa, Europe, Asia, and Australasia and Oceania. Each country, or group of countries, then has its own map that shows cities, towns, and main geographical features such as rivers, lakes, and mountain ranges. Photographs and text provide detailed information about life in that country – its people, traditions, politics, and economy. Each continental section has a different colour border to help you locate that section. There is also a gazetteer and an index to help you access information.

MAP LOCATOR
This map shows, in red, the location of each country, part of a country, or group of countries in relation to the whole planet. There is a locator for each map in the book.

MAP COLOURS
The colours shown on the maps are built up from numerous satellite photographs and reflect the true colours of the land, averaged over the seasons. Certain colours give clues to what the land is like – whether it is forested or farmland, mountains or desert.

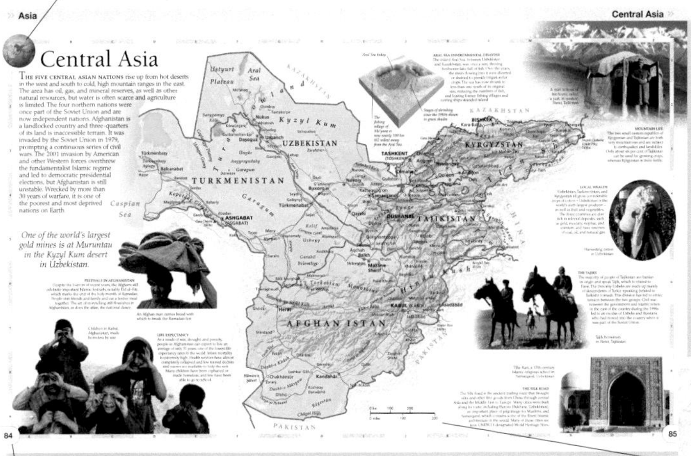

Land appearing sandy tends to be desert, semi-desert, or scrub.

Mountainous desert looks like this, with shadows on the sandy background colour.

Pale green is usually grassland or crop land.

Darker greens usually indicate wooded land or pasture.

White shows land under permanent cover by snow and ice.

FOREIGN NAMES
Features on the maps are generally labelled in the language of that country. For example, it would be:
Lake on English-speaking countries
Lago on Spanish-speaking countries
Lac on French-speaking countries
However, if a feature is well-known or mentioned in the main text on the page, it will appear there in English so that readers can find it easily.

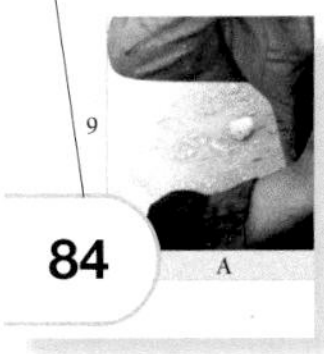

USING THE GRID REFERENCES
The letters and numbers around the outside of the page form a grid to help you find places on the map. For example, to find Kabul, look up its name in the gazetteer (see pp.112–133), and you'll find the reference 85 J7. The first number is the page, the letter and number refer to the square made by following up or down from J and across from 7 to form J7.

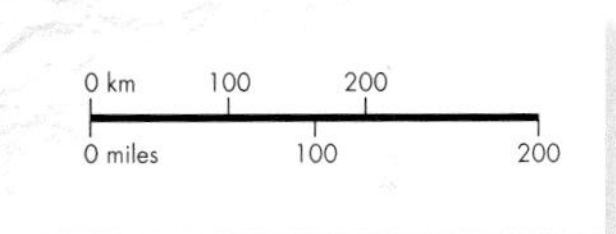

SCALE
Each map features a scale that shows how distances on the map relate to kilometres and miles. The scale guide can be used to see how big a country is. Not all maps in the book are drawn to the same scale.

KEY TO MAP SYMBOLS

Borders
- International border: Border between countries which is mutually recognized.
- State border: Border used in some large countries to show internal divisions.
- Disputed border: Border used in practice, but not mutually agreed between two countries.
- Claimed border: Border which is not mutually recognized – where territory belonging to one country is claimed by another.
- Ceasefire line
- Undefined boundary

Physical Features
- Mountain
- Depression
- Volcano
- Pass/Tunnel

Drainage Features
- Major river
- Minor river
- Seasonal river
- Dam
- Canal
- Waterfall
- Seasonal lake

Miscellaneous Features
- Site of interest
- Ancient wall

Communications
- Highway
- Major road
- Minor road
- Rail
- Airport

Towns & Cities
- More than 500,000
- 100,000 – 500,000
- 50,000 – 100,000
- Less than 50,000
- National capital
- Internal administrative capital
- Polar research station

Latitude & Longitude
- Equator
- Tropics/Circles

Names
REGIONS
- FRANCE — Country
- JERSEY (British Crown Dependency) — Dependent territory
- KANSAS — Administrative region
- Dordogne — Cultural region

TOWNS & CITIES
- PARIS — National capital
- SAN JUAN — Dependent territory capital city
- Seattle, Limón, Genk, San José — Other towns & cities

Names *continued*
PHYSICAL
- *Andes*, *Ardennes* — Landscape features
- *Balearic Islands* — Island group
- *Majorca* — Island
- *Lake Baikal* — Lake/River /Canal
- PACIFIC OCEAN, *Gulf of Mexico*, *Bay of Campeche* — Sea features
- *Chile Rise* — Undersea feature

OTHER FEATURES
- *Tropic of Cancer* — Graticule text

NORTH AMERICA

The North American continent extends from the frozen wastes of Arctic Canada to the Caribbean islands and the tropical jungles of Panama. It is dominated politically by the United States, the richest nation on Earth, yet life in countries such as Mexico and Nicaragua is still a struggle. The data below is arranged in order of each nation's size.

Canada
9,984,670 sq km
3,855,103 sq miles
35,363,000
Ottawa
English, French, Punjabi, Italian, Spanish, German, Cantonese, Tagalog, Arabic, Inuktitut, Cree

Mexico
1,964,375 sq km
758,449 sq miles
123,167,000
Mexico City
Spanish, Nahuatl, Mayan, Zapotec, Mixtec, Otomi, Totonac, Tzotzil, Tzeltal

Honduras
112,090 sq km
43,278 sq miles
8,893,000
Tegucigalpa
Spanish, Garífuna (Carib), English Creole

The warm seas and glorious beaches of the Caribbean make islands like St Lucia magnets for tourists. The wealth they bring is vital to the local economy.

United States of America
9,833,517 sq km
3,796,742 sq miles
323,996,000
Washington, DC
English, Spanish, Chinese, French, German, Tagalog, Vietnamese, Italian, Korean, Russian, Polish

Nicaragua
130,370 sq km
50,336 sq miles
5,967,000
Managua
Spanish, English Creole, Miskito

Cuba
110,860 sq km
42,803 sq miles
11,180,000
Havana
Spanish

Panama
75,420 sq km
29,120 sq miles
3,705,000
Panama City
English Creole, Spanish, Amerindian languages, Chibchan languages

Dominican Republic
48,670 sq km
18,792 sq miles
10,607,000
Santo Domingo
Spanish, French Creole

Guatemala
108,889 sq km
42,042 sq miles
15,190,000
Guatemala City
Quiché, Mam, Kakchiquel, Kekchí, Spanish

Haiti
27,750 sq km
10,714 sq miles
10,486,000
Port-au-Prince
French Creole, French

The Statue of Liberty in New York Harbour has long been a potent symbol of freedom, especially for those arriving here by ship to seek a new life.

Costa Rica
51,100 sq km
19,730 sq miles
4,873,000
San José
Spanish, English Creole, Bribri, Cabecar

Belize
22,966 sq km
8,867 sq miles
353,800
Belmopan
English Creole, Spanish, English, Mayan, Garifuna (Carib)

El Salvador
21,041 sq km
8,124 sq miles
6,157,000
San Salvador
Spanish

Dominica
751 sq km
290 sq miles
73,700
Roseau
French Creole, English

The Bahamas
13,880 sq km
5,359 sq miles
327,300
Nassau
English, English Creole, French Creole

St Lucia
616 sq km
238 sq miles
164,500
Castries
English, French Creole

Antigua and Barbuda
443 sq km
171 sq miles
93,600
St John's
English, English Patois

Jamaica
10,991 sq km
4,244 sq miles
2,970,000
Kingston
English Creole, English

Grenada
344 sq km
133 sq miles
111,200
St George's
English, English Creole

Much of Canada is still untamed wilderness – a land of huge, dramatic landscapes like this lake high up in the rugged, frost-shattered Rocky Mountains.

Trinidad and Tobago
5,128 sq km
1,980 sq miles
1,220,000
Port-of-Spain
English Creole, English

Barbados
430 sq km
166 sq miles
291,500
Bridgetown
Bajan (Barbadian English)

St Vincent and the Grenadines
389 sq km
150 sq miles
102,300
Kingstown
English, English Creole

St Kitts and Nevis
261 sq km
101 sq miles
52,300
Basseterre
English, English Creole

Western Canada and Alaska

CANADA IS A HUGE COUNTRY and its western half stretches from the flat prairies in the east to the towering Rocky Mountains in the west, and from the relatively mild south to the permanently frozen area north of the Arctic Circle. Harsh conditions over much of the region mean that most of the population is concentrated in cities in the south, such as Vancouver, Calgary, and Winnipeg. The Prairies – once a vast expanse of grassland – are now used mainly for growing wheat on huge mechanized farms. Oil and natural gas are found there as well. These natural resources are also important in Alaska, a part of the United States. The majority of Alaska's people moved there to work in these lucrative industries.

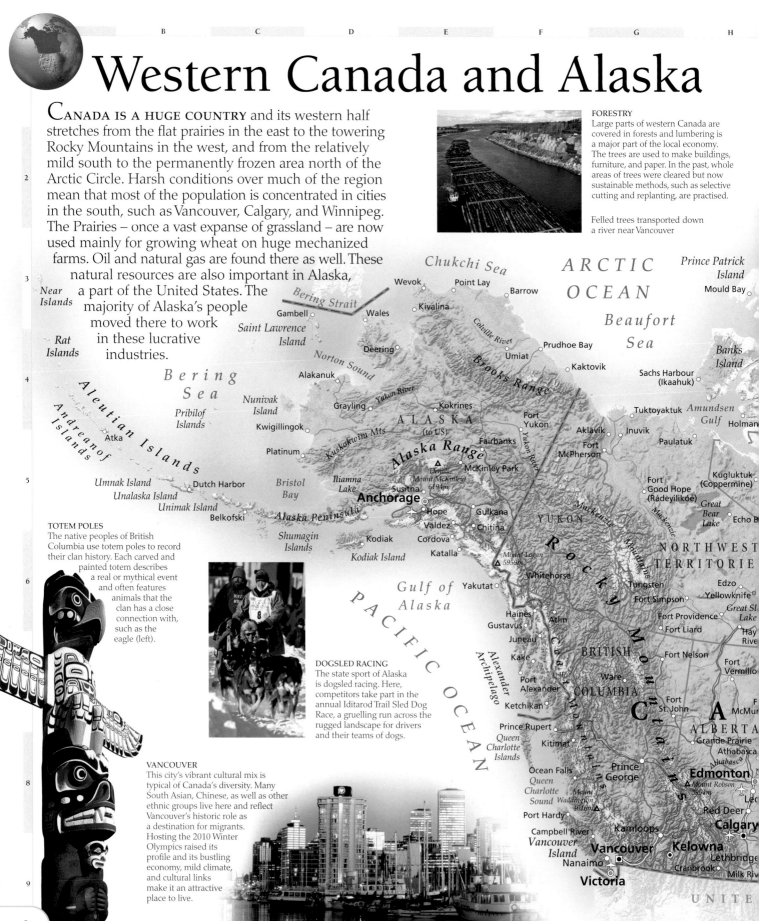

FORESTRY
Large parts of western Canada are covered in forests and lumbering is a major part of the local economy. The trees are used to make buildings, furniture, and paper. In the past, whole areas of trees were cleared but now sustainable methods, such as selective cutting and replanting, are practised.

Felled trees transported down a river near Vancouver

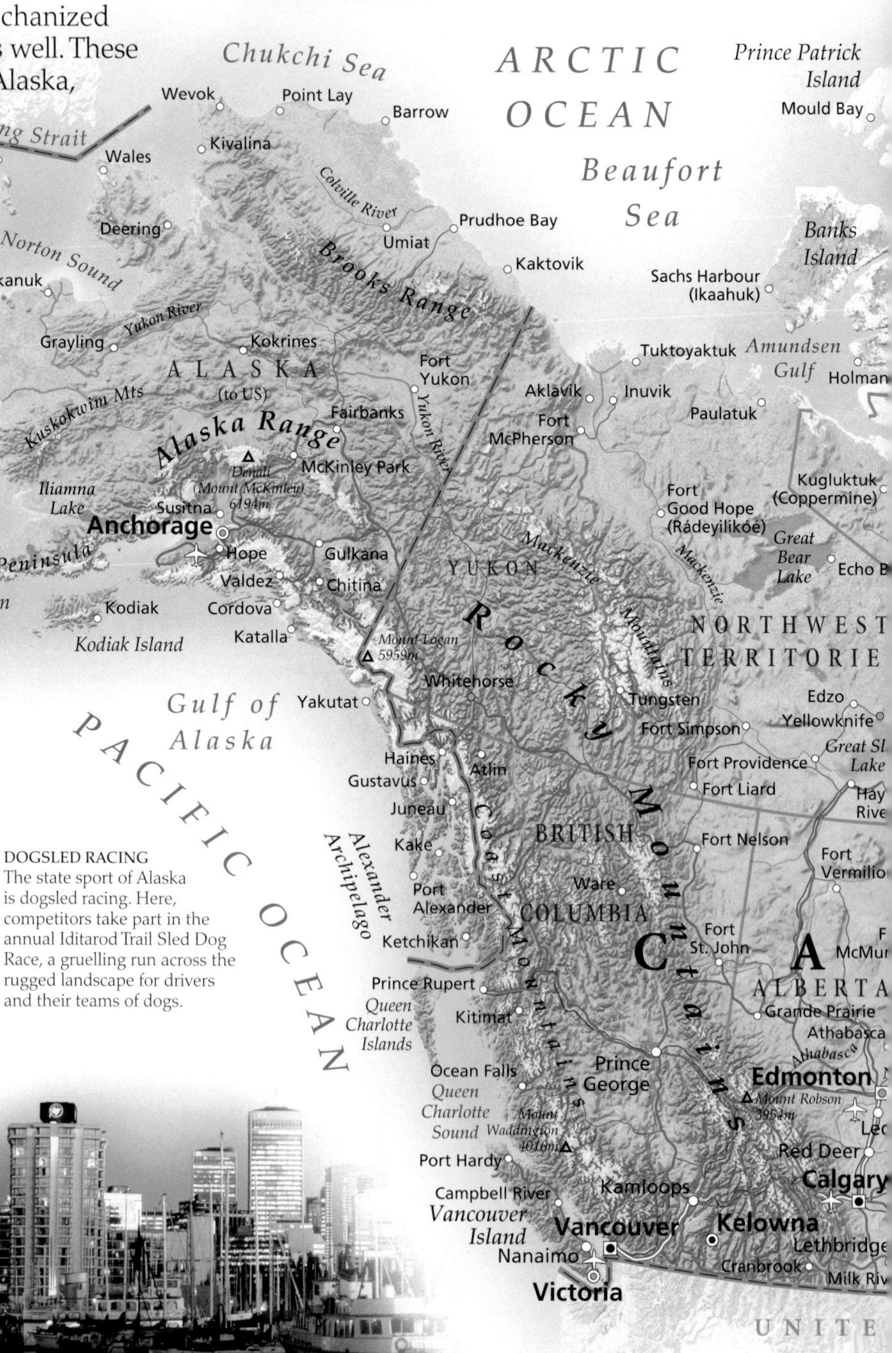
B
C
D
E
F
G
H
2
3
4
5
6
8
9
Chukchi Sea
ARCTIC OCEAN
Prince Patrick Island
Mould Bay
Wevok
Point Lay
Barrow
Near Islands
Bering Strait
Gambell
Wales
Kivalina
Colville River
Beaufort Sea
Saint Lawrence Island
Rat Islands
Deering
Prudhoe Bay
Umiat
Banks Island
Norton Sound
Kaktovik
Brooks Range
Bering Sea
Alakanuk
Sachs Harbour (Ikaahuk)
Aleutian Islands
Yukon River
Nunivak Island
Grayling
Kokrines
Tuktoyaktuk
Amundsen Gulf
Andreanof Islands
Pribilof Islands
ALASKA (to US)
Fort Yukon
Holman
Kwigillingok
Aklavik
Inuvik
Atka
Kuskokwim Mts
Fairbanks
Paulatuk
Platinum
Alaska Range
Yukon River
Fort McPherson
Denali (Mount McKinley) 6194m
McKinley Park
Kugluktuk (Coppermine)
Umnak Island
Dutch Harbor
Bristol Bay
Iliamna Lake
Susitna
Fort Good Hope (Rádeyilikóé)
Unalaska Island
Anchorage
Mackenzie
Great Bear Lake
Unimak Island
Hope
Gulkana
YUKON
Echo B
Belkofski
Alaska Peninsula
Valdez
Chitina
Shumagin Islands
Kodiak
Cordova
Rocky
NORTHWEST TERRITORIE
Katalla
Kodiak Island
Mount Logan 5959m
Mountains
Whitehorse
Tungsten
Edzo
Gulf of Alaska
Yakutat
Fort Simpson
Yellowknife
PACIFIC OCEAN
Haines
Atlin
Fort Providence
Great Sl Lake
Gustavus
Fort Liard
Hay Rive
Juneau
Mountains
Alexander Archipelago
Kake
BRITISH
Fort Nelson
Coast
Fort Vermilio
Port Alexander
Ware
COLUMBIA
Ketchikan
Fort St. John
CA
McMur
Prince Rupert
ALBERTA
Queen Charlotte Islands
Kitimat
Grande Prairie
Athabasca
Ocean Falls
Prince George
Edmonton
Queen Charlotte Sound
Mount Robson 3954m
Mount Waddington 4016m
Port Hardy
Red Deer
Campbell River
Kamloops
Calgary
Vancouver Island
Vancouver
Kelowna
Lethbridge
Nanaimo
Cranbrook
Milk Riv
Victoria
UNITE

TOTEM POLES
The native peoples of British Columbia use totem poles to record their clan history. Each carved and painted totem describes a real or mythical event and often features animals that the clan has a close connection with, such as the eagle (left).

DOGSLED RACING
The state sport of Alaska is dogsled racing. Here, competitors take part in the annual Iditarod Trail Sled Dog Race, a gruelling run across the rugged landscape for drivers and their teams of dogs.

VANCOUVER
This city's vibrant cultural mix is typical of Canada's diversity. Many South Asian, Chinese, as well as other ethnic groups live here and reflect Vancouver's historic role as a destination for migrants. Hosting the 2010 Winter Olympics raised its profile and its bustling economy, mild climate, and cultural links make it an attractive place to live.

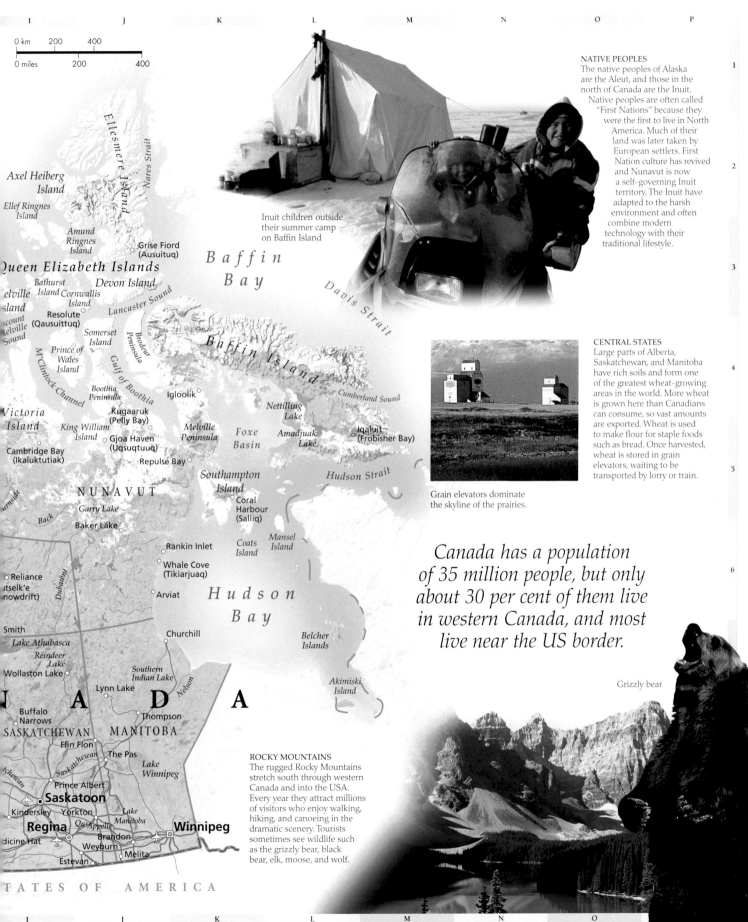

I J K L M N O P
1 2 3 4 5 6
0 km 200 400
0 miles 200 400
Ellesmere Island
Nares Strait
Axel Heiberg Island
Ellef Ringnes Island
Amund Ringnes Island
Grise Fiord (Ausuituq)
Queen Elizabeth Islands
Baffin Bay
Davis Strait
Bathurst Island
Devon Island
Cornwallis Island
Lancaster Sound
Resolute (Qausuittuq)
Somerset Island
Brodeur Peninsula
Prince of Wales Island
M'Clintock Channel
Gulf of Boothia
Boothia Peninsula
Baffin Island
Cumberland Sound
Igloolik
Victoria Island
Kugaaruk (Pelly Bay)
King William Island
Gjoa Haven (Uqsuqtuuq)
Cambridge Bay (Ikaluktutiak)
Melville Peninsula
Nettilling Lake
Amadjuak Lake
Foxe Basin
Iqaluit (Frobisher Bay)
Repulse Bay
Southampton Island
Hudson Strait
Coral Harbour (Salliq)
NUNAVUT
Garry Lake
Back
Baker Lake
Rankin Inlet
Coats Island
Mansel Island
Whale Cove (Tikiarjuaq)
Reliance
Dubawnt
Arviat
Hudson Bay
Churchill
Lake Athabasca
Reindeer Lake
Belcher Islands
Wollaston Lake
Southern Indian Lake
Nelson
Akimiski Island
Lynn Lake
A D A
Buffalo Narrows
Thompson
SASKATCHEWAN
MANITOBA
Flin Flon
The Pas
Saskatchewan
Lake Winnipeg
Prince Albert
Saskatoon
Kindersley
Yorkton
Lake Manitoba
Regina
Qu'Appelle
Winnipeg
Brandon
Weyburn
Melita
Estevan
TATES OF AMERICA
I J K L M N O

Inuit children outside their summer camp on Baffin Island

NATIVE PEOPLES
The native peoples of Alaska are the Aleut, and those in the north of Canada are the Inuit. Native peoples are often called "First Nations" because they were the first to live in North America. Much of their land was later taken by European settlers. First Nation culture has revived and Nunavut is now a self-governing Inuit territory. The Inuit have adapted to the harsh environment and often combine modern technology with their traditional lifestyle.

Grain elevators dominate the skyline of the prairies.

CENTRAL STATES
Large parts of Alberta, Saskatchewan, and Manitoba have rich soils and form one of the greatest wheat-growing areas in the world. More wheat is grown here than Canadians can consume, so vast amounts are exported. Wheat is used to make flour for staple foods such as bread. Once harvested, wheat is stored in grain elevators, waiting to be transported by lorry or train.

Canada has a population of 35 million people, but only about 30 per cent of them live in western Canada, and most live near the US border.

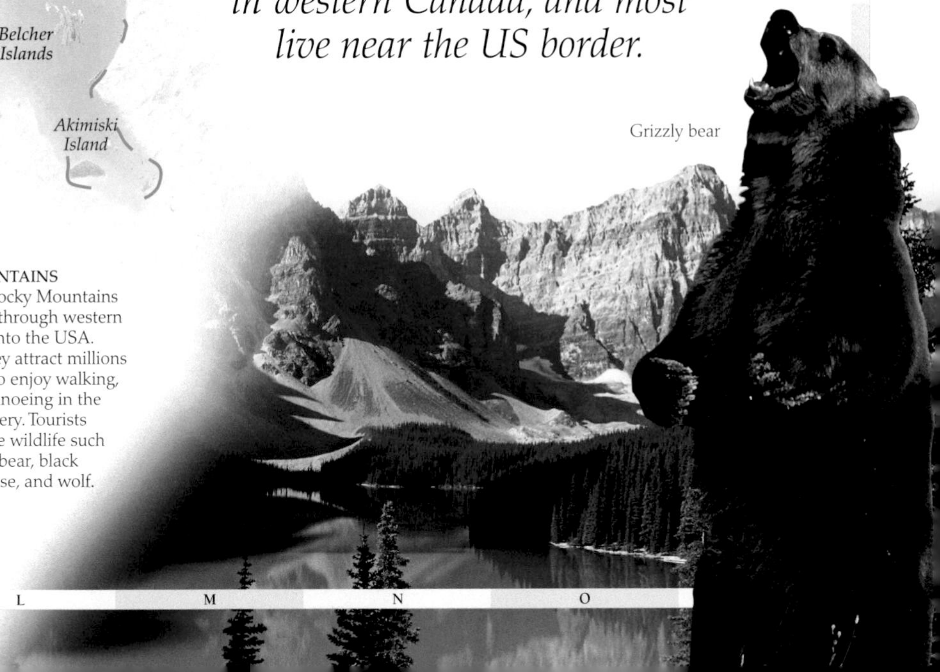

Grizzly bear

ROCKY MOUNTAINS
The rugged Rocky Mountains stretch south through western Canada and into the USA. Every year they attract millions of visitors who enjoy walking, hiking, and canoeing in the dramatic scenery. Tourists sometimes see wildlife such as the grizzly bear, black bear, elk, moose, and wolf.

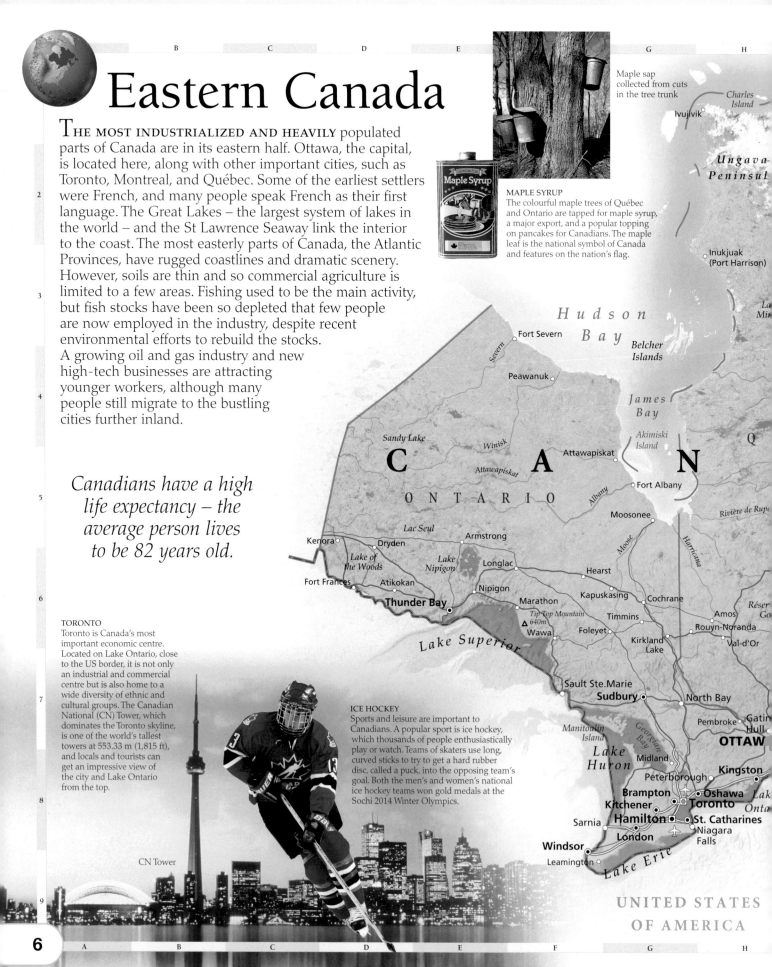

Eastern Canada

THE MOST INDUSTRIALIZED AND HEAVILY populated parts of Canada are in its eastern half. Ottawa, the capital, is located here, along with other important cities, such as Toronto, Montreal, and Québec. Some of the earliest settlers were French, and many people speak French as their first language. The Great Lakes – the largest system of lakes in the world – and the St Lawrence Seaway link the interior to the coast. The most easterly parts of Canada, the Atlantic Provinces, have rugged coastlines and dramatic scenery. However, soils are thin and so commercial agriculture is limited to a few areas. Fishing used to be the main activity, but fish stocks have been so depleted that few people are now employed in the industry, despite recent environmental efforts to rebuild the stocks. A growing oil and gas industry and new high-tech businesses are attracting younger workers, although many people still migrate to the bustling cities further inland.

Canadians have a high life expectancy – the average person lives to be 82 years old.

Maple sap collected from cuts in the tree trunk

MAPLE SYRUP
The colourful maple trees of Québec and Ontario are tapped for maple syrup, a major export, and a popular topping on pancakes for Canadians. The maple leaf is the national symbol of Canada and features on the nation's flag.

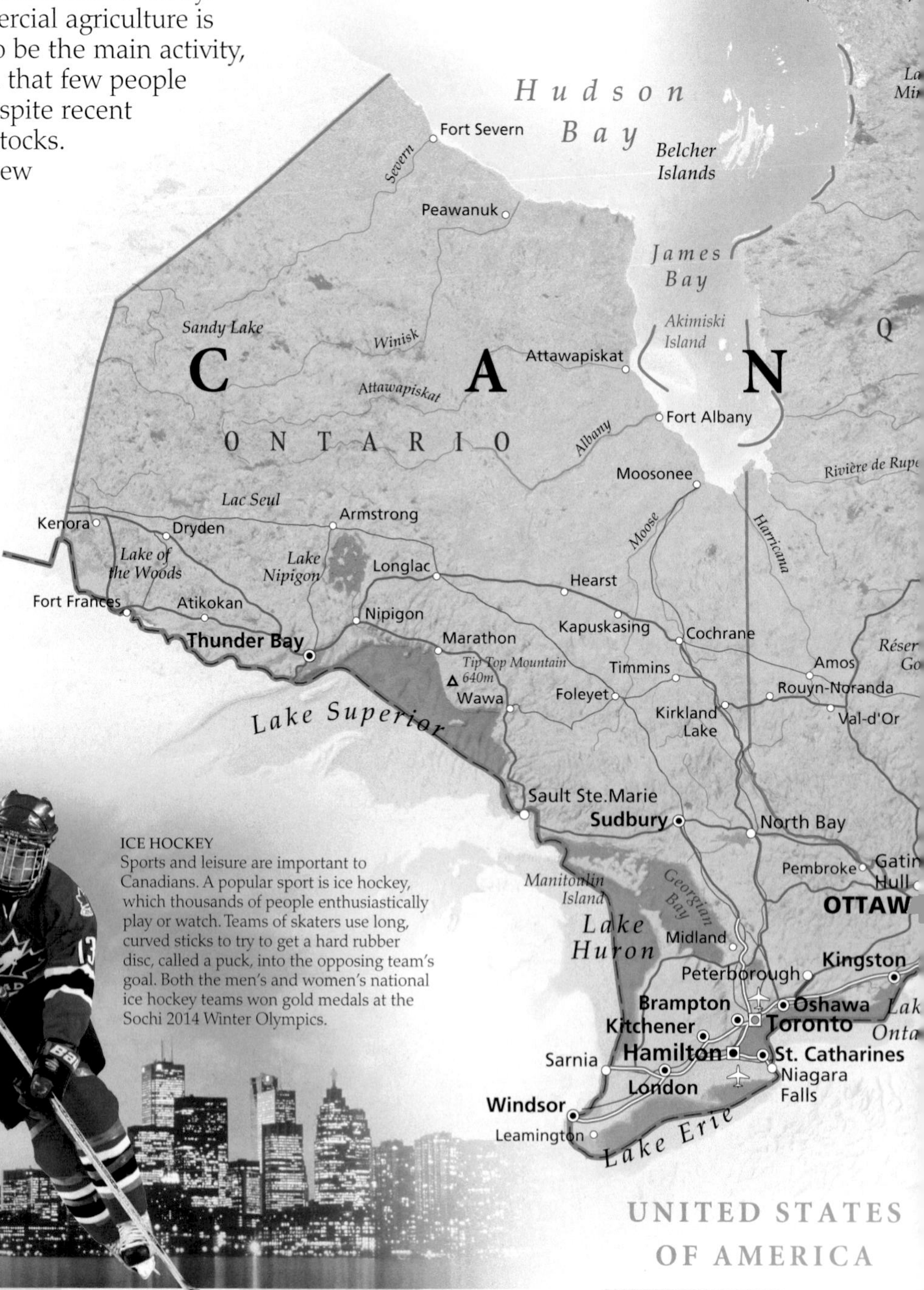

TORONTO
Toronto is Canada's most important economic centre. Located on Lake Ontario, close to the US border, it is not only an industrial and commercial centre but is also home to a wide diversity of ethnic and cultural groups. The Canadian National (CN) Tower, which dominates the Toronto skyline, is one of the world's tallest towers at 553.33 m (1,815 ft), and locals and tourists can get an impressive view of the city and Lake Ontario from the top.

ICE HOCKEY
Sports and leisure are important to Canadians. A popular sport is ice hockey, which thousands of people enthusiastically play or watch. Teams of skaters use long, curved sticks to try to get a hard rubber disc, called a puck, into the opposing team's goal. Both the men's and women's national ice hockey teams won gold medals at the Sochi 2014 Winter Olympics.

I
J
K
L
M
N
O
P
Baffin Island
Hudson Strait
Resolution Island
Button Islands
Akpatok Island
Ungava Bay
Rivière aux Feuilles
Kuujjuaq
Koksoak
Caniapiscau
Rivière à la Baleine
Nain
Labrador
Hopedale
Makkovik
Cape Harrison
Cartwright
Labrador Sea
Lac Bienville
Schefferville
Smallwood Reservoir
Lake Melville
Churchill
NEWFOUNDLAND & LABRADOR
Réservoir de Caniapiscau
St.Anthony
QUEBEC
CANADA
Gagnon
Laurentian Mountains
Strait of Belle Isle
Gander
Réservoir Manicouagan
Havre-St-Pierre
Grand Falls
St.John's
Île d'Anticosti
Corner Brook
Newfoundland
Lac Mistassini
Sept-Îles
Chibougamau
Gaspé
Gulf of St. Lawrence
Channel-Port aux Basques
Cape Race
Baie-Comeau
St. Lawrence
Péninsule de Gaspé
Lac St-Jean
Matane
Îles de la Madeleine
Cabot Strait
ST PIERRE & MIQUELON (to France)
Chicoutimi
Rimouski
Jonquière
Bathurst
PRINCE EDWARD ISLAND
Rivière-du-Loup
Edmundston
Glace Bay
La Tuque
NEW BRUNSWICK
Sydney
Charlesbourg
Charlottetown
Cape Breton Island
Québec
Moncton
Amherst
New Glasgow
Trois-Rivières
St-Georges
Oromocto
Truro
Fredericton
NOVA SCOTIA
Sable Island
Laval
Drummondville
Saint John
Bay of Fundy
Dartmouth
Halifax
Sherbrooke
Montréal
Liverpool
Yarmouth
ATLANTIC OCEAN
0 km 100 200
0 miles 100 200
1
2
3
4
5
6
7
8
9

ATLANTIC PROVINCES
Nova Scotia, New Brunswick, Prince Edward Island, and Newfoundland and Labrador attract tourists for their landscape, wildlife, and quaint seaside villages. Icebergs are a regular sight off the coast of Newfoundland and Labrador as they drift south from the Arctic.

FISHERIES
The Grand Banks, off the coast of Newfoundland, are shallow waters that once contained huge stocks of fish. Stocks have declined, however, due to overfishing, and now catches are severely restricted. Tourism has been a valuable alternative for those who relied on fishing for their livelihood.

Ibiza
Le Portal

French signs in Québec city

FRENCH CANADA
Québec province is the main French-speaking part of Canada. With a different language and cultural traditions from other parts of the country, there have been calls in the past for Québec to become independent from the rest of Canada.

ST LAWRENCE SEAWAY
Stretching far inland, the St Lawrence Seaway provides a link from the Great Lakes to the Atlantic. A series of huge locks descends from Lake Ontario to sea level, allowing ocean-going ships to transport their cargo as far inland as Lake Superior. Large amounts of iron ore, for example, are transported inland from Labrador to Ontario for processing. Corn, soy, and other agricultural products move in the opposite direction, from the prairies east to the markets of the world.

USA: Northeast

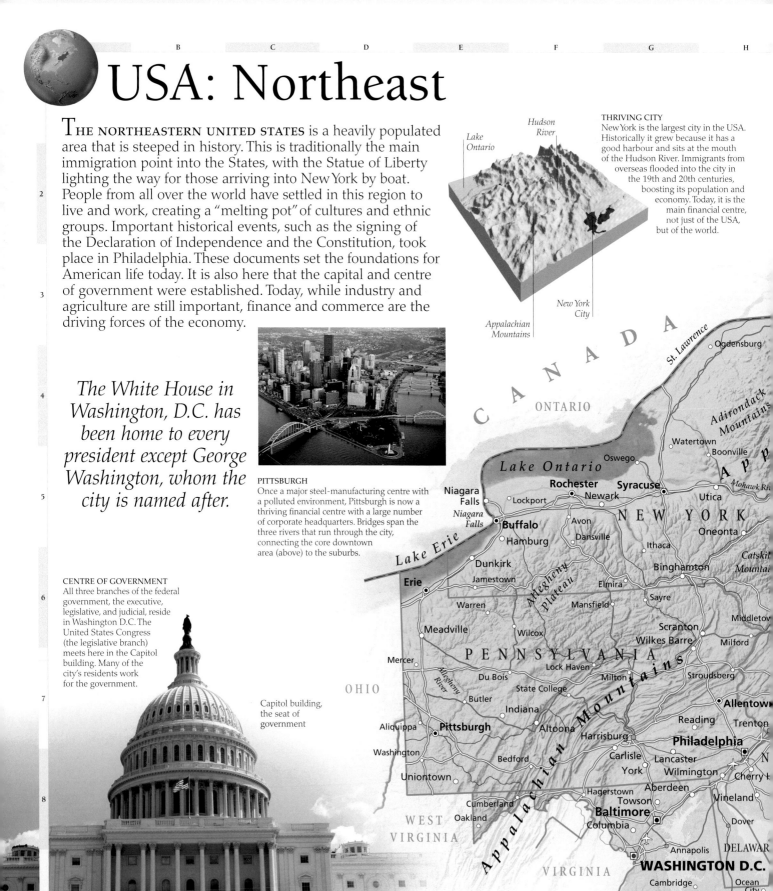

THE NORTHEASTERN UNITED STATES is a heavily populated area that is steeped in history. This is traditionally the main immigration point into the States, with the Statue of Liberty lighting the way for those arriving into New York by boat. People from all over the world have settled in this region to live and work, creating a "melting pot" of cultures and ethnic groups. Important historical events, such as the signing of the Declaration of Independence and the Constitution, took place in Philadelphia. These documents set the foundations for American life today. It is also here that the capital and centre of government were established. Today, while industry and agriculture are still important, finance and commerce are the driving forces of the economy.

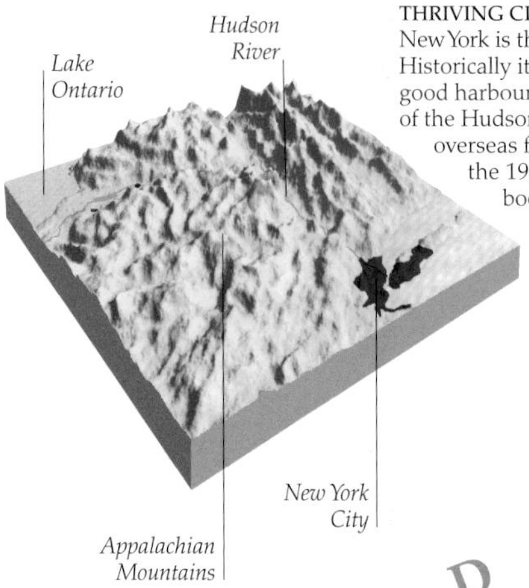

THRIVING CITY
New York is the largest city in the USA. Historically it grew because it has a good harbour and sits at the mouth of the Hudson River. Immigrants from overseas flooded into the city in the 19th and 20th centuries, boosting its population and economy. Today, it is the main financial centre, not just of the USA, but of the world.

The White House in Washington, D.C. has been home to every president except George Washington, whom the city is named after.

PITTSBURGH
Once a major steel-manufacturing centre with a polluted environment, Pittsburgh is now a thriving financial centre with a large number of corporate headquarters. Bridges span the three rivers that run through the city, connecting the core downtown area (above) to the suburbs.

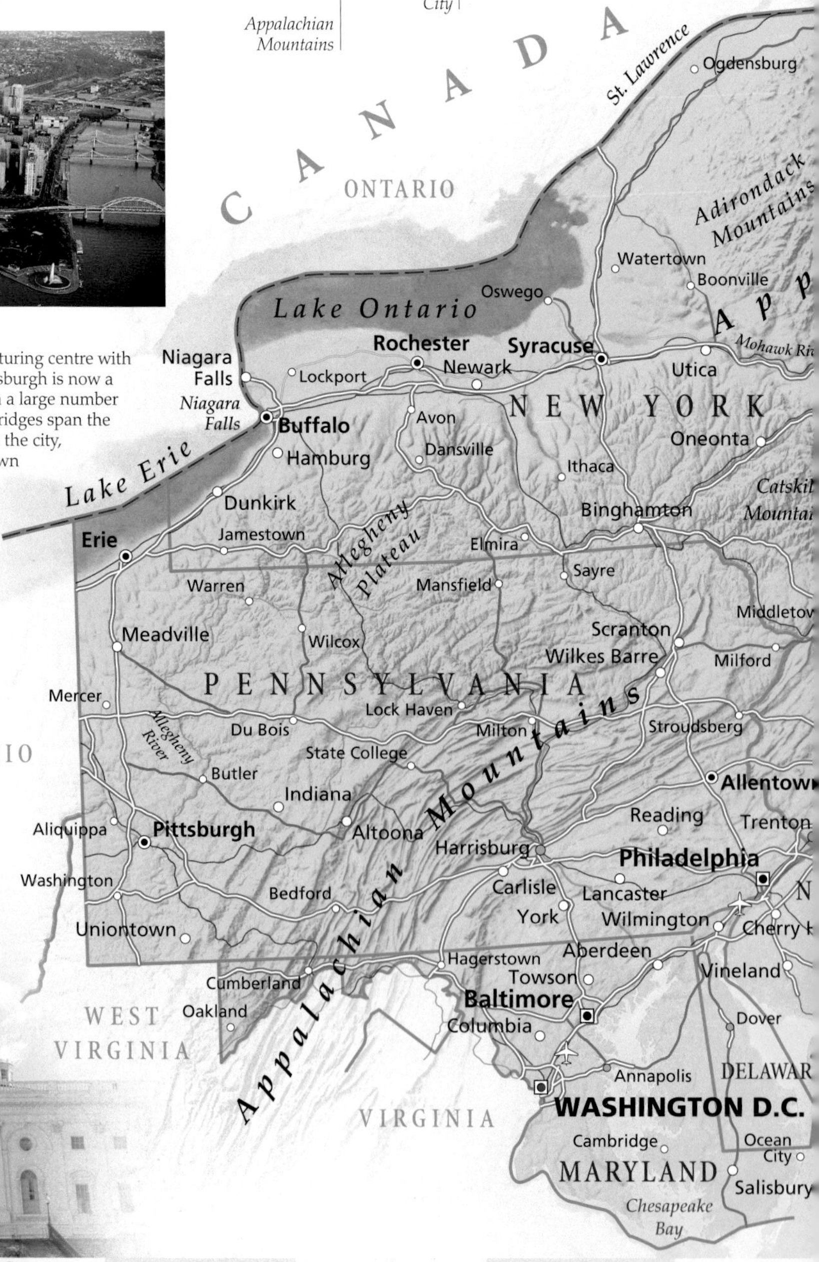

CENTRE OF GOVERNMENT
All three branches of the federal government, the executive, legislative, and judicial, reside in Washington D.C. The United States Congress (the legislative branch) meets here in the Capitol building. Many of the city's residents work for the government.

Capitol building, the seat of government

CRANBERRIES
The northeast USA is a major cranberry-growing region. Cranberries grow in flooded bogs, and once harvested – often with high-tech equipment (above) – they can be eaten in pies and sauces.

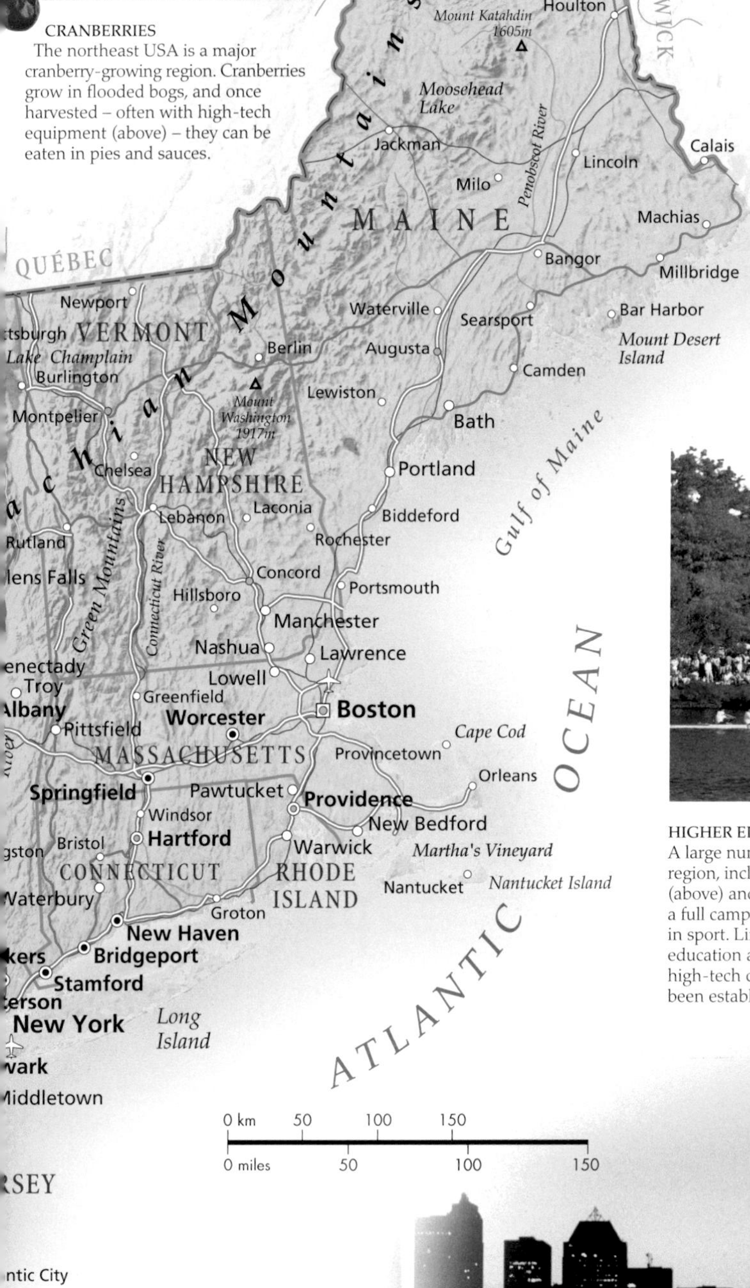

MAINE
Although Maine is a large state, it is relatively sparsely populated. Early settlers were attracted to its coastline, and fishing communities gradually sprang up. To this day, fishing remains an important activity, while colourful foliage attracts tourists in the autumn.

Maine (above), famous for its clam chowder and lobsters (right)

HIGHER EDUCATION
A large number of universities are located in this region, including two of the most famous – Harvard (above) and Yale. As well as studying, students enjoy a full campus life, including taking part in sport. Links between industry and education are strong, so many high-tech companies have been established here.

THANKSGIVING
The first Thanksgiving was held in 1621 as a gesture of friendship between American Indians and the Pilgrims after the Pilgrims' first successful harvest. Americans honour that tradition every November by gathering with family and friends to give thanks for life's blessings and to share a meal.

The Statue of Liberty has stood in New York harbour since 1886.

NEW YORK CITY
The centre of US commerce and business is New York City. People living here have a fast-paced lifestyle, and many travel by train or ferry from the suburbs to work in the towering high-rise office blocks of Manhattan. People travelling by boat across the harbour pass the Statue of Liberty, a huge monument that represents freedom and opportunity to Americans.

USA: South

THE SOUTHERN STATES of the USA have a varied landscape and an interesting mix of people, both culturally and economically. Some areas of the region are poor, especially the Appalachian Mountain communities, while other parts, such as the Florida coast, are wealthy and attract many people from other states and countries. The cultural mix includes people of Latin American origin, African-Americans, Cajuns (French-Canadians), and European Americans, giving rise to diverse music styles, dialects, pastimes, and food. While coal mining in the Appalachian Mountains has declined in recent years, agriculture is still important, as are tourism and industry. Tourism is particularly important in Florida and in New Orleans near the mouth of the mighty Mississippi River.

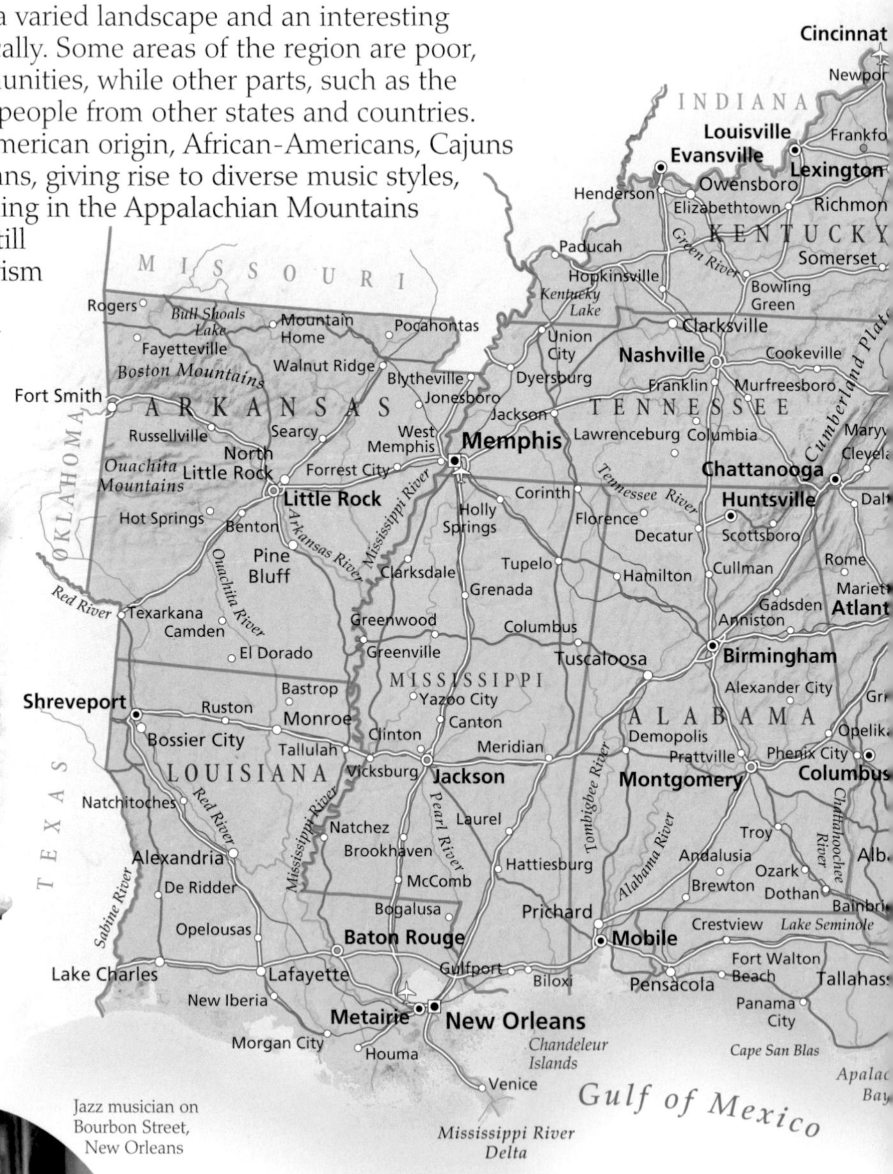

B C D E F G H
2 3 4 5 6 7 8 9
A B C D E F G H
0 km 50 100 150 200
0 miles 50 100 150 200
Cincinnat
Newpor
INDIANA
Louisville
Frankfo
Evansville
Lexington
Henderson
Owensboro
Elizabethtown
Richmon
KENTUCKY
Paducah
Somerset
Green River
Hopkinsville
Kentucky Lake
Bowling Green
MISSOURI
Rogers
Bull Shoals Lake
Mountain Home
Pocahontas
Fayetteville
Boston Mountains
Walnut Ridge
Union City
Clarksville
Nashville
Cookeville
Cumberland Plat
Fort Smith
Blytheville
Jonesboro
Dyersburg
Franklin
Murfreesboro
ARKANSAS
Jackson
TENNESSEE
OKLAHOMA
Russellville
Searcy
West Memphis
Memphis
Lawrenceburg
Columbia
Mary
Clevela
North Little Rock
Ouachita Mountains
Forrest City
Chattanooga
Little Rock
Mississippi River
Corinth
Tennessee River
Huntsville
Dal
Hot Springs
Benton
Holly Springs
Florence
Decatur
Scottsboro
Pine Bluff
Arkansas River
Ouachita River
Clarksdale
Tupelo
Hamilton
Cullman
Rome
Grenada
Mariet
Red River
Texarkana
Gadsden
Atlant
Camden
Greenwood
Columbus
Anniston
El Dorado
Greenville
Tuscaloosa
Birmingham
MISSISSIPPI
Bastrop
Alexander City
Shreveport
Ruston
Yazoo City
Gri
Monroe
Canton
ALABAMA
Bossier City
Clinton
Demopolis
Opelik
Tallulah
Meridian
Prattville
Phenix City
LOUISIANA
Vicksburg
Jackson
Montgomery
Columbus
TEXAS
Natchitoches
Red River
Tombigbee River
Chattahoochee River
Laurel
Troy
Natchez
Pearl River
Alabama River
Alexandria
Brookhaven
Hattiesburg
Andalusia
Ozark
Alb
De Ridder
McComb
Brewton
Dothan
Sabine River
Bogalusa
Prichard
Bainbri
Opelousas
Baton Rouge
Mobile
Crestview
Lake Seminole
Gulfport
Fort Walton Beach
Lake Charles
Lafayette
Biloxi
Pensacola
Tallahas
New Iberia
Panama City
Metairie
New Orleans
Morgan City
Chandeleur Islands
Cape San Blas
Houma
Apalac Bay
Venice
Gulf of Mexico
Mississippi River Delta

COTTON CROPS
Cotton was once the mainstay crop of the south and was grown by African-American slaves. Today, cotton is still important for the economy of the region and is grown in large fields and harvested with huge machinery. Cotton has many uses, primarily as the raw material for textiles.

Cotton pod, or boll

The Mississippi is the largest river in North America and the third largest in the world.

Jazz musician on Bourbon Street, New Orleans

MUSICAL ORIGINS
The southern USA is famous for its music, much of which reflects the cultural mix of the region. New Orleans and other parts of Louisiana are the birthplaces of jazz and Cajun music, while bluegrass and country have origins in Nashville and Memphis. These music styles started here, but quickly spread throughout the country and developed even further in the cities.

Chef holding a skillet of jambalaya, a Cajun dish

CAJUN CULTURE
The Cajuns in this region are French-speaking people who were expelled from Canada in the 18th century. They mixed with other cultures in Louisiana, but their French influence can be seen in the music, food, and place names, such as Lafayette.

FLORIDA EVERGLADES
The increasing population of Florida means that the Everglades, swampy plains inhabited by alligators and other wildlife, are under threat as land is needed for houses and farms. However, the Everglades National Park protects part of this important ecosystem.

KENTUCKY DERBY
Every year on the first Saturday of May, the Kentucky Derby takes place in Louisville. This horse race, and the festivities based around it, mark the beginning of spring for people in the area. The best horses and jockeys, as well as massive crowds of spectators from around the country, travel here for the event.

Kumba roller coaster, a popular ride at Busch Gardens Tampa Bay, Florida

TOURISM
Tourism is an important industry in the south, especially for Florida. As well as warm weather and appealing scenery, tourists are attracted to the theme parks around Orlando. Jobs and income are generated by tourism, with many people working in retail outlets, restaurants, hotels, and theme parks.

MARTIN LUTHER KING, JR
Martin Luther King, Jr, (left) was born in Atlanta in 1929. In the 1960s, he led many peaceful protests to end the laws that discriminated against black Americans. King was assassinated in 1969 and has since been seen as a symbol of the struggle for racial equality. Many African-Americans live in the southern USA where, before the Civil War (1861–65), their ancestors were forced to work on cotton plantations and farms.

Martin Luther King, Jr, speaking at the final rally of the March Against Fear, Mississippi, 1966

FLORIDA'S SUNSHINE COAST
Florida's sunny weather and sandy beaches have traditionally attracted many retired people, many of whom live in apartments along the coast in resorts such as Miami Beach (right). Florida also attracts young people, particularly to the vibrant city of Miami, where many immigrants from Central America, Cuba, and other Caribbean islands live, and Spanish is spoken by half the population. The Florida Keys, an island chain in the south of the peninsula, is also popular with tourists, and contains some of the largest living coral formations in North America.

USA: Midwest

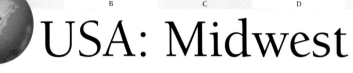

THE AMERICAN MIDWEST is dominated by the Great Plains, once the home of cattle ranches, cowboys, and American Indian peoples. However, the discovery of gold in South Dakota brought a rush of settlers to the area. This, combined with a decline in bison numbers, led to the eventual displacement of the American Indians from the Plains. The area is prone to dramatic weather – tornadoes, freezing blizzards, and blazing hot summers. To the west, vast areas of farmland generate more wheat and maize than anywhere else in the world. East of the Mississippi the landscape varies and, although farming is still important, it is an industrial heartland. The greater Detroit area and other parts of Michigan make up a big manufacturing centre, with other hubs in Ohio, Indiana, and Illinois.

BUFFALO ON THE PLAINS
Up to 100 million bison, locally known as buffalo, once grazed on the Great Plains. They provided local American Indians with food for the family, and skin for clothes and tepees. The Dakota people used bison bones to make shields and tools, and the animal's bladder into a bag for carrying water. But over-hunting and the destruction of the bison's habitat by early European settlers drastically reduced the number of animals. The bison is now a protected species and lives in reserves.

Bison herd on a reserve, South Dakota

MOUNT RUSHMORE NATIONAL MEMORIAL
Mount Rushmore, in the Black Hills of South Dakota, was created as a tribute to the American presidency. Four of the United States' greatest presidents – (left to right) Washington, Jefferson, Roosevelt, and Lincoln – were carved into the granite cliff between 1927 and 1941. Teams of workers hung from saddles anchored to the mountain to complete the work, often enduring harsh winds or blazing sun. Today, it is a popular tourist attraction.

Each carved face is about 18 m (60 ft) high.

TORNADO ALLEY
Dramatic tornadoes, or "twisters", regularly tear through the states of Kansas and Oklahoma, along a path known as Tornado Alley. Tornadoes occur when warm and cold air masses meet. As the warm air rises, it cools, and under the right conditions, it can suck in more and more air until a whirling twister develops. The more air that is drawn in, the greater the power of the tornado.

RURAL AMERICA
Although most Americans today live in cities and large towns, there are still many small towns with populations of less than 10,000 people. These towns are often in farming communities and are where people go to shop or to attend church. Children, such as these boys from Iowa (left), often have to be taken to and from school by special bus.

The Great Lakes contain one-fifth of Earth's fresh water.

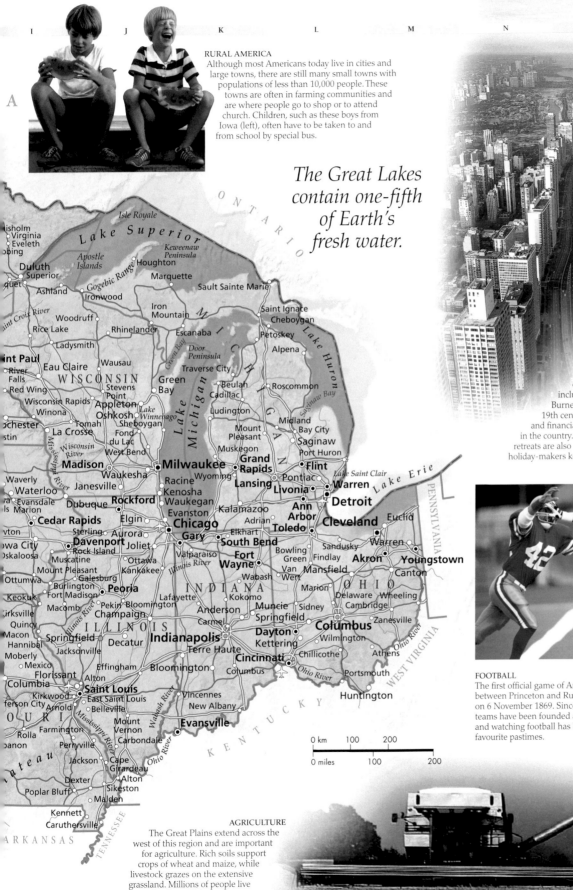

GREAT LAKES
Several large cities are located on the shores of the Great Lakes, including Chicago on Lake Michigan. Burned to the ground in the late 19th century, it is now a leading industrial and financial centre and the third-largest city in the country. The Great Lakes and their lakeside retreats are also a popular tourist destination for holiday-makers keen on watersports.

FOOTBALL
The first official game of American football was played between Princeton and Rutgers universities in New Jersey on 6 November 1869. Since then, college and professional teams have been founded all over the country, and playing and watching football has become one of America's favourite pastimes.

AGRICULTURE
The Great Plains extend across the west of this region and are important for agriculture. Rich soils support crops of wheat and maize, while livestock grazes on the extensive grassland. Millions of people live on the Great Plains, many on family-owned and -run farms.

USA: West

The Rocky Mountains separate the coastal region from the drier inland states. Large and fast-growing cities, such as San Francisco, Los Angeles, and San Diego, hug the Pacific coast, and have attracted many migrants because of good job opportunities. Inland, blazing desert and towering mountains provide some of the most dramatic landscapes in the country. National parks, such as Yellowstone in northwestern Wyoming and Montana, and Yosemite in central California, protect some of these wilderness areas. Further east, the foothills of the Rockies give way to vast plains grazed by large herds of cattle.

NORTHERN FORESTS
The coastal areas of Oregon and Washington contain large forests. These produce economically important timber, but much land is also left in its natural state and is popular with hikers. Most people here live in large cities like Seattle, and in the fertile inland valleys.

CALIFORNIA AGRICULTURE
California is warm, fertile, and, with irrigation, ideal for agriculture. Grapes are an important crop north of San Francisco in the Napa Valley. Further south, citrus crops such as oranges also flourish. Premium farming land is under threat, however, as the population expands.

The American Indian name for Death Valley is Tomesha, which means "land where the ground is on fire".

LOS ANGELES
This sprawling city – the second largest in the USA – is home to migrants from all over the world, as well as from other states in the country. Sandwiched between the coast and the mountains, the city has massive air pollution problems. This mostly arises from the exhaust fumes from the high number of cars used by commuters on the city's highways.

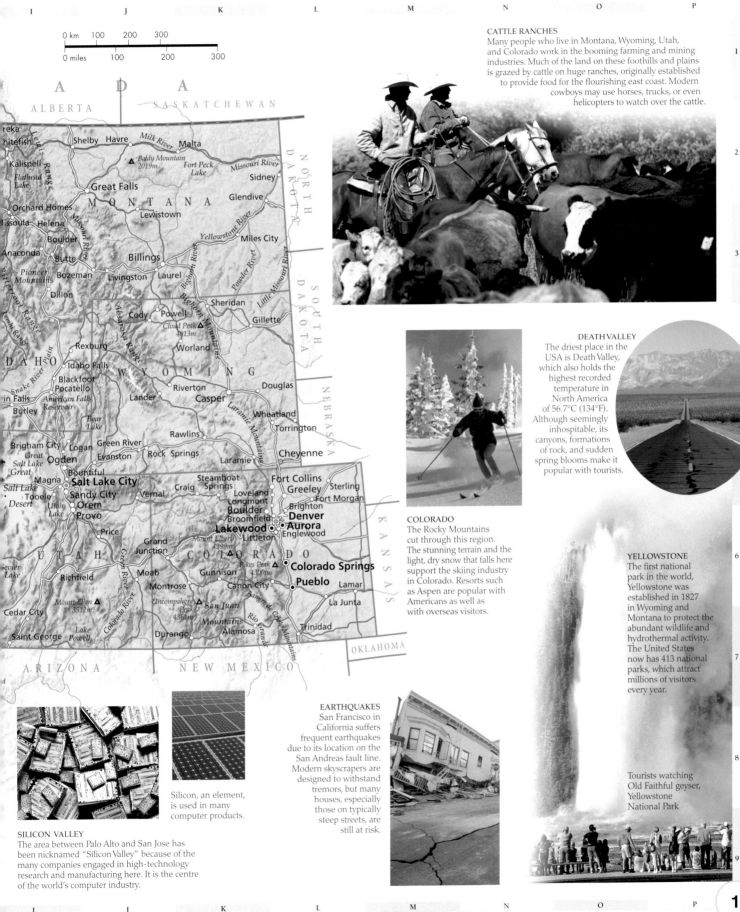

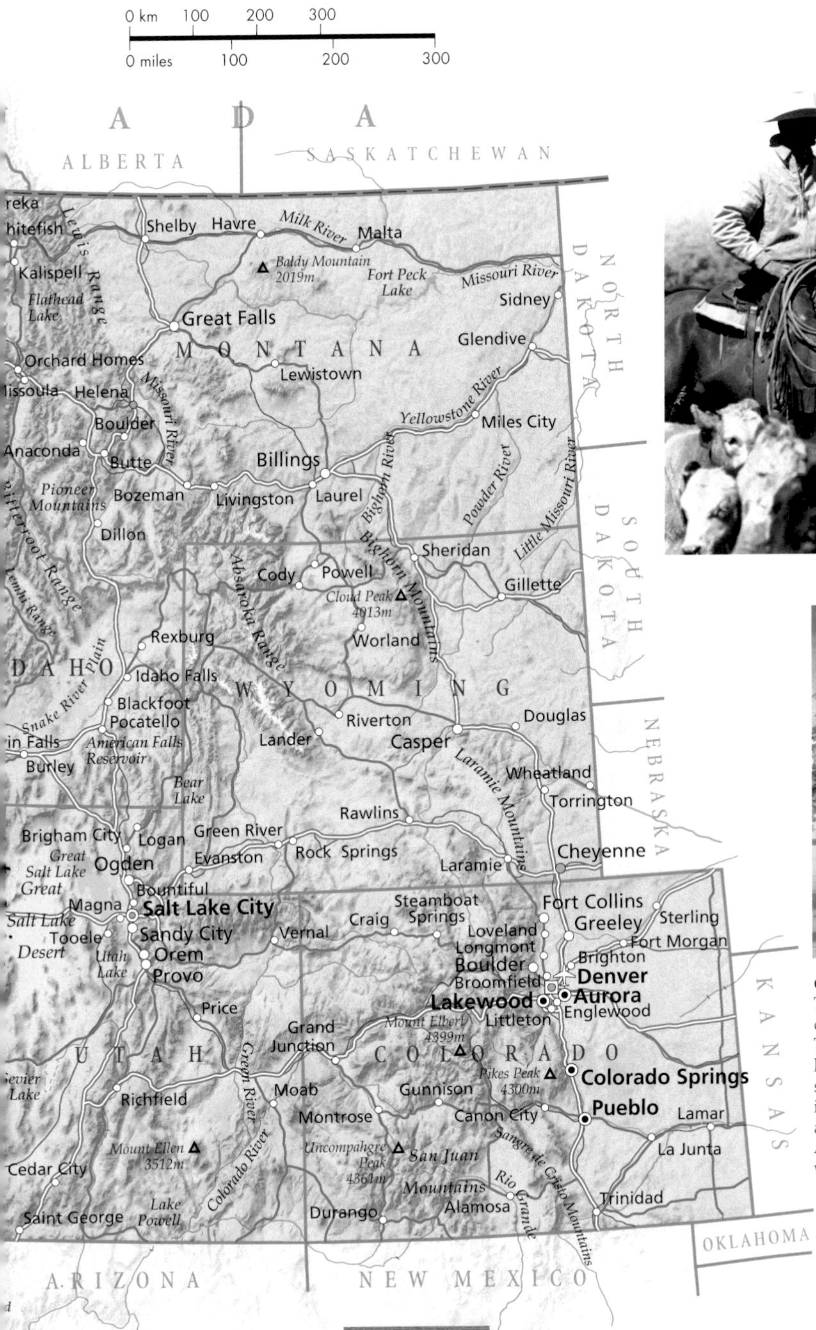
0 km 100 200 300
0 miles 100 200 300
ALBERTA
SASKATCHEWAN
MONTANA
NORTH DAKOTA
SOUTH DAKOTA
WYOMING
NEBRASKA
UTAH
COLORADO
KANSAS
OKLAHOMA
ARIZONA
NEW MEXICO
Shelby
Havre
Milk River
Malta
Baldy Mountain 2019m
Fort Peck Lake
Missouri River
Sidney
Kalispell
Flathead Lake
Great Falls
Glendive
Orchard Homes
Lewistown
Helena
Missouri River
Yellowstone River
Miles City
Boulder
Anaconda
Butte
Billings
Bighorn River
Powder River
Little Missouri River
Pioneer Mountains
Bozeman
Livingston
Laurel
Dillon
Sheridan
Bighorn Mountains
Cody
Powell
Cloud Peak 4013m
Gillette
Absaroka Range
Rexburg
Worland
Idaho Falls
Snake River
Blackfoot
Pocatello
Riverton
Douglas
American Falls Reservoir
Lander
Casper
Burley
Laramie Mountains
Wheatland
Bear Lake
Torrington
Rawlins
Brigham City
Logan
Green River
Great Salt Lake
Ogden
Evanston
Rock Springs
Laramie
Cheyenne
Bountiful
Magna
Salt Lake City
Steamboat Springs
Fort Collins
Greeley
Sterling
Tooele
Sandy City
Vernal
Craig
Loveland
Longmont
Fort Morgan
Utah Lake
Orem
Provo
Boulder
Brighton
Broomfield
Denver
Lakewood
Aurora
Englewood
Price
Littleton
Mount Elbert 4399m
Grand Junction
Green River
Pikes Peak 4300m
Colorado Springs
Moab
Gunnison
Richfield
Montrose
Cañon City
Pueblo
Lamar
Mount Ellen 3512m
Uncompahgre Peak 4361m
San Juan Mountains
Colorado River
La Junta
Cedar City
Rio Grande
Sangre de Cristo Mountains
Trinidad
Saint George
Lake Powell
Durango
Alamosa

CATTLE RANCHES

Many people who live in Montana, Wyoming, Utah, and Colorado work in the booming farming and mining industries. Much of the land on these foothills and plains is grazed by cattle on huge ranches, originally established to provide food for the flourishing east coast. Modern cowboys may use horses, trucks, or even helicopters to watch over the cattle.

DEATH VALLEY

The driest place in the USA is Death Valley, which also holds the highest recorded temperature in North America of 56.7°C (134°F). Although seemingly inhospitable, its canyons, formations of rock, and sudden spring blooms make it popular with tourists.

COLORADO

The Rocky Mountains cut through this region. The stunning terrain and the light, dry snow that falls here support the skiing industry in Colorado. Resorts such as Aspen are popular with Americans as well as with overseas visitors.

YELLOWSTONE

The first national park in the world, Yellowstone was established in 1827 in Wyoming and Montana to protect the abundant wildlife and hydrothermal activity. The United States now has 413 national parks, which attract millions of visitors every year.

Tourists watching Old Faithful geyser, Yellowstone National Park

Silicon, an element, is used in many computer products.

SILICON VALLEY

The area between Palo Alto and San Jose has been nicknamed "Silicon Valley" because of the many companies engaged in high-technology research and manufacturing here. It is the centre of the world's computer industry.

EARTHQUAKES

San Francisco in California suffers frequent earthquakes due to its location on the San Andreas fault line. Modern skyscrapers are designed to withstand tremors, but many houses, especially those on typically steep streets, are still at risk.

USA: Southwest

THE SOUTHWEST is an area of great contrasts. Much of Oklahoma and Texas consists of flat, rolling grasslands and huge farms, while both Arizona and New Mexico are hot, arid, and mountainous, with vast canyons and river valleys carving their way through the land. Since the discovery of oil in 1901, Texas has become the country's top oil producer with Houston as the centre of the billion-dollar industry. Tourism is also important to the Southwest, as visitors flock to see the Grand Canyon, the Painted Desert, and other natural wonders. Buildings here reflect the mix of Latino, American Indian, European American, and modern American cultures.

Suburbs of Phoenix, Arizona

HOT PLACE TO LIVE
The climate across much of the Southwest is hot and dry, with summer temperatures often reaching 38°C (100°F). Although water can be scarce, many people have a swimming pool in their garden so they can cool off.

DESERT LIFE
The saguaro cactus can reach up to 15 m (50 ft) tall, grow as many as 40 branches, and live for 200 years. Cacti, yucca, and other plants have all adapted to the hot, dry desert conditions found in the Southwest. So, too, have many animals, including the deadly rattlesnake.

Saguaro cacti in the Sonoran Desert

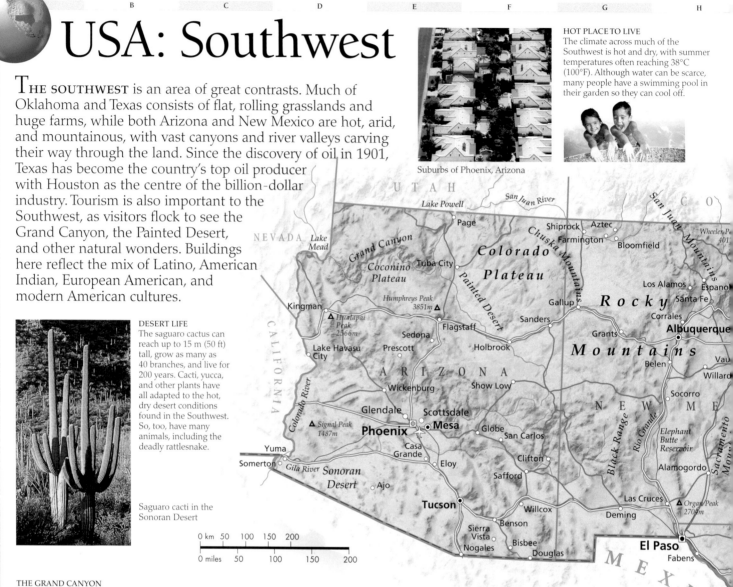

THE GRAND CANYON
The Grand Canyon in northern Arizona is one of the natural wonders of the world. This incredibly deep gorge was slowly cut out of the rock, beginning 6 million years ago, by the Colorado River. People can hike around its edge or venture down into the canyon to camp for the night.

AMERICAN-INDIAN CULTURES
American Indians, including Navajo, Hopi, and Apache, used to live across the Southwest but are now concentrated in reservations set up by the US government. The largest of these is in Arizona and New Mexico, and is home to the Navajo people. The Navajo farm the land and produce crafts, like the woven blanket wrapped around these Navajo children.

Kachina doll made by the Hopi

ADOBE HOUSES
Traditional homes of the Pueblo peoples of the Southwest were made from adobe bricks of sun-baked earth and straw covered with plaster. Dwellings had a flat roof and smooth walls. Modern adobe-style buildings can still be seen in the Southwest, but are often made of concrete and then painted to look like adobe. Here, a woman demonstrates baking bread in an adobe oven.

Astronaut leaving the shuttle by means of a manned manoeuvring unit (MMU)

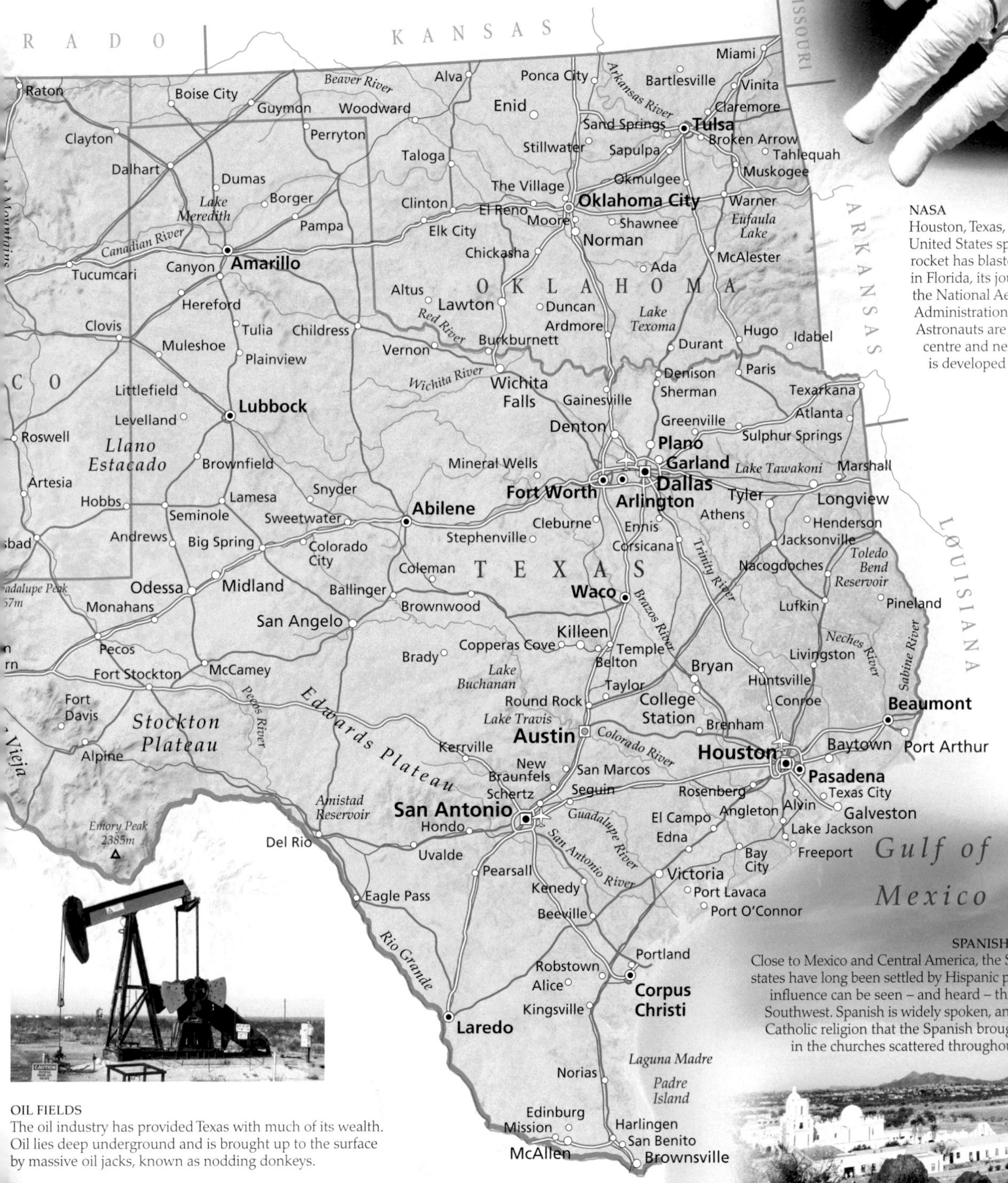

NASA
Houston, Texas, is the centre of the United States space programme. After a rocket has blasted off from Cape Canaveral in Florida, its journey is controlled by the National Aeronautics and Space Administration (NASA) from Houston. Astronauts are also trained at the centre and new space technology is developed here.

The Grand Canyon is up to 1.6 km (1 mile) deep, 29 km (18 miles) wide, and stretches for 349 km (217 miles).

OIL FIELDS
The oil industry has provided Texas with much of its wealth. Oil lies deep underground and is brought up to the surface by massive oil jacks, known as nodding donkeys.

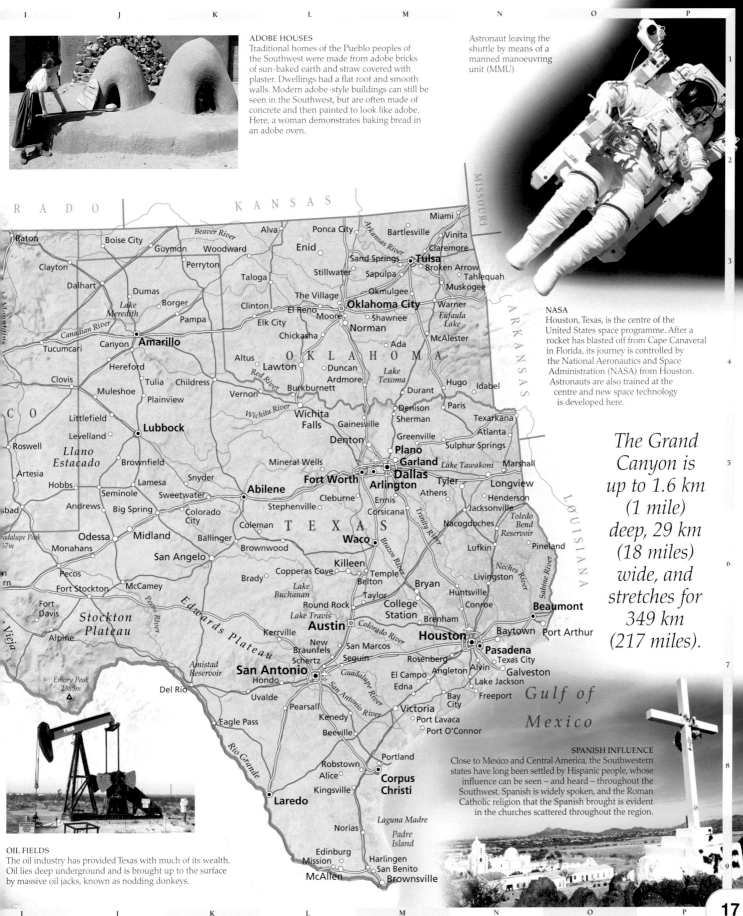

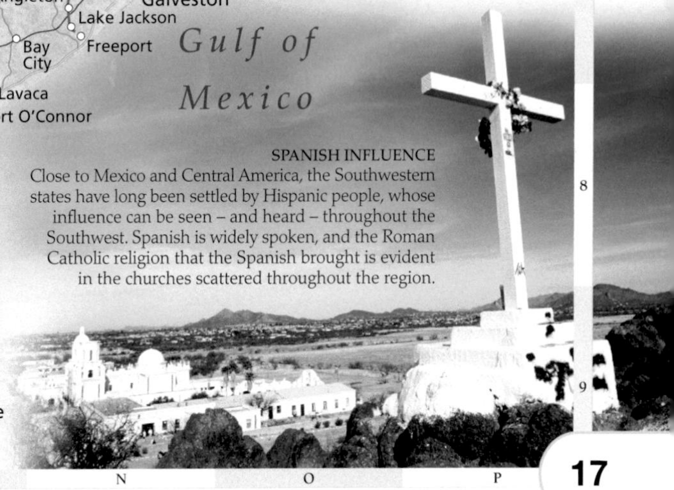

SPANISH INFLUENCE
Close to Mexico and Central America, the Southwestern states have long been settled by Hispanic people, whose influence can be seen – and heard – throughout the Southwest. Spanish is widely spoken, and the Roman Catholic religion that the Spanish brought is evident in the churches scattered throughout the region.

Mexico

ONCE HOME TO THE GREAT Aztec and Mayan civilizations and then the focus of Spanish conquistadors who came in search of wealth, Mexico today reflects its colourful past through its culture and architecture. The majority of Mexicans is mestizo (mixed race), of Spanish and native Indian descent. Mexico City, site of the ancient Aztec capital, is today one of the largest cities in the world, with a population of around 21 million. Despite oil and natural gas reserves, and a plentiful supply of labour, large numbers of Mexicans are still poor, especially in the rural areas and the urban slums.

ALONG THE BORDER
In 1994, Mexico signed the North American Free Trade Agreement (NAFTA), which effectively bound its economy to that of the USA. A large industrial area has developed along the Mexican border with the USA.

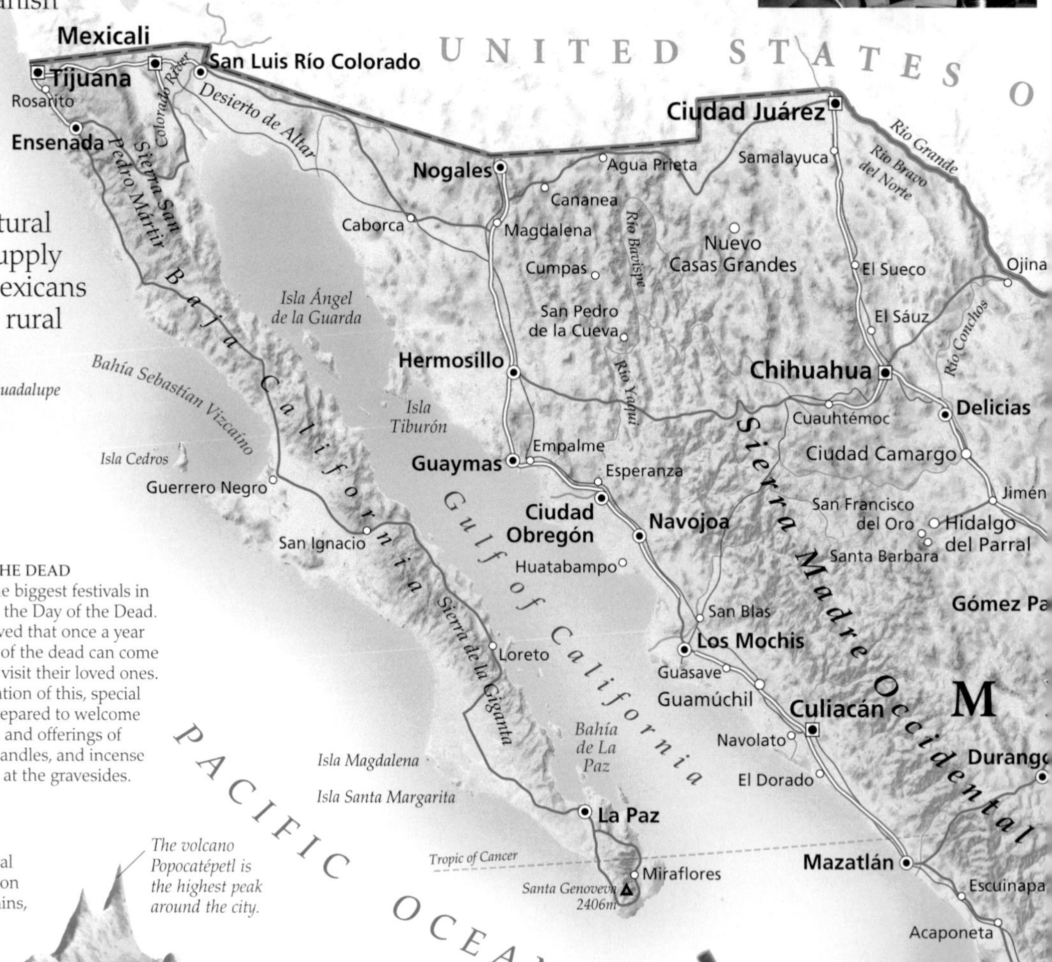
UNITED STATES O
Mexicali
Tijuana
Rosarito
Ensenada
San Luis Río Colorado
Colorado River
Desierto de Altar
Sierra San Pedro Mártir
Baja California
Nogales
Agua Prieta
Cananea
Caborca
Magdalena
Cumpas
Río Bavispe
Nuevo Casas Grandes
Ciudad Juárez
Samalayuca
Río Grande
Río Bravo del Norte
El Sueco
Ojina
El Sáuz
Río Conchos
Isla Ángel de la Guarda
San Pedro de la Cueva
Río Yaqui
Hermosillo
Chihuahua
Cuauhtémoc
Delicias
Isla Guadalupe
Bahía Sebastián Vizcaíno
Isla Tiburón
Isla Cedros
Guerrero Negro
Empalme
Guaymas
Esperanza
Ciudad Camargo
Jimén
Ciudad Obregón
Navojoa
San Francisco del Oro
Hidalgo del Parral
Santa Barbara
San Ignacio
Huatabampo
Gulf of California
Sierra Madre Occidental
Gómez Pa
San Blas
Los Mochis
Loreto
Sierra de la Giganta
Guasave
Guamúchil
Culiacán
M
Bahía de La Paz
Navolato
Durang
El Dorado
Isla Magdalena
PACIFIC OCEAN
Isla Santa Margarita
La Paz
Tropic of Cancer
Mazatlán
Miraflores
Santa Genoveva 2406m
Escuinapa
Acaponeta
Tuxpan
Tepic
Islas Marías
Puerto Vallarta
Manza

DAY OF THE DEAD
One of the biggest festivals in Mexico is the Day of the Dead. It is believed that once a year the souls of the dead can come back and visit their loved ones. In celebration of this, special food is prepared to welcome the souls, and offerings of flowers, candles, and incense are made at the gravesides.

LIFE IN THE CITY
Mexico City is the political, economic, and cultural hub of the country, and is home to some 16 million people. Its site, in a basin surrounded by mountains, means that expansion is difficult. Air pollution from factories and cars cannot escape, so on most days a thick layer of smog builds up over the city. Attempts to deal with the pollution, including banning cars from some parts, have had limited success.

The volcano Popocatépetl is the highest peak around the city.

Mexico City is contained within a ring of mountains.

WORKING ON THE LAND
Agriculture employs 6.5 million people – about one-eighth of Mexico's work force. However, only 12 per cent of the land is suitable for farming because it is so mountainous and dry. The peasant communities of the south rely on farming for their food, while communities in the north are more industrialized. Here, the agave plant is being harvested near the town of Tequila.

Mexican selling baskets, Puerto Escondido

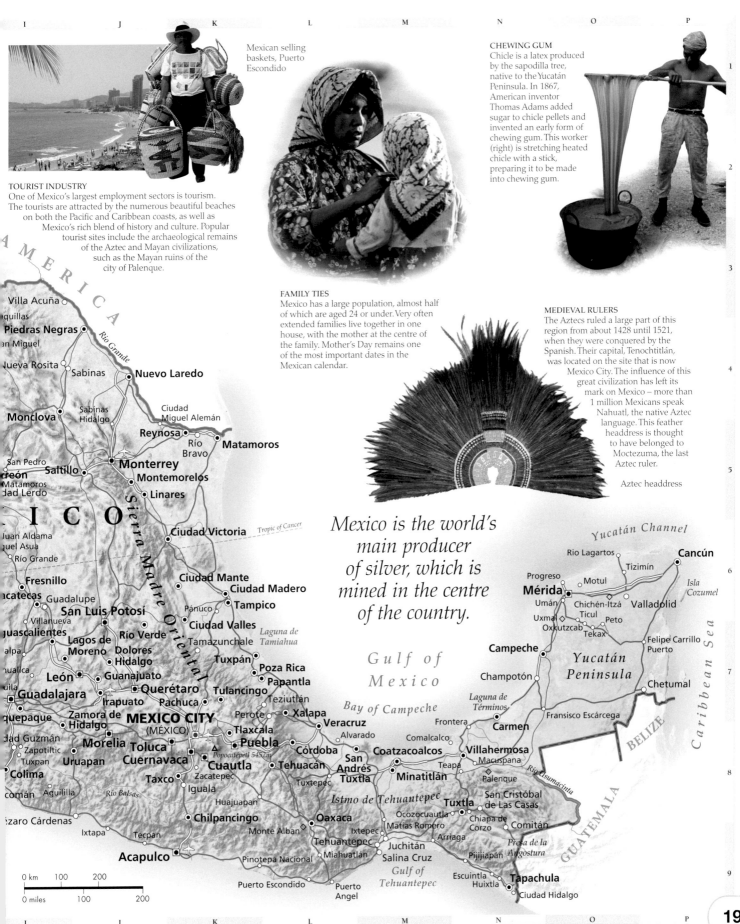

TOURIST INDUSTRY
One of Mexico's largest employment sectors is tourism. The tourists are attracted by the numerous beautiful beaches on both the Pacific and Caribbean coasts, as well as Mexico's rich blend of history and culture. Popular tourist sites include the archaeological remains of the Aztec and Mayan civilizations, such as the Mayan ruins of the city of Palenque.

FAMILY TIES
Mexico has a large population, almost half of which are aged 24 or under. Very often extended families live together in one house, with the mother at the centre of the family. Mother's Day remains one of the most important dates in the Mexican calendar.

CHEWING GUM
Chicle is a latex produced by the sapodilla tree, native to the Yucatán Peninsula. In 1867, American inventor Thomas Adams added sugar to chicle pellets and invented an early form of chewing gum. This worker (right) is stretching heated chicle with a stick, preparing it to be made into chewing gum.

MEDIEVAL RULERS
The Aztecs ruled a large part of this region from about 1428 until 1521, when they were conquered by the Spanish. Their capital, Tenochtitlán, was located on the site that is now Mexico City. The influence of this great civilization has left its mark on Mexico – more than 1 million Mexicans speak Nahuatl, the native Aztec language. This feather headdress is thought to have belonged to Moctezuma, the last Aztec ruler.

Aztec headdress

Mexico is the world's main producer of silver, which is mined in the centre of the country.

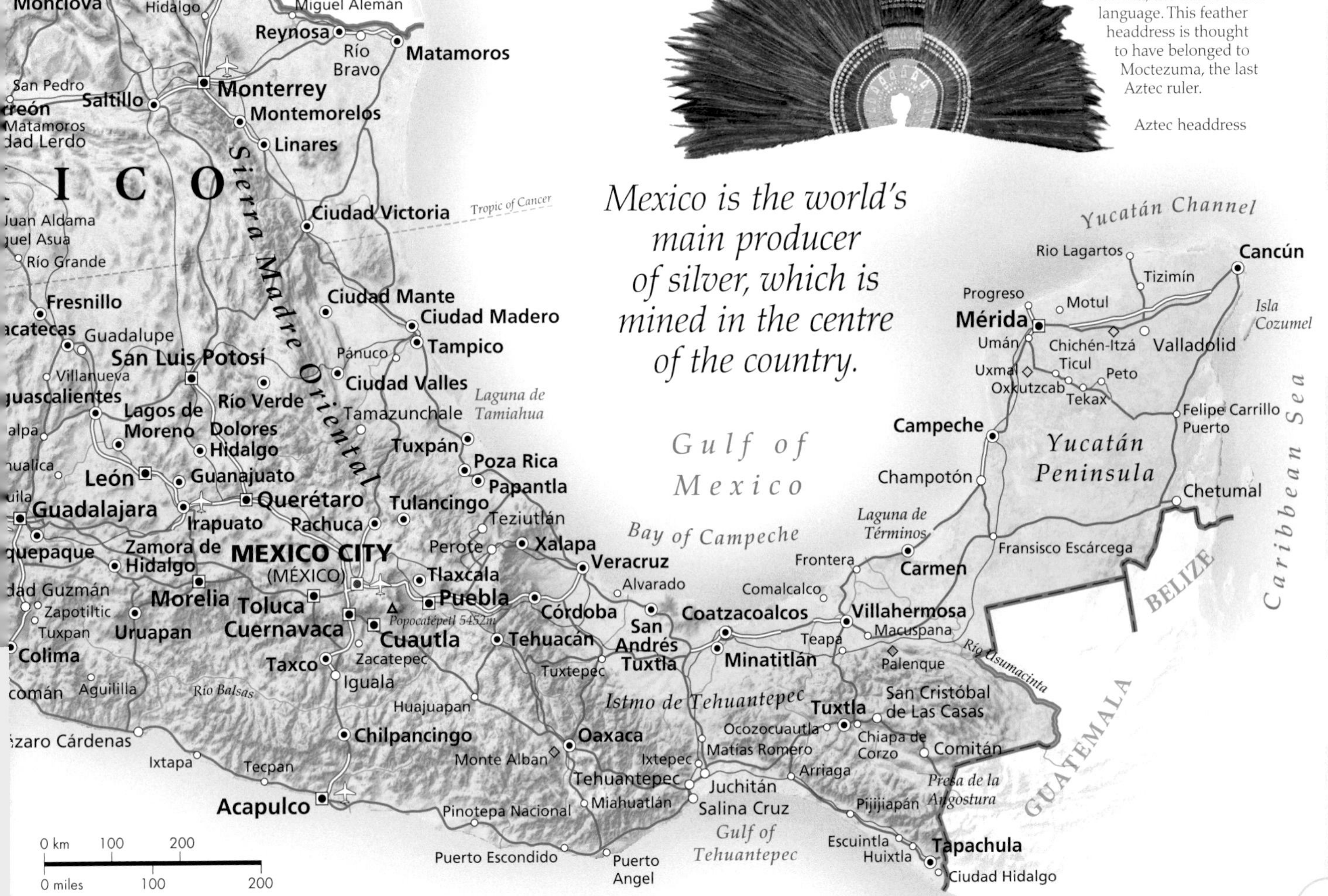

I J K L M N O P
1 2 3 4 5 6 7 8 9
AMERICA
Villa Acuña
Piedras Negras
Río Grande
Nueva Rosita
Sabinas
Nuevo Laredo
Monclova
Sabinas Hidalgo
Ciudad Miguel Alemán
Reynosa
Río Bravo
Matamoros
San Pedro
Saltillo
Monterrey
Montemorelos
Linares
Sierra Madre Oriental
ICO
Ciudad Victoria
Tropic of Cancer
Juan Aldama
Río Grande
Fresnillo
Ciudad Mante
Ciudad Madero
Guadalupe
Tampico
San Luis Potosí
Pánuco
Villanueva
Ciudad Valles
Laguna de Tamiahua
Río Verde
Lagos de Moreno
Dolores Hidalgo
Tamazunchale
Tuxpán
Poza Rica
León
Guanajuato
Papantla
Querétaro
Tulancingo
Guadalajara
Irapuato
Pachuca
Teziutlán
Zamora de Hidalgo
MEXICO CITY (MÉXICO)
Perote
Xalapa
Veracruz
Tlaxcala
Puebla
Alvarado
Morelia
Toluca
Córdoba
Popocatépetl 5452m
Zapotiltic
Uruapan
Cuernavaca
Cuautla
Tehuacán
San Andrés Tuxtla
Colima
Taxco
Zacatepec
Iguala
Tuxtepec
Aguililla
Río Balsas
Huajuapan
Chilpancingo
Oaxaca
Monte Albán
Ixtapa
Tecpan
Acapulco
Pinotepa Nacional
Miahuatlán
Puerto Escondido
Puerto Angel
Gulf of Mexico
Bay of Campeche
Coatzacoalcos
Minatitlán
Istmo de Tehuantepec
Ixtepec
Matías Romero
Tehuantepec
Juchitán
Salina Cruz
Gulf of Tehuantepec
Comalcalco
Frontera
Villahermosa
Teapa
Macuspana
Palenque
Río Usumacinta
Tuxtla
San Cristóbal de Las Casas
Ocozocuautla
Chiapa de Corzo
Comitán
Arriaga
Presa de la Angostura
Pijijiapan
Escuintla
Huixtla
Tapachula
Ciudad Hidalgo
GUATEMALA
BELIZE
Laguna de Términos
Carmen
Champotón
Campeche
Fransisco Escárcega
Chetumal
Yucatán Peninsula
Felipe Carrillo Puerto
Caribbean Sea
Yucatán Channel
Río Lagartos
Cancún
Tizimín
Progreso
Motul
Mérida
Umán
Chichén-Itzá
Valladolid
Isla Cozumel
Uxmal
Ticul
Peto
Oxkutzcab
Tekax
0 km 100 200
0 miles 100 200

Central America

VOLCANOES, EARTHQUAKES, and hurricanes threaten the livelihoods of people in the seven countries of Central America. People here have also struggled with poverty and civil war. In more recent years, however, peace and economic recovery have offered hope, and education is now free in all countries. Remains of the ancient Mayan civilization that flourished until the 16th century, when the Spanish invaded, can be seen throughout the region. Large numbers of the native population died after the invasion, mostly from disease. Today, Spanish is the main language of the region.

Lake Nicaragua is the only freshwater lake in the world that contains sharks.

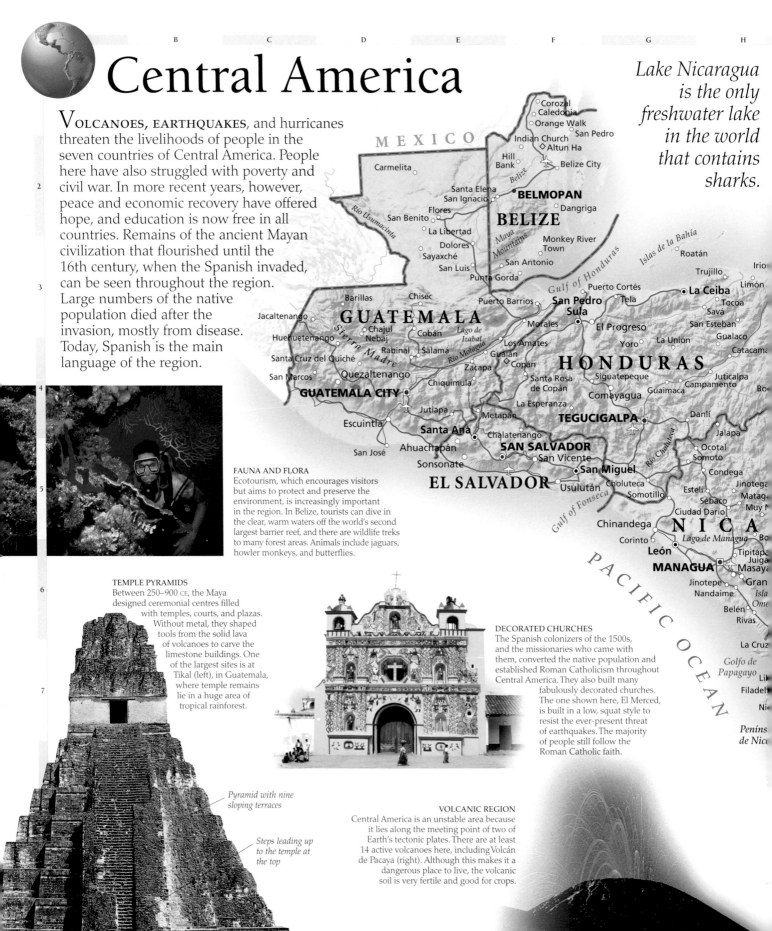

FAUNA AND FLORA
Ecotourism, which encourages visitors but aims to protect and preserve the environment, is increasingly important in the region. In Belize, tourists can dive in the clear, warm waters off the world's second largest barrier reef, and there are wildlife treks to many forest areas. Animals include jaguars, howler monkeys, and butterflies.

TEMPLE PYRAMIDS
Between 250–900 CE, the Maya designed ceremonial centres filled with temples, courts, and plazas. Without metal, they shaped tools from the solid lava of volcanoes to carve the limestone buildings. One of the largest sites is at Tikal (left), in Guatemala, where temple remains lie in a huge area of tropical rainforest.

Pyramid with nine sloping terraces

Steps leading up to the temple at the top

DECORATED CHURCHES
The Spanish colonizers of the 1500s, and the missionaries who came with them, converted the native population and established Roman Catholicism throughout Central America. They also built many fabulously decorated churches. The one shown here, El Merced, is built in a low, squat style to resist the ever-present threat of earthquakes. The majority of people still follow the Roman Catholic faith.

VOLCANIC REGION
Central America is an unstable area because it lies along the meeting point of two of Earth's tectonic plates. There are at least 14 active volcanoes here, including Volcán de Pacaya (right). Although this makes it a dangerous place to live, the volcanic soil is very fertile and good for crops.

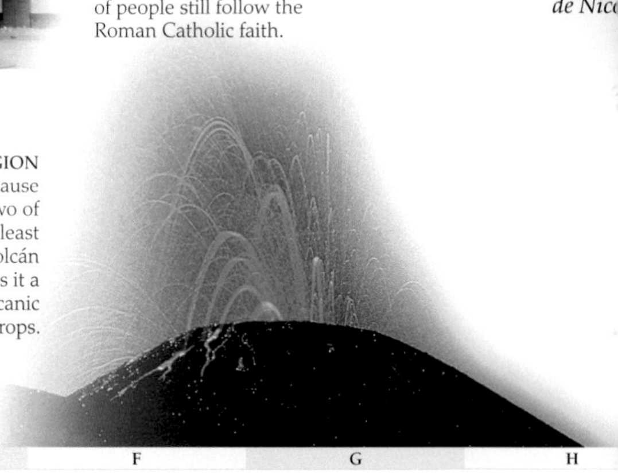

FOOD MARKETS

Coffee, bananas, and sugar cane are all key exports from here to the food markets of the world. Most are cultivated on large plantations. However, food for the local population, such as potatoes, avocados, rice, and maize, is grown on small farms and sold at local markets.

Markets, selling fresh fruit and vegetables

NATIVE PEOPLES

These Cuna Indians of Panama wear traditional embroidered clothes. Native Indians and mestizos (people of mixed heritage) form a small minority in the region, although the ethnic mix varies from country to country. In Guatemala, more than half the people are direct descendants of the Maya Indians.

BANANA INDUSTRY

The hot, wet climate of Honduras is perfect for cultivating fruit, such as bananas. These are often grown on huge plantations, which employ local people who may work long hours for very little pay. Once cut down, the bananas are washed, inspected, and packed into boxes to be sent abroad. Bananas are a major export for Honduras.

As bananas grow, they begin to point upwards.

COFFEE BEANS

Costa Rica was the first country in Central America to grow coffee and today produces more than 150,000 tonnes each year. Coffee is harvested from the fruit of the coffee bush. Once picked, the beans are left to dry in the sun. This worker is raking the beans as they dry.

PANAMA CANAL

Forming a vital link between the Atlantic and Pacific Oceans, the Panama Canal is one of the world's busiest waterways. After sharing the canal with the US, Panama took full control in 1999. Over the years, trade has made Panama City a major financial centre.

The Caribbean

THIS REGION CONSISTS of thousands of islands stretching from Cuba in the west to Trinidad and Tobago in the southeast. European colonists wanted control of the islands in the 1500s, but the diseases they brought wiped out most of the local Carib and Arawak peoples. African slaves, imported to work on plantations, replaced local peoples and today most of the population are descended from those Africans. English, Spanish, and French are spoken in different countries, depending on which European power claimed the territory. Tourism and agriculture are major sources of employment.

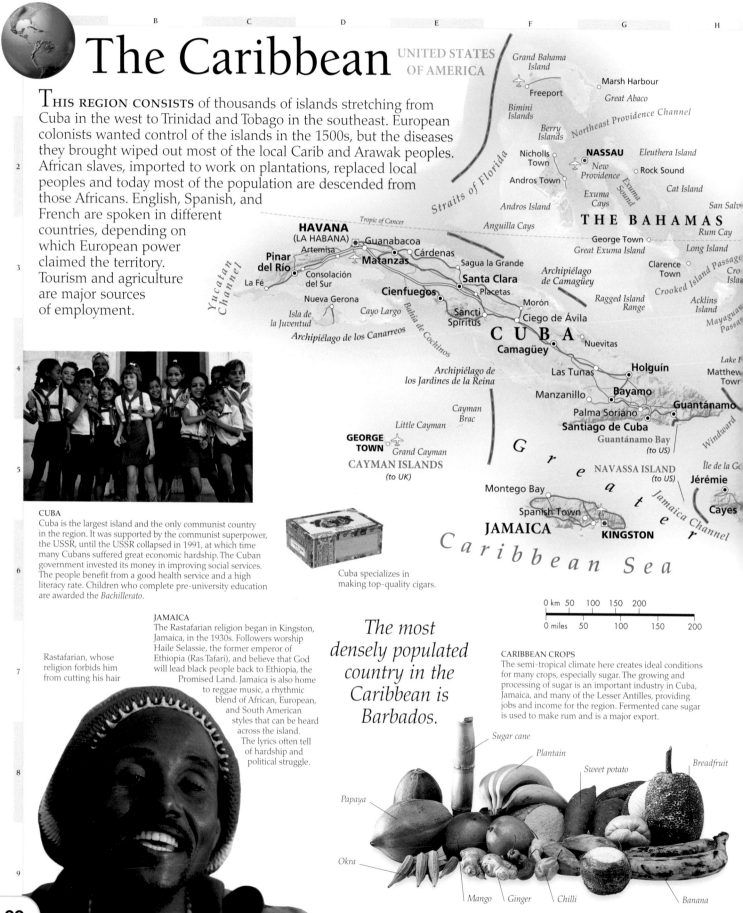

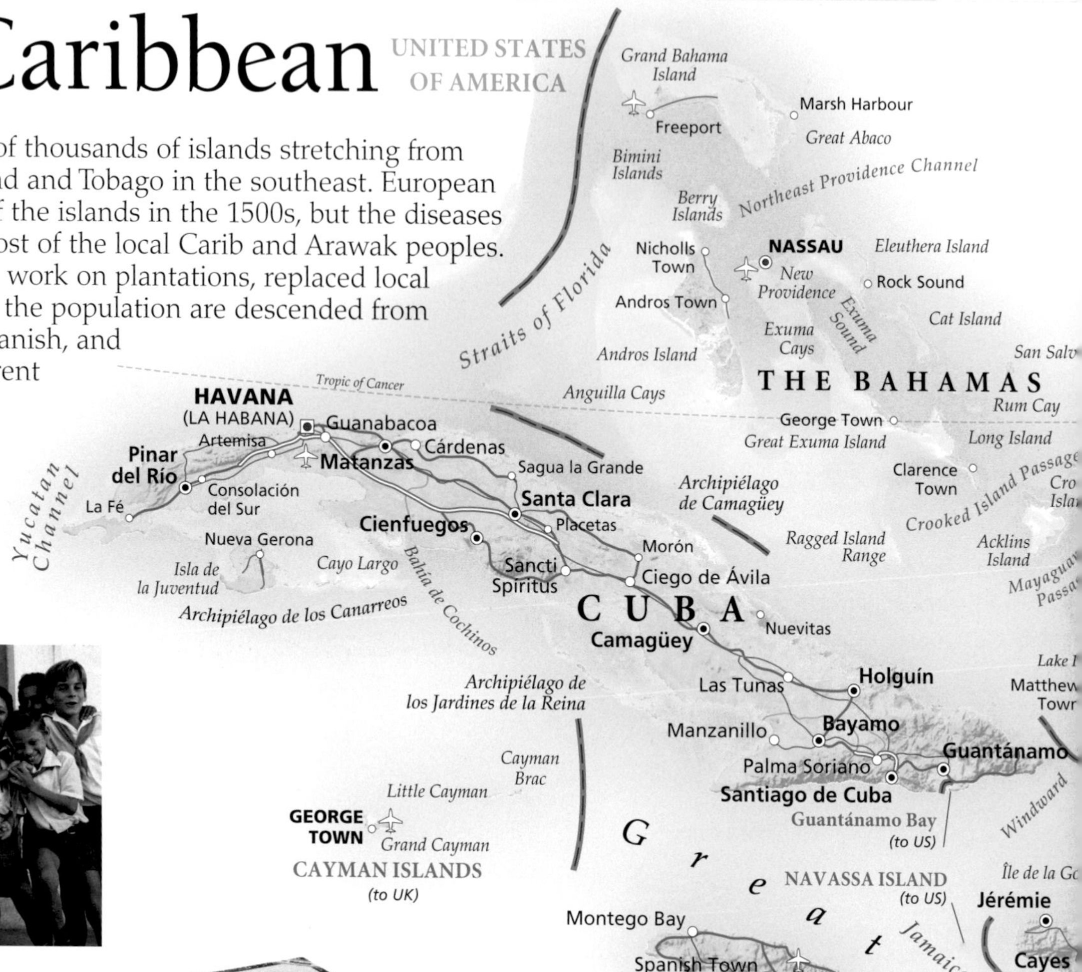
UNITED STATES OF AMERICA
Grand Bahama Island
Freeport
Marsh Harbour
Great Abaco
Bimini Islands
Berry Islands
Northeast Providence Channel
Nicholls Town
NASSAU
New Providence
Eleuthera Island
Rock Sound
Andros Town
Exuma Sound
Exuma Cays
Cat Island
Straits of Florida
Andros Island
San Salv
THE BAHAMAS
Anguilla Cays
Rum Cay
George Town
Great Exuma Island
Long Island
Tropic of Cancer
HAVANA (LA HABANA)
Guanabacoa
Artemisa
Cárdenas
Pinar del Río
Matanzas
Sagua la Grande
Archipiélago de Camagüey
Clarence Town
Crooked Island Passage
Yucatan Channel
La Fé
Consolación del Sur
Santa Clara
Placetas
Cienfuegos
Ragged Island Range
Acklins Island
Nueva Gerona
Morón
Isla de la Juventud
Cayo Largo
Bahía de Cochinos
Sancti Spíritus
Ciego de Ávila
Mayaguana Passage
Archipiélago de los Canarreos
CUBA
Camagüey
Nuevitas
Archipiélago de los Jardines de la Reina
Las Tunas
Holguín
Matthew Town
Manzanillo
Bayamo
Cayman Brac
Palma Soriano
Guantánamo
Little Cayman
Santiago de Cuba
GEORGE TOWN
Guantánamo Bay (to US)
Grand Cayman
Windward
CAYMAN ISLANDS (to UK)
Greater
NAVASSA ISLAND (to US)
Jérémie
Montego Bay
Jamaica Channel
Cayes
Spanish Town
JAMAICA
KINGSTON
Caribbean Sea
0 km 50 100 150 200
0 miles 50 100 150 200

CUBA
Cuba is the largest island and the only communist country in the region. It was supported by the communist superpower, the USSR, until the USSR collapsed in 1991, at which time many Cubans suffered great economic hardship. The Cuban government invested its money in improving social services. The people benefit from a good health service and a high literacy rate. Children who complete pre-university education are awarded the *Bachillerato*.

Cuba specializes in making top-quality cigars.

JAMAICA
The Rastafarian religion began in Kingston, Jamaica, in the 1930s. Followers worship Haile Selassie, the former emperor of Ethiopia (Ras Tafari), and believe that God will lead black people back to Ethiopia, the Promised Land. Jamaica is also home to reggae music, a rhythmic blend of African, European, and South American styles that can be heard across the island. The lyrics often tell of hardship and political struggle.

Rastafarian, whose religion forbids him from cutting his hair

The most densely populated country in the Caribbean is Barbados.

CARIBBEAN CROPS
The semi-tropical climate here creates ideal conditions for many crops, especially sugar. The growing and processing of sugar is an important industry in Cuba, Jamaica, and many of the Lesser Antilles, providing jobs and income for the region. Fermented cane sugar is used to make rum and is a major export.

Sugar cane
Plantain
Sweet potato
Breadfruit
Papaya
Okra
Mango
Ginger
Chilli
Banana

I J K L M N O P

HURRICANES
The Caribbean islands can be devastated by hurricanes between May and October each year. These powerful and damaging storms occur when a normal storm builds up energy as it moves across the Atlantic Ocean. Eventually, violent winds and torrential rain are released on the islands.

FAMILY LIFE
Family is very important here, and is usually the centre of everyday life. Some Caribbean people migrated to other countries, such as the UK, but return when they retire – often bringing considerable money back with them.

TROPICAL ISLES
White sands and warm seas attract vast numbers of visitors to these islands. Tourism is important to the economies of many countries including the Bahamas and the Dominican Republic. Many people work in tourism-related jobs, such as in hotels.

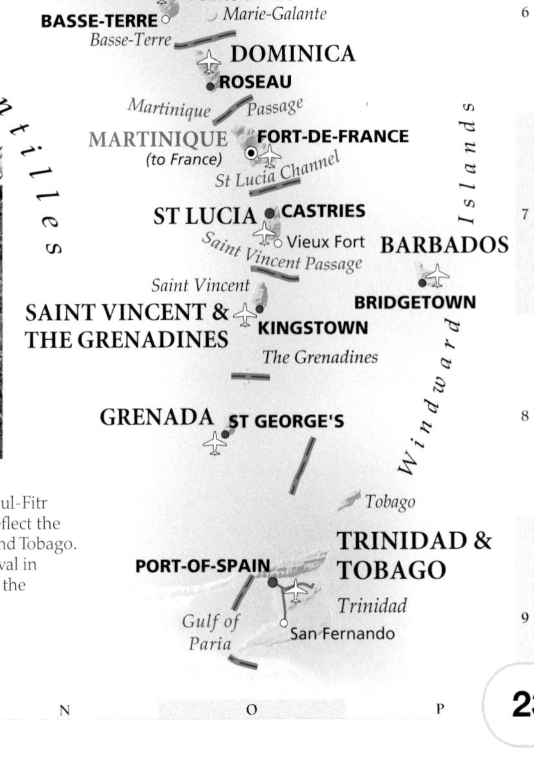
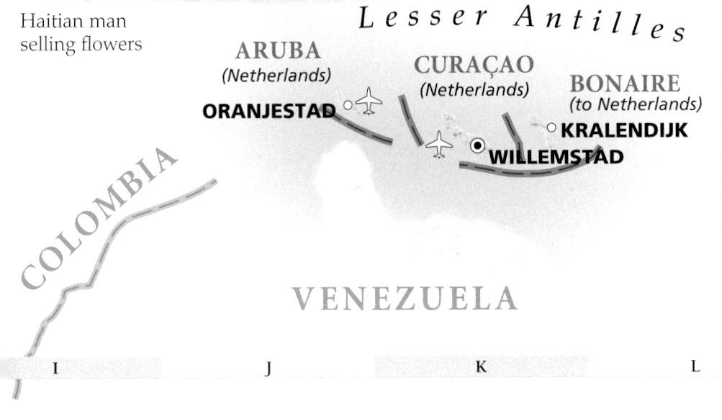
Tropic of Cancer
yaguana
cos Passage
TURKS & CAICOS ISLANDS
(to UK)
COCKBURN TOWN
tle Inagua
at Inagua
DOMINICAN REPUBLIC
Cap-aïtien
Monte Cristi
Puerto Plata
Santiago
Gonaïves
San Francisco de Macorís
HAITI
Cordillera Central
La Vega
La Romana
PORT-AU-PRINCE
SANTO DOMINGO
cmel
Isla Saona
Mona Passage
Isla Mona
Isla Beata
SAN JUAN
Mayagüez
Caguas
Ponce
PUERTO RICO
(to US)
VIRGIN ISLANDS
(to US)
BRITISH VIRGIN ISLANDS
(to UK)
ROAD TOWN
CHARLOTTE AMALIE
St Croix
ANGUILLA
(to UK)
THE VALLEY
Sint Maarten
(to Netherlands)
Saba
(to Netherlands)
BASSETERRE
SAINT KITTS & NEVIS
ANTIGUA & BARBUDA
Barbuda
ST JOHN'S
Antigua
BRADES
MONTSERRAT
(to UK)
Grande Terre
GUADELOUPE
(to France)
Pointe-à-Pitre
Marie-Galante
BASSE-TERRE
Basse-Terre
DOMINICA
ROSEAU
Martinique Passage
MARTINIQUE
(to France)
FORT-DE-FRANCE
St Lucia Channel
ST LUCIA
CASTRIES
Vieux Fort
Saint Vincent Passage
BARBADOS
Saint Vincent
BRIDGETOWN
SAINT VINCENT & THE GRENADINES
KINGSTOWN
The Grenadines
GRENADA
ST GEORGE'S
Tobago
TRINIDAD & TOBAGO
PORT-OF-SPAIN
Trinidad
Gulf of Paria
San Fernando
ATLANTIC OCEAN
Leeward Islands
Lesser Antilles
Windward Islands
tilles
Lesser Antilles
ARUBA
(Netherlands)
ORANJESTAD
CURAÇAO
(Netherlands)
WILLEMSTAD
BONAIRE
(to Netherlands)
KRALENDIJK
COLOMBIA
VENEZUELA

HAITI
Haiti was the first Caribbean country to become independent. However, political unrest, combined with poor soil and natural disasters, have made Haiti one of the poorest countries in the world. Health care and sanitation levels are poor and, as a result, life expectancy is low.

Haitian man selling flowers

A TIME TO CELEBRATE
The celebration of Diwali (Hindu), Eid ul-Fitr (Muslim), and Christmas (Christian) reflect the varied religions of people in Trinidad and Tobago. The woman above is dressed for Carnival in Port of Spain to mark the beginning of the Christian season of Lent.

1 2 3 4 5 6 7 8 9

I J K L M N O P

SOUTH AMERICA

Although South America is much poorer than its northern neighbour, it is rich in natural resources. Its mineral wealth led to its invasion by the Portuguese and Spanish in the 1500s, and their languages and culture still shape the lives of the people here. The nations below are listed in order of area, headed by Brazil – the world's fifth largest country.

Brazil
8,515,770 sq km
3,287,957 sq miles
205,824,000
Brasília
Portuguese, German, Italian, Spanish, Polish, Japanese, Amerindian languages

Venezuela
912,050 sq km
352,144 sq miles
30,912,000
Caracas
Spanish, Amerindian languages

Latin American culture is world famous, thanks to its infectious music and dance. Here a couple in Buenos Aires, Argentina, demonstrate the art of the tango.

Bolivia
1,098,581 sq km
424,164 sq miles
10,970,000
La Paz
Aymara, Quechua, Spanish

Chile
756,102 sq km
291,933 sq miles
17,650,000
Santiago
Spanish, Amerindian languages

Argentina
2,780,400 sq km
1,073,518 sq miles
43,887,000
Buenos Aires
Spanish, Italian, Amerindian languages

Paraguay
406,752 sq km
157,048 sq miles
6,863,000
Asunción
Guaraní, Spanish, German

Ecuador
283,561 sq km
109,484 sq miles
16,081,000
Quito
Spanish, Quechua, other Amerindian languages

Peru
1,285,216 sq km
496,225 sq miles
30,741,000
Lima
Spanish, Quechua, Aymara

Guyana
214,969 sq km
83,000 sq miles
736,000
Georgetown
English Creole, Hindi, Tamil, Amerindian languages, English

Uruguay
176,215 sq km
68,037 sq miles
3,351,000
Montevideo
Spanish

Colombia
1,138,910 sq km
439,736 sq miles
47,221,000
Bogotá
Spanish, Wayuu, Páez, and other Amerindian languages

Football is a national passion in Brazil. Most of these barefoot boys on Ipanema beach, Rio de Janeiro, will be dreaming of playing for Brazil in the World Cup.

Suriname
163,820 sq km
63,251 sq miles
585,800
Paramaribo
Sranan (creole), Dutch, Javanese, Sarnami Hindi, Saramaccan (creole), Chinese, Carib

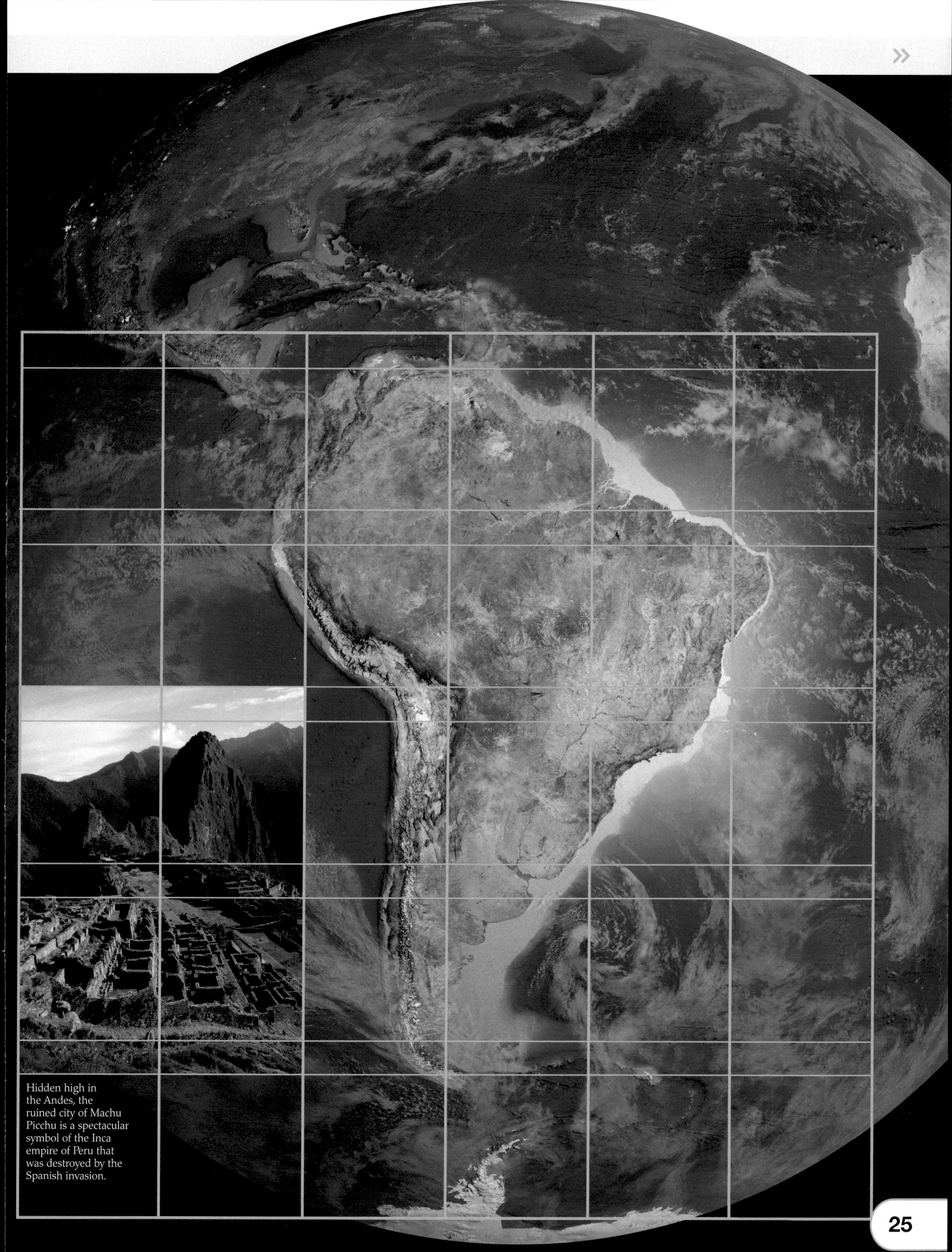

Hidden high in the Andes, the ruined city of Machu Picchu is a spectacular symbol of the Inca empire of Peru that was destroyed by the Spanish invasion.

Northwest South America

HIGH MOUNTAINS AND PLATEAUS, dense tropical rainforest, and coastal swamps are found in this region. In the 16th century, promises of untold riches attracted the Spanish to the countries here. They found the vast empire of the Incas, which stretched from what is now Peru into northern Colombia. To the north and east, other colonizers – Dutch, English, and French – arrived. Today, although the countries are independent, with the exception of French Guiana, Spanish remains the main language. The population is mainly a mix of native peoples and Europeans, except along the Caribbean coast where descendants of former African slaves live.

ANDES MOUNTAINS
The Andes, the world's longest mountain chain, extends 7,250 km (4,505 miles) down the western edge of South America. Barley, wheat, and potatoes grow well in highland areas, and are cultivated on the terraced hillsides.

FRENCH GUIANA
French Guiana is the only remaining colony in South America, and is governed by France. Tropical forests cover more than four-fifths of its land. In 1968, the European Space Agency established a launch site on the coast at Kourou, which is still used today.

CARACAS
Venezuela's population is growing rapidly and more than 89 per cent of its people now live in cities. The oil industry brings in considerable wealth, but many people are still poor. Although Caracas, Venezuela's capital city, is an important financial centre, it has many shantytowns.

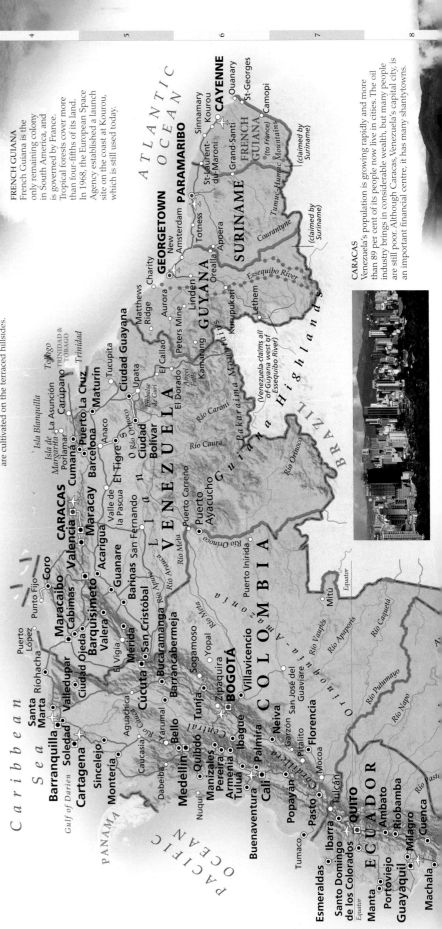

0 km 100 200 300 400
0 miles 100 200 300 400
P E R U
B O L I V I A
B R A Z I L
PARAGUAY
ARGENTINA
CHILE
PACIFIC OCEAN
Andes
Cordillera Occidental
Altiplano
Tropic of Capricorn
Piura
Ferreñafe
Chiclayo
San Pedro de Lloc
Trujillo
Chimbote
Huaraz
Huarmey
Chiquián
Huacho
Callao
LIMA
Pisco
Ica
Nazca
Lomas
Camaná
Chachapoyas
Cajamarca
Tarapoto
Pucallpa
Aguaytía
Huánuco
Cerro de Pasco
Huancayo
Ayacucho
Quillabamba
Machu Picchu
Cusco
Puerto Maldonado
Ayaviri
Juliaca
Puno
Arequipa
Moquegua
Tacna
Nevado Ampato 6310m
Nevado Pupuya 5818m
Nevado Sajama 6520m
Lake Titicaca
Copacabana
LA PAZ
Cochabamba
Oruro
Lago Poopó
Sabaya
Uncía
Aiquile
SUCRE
Potosí
Uyuni
Villa Martín
Tupiza
Villazón
Tarija
Monteagudo
Santa Cruz
Buena Vista
Montero
San José
San Matías
Puerto Suárez
Trinidad
Magdalena
Reyes
Cobija
Riberalta
Fortaleza
Río Abunã
Río Beni
Río Madre de Dios
Río Mamoré
Río Guaporé
Río San Miguel
Río Huallaga
Río Ucayali

ANGEL FALLS
Each year thousands of tourists visit the spectacular Angel Falls on the River Churún in eastern Venezuela. They were spotted by an American pilot, Jimmy Angel, in 1935, and later named after him. The water drops for 807 m (2,648 ft), making Angel Falls the highest uninterrupted waterfall in the world.

MACHU PICCHU
The conquering Spaniards never found the remains of this important Inca city – it remained a secret until Hiram Bingham, an American archaeologist and explorer, discovered its ruins hidden in the forest in 1911. Situated on a high ridge northwest of Cusco, this magnificent ruined city covers 13 sq km (5 sq miles), and has small houses, temples, and stairways built around a central square.

The railway from Lima climbs 4,818 m (15,807 ft) into the Andes and is the highest in the Americas.

Quechua woman in Peru

THE INCAS
The Incas first lived in the mountainous area near Cusco in Peru. By the time of the Spanish invasion, the Inca Empire extended north into southern Colombia and south through Bolivia and into Argentina and Chile. The Quechua Indians were the most powerful group in the empire, and theirs was the official language. The Quechua and Aymara peoples now live on the high plains in the Andes.

MINERALS
Many countries in this area have extensive reserves of gold, silver, copper, and gems. Colombia produces more than half the world's emeralds. The Incas made good use of these resources and created many beautiful golden objects, such as this llama.

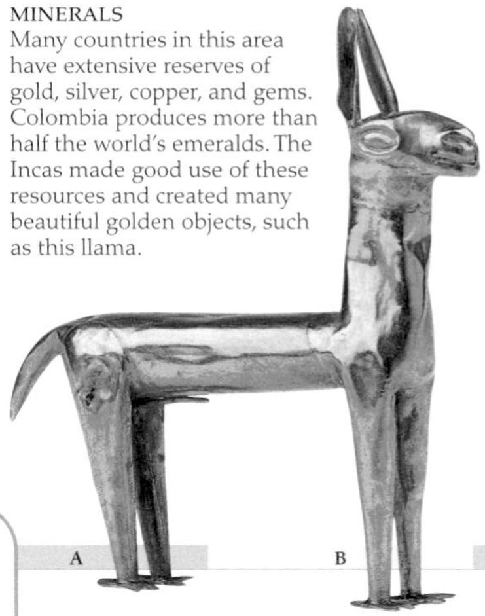

LAKE TITICACA
At 3,812 m (12,507 ft), Lake Titicaca is the highest navigable lake in the world. It is also South America's largest lake. The Uru people live here in houses built on huge, floating reed islands. They grow potatoes, hunt birds, and catch fish, using boats made from tightly bundled reeds.

LIFE ON THE HIGH PLAINS
The Altiplano is a cold plateau at high altitude between two ranges of the Andes Mountains in southwest Bolivia and southern Peru. The native peoples who live here graze sheep and llamas on the windy plains. They have generally retained their own language and customs.

Brazil

THE VIBRANT CULTURE OF BRAZIL – with its fusion of music and dance – reflects the rich mix of its ethnic groups. The country also boasts immense natural resources with well-developed mining and manufacturing industries. Brazil grows all its own food and exports large quantities of coffee, sugar cane, soya beans, oranges, and cotton. However, the wealth is not evenly distributed, with some people living in luxury while most struggle with poverty. São Paulo is home to more than 21 million people, but poverty and lack of housing means that many live in shantytowns without running water or sanitation. Brazil was colonized in the 16th century by the Portuguese, who established their language and their Roman Catholic faith. It remains a deeply Catholic country with a strong emphasis on family life.

COFFEE
Brazil produces about one-quarter of the world's coffee, which is grown on large plantations in the states of Paraná and São Paulo. However, because world coffee prices go up and down so much, Brazilians are now growing other crops for export as well.

VENEZUELA
COLOMBIA
Guiana Highlands
Uraricoera
Boa Vista
Caracaraí
Roraima
Pico da Neblina 3014m
Equator
Represa Balbina
Rio Negro
Rio Japurá
Rio Içá
Manaus
Tefé
Amazon
Coari
Rio Juruá
Rio Purus
Rio Madeira
Rio Javari
Amazon Basin
Humaitá
Japiim
Feijó
PERU
Acre
B
R
Porto Velho
Rio Abunã
Rondônia
Chapada dos Parecis
Guaporé
Vilhena
BOLIVIA

AMAZON RAINFOREST
Covering more than one-third of Brazil, the rainforest is home to a huge variety of animal and plant life. At one time, more than 5 million native Indians also lived here, but now only about 200,000 remain. Over the years, vast areas of forest have been cut down to provide timber for export, to make way for farmland, or to mine minerals such as gold, silver, and iron. The Kaxinawa Indians (left) still cultivate root vegetables as a food crop.

Brazilian morpho butterfly with brilliant blue wings, lives in rainforests from Brazil to Venezuela.

BRASÍLIA
Brasília replaced Rio de Janeiro as Brazil's capital in 1960 as part of a scheme to develop the interior of the country. Situated on land that was once rainforest, the city is laid out in the shape of an aeroplane. Government buildings are in the "cockpit", and residential areas are in the "wings".

FOOTBALL ENTHUSIASTS
Brazilians are passionate about football, which is played everywhere from beaches to shantytowns. There is fervent support for the national team, which has won the World Cup more times than any other country, most recently in 2002.

PEOPLE OF BRAZIL
Brazilians come from a variety of different ethnic groups, including descendants of the original native Indians, the Portuguese colonizers, African slaves brought over to work in the sugar plantations, and European migrants.

I
J
K
L
M
N
O
P
1
2
3
4
5
6
7
8
9
0 km 200 400
0 miles 200 400
FRENCH GUIANA (to France)
SURINAME
Tumuc-Humac Mountains
Mouths of the Amazon
ATLANTIC OCEAN
Amapá
Macapá
Ilha Caviana de Fora
Equator
Baía de Marajó
Ilha de Marajó
Belém
Baía de São Marcos
Alenquer
Amazon
Santarém
Altamira
São Luís
Parnaíba
Camocim
Fortaleza
Itaituba
Represa de Tucuruí
Piripiri
Bacabal
Teresina
Rio Tapajós
Rio Xingu
Marabá
Imperatriz
Ceará
Cabo de São Roque
Mossoró
Assu
Maranhão
Rio Grande do Norte
Natal
João Pessoa
Floriano
Pará
Serra do Cachimbo
Carolina
Picos
Paraíba
Araguaína
Balsas
Juazeiro do Norte
Campina Grande
Piauí
Pernambuco
Recife
BRAZIL
Cachimbo
Rio Tocantins
Represa de Sobradinho
Alagoas
Juazeiro
Rio São Manuel
Serra Formosa
Serra dos Gradaús
Palmas do Tocantis
Maceió
Chapada Diamantina
Rio São Francisco
Aracaju
Estância
Tocantins
Barreiras
Mato Grosso
Taguatinga
Feira de Santana
Bahia
Salvador
Baía de Todos os Santos
Rio Araguaia
Goiás
Planalto Central
Vitória da Conquista
Itabuna
Cuiabá
BRASÍLIA
Janaúba
Canavieiras
Anápolis
Rondonópolis
Goiânia
Montes Claros
Minas Gerais
Araçuaí
Jataí
Pantanal
Caravelas
Araguari
Mato Grosso do Sul
Governador Valadares
Espírito Santo
Uberlândia
Uberaba
Campo Grande
Belo Horizonte
Aquidauana
São José do Rio Preto
Divinópolis
Vitória
Ribeirão Preto
Presidente Epitácio
Juiz de Fora
Campos dos Goytacazes
Marília
Campinas
Londrina
Nova Iguaçu
Rio de Janeiro
Maringá
São Paulo
Tropic of Capricorn
PARAGUAY
Paraná
Santos
Represa de Itaipú
Ponta Grossa
Curitiba
Saltos do Iguaçu
Rio Iguaçu
Joinville
Blumenau
Santa Catarina
Florianópolis
ATLANTIC OCEAN
Passo Fundo
Rio Grande do Sul
Santa Maria
Canoas
Porto Alegre
Bagé
Lagoa dos Patos
Rio Grande
URUGUAY
Mirim Lagoon

AMAZON TRANSPORT
The River Amazon provides Brazil with its most important transport link, not only for tourists but also for trade. Large boats can travel as far inland as the city of Manaus.

RIO CARNIVAL
During the five days leading up to Lent, Rio de Janeiro celebrates Carnival. There are street parties, balls, and parades in the streets, and samba schools compete for awards for best costume and best float.

São Paulo has the world's largest Japanese community outside Japan.

BEACH CULTURE
Wide, sandy beaches along the eastern coast of Brazil provide a playground for large numbers of Brazilians who come here to relax, meet friends, and play volleyball or football. By far the most popular beach is Copacabana (right) in Rio de Janeiro. Only the strongest swimmers brave the strong tides of the Atlantic.

Southern South America

Towering mountains, vast grassy plains, and hot deserts create a very diverse geographical landscape. The four countries in this region – Chile, Paraguay, Uruguay, and Argentina – were once Spanish colonies but gained their independence in the early 1800s. Each country has an elected government but their economies remain fragile. Most of the population speak Spanish and are mestizo – of mixed Spanish and native Indian descent – except for Argentina, where up to 97 per cent are descended from Europeans.

ITAIPÚ DAM
The enormous Itaipú dam on the Paraná River in Paraguay is one of the world's largest hydroelectric projects. It generates 75 per cent of the electricity Paraguay needs as well as large amounts for export.

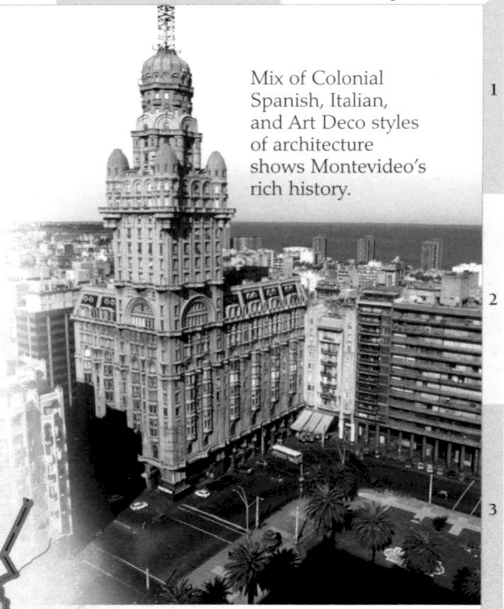

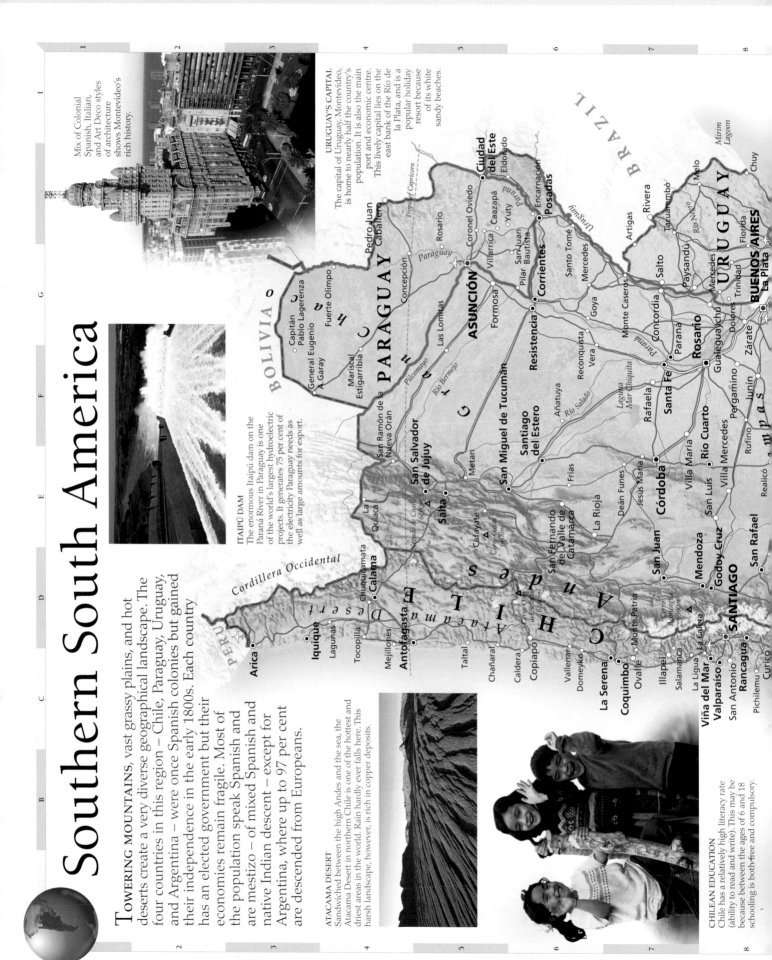

Mix of Colonial Spanish, Italian, and Art Deco styles of architecture shows Montevideo's rich history.

URUGUAY'S CAPITAL
The capital of Uruguay, Montevideo, is home to nearly half the country's population. It is also the main port and economic centre. This lively capital lies on the east bank of the Río de la Plata, and is a popular holiday resort because of its white sandy beaches.

ATACAMA DESERT
Sandwiched between the high Andes and the sea, the Atacama Desert in northern Chile is one of the hottest and driest areas in the world. Rain hardly ever falls here. This harsh landscape, however, is rich in copper deposits.

CHILEAN EDUCATION
Chile has a relatively high literacy rate (ability to read and write). This may be because between the ages of 6 and 18 schooling is both free and compulsory.

WINES FROM CHILE
About 90 per cent of Chileans live in the central region, where the rich soil is ideal for a wide range of agriculture. Vines were brought to Chile by the Spaniards, and the country now has an important wine-making industry that exports wine all over the world.

0 km 200 400
0 miles 200 400
Talcahuano
Chillán
Concepción
Los Ángeles
Lebu
Río Bío Bío
Temuco
Loncoche
Valdivia
Osorno
Puerto Varas
Puerto Montt
Ancud
Castro
Isla de Chiloé
Golfo Corcovado
Archipiélago de los Chonos
Puerto Aisén
Coihaique
Chile Chico
Cerro San Valentín 4058m
Golfo de Penas
Cochrane
Cerro Melliso Sur 3050m
Isla Wellington
Cerro Paine 2670m
Puerto Natales
Punta Arenas
Porvenir
Tierra del Fuego
Ushuaia
Beagle Channel
Cape Horn
(Cabo de Hornos)
Isla de los Estados
PACIFIC OCEAN
CHILE
ARGENTINA
Andes
Patagonia
Zapala
Cipolletti
Neuquén
Río Colorado
Lago Nahuel Huapi
San Carlos de Bariloche
Maquinchao
Esquel
Río Chubut
Paso de Indios
Lago Musters
Río Chico
Sarmiento
Lago Buenos Aires
Perito Moreno
Río Deseado
Río Chico
Río Santa Cruz
El Calafate
Bahía Grande
Río Gallegos
Strait of Magellan
Puerto San Julián
Puerto Deseado
Caleta Olivia
Comodoro Rivadavia
Golfo San Jorge
Trelew
Rawson
Golfo Nuevo
Peninsula Valdés
Golfo San Matías
San Antonio Oeste
Viedma
Río Negro
Choele Choel
Bahía Blanca
Punta Alta
Coronel Dorrego
Bahía Blanca
Santa Rosa
Lauquen
Olavarría
Azul
Tandil
Tres Arroyos
Balcarce
Mar del Plata
Necochea
Dolores
ATLANTIC OCEAN

ANDES MOUNTAIN WEATHER
The Andes stretch the entire length of South America, and this has a major effect on the weather. As westerly air from the Pacific Ocean rises over the mountains, its moisture can fall as rain and snow. By the time it reaches the eastern side, the air is much drier and the landscape is more arid.

DANCING THE TANGO
Popular around the world today, the tango originated in the slums of Buenos Aires in the late 1800s. This passionate dance with its characteristic rhythm is accompanied by music on a type of concertina known as a *bandoneón*, together with piano and violin.

BUENOS AIRES
More than one-third of Argentina's population lives in or around the capital Buenos Aires. A thriving port on the River Plate estuary, it is the largest city in Argentina. The colourful La Boca district with its painted walls is home to the descendants of Italian immigrants.

Chile has a large concentration of astronomical observatories because of its exceptionally clear skies.

Gaucho herding cattle in the Pampas region

PAMPAS
Vast, treeless plains called the Pampas – which means "flat" in Spanish – cover much of southern and western Argentina. The Pampas are used to grow cereals and raise cattle. *Gauchos*, Argentinian cowboys, work on large ranches, or *estancias*.

Atlantic Ocean

THE WORLD'S SECOND-LARGEST OCEAN, the Atlantic separates the Americas from Europe and Africa. The Atlantic is the world's youngest ocean, starting to form about 180 million years ago, as the continental plates began to separate. This movement continues today, as the oceanic plates that meet at the Mid-Atlantic Ridge continue to pull apart. The Atlantic is a major source of fish but, due to overfishing, stocks are now low. Many shipping routes cross the Atlantic, and pollution is an international problem as ships dump chemicals and waste. There are substantial reserves of oil and gas in the Gulf of Mexico, off the coast of west Africa, and in the north Atlantic.

GREENLAND
The largest island in the world, Greenland is a self-governing part of Denmark. Most Greenlanders live on the southwest coast. Mainly Inuit, with some Danish-Norwegian influences, they make their living by seal hunting, fishing, and fur trapping.

Fishing for halibut

TOURISM
The volcanic islands and black beaches of the eastern Atlantic, especially the Canaries (left), Madeira, and the Azores, are popular with tourists, who are attracted by the scenery and subtropical climate.

WARM CURRENTS
The Gulf Stream flows up the east coast of North America and across the Atlantic. It brings warm water and a mild climate to northern Europe, which would otherwise be cooler.

Mid-Atlantic Ridge

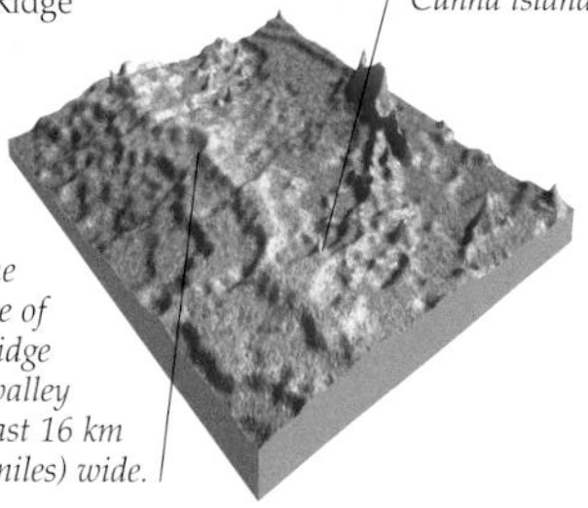

Tristan da Cunha island

At the centre of the ridge is a valley at least 16 km (10 miles) wide.

UNDERWATER MOUNTAINS
The Mid-Atlantic Ridge is a great underwater mountain chain that runs the entire length of the Atlantic. It was formed by magma that oozed up from the sea bed, cooled to create solid rock, and gradually built up to form a ridge. Some peaks are so high that they break the surface to form volcanic islands, such as the country of Iceland.

ATLANTIC FISHING INDUSTRY
The Atlantic Ocean contains more than half the world's total stock of fish. Herring, anchovy, sardine, cod, flounder, and tuna are among the most important fish found here. However, overfishing, particularly of cod and tuna, has caused a significant decline in numbers.

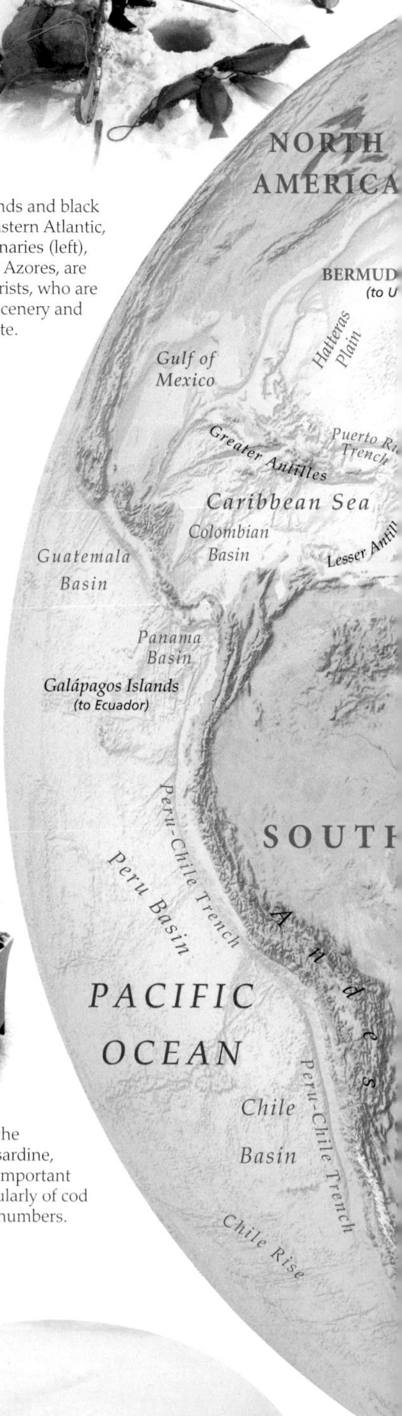

NORTH AMERICA
BERMUD
(to U
Gulf of Mexico
Hatteras Plain
Greater Antilles
Puerto Ri Trench
Caribbean Sea
Colombian Basin
Lesser Antil
Guatemala Basin
Panama Basin
Galápagos Islands
(to Ecuador)
SOUTH
Peru-Chile Trench
Peru Basin
Andes
PACIFIC OCEAN
Chile Basin
Peru-Chile Trench
Chile Rise

WHALES
Many whales live in the Atlantic, migrating from summer feeding grounds in the cold polar regions to warmer waters in the Caribbean for the winter. They give birth and mate again before returning north.

Humpback whale breaching

FALKLANDS
Set in the windy south Atlantic off the coast of Argentina, the Falkland Islands belong to the UK but are also claimed by Argentina. Fishing and sheep farming are important. The land is rocky, mountainous, boggy, and almost treeless.

GREENLAND
(to Denmark)
Labrador Sea
Denmark Strait
ICELAND
REYKJAVIK
FAROE ISLANDS
(to Denmark)
Labrador Basin
Reykjanes Basin
Iceland Basin
Rockall Bank
British Isles
North Sea
Baltic Sea
Charlie-Gibbs Fracture Zone
EUROPE
Newfoundland
Grand Banks of Newfoundland
Newfoundland Basin
Bay of Biscay
Alps
Azores
(to Portugal)
Mediterranean Sea
East Azores Fracture Zone
Sohm Plain
Madeira
(to Portugal)
Atlas Mountains
Great Meteor Tablemount
Canary Islands
(to Spain)
Madeira Plain
Mid-Atlantic Ridge
Sahara
Cape Verde Plain
Kane Fracture Zone
Cape Verde Basin
PRAIA
CAPE VERDE
Sahel
ATLANTIC
AFRICA
Doldrums Fracture Zone
Sierra Leone Rise
Sierra Leone Basin
OCEAN
Amazon Fan
Guinea Basin
Gulf of Guinea
Ceará Plain
Fernando de Noronha
(to Brazil)
Pernambuco Plain
Ascension Fracture Zone
ASCENSION ISLAND
(to UK)
Brazil Basin
Angola Basin
ST HELENA
(to UK)
Zubov Seamount
Vitória Seamount
Ilha da Trindade
(to Brazil)
Walvis Ridge
Orange Fan
Santos Plateau
Cape Basin
Rio Grande Rise
Cape of Good Hope
TRISTAN DA CUNHA
(to UK)
Argentine Basin
Gough Island
(to Tristan da Cunha)
Gough Fracture Zone
FALKLAND ISLANDS
(to UK)
Zapiola Ridge
Scotia Sea
SOUTH SANDWICH ISLANDS
(to UK)
BOUVET ISLAND
(to Norway)
SOUTH GEORGIA
(to UK)
Drake Passage
SOUTHERN OCEAN
East Scotia Basin

Mineral-rich waters in the Blue Lagoon, Iceland, are said to be beneficial to people's health.

ICELAND

Iceland is situated in the north Atlantic on the Mid-Atlantic Ridge. As a result, it has at least 20 active volcanoes and suffers frequent earthquakes. There are numerous thermal springs with boiling mud lakes and geysers. Water from hot springs (above) is used to provide hot water and heating for much of Iceland's population, most of whom live on the coast. The warm Gulf Stream ensures that the country's ports stay ice-free in winter.

The Atlantic covers one-fifth of Earth's surface.

ICEBERGS

Icebergs in the Atlantic Ocean are formed when icesheets and glaciers reach the sea. Parts break off and start to drift, driven by winds and currents.

AFRICA

Covering one-fifth of the world's land area, Africa has a rapidly growing population. Many of its 53 nations – listed below in order of size – are desperately poor. This is partly due to hostile climates, especially in and around the vast Sahara desert, but also because of a history of political turmoil, ethnic tension or conflict and, in some countries, war. Despite this, African culture is among the most vibrant on Earth.

Algeria
2,381,741 sq km
919,595 sq miles
40,264,000
Algiers
Arabic, Tamazight (Berber: Kabyle, Shawia, Tamashek), French

Chad
1,284,000 sq km
495,755 sq miles
11,852,000
N'Djamena
French, Sara, Arabic, Maba

Ethiopia
1,104,300 sq km
426,373 sq miles
102,374,000
Addis Ababa
Amharic, Tigrinya, Galla, Sidamo, Somali, English, Arabic (Oromu)

Namibia
824,292 sq km
318,261 sq miles
2,436,000
Windhoek
Ovambo, Kavango, English, Bergdama, German, Afrikaans

South Sudan
644,329 sq km
248,777 sq miles
12,531,000
Juba
Dinka, Nuer, Zande, Bari, Shilluk, Lotuko, Arabic

Morocco
446,550 sq km
172,414 sq miles
33,656,000
Rabat
Arabic, Tamazight (Berber), French, Spanish

Congo, Dem Rep of the
2,344,858 sq km
905,355 sq miles
81,331,000
Kinshasa
Kiswahili, Tshiluba, Kikongo, Lingala, French

Niger
1,267,000 sq km
489,191 sq miles
18,639,000
Niamey
Hausa, Djerma, Fula, Tuareg, Teda, French

Mauritania
1,030,700 sq km
397,955 sq miles
3,677,000
Nouakchott
Hassaniyah Arabic, Wolof, French

Mozambique
799,380 sq km
308,642 sq miles
25,930,000
Maputo
Makua, Xitsonga, Sena, Lomwe, Portuguese

Madagascar
587,041 sq km
226,658 sq miles
24,430,000
Antananarivo
Malagasy, French

Zimbabwe
390,757 sq km
150,872 sq miles
14,547,000
Harare
Shona, isiNdebele, English

Congo, Republic of
342,000 sq km
132,946 sq miles
4,852,000
Brazzaville
Kikongo, Teke, Lingala, French

Angola
1,246,700 sq km
481,354 sq miles
20,172,000
Luanda
Portuguese, Umbundu, Kimbundu, Kikongo

Egypt
1,001,450 sq km
386,662 sq miles
94,667,000
Cairo
Arabic, French, English, Berber

Zambia
752,618 sq km
290,587 sq miles
15,511,000
Lusaka
Bemba, Tongan, Nyanja, Lozi, Lala-Bisa, Nsenga, English

Botswana
581,730 sq km
224,607 sq miles
2,209,000
Gaborone
Setswana, English, Shona, San, Khoikhoi, isiNdebele

Ivory Coast
322,463 sq km
124,504 sq miles
23,740,000
Yamoussoukro
Akan, French, Kru, Voltaïque

Sudan
1,861,484 sq km
718,723 sq miles
36,730,000
Khartoum
Arabic, Nubian, Beja, Fur

Mali
1,240,192 sq km
478,841 sq miles
17,467,000
Bamako
Bambara, Fula, Senufo, Soninke, French

Tanzania
947,300 sq km
365,755 sq miles
52,483,000
Dodoma
Kiswahili, Sukuma,Kichagga, Nyamwezi, Hehe, Makonde, Yao, Sandawe, English

Somalia
637,657 sq km
246,201 sq miles
10,817,000
Mogadishu
Somali, Arabic, English, Italian

Kenya
580,367 sq km
224,081 sq miles
46,791,000
Nairobi
Kiswahili, English, Kikuyu, Luo, Kalenjin, Kamba

Burkina Faso
274,200 sq km
105,869 sq miles
19,513,000
Ouagadougou
Mossi, Fulani, French, Tuareg, Diyula, Songhai

Libya
1,759,540 sq km
679,362 sq miles
6,542,000
Tripoli
Arabic, Tuareg

South Africa
1,219,090 sq km
470,693 sq miles
54,301,000
Pretoria
English, isiZulu, isiXhosa, Afrikaans, Sepedi, Setswana, Sesotho, Xitsonga, siSwati, Tshivenda, isiNdebele

Nigeria
923,768 sq km
356,669 sq miles
186,053,000
Abuja
Hausa, English, Yoruba, Igbo

Central African Republic
622,984 sq km
240,535 sq miles
5,507,000
Bangui
Sango, Banda, Gbaya, French

Cameroon
475,440 sq km
183,568 sq miles
24,361,000
Yaoundé
Bamileke, Fang, Fula, French, English

Gabon
267,667 sq km
103,347 sq miles
1,739,000
Libreville
Fang, French, Punu, Sira, Nzebi, Mpongwe

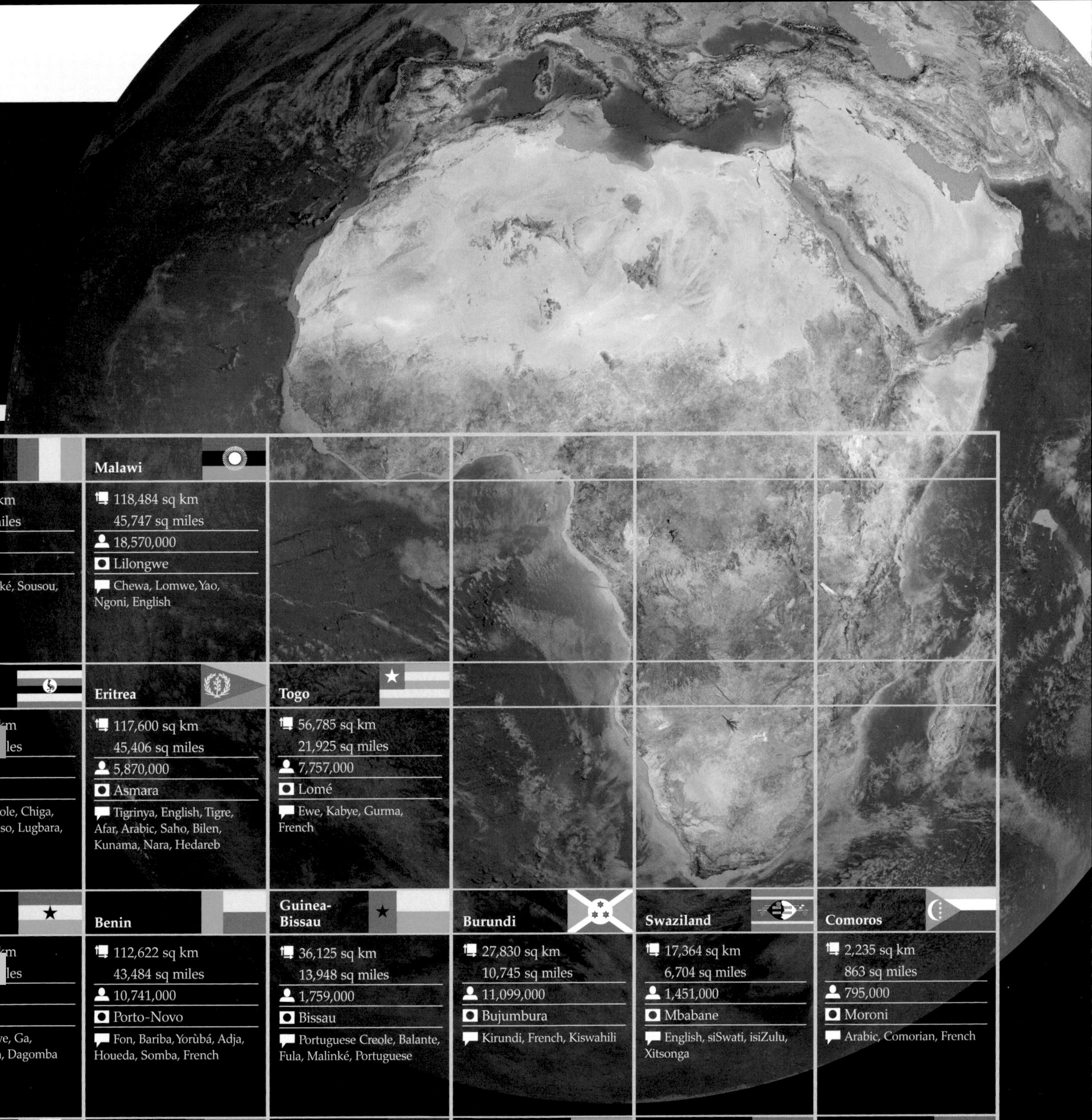

Guinea
245,857 sq km
94,926 sq miles
12,093,000
Conakry
Pulaar, Malinké, Sousou, French

Malawi
118,484 sq km
45,747 sq miles
18,570,000
Lilongwe
Chewa, Lomwe, Yao, Ngoni, English

Uganda
241,03[redacted]m
93,06[redacted]les
38,319,000
Kampala
Luganda, Nkole, Chiga, Lango, Acholi, Teso, Lugbara, English

Eritrea
117,600 sq km
45,406 sq miles
5,870,000
Asmara
Tigrinya, English, Tigre, Afar, Arabic, Saho, Bilen, Kunama, Nara, Hedareb

Togo
56,785 sq km
21,925 sq miles
7,757,000
Lomé
Ewe, Kabye, Gurma, French

Ghana
238,53[redacted]m
92,09[redacted]les
26,908,000
Accra
Twi-Fanti, Ewe, Ga, Adangbe, Gurma, Dagomba (Dagbani)

Benin
112,622 sq km
43,484 sq miles
10,741,000
Porto-Novo
Fon, Bariba, Yorùbá, Adja, Houeda, Somba, French

Guinea-Bissau
36,125 sq km
13,948 sq miles
1,759,000
Bissau
Portuguese Creole, Balante, Fula, Malinké, Portuguese

Burundi
27,830 sq km
10,745 sq miles
11,099,000
Bujumbura
Kirundi, French, Kiswahili

Swaziland
17,364 sq km
6,704 sq miles
1,451,000
Mbabane
English, siSwati, isiZulu, Xitsonga

Comoros
2,235 sq km
863 sq miles
795,000
Moroni
Arabic, Comorian, French

Senegal
196,72[redacted]m
75,95[redacted]les
14,320,000
Dakar
Wolof, Pulaar, Serer, Diyula, Mandinka, Malinké, Soninke, French

Liberia
111,369 sq km
43,000 sq miles
4,300,000
Monrovia
Kpelle, Vai, Bassa, Kru, Grebo, Kissi, Gola, Loma, English

Lesotho
30,355 sq km
11,720 sq miles
1,953,000
Maseru
English, Sesotho, isiZulu

Rwanda
26,338 sq km
10,169 sq miles
12,988,000
Kigali
Kinyarwanda, French, Kiswahili, English

Gambia, The
11,300 sq km
4,363 sq miles
2,010,000
Banjul
Mandinka, Fula, Wolof, Jola, Soninke, English

Mauritius
2,040 sq km
788 sq miles
1,348,000
Port Louis
French Creole, Hindi, Urdu, Tamil, Chinese, English, French

Tunisia
163,61[redacted]m
63,17[redacted]les
11,135,000
Tunis
Arabic, French

Sierra Leone
71,740 sq km
27,699 sq miles
6,019,000
Freetown
Mende, Temne, Krio, English

Equatorial Guinea
28,051 sq km
10,831 sq miles
759,400
Malabo
Spanish, Fang, Bubi, French

Djibouti
23,200 sq km
8,958 sq miles
846,700
Djibouti City
Somali, Afar, French, Arabic

Cape Verde
4,033 sq km
1,557 sq miles
553,400
Praia
Portuguese Creole, Portuguese

São Tomé and Príncipe
964 sq km
372 sq miles
197,500
São Tomé
Portuguese Creole, Portuguese

Northwest Africa

FOUR COUNTRIES, plus the disputed area of Western Sahara, make up this part of Africa. Algeria, Libya, and Tunisia have rich supplies of oil and natural gas that boost their economies. Morocco relies on tourism, phosphates used for chemicals and fertilizer, and agriculture. In the fertile valleys of the Atlas Mountains, farmers grow grapes, citrus fruit, dates, and olives. The area also attracts tourists to its colourful markets, historical sites, and sandy beaches. The Sahara Desert dominates the region, particularly in Algeria and Libya.

SUN AND SEA
Many tourists visit Tunisia and Morocco each year to enjoy the warm climate and sandy beaches. Tourism provides jobs for the local people and brings much-needed income.

MOROCCAN MARKET
In a souk, or market, craftworkers sell handmade products to tourists. Goods are displayed in booths along the bustling streets.

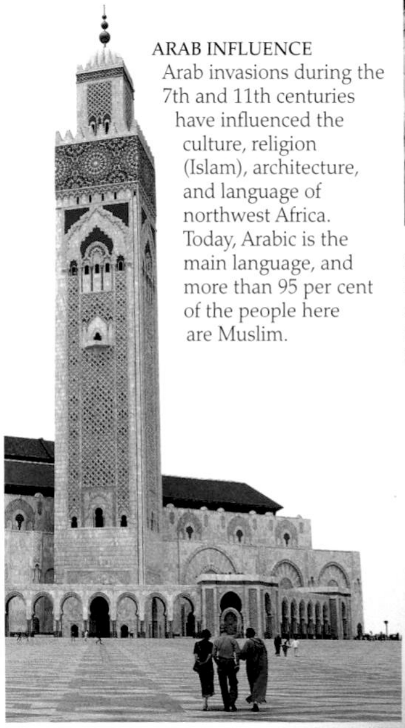

ARAB INFLUENCE
Arab invasions during the 7th and 11th centuries have influenced the culture, religion (Islam), architecture, and language of northwest Africa. Today, Arabic is the main language, and more than 95 per cent of the people here are Muslim.

Muslims going to worship at the Hassan II mosque in Casablanca, Morocco

BERBERS
The Berber people were the original inhabitants of northwest Africa. Most now live in the Atlas Mountains or the desert. Although most Berbers converted to Islam when the Arabs arrived, they kept their own language and way of life. In 2001, Algeria recognized Berber (Tamazight) as an official language.

Berber woman working on the land in the Atlas Mountains

I J K M N O P

DATE PALMS
Dates are an important crop for Algeria and Tunisia. Date palms are often grown at oases, where water lies close to the surface of the desert. Here, the clusters of dates are shown ripening beneath polythene. Leaves from the trees can be used for thatch and the trunk is cut for timber.

ANCIENT RUINS
Phoenicians, Romans, and Greeks from ancient times have all left their mark on this part of Africa. Today, tourists come to admire the historical sites along the coast. These ruins of Carthage, near Tunis, date from 146 BCE, when Romans laid waste to this city. The Romans went on to control all of the north African coast.

Ruins of a Roman bath at Carthage

The stones from dates can be roasted and ground to make a traditional date coffee.

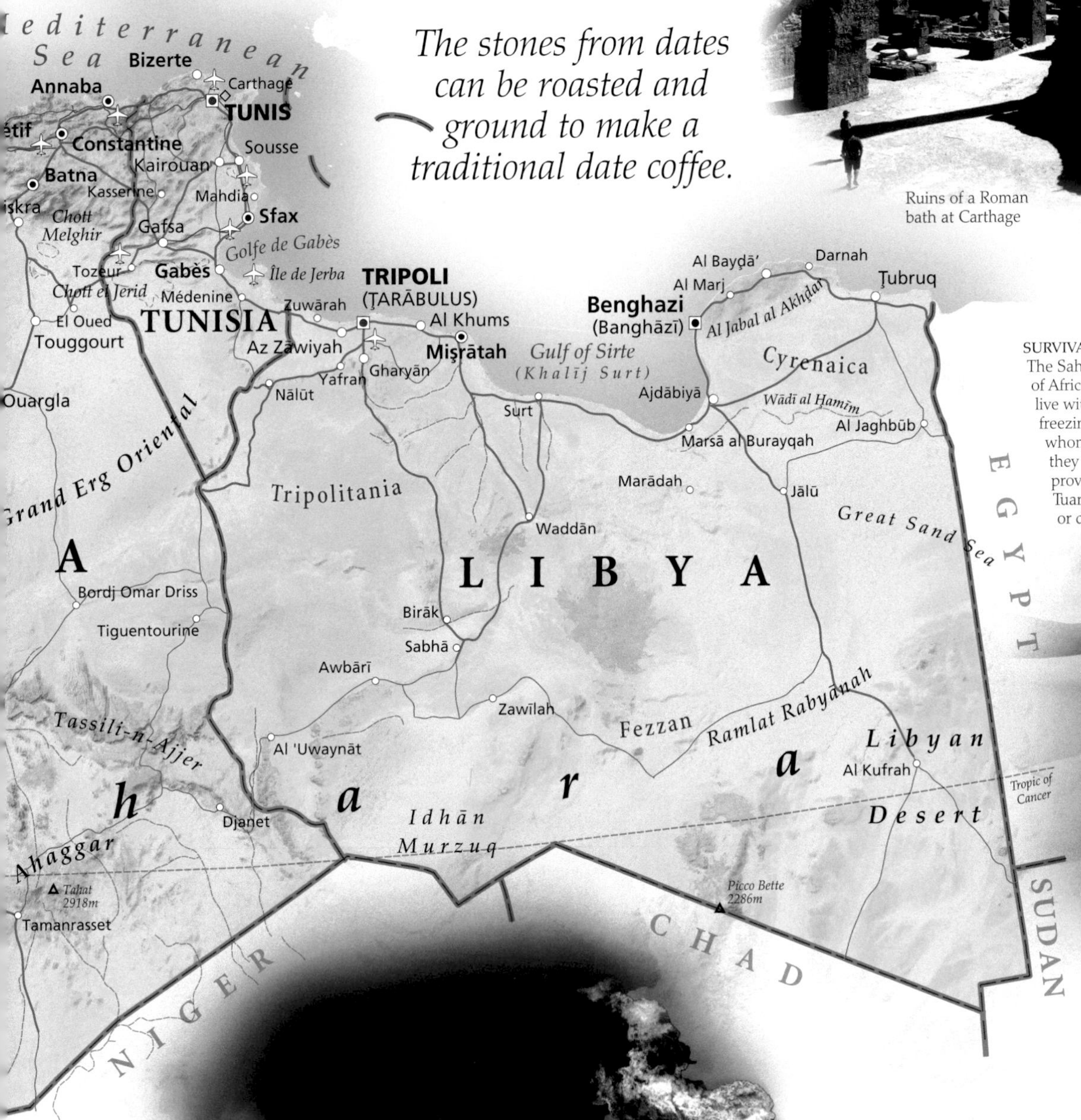
Mediterranean Sea
Bizerte
Annaba
Carthage
TUNIS
Sétif
Constantine
Sousse
Batna
Kairouan
Kasserine
Mahdia
Biskra
Chott Melghir
Gafsa
Sfax
Golfe de Gabès
Tozeur
Gabès
Île de Jerba
Chott el Jerid
Médenine
TRIPOLI
(ṬARĀBULUS)
El Oued
TUNISIA
Zuwārah
Touggourt
Az Zāwiyah
Al Khums
Benghazi
(Banghāzī)
Miṣrātah
Gulf of Sirte
(Khalīj Surt)
Gharyān
Yafran
Nālūt
Ouargla
Grand Erg Oriental
Surt
Ajdābiyā
Al Bayḍā'
Darnah
Al Marj
Ṭubruq
Al Jabal al Akhḍar
Cyrenaica
Wādī al Hamīm
Al Jaghbūb
Marsá al Burayqah
Tripolitania
Marādah
Jālū
Great Sand Sea
Waddān
EGYPT
A
LIBYA
Bordj Omar Driss
Tiguentourine
Birāk
Sabhā
Awbārī
Zawīlah
Fezzan
Ramlat Rabyānah
Tassili-n-Ajjer
Al 'Uwaynāt
Libyan Desert
Al Kufrah
Tropic of Cancer
h a r a
Djanet
Idhān Murzuq
Ahaggar
Tahat 2918m
Picco Bette 2286m
Tamanrasset
SUDAN
CHAD
NIGER

SURVIVAL IN THE SAHARA
The Sahara Desert covers almost one-third of Africa and is an inhospitable place to live with high daytime temperatures and freezing nights. The Tuareg are nomads for whom the desert is home. Traditionally, they keep camels for transport and to provide meat, milk, and hides. Many Tuareg now live in mountain areas or dwell in the cities.

Tuareg nomads in the Sahara carrying salt to trade in markets

0 km 100 200
0 miles 100 200

Libyan oil field

LIBYAN OIL RESOURCES
The discovery of oil and gas in 1959 brought considerable wealth to Libya, and by 2010 oil and gas made up 95 per cent of the country's exports. Since 2015, however, civil war, political chaos, and low oil prices have made life hard for Libyans.

1 2 3 4 5 6 7 8 9

I J K L M N O P

Northeast Africa

THIS REGION, KNOWN AS the Horn of Africa, contains the oldest civilizations in the continent, and some of its poorest countries. The borders that divide the countries today were mostly created by colonial rulers in the last hundred years. Pastoral nomads with their herds of animals often cross these borders in search of pasture. Most people still live in the countryside and farm the land, but many people now live in the cities. Tourism and agriculture are important sources of income for Egypt and Kenya, two of the richest and fastest-growing countries in the region. Elsewhere, tribal rivalries and disputes over land and resources have sometimes erupted into full-scale war and these, together with drought and poverty, have blighted the lives of millions of people in this region.

ABU SIMBEL
Tourists come to Egypt to see the pyramids at Giza and the temples along the Nile, such as these two built at Abu Simbel, south of Aswan. Tourism brings in money to preserve these historical sites.

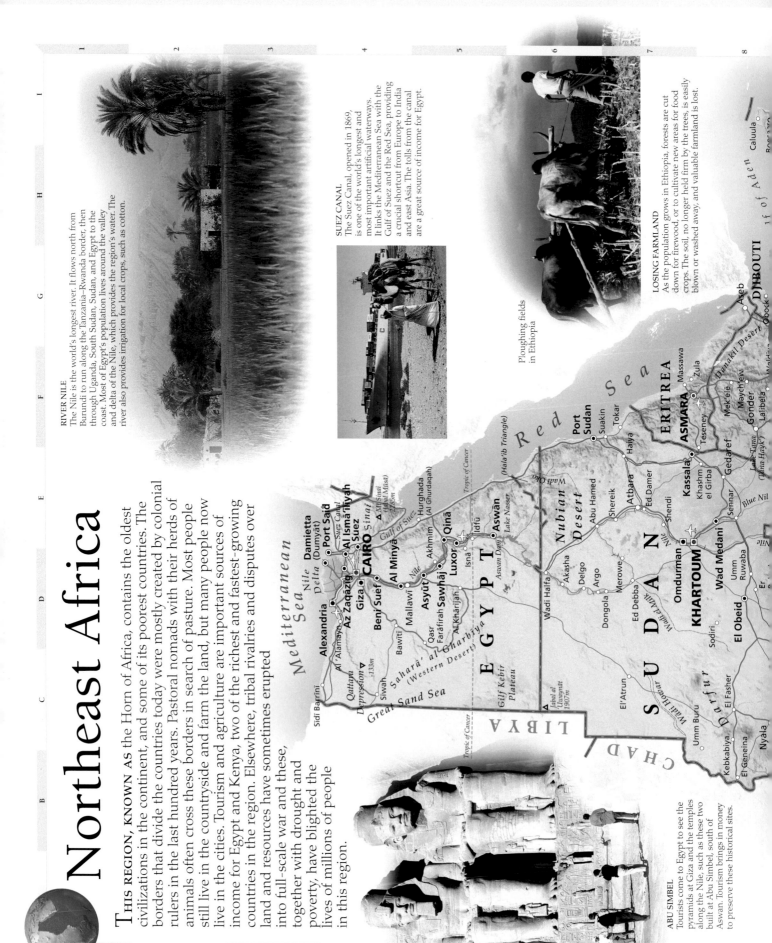

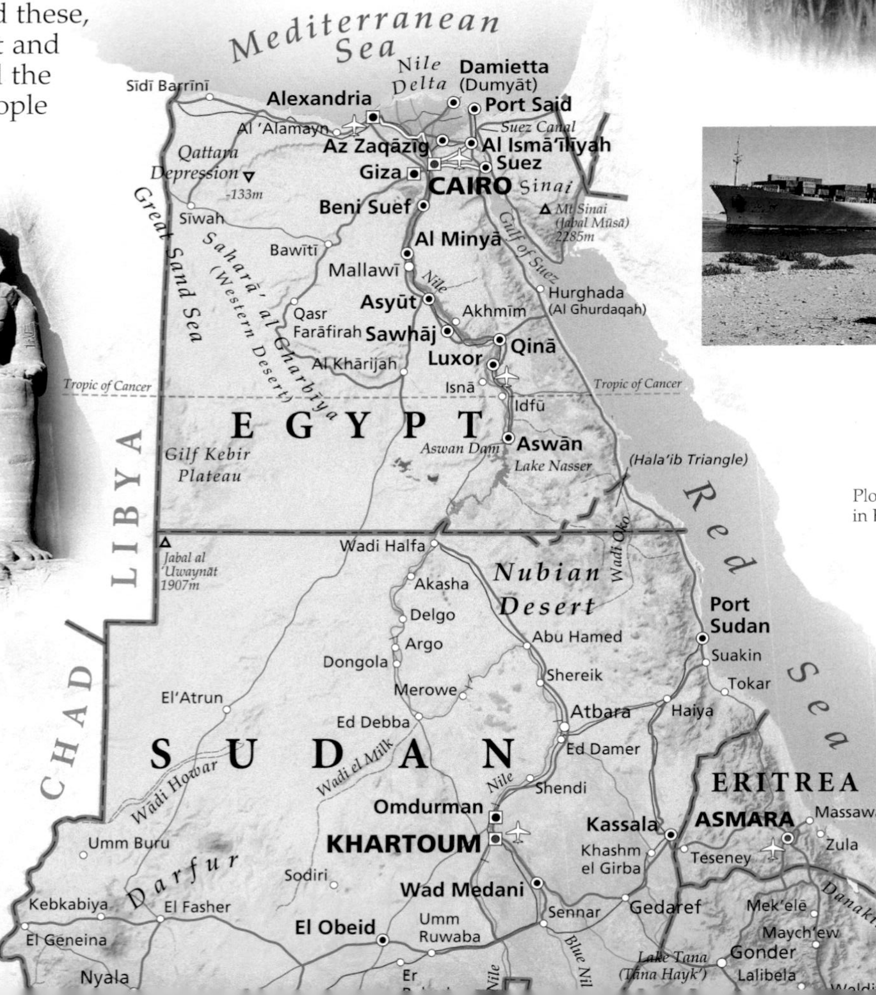

RIVER NILE
The Nile is the world's longest river. It flows north from Burundi to run along the Tanzania–Rwanda border, then through Uganda, South Sudan, Sudan, and Egypt to the coast. Most of Egypt's population lives around the valley and delta of the Nile, which provides the region's water. The river also provides irrigation for local crops, such as cotton.

SUEZ CANAL
The Suez Canal, opened in 1869, is one of the world's longest and most important artificial waterways. It links the Mediterranean Sea with the Gulf of Suez and the Red Sea, providing a crucial shortcut from Europe to India and east Asia. The tolls from the canal are a great source of income for Egypt.

Ploughing fields in Ethiopia

LOSING FARMLAND
As the population grows in Ethiopia, forests are cut down for firewood, or to cultivate new areas for food crops. The soil, no longer held firm by the trees, is easily blown or washed away, and valuable farmland is lost.

احمد عثمان
عطارة وبقالة حلويات

Busy street bazaar in Cairo

CAIRO
The largest city in Africa is Cairo, the capital of Egypt, with a population of more than 18 million. Here, Arab, African, and European influences exist alongside more traditional Egyptian customs.

Young Dinka man

THE DINKA OF SOUTH SUDAN
There are more than 500 tribes in Sudan and South Sudan. They speak more than 100 languages and dialects. Like many tribal people here, the Dinka are nomadic – their cattle graze on the plains east of the Nile. Cattle are central to their lives – young Dinka men officially become adults with an initiation ceremony in which they are given an ox of their own.

SOUTH SUDAN
CENTRAL AFRICAN REPUBLIC
ETHIOPIA
SOMALIA
Somaliland
Puntland
KENYA
UGANDA
RWANDA
BURUNDI
TANZANIA
DEM. REP. CONGO
ZAMBIA
MALAWI
MOZAMBIQUE
INDIAN OCEAN
Highlands
ADDIS ABABA
(ĀDĪS ĀBEBA)
Dirē Dawa
Hargeysa
Mī'ēso
Āwash
Hārer
Nazrēt
Gorē
Āgaro
Jīma
Ogaden
Dooxo Nugaaleed
Garoowe
Sinujiif
Gaalkacyo
Gellinsoor
Dhuusa Marreeb
Shilabo
Shebeli
Beledweyne
Ābaya Hāyk'
Negēlē
Great Rift Valley
Yabēlo
Doolow
Xuddur
Luuq
Baydhabo
Buulobarde
Jawhar
MOGADISHU
(MUQDISHO)
Wanlaweyn
Baardheere
Marka
Baraawe
Juba
Jilib
Jamaame
Kismaayo
Afmadow
Garissa
Buur Gaabo
Equator
Malakal
Raga
Jur
Sudd
Wau
Tonj
Rumbek
Sue
Tambura
Duk Faiwil
Kongor
White Nile
Bor
Amadi
Elemi Triangle
(administered by Kenya)
JUBA
Kapoeta
Kinyeti 3187m
Lotagipi Swamp
Lokitaung
Lake Turkana
Marsabit
Maridi
Yambio
Arua
Gulu
Lira
Lodwar
Masindi
Lake Albert
KAMPALA
Mbale
Jinja
Eldoret
Kisumu
Meru
Kirinyaga 5200m
Entebbe
Nakuru
Nyeri
NAIROBI
Lake Edward
Masaka
Mbarara
Kabale
Lake Victoria
Lake Kivu
KIGALI
Bukoba
Musoma
Biharamulo
Mwanza
Garsen
Malindi
Kilimanjaro 5895m
Arusha
Moshi
BUJUMBURA
Nyantakara
Shinyanga
Nzega
Kasulu
Malagarasi
Tabora
Singida
Masai Steppe
Mombasa
Pemba
Tanga
Kigoma
Lake Tanganyika
Zanzibar
DODOMA
Morogoro
DAR ES SALAAM
Great Ruaha
Rufiji
Mafia
Kipili
Lake Rukwa
Sumbawanga
Iringa
Mohoro
Sao Hill
Mbeya
Njombe
Kilwa Kivinje
Luwego
Lindi
Nyamtumbo
Masasi
Mtwara
Songea
Tunduru
Newala
Lake Nyasa
0 km 200 400
0 miles 100 200 300 400

Water makes up almost one-fifth of the surface area of Uganda.

Coptic cross

RELIGIOUS BELIEFS
The Ethiopian Orthodox Union Church has existed since the 4th century CE. It is a branch of the Coptic Church and mixes Christian beliefs, such as Catholic saints, with some traditional African spiritual beliefs.

MOUNTAIN GORILLAS
The Volcanoes National Park in Rwanda is one of the few places where you can still see a mountain gorilla (right) in the wild. These animals are threatened with extinction because of poachers and the destruction of their habitat. Tanzania and Kenya also have many important game reserves, which preserve the wildlife of the savannah.

TEA IN KENYA
Kenya is an important world producer of tea, which is grown on plantations in the highland areas (such as this one below). High rainfall here ensures a good crop. Coffee is also a valuable export.

Kenyan workers carefully select tea leaves for picking.

West Africa

DRAMATICALLY DIFFERENT CLIMATES and landscapes influence life in west Africa. In the hot, dry north, it is difficult to grow crops. Only oases in the Sahara and seasonal rainfall in the Sahel make crop-growing possible. To the south, the climate is warm and wet, and crops such as cocoa and coffee are grown on large plantations. This region also has many valuable minerals. Despite these rich resources, most countries are poor. Since independence from colonial powers, there has been much political unrest, often sparked by poverty and tribal rivalries in the region. West Africa is also divided by religion, with Islam dominant in the north and Christianity in the south.

GAMBIA
In recent years, tourism has become increasingly important to the economy of Gambia. Visitors come to see wildlife along the River Gambia and to visit the Atlantic coast beaches. These safari tourists are admiring a giant termite mound.

PEOPLE OF GHANA
Family ties and a sense of community are important to the people of Ghana, and ceremonies throughout each year mark the events of childbirth, puberty, marriage, and death. About half of Ghanaians are Ashanti people whose ancestors developed one of the richest and most notable civilizations in Africa.

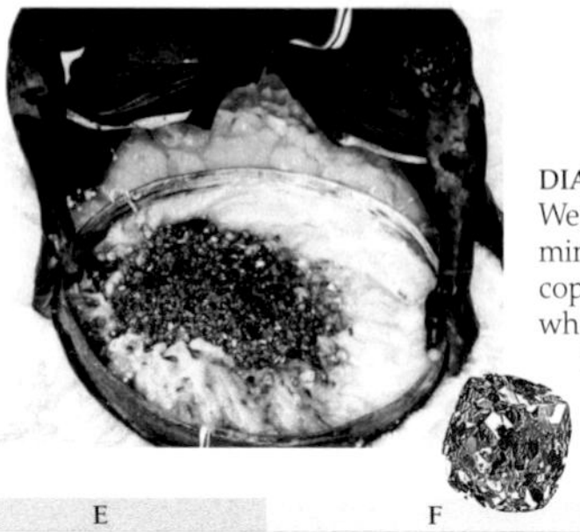

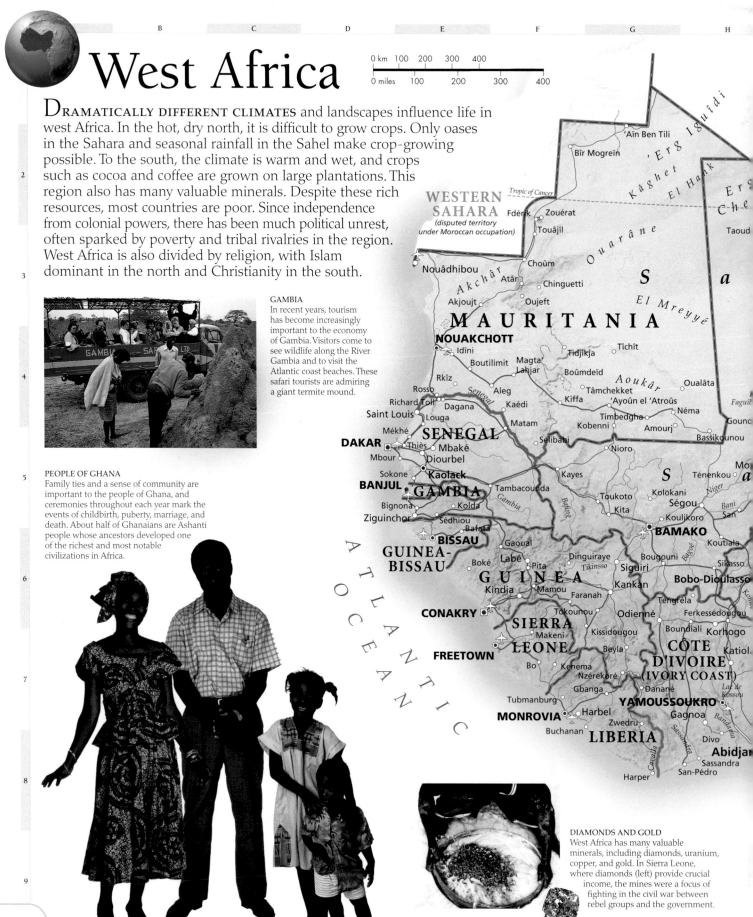

DIAMONDS AND GOLD
West Africa has many valuable minerals, including diamonds, uranium, copper, and gold. In Sierra Leone, where diamonds (left) provide crucial income, the mines were a focus of fighting in the civil war between rebel groups and the government.

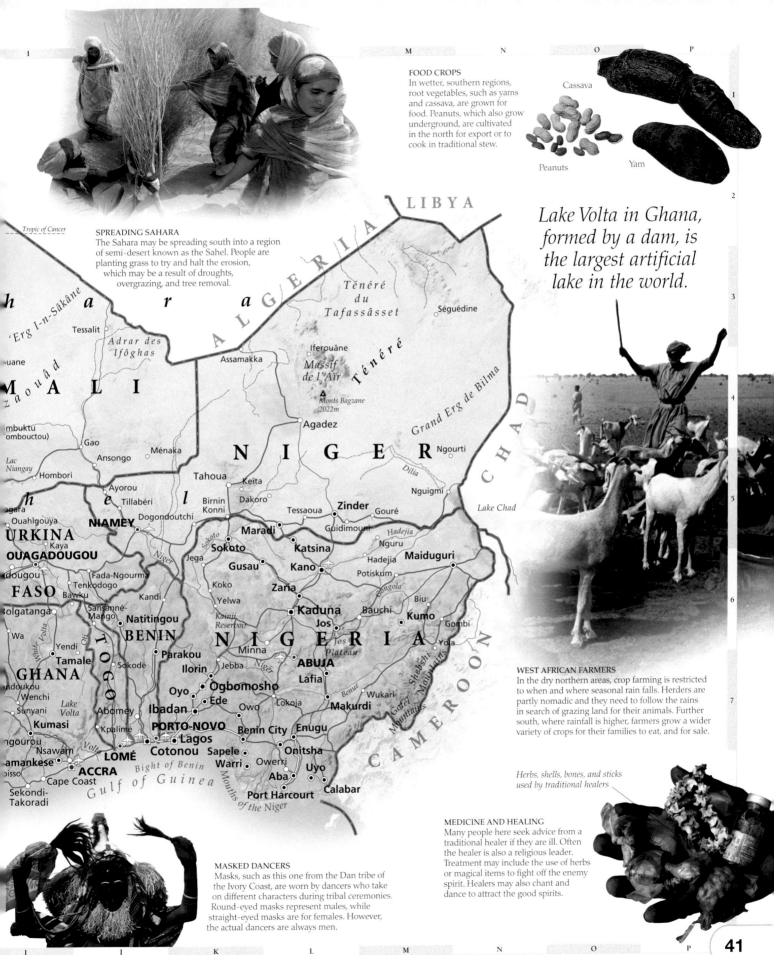

FOOD CROPS
In wetter, southern regions, root vegetables, such as yams and cassava, are grown for food. Peanuts, which also grow underground, are cultivated in the north for export or to cook in traditional stew.

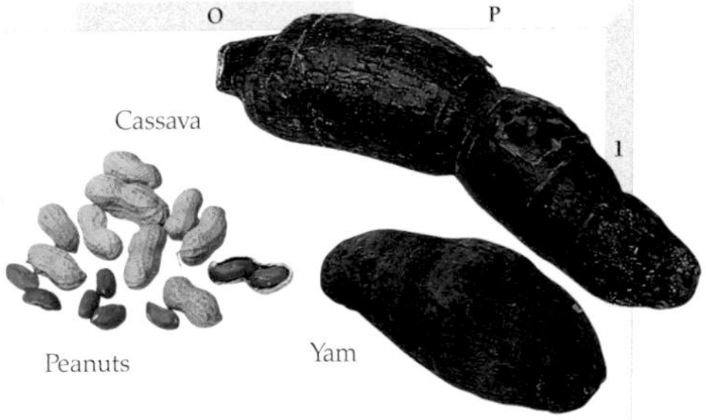

Lake Volta in Ghana, formed by a dam, is the largest artificial lake in the world.

SPREADING SAHARA
The Sahara may be spreading south into a region of semi-desert known as the Sahel. People are planting grass to try and halt the erosion, which may be a result of droughts, overgrazing, and tree removal.

WEST AFRICAN FARMERS
In the dry northern areas, crop farming is restricted to when and where seasonal rain falls. Herders are partly nomadic and they need to follow the rains in search of grazing land for their animals. Further south, where rainfall is higher, farmers grow a wider variety of crops for their families to eat, and for sale.

Herbs, shells, bones, and sticks used by traditional healers

MEDICINE AND HEALING
Many people here seek advice from a traditional healer if they are ill. Often the healer is also a religious leader. Treatment may include the use of herbs or magical items to fight off the enemy spirit. Healers may also chant and dance to attract the good spirits.

MASKED DANCERS
Masks, such as this one from the Dan tribe of the Ivory Coast, are worn by dancers who take on different characters during tribal ceremonies. Round-eyed masks represent males, while straight-eyed masks are for females. However, the actual dancers are always men.

Central Africa

ALL EIGHT COUNTRIES IN central Africa were European colonies with a painful history of slavery. Since the 1960s, independence has brought them mixed success. Rich mineral deposits and the discovery of offshore oil have provided income for Cameroon, Congo, and Gabon, while civil war and repressive governments have damaged other countries in the region. These include Chad and the Central African Republic, two of the world's poorest countries. Although the north is mainly arid, Africa's largest tropical rainforest dominates the south, with the powerful Congo River linking the interior with the coast. The tiny, volcanic country of São Tomé and Príncipe lies off the coast of Gabon.

FISHING IN LAKE CHAD
Lake Chad is an important source of food, but it is shrinking at an alarming rate. A shallow lake, it is now only about 2–4 m (6.5–13 ft) deep on average. Its surface area has also reduced, due to droughts and the demand for water to irrigate the land.

RELIGIOUS BELIEFS
Although Christianity is the main religion here, many people also follow traditional beliefs. These suggest that natural objects, such as mountains and rivers, have a spirit. Masks, like this Bambuku head, are sometimes used to scare off evil spirits.

Mud-brick home

VILLAGE LIFE
Most people in rural areas live in villages or small towns. Some grow crops, such as cotton or cassava, for sale, but many exist by growing food just for their family.

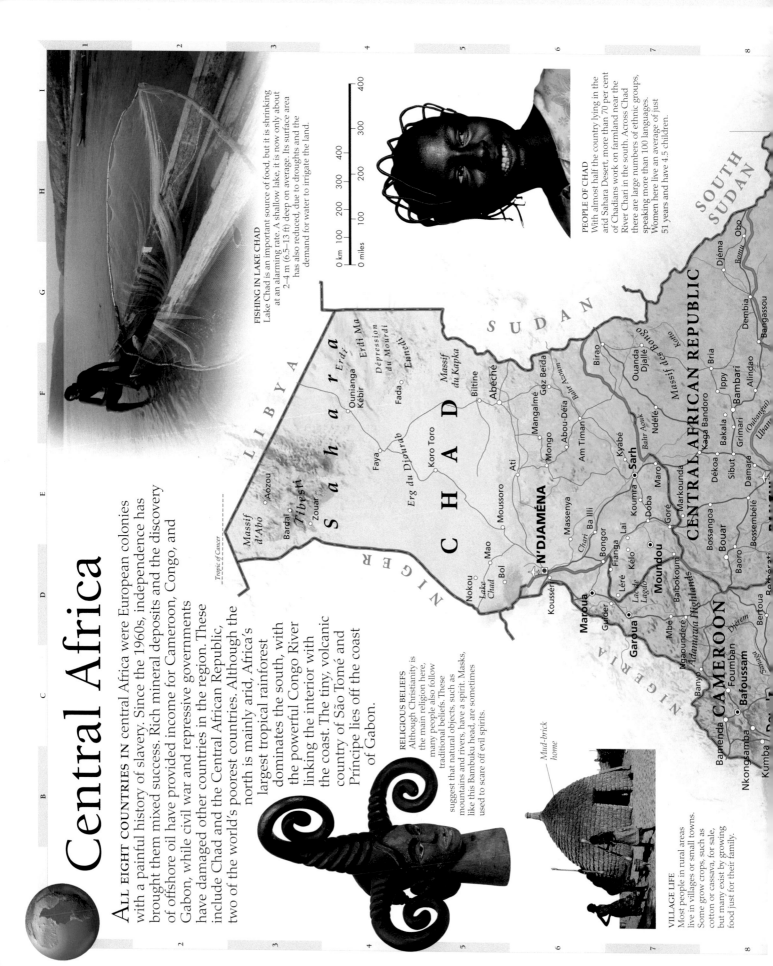

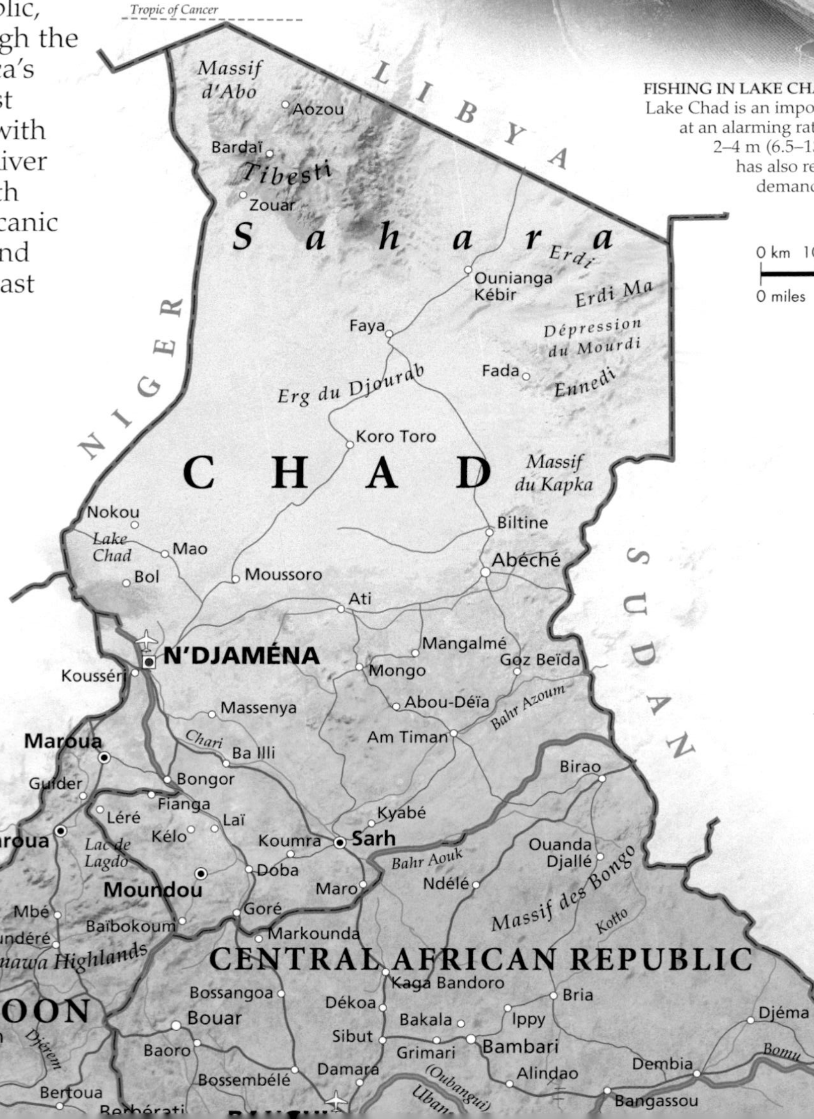
Tropic of Cancer
LIBYA
NIGER
CHAD
SUDAN
NIGERIA
CAMEROON
CENTRAL AFRICAN REPUBLIC
SOUTH SUDAN
Sahara
Massif d'Abo
Aozou
Bardaï
Tibesti
Zouar
Erdi
Ouniang Kébir
Erdi Ma
Dépression du Mourdi
Faya
Fada
Ennedi
Erg du Djourab
Koro Toro
Massif du Kapka
Nokou
Lake Chad
Mao
Bol
Moussoro
Biltine
Abéché
Ati
N'DJAMÉNA
Mangalmé
Goz Beïda
Mongo
Kousséri
Massenya
Abou-Déïa
Bahr Azoum
Am Timan
Maroua
Chari
Ba Illi
Birao
Guider
Bongor
Fianga
Léré
Laï
Kyabé
Garoua
Lac de Lagdo
Kélo
Koumra
Sarh
Ouanda Djallé
Bahr Aouk
Doba
Ndélé
Moundou
Maro
Mbé
Baïbokoum
Goré
Massif des Bongo
Kotto
Ngaoundéré
Markounda
Adamawa Highlands
Banyo
Kaga Bandoro
Bossangoa
Bria
Bamenda
Dékoa
Foumban
Bouar
Bakala
Ippy
Djéma
Sibut
Bafoussam
Grimari
Bambari
Nkongsamba
Djérem
Baoro
Damara
Dembia
Bomu
Obo
Bossembélé
Alindao
Sanaga
Bertoua
(Oubangui)
Bangassou
Kumba
0 km 100 200 300 400
0 miles 100 200 300 400

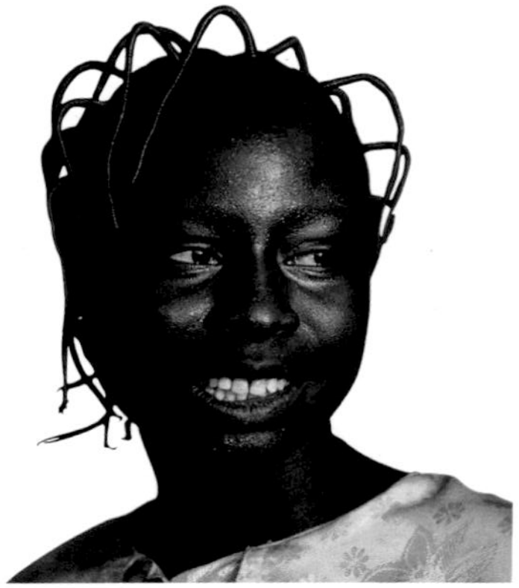

PEOPLE OF CHAD
With almost half the country lying in the arid Sahara Desert, more than 70 per cent of Chadians work on farmland near the River Chari in the south. Across Chad there are large numbers of ethnic groups, speaking more than 100 languages. Women here live an average of just 51 years and have 4.5 children.

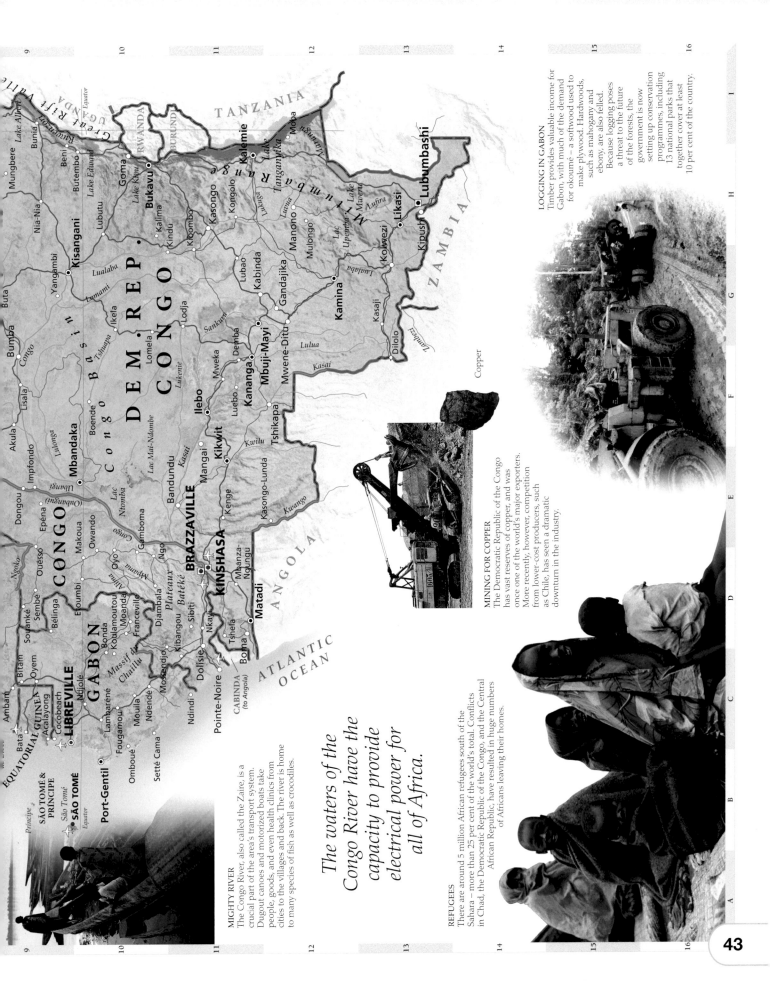

Príncipe
SÃO TOMÉ & PRÍNCIPE
São Tomé
SÃO TOMÉ
Equator
EQUATORIAL GUINEA
Bata
Ambam
Bitam
Oyem
Acalayong
Cocobeach
LIBREVILLE
Ndjolé
GABON
Port-Gentil
Lambaréné
Fougamou
Omboué
Mouila
Ndendé
Setté Cama
Bonda
Koulamoutou
Moanda
Franceville
Massif du Chaillu
Mossendjo
Djambala
Plateaux Batéké
Kibangou
Sibiti
Ndindi
Dolisie
Pointe-Noire
CABINDA (to Angola)
Boma
Tshela
Nkayi
Matadi
Mbanza-Ngungu
ATLANTIC OCEAN
ANGOLA
Souanké
Sembé
Bélinga
Ouésso
Ngoko
CONGO
Etoumbi
Makoua
Owando
Oyo
Alima
Mpama
Gamboma
Ngo
BRAZZAVILLE
KINSHASA
Dongou
Epéna
(Oubangui)
Ubangi
Impfondo
Akula
Lisala
Bumba
Buta
Congo
Mbandaka
Lulonga
Lac Ntomba
Lac Mai-Ndombe
Bandundu
Kasai
Mangai
Kikwit
Kenge
Kasongo-Lunda
Kwango
Kwilu
Tshikapa
Ilebo
Mweka
Luebo
Kananga
Demba
Mbuji-Mayi
Mwene-Ditu
Lulua
Kasai
Boende
Congo Basin
Tshuapa
Ikela
Lomami
Lualaba
DEM. REP. CONGO
Lomela
Lukenie
Lodja
Sankuru
Yangambi
Kisangani
Nia-Nia
Mungbere
Bunia
Lake Albert
Beni
Butembo
Lake Edward
Ruwenzori
Great Rift Valley
UGANDA
Equator
Lubutu
Goma
Lake Kivu
RWANDA
Bukavu
BURUNDI
Kalima
Kindu
Kibombo
Kasongo
Kongolo
Lubao
Kabinda
Gandajika
Lukuga
Kalemie
Lake Tanganyika
Moba
Marungu
TANZANIA
Mitumba Range
Manono
Luvua
Mulongo
Kamina
Lualaba
Lac Upemba
Lake Mweru
Lufira
Kasaji
Dilolo
Zambezi
Kolwezi
Likasi
Kipushi
Lubumbashi
ZAMBIA

MIGHTY RIVER
The Congo River, also called the Zaire, is a crucial part of the area's transport system. Dugout canoes and motorized boats take people, goods, and even health clinics from cities to the villages and back. The river is home to many species of fish as well as crocodiles.

The waters of the Congo River have the capacity to provide electrical power for all of Africa.

1605
90

Copper

MINING FOR COPPER
The Democratic Republic of the Congo has vast reserves of copper, and was once one of the world's major exporters. More recently, however, competition from lower-cost producers, such as Chile, has seen a dramatic downturn in the industry.

REFUGEES
There are around 5 million African refugees south of the Sahara – more than 25 per cent of the world's total. Conflicts in Chad, the Democratic Republic of the Congo, and the Central African Republic, have resulted in huge numbers of Africans leaving their homes.

LOGGING IN GABON
Timber provides valuable income for Gabon, with much of the demand for okoumé – a softwood used to make plywood. Hardwoods, such as mahogany and ebony, are also felled. Because logging poses a threat to the future of the forests, the government is now setting up conservation programmes, including 13 national parks that together cover at least 10 per cent of the country.

Southern Africa

FROM THE DRAMATIC Namib and Kalahari deserts in the west, to the tropical forests in the north, southern Africa is a region of contrasts. Oil, diamonds, gold, and other precious metals are all mined here. There are huge inland plains that are home to a variety of wildlife, and large areas devoted to agriculture. But flooding and droughts, together with civil unrest, have hampered development so that, despite an abundance of natural resources, many countries remain poor.

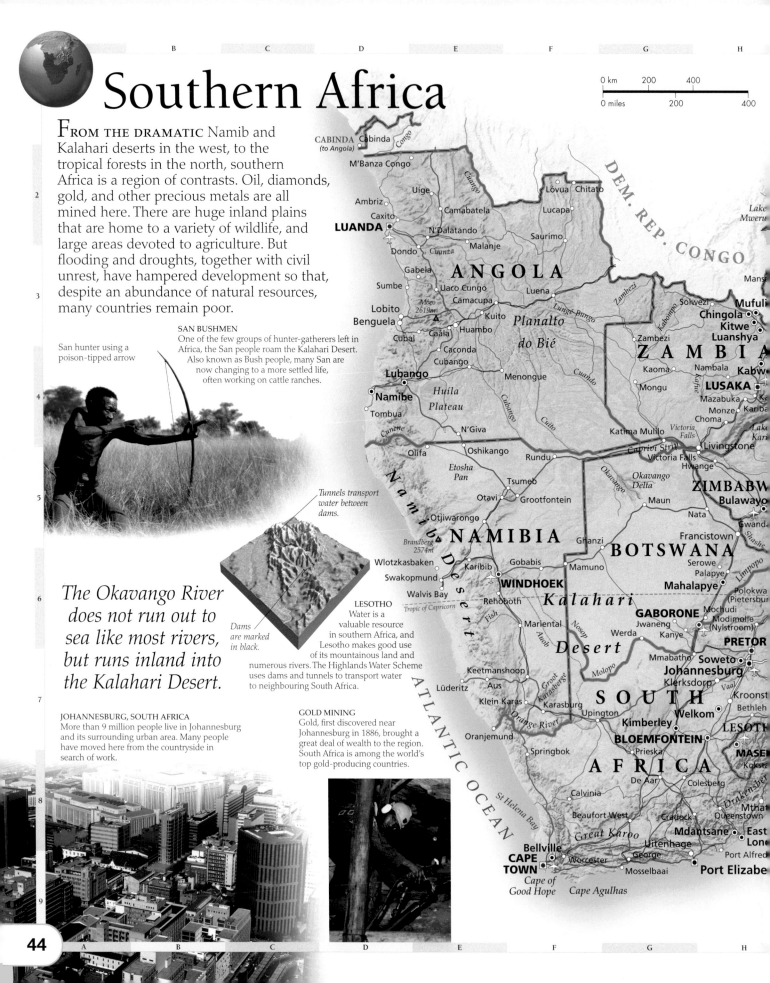

B C D E F G H
0 km 200 400
0 miles 200 400
CABINDA (to Angola)
Cabinda
Congo
M'Banza Congo
DEM. REP. CONGO
Lake Mweru
Cuango
Uige
Lóvua
Chitato
Ambriz
Caxito
Camabatela
Lucapa
LUANDA
N'Dalatando
Saurimo
Dondo
Cuanza
Malanje
Gabela
ANGOLA
Sumbe
Uaco Cungo
Luena
Lobito
Moco 2619m
Camacupa
Benguela
Kuito
Planalto do Bié
Lungé-Bungo
Zambezi
Cubal
Caála
Huambo
Caconda
Cubango
Lubango
Menongue
Cuando
Namibe
Huíla Plateau
Tombua
Cubango
Cuito
Cunene
N'Giva
Olifa
Oshikango
Rundu
Etosha Pan
Tsumeb
Otavi
Grootfontein
Namib Desert
Otjiwarongo
Brandberg 2574m
NAMIBIA
Wlotzkasbaken
Karibib
Gobabis
Swakopmund
WINDHOEK
Walvis Bay
Rehoboth
Tropic of Capricorn
Fish
Kalahari Desert
Mariental
Auob
Nosop
Keetmanshoop
Lüderitz
Aus
Klein Karas
Groot Karasberge
Karasburg
Orange River
Oranjemund
ATLANTIC OCEAN
Springbok
St Helena Bay
Okavango
Okavango Delta
Maun
Nata
Ghanzi
BOTSWANA
Mamuno
Serowe
Palapye
Mahalapye
Francistown
GABORONE
Mochudi
Jwaneng
Kanye
Werda
Molopo
Mmabatho
Upington
SOUTH AFRICA
Kimberley
BLOEMFONTEIN
Prieska
Calvinia
De Aar
Colesberg
Beaufort West
Cradock
Great Karoo
Queenstown
Mdantsane
Uitenhage
George
Bellville
Worcester
Mosselbaai
CAPE TOWN
Cape of Good Hope
Cape Agulhas
Port Elizabe
Port Alfred
East Lon
Mtha
Drakensber
Kokstа
MASE
LESOTH
Bethleh
Kroonst
Welkom
Vaal
Klerksdorp
Johannesburg
Soweto
PRETOR
Modimolle (Nylstroom)
Polokwa (Pietersbur
Limpopo
Shashe
Gwanda
Bulawayo
ZIMBABW
Hwange
Victoria Falls
Livingstone
Caprivi Strip
Katima Mulilo
Victoria Falls
Choma
Monze
Kariba
Mazabuka
LUSAKA
Kafue
Nambala
Kabw
Mongu
Kaoma
ZAMBIA
Zambezi
Kabompo
Solwezi
Chingola
Mufuli
Kitwe
Luanshya
Mans

SAN BUSHMEN
One of the few groups of hunter-gatherers left in Africa, the San people roam the Kalahari Desert. Also known as Bush people, many San are now changing to a more settled life, often working on cattle ranches.

San hunter using a poison-tipped arrow

Tunnels transport water between dams.

Dams are marked in black.

LESOTHO
Water is a valuable resource in southern Africa, and Lesotho makes good use of its mountainous land and numerous rivers. The Highlands Water Scheme uses dams and tunnels to transport water to neighbouring South Africa.

The Okavango River does not run out to sea like most rivers, but runs inland into the Kalahari Desert.

JOHANNESBURG, SOUTH AFRICA
More than 9 million people live in Johannesburg and its surrounding urban area. Many people have moved here from the countryside in search of work.

GOLD MINING
Gold, first discovered near Johannesburg in 1886, brought a great deal of wealth to the region. South Africa is among the world's top gold-producing countries.

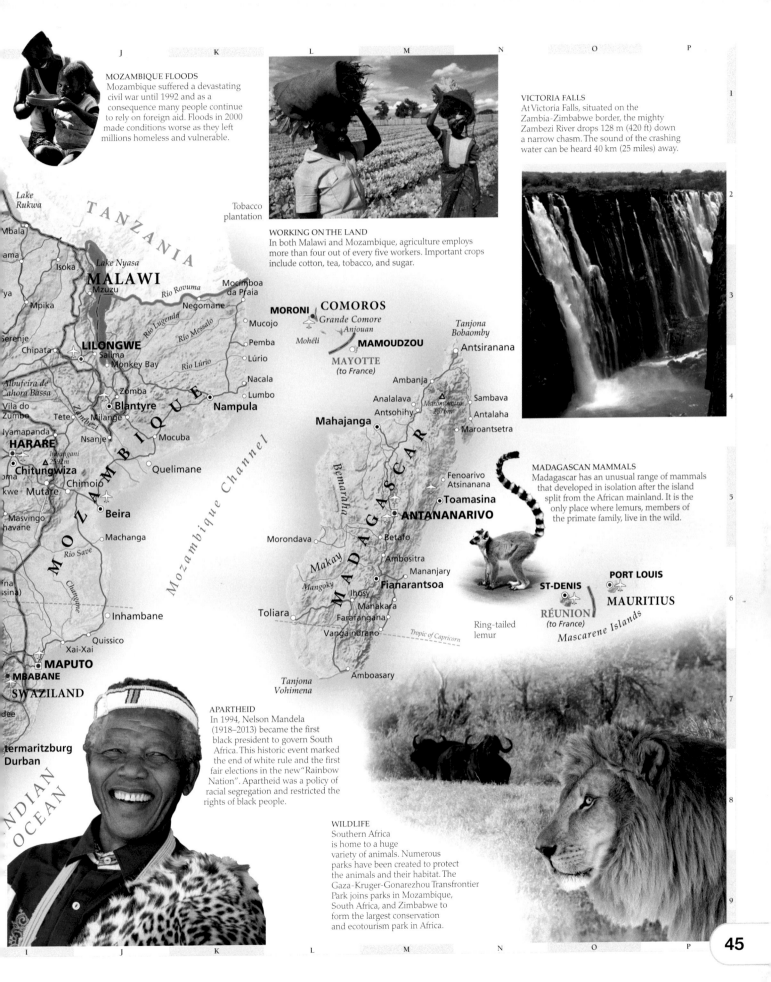

MOZAMBIQUE FLOODS
Mozambique suffered a devastating civil war until 1992 and as a consequence many people continue to rely on foreign aid. Floods in 2000 made conditions worse as they left millions homeless and vulnerable.

Tobacco plantation

WORKING ON THE LAND
In both Malawi and Mozambique, agriculture employs more than four out of every five workers. Important crops include cotton, tea, tobacco, and sugar.

VICTORIA FALLS
At Victoria Falls, situated on the Zambia-Zimbabwe border, the mighty Zambezi River drops 128 m (420 ft) down a narrow chasm. The sound of the crashing water can be heard 40 km (25 miles) away.

Lake Rukwa
TANZANIA
Mbala
Isoka
Lake Nyasa
MALAWI
Mzuzu
Mpika
Rio Rovuma
Mocímboa da Praia
Negomane
Rio Lugenda
Rio Messalo
Serenje
Chipata
LILONGWE
Salima
Monkey Bay
Rio Lúrio
Mucojo
Pemba
Lúrio
Nacala
Lumbo
Albufeira de Cahora Bassa
Zomba
Blantyre
Nampula
Vila do Zumbo
Tete
Zambezi
Milange
MOZAMBIQUE
Nyamapanda
Nsanje
Mocuba
HARARE
Inyangani 2592m
Chitungwiza
Quelimane
Chimoio
Mutare
Beira
Masvingo
Machanga
Rio Save
Changane
Inhambane
Quissico
Xai-Xai
MAPUTO
MBABANE
SWAZILAND
Pietermaritzburg
Durban
INDIAN OCEAN
Mozambique Channel
MORONI
COMOROS
Grande Comore
Anjouan
Mohéli
MAMOUDZOU
MAYOTTE
(to France)
Tanjona Bobaomby
Antsiranana
Ambanja
Analalava
Maromokotro 2876m
Sambava
Antsohihy
Antalaha
Mahajanga
Maroantsetra
MADAGASCAR
Bemaraha
Fenoarivo Atsinanana
Toamasina
ANTANANARIVO
Morondava
Betafo
Ambositra
Makay
Mananjary
Mangoky
Fianarantsoa
Ihosy
Manakara
Toliara
Farafangana
Vangaindrano
Tropic of Capricorn
Amboasary
Tanjona Vohimena
ST-DENIS
PORT LOUIS
MAURITIUS
RÉUNION
(to France)
Mascarene Islands

Ring-tailed lemur

MADAGASCAN MAMMALS
Madagascar has an unusual range of mammals that developed in isolation after the island split from the African mainland. It is the only place where lemurs, members of the primate family, live in the wild.

APARTHEID
In 1994, Nelson Mandela (1918–2013) became the first black president to govern South Africa. This historic event marked the end of white rule and the first fair elections in the new "Rainbow Nation". Apartheid was a policy of racial segregation and restricted the rights of black people.

WILDLIFE
Southern Africa is home to a huge variety of animals. Numerous parks have been created to protect the animals and their habitat. The Gaza-Kruger-Gonarezhou Transfrontier Park joins parks in Mozambique, South Africa, and Zimbabwe to form the largest conservation and ecotourism park in Africa.

EUROPE

Separated from Asia by the ridge of the Ural Mountains, Europe is a continent of very different nations, listed below in order of their land area. Each nation has its own language and culture, but they share a 2,000-year history of civilization that has inspired some of the world's greatest political ideas, works of art, and innovations in technology.

Russia (Russian Federation)
17,098,242 sq km
6,601,668 sq miles
142,355,000
Moscow
Russian, Tatar, Ukrainian, Chuvash, various other national languages

Germany
357,022 sq km
137,847 sq miles
80,723,000
Berlin
German, Turkish

United Kingdom
243,610 sq km
94,058 sq miles
64,430,000
London
English, Welsh, Scottish Gaelic, Irish Gaelic

Iceland
103,000 sq km
39,769 sq miles
335,900
Reykjavík
Icelandic

Serbia
77,474 sq km
29,913 sq miles
7,144,000
Belgrade
Serbian, Hungarian (Magyar)

Bosnia and Herzegovina
51,197 sq km
19,767 sq miles
3,862,000
Sarajevo
Bosnian, Serbian, Croatian

France
551,500 sq km
212,935 sq miles
66,836,000
Paris
French, Provençal, German, Breton, Catalan, Basque

Finland
338,145 sq km
130,559 sq miles
5,498,000
Helsinki
Finnish, Swedish, Sami

Romania
238,391sq km
92,043 sq miles
21,600,000
Bucharest
Romanian, Hungarian (Magyar), Romany, German

Hungary
93,028 sq km
35,918 sq miles
9,875,000
Budapest
Hungarian (Magyar)

Ireland
70,273 sq km
27,133 sq miles
4,952,000
Dublin
English, Irish Gaelic

Slovakia
49,035 sq km
18,933 sq miles
5,446,000
Bratislava
Slovak, Hungarian (Magyar), Czech

Ukraine
603,550 sq km
233,032 sq miles
44,210,000
Kiev
Ukrainian, Russian, Tatar

Norway
323,802 sq km
125,021 sq miles
5,265,000
Oslo
Norwegian (*Bokmål*, "book language", and *Nynorsk* "new Norsk"), Sami

Belarus
207,600 sq km
180,155 sq miles
9,570,000
Minsk
Belarussian, Russian

Portugal
92,090 sq km
35,556 sq miles
10,834,000
Lisbon
Portuguese

Lithuania
65,300 sq km
25,212 sq miles
2,854,000
Vilnius
Lithuanian, Russian

Estonia
45,228 sq km
17,463 sq miles
1,259,000
Tallinn
Estonian, Russian

Spain
505,370 sq km
195,124 sq miles
48,563,000
Madrid
Spanish, Catalan, Galician, Basque

Poland
312,685 sq km
120,728 sq miles
38,523,000
Warsaw
Polish

Greece
131,957 sq km
50,949 sq miles
10,773,000
Athens
Greek, Turkish, Macedonian, Albanian

Austria
83,871 sq km
32,383 sq miles
8,712,000
Vienna
German, Croatian, Slovenian, Hungarian (Magyar)

Latvia
64,589 sq km
24,938 sq miles
1,966,000
Riga
Latvian, Russian

Denmark
43,094 sq km
16,639 sq miles
5,725,000
Copenhagen
Danish

Sweden
450,295 sq km
173,860 sq miles
9,881,000
Stockholm
Swedish, Finnish, Sami

Italy
301,340 sq km
116,348 sq miles
62,008,000
Rome
Italian, German, French

Bulgaria
110,879 sq km
42,811 sq miles
7,145,000
Sofia
Bulgarian, Turkish, Romany

Czechia
78,867 sq km
30,451 sq miles
10,645,000
Prague
Czech, Slovak, Hun[illegible]

Croatia
56,594 sq km
21,851 sq miles
4,314,000
Zagreb
Croatian

Netherlands
41,543 sq km
16,040 sq miles
17,017,000
Amsterdam
Dutch, Frisian

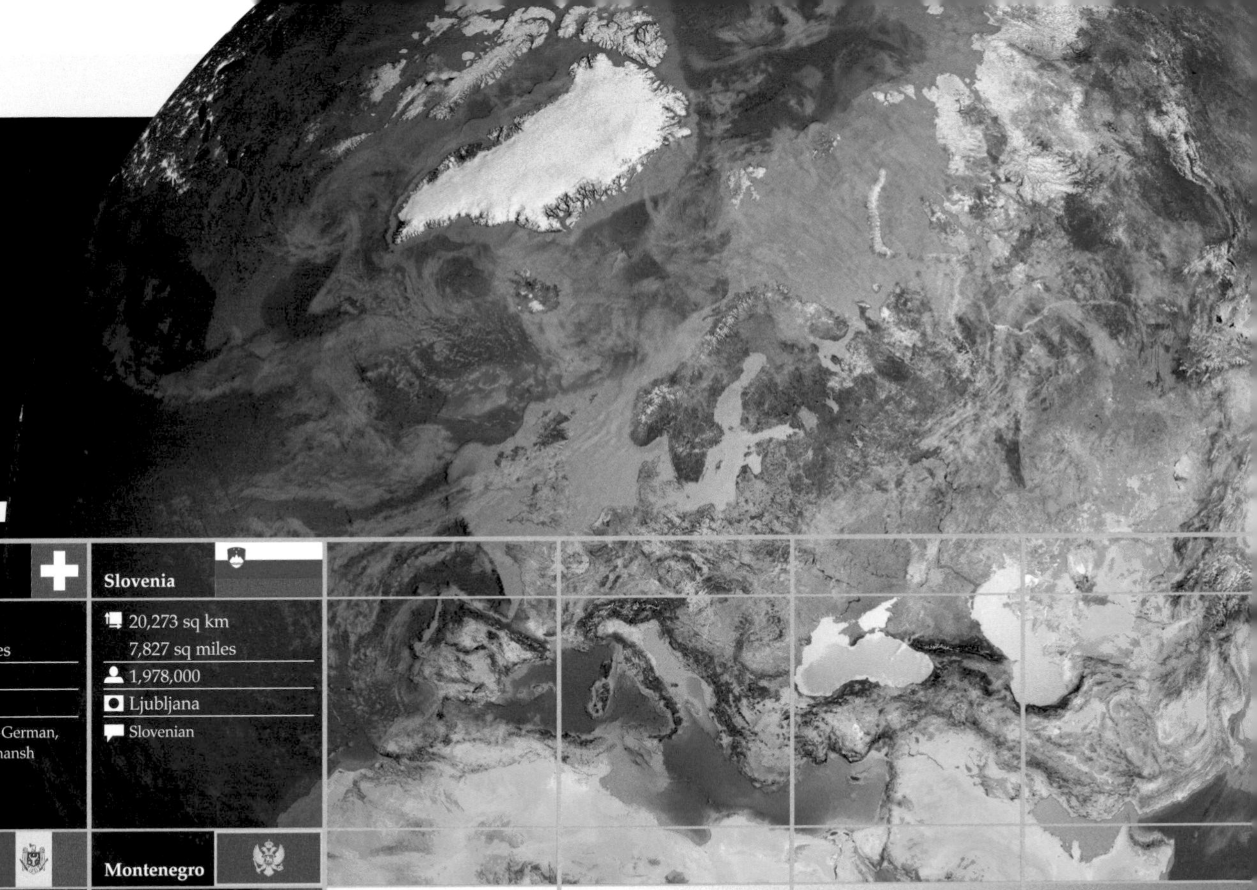

Switzerland
41,277 sq km
15,937 sq miles
8,179,000
Bern
German, Swiss-German, French, Italian, Romansh

Slovenia
20,273 sq km
7,827 sq miles
1,978,000
Ljubljana
Slovenian

Moldova
33,851 sq km
13,070 sq miles
3,510,000
Chisinau
Moldovan, Ukrainian, Russian

Montenegro
13,812 sq km
5,333 sq miles
644,600
Podgorica
Montenegrin, Serbian, Albanian, Bosnian, Croatian

Belgium
30,528 sq km
11,787 sq miles
11,409,000
Brussels
Dutch, French, German

The cathedral dome of Santa Maria del Fiore dominates the skyline of Florence, Italy – one of the world's most beautiful cities.

Albania
28,748 sq km
11,100 sq miles
3,039,000
Tirana
Albanian, Greek

Kosovo
10,887 sq km
4,203 sq miles
1,883,000
Pristina
Albanian, Serbian, Bosnian, Gorani, Romany, Turkish

Luxembourg
2,586 sq km
998 sq miles
582,300
Luxembourg
Luxembourgish, German, French

Malta
316 sq km
122 sq miles
415,200
Valletta
Maltese, English

San Marino
61 sq km
24 sq miles
33,300
San Marino
Italian

Vatican City
0.44 sq km
0.17 sq miles
1,000
Vatican City
Italian, Latin

Macedonia
25,713 sq km
9,928 sq miles
2,100,000
Skopje
Macedonian, Albanian,

Cyprus
9,251 sq km
3,572 sq miles
1,205,600
Nicosia
Greek, Turkish

Andorra
468 sq km
181 sq miles
85,700
Andorra la Vella
Spanish, Catalan, French,

Liechtenstein
160 sq km
62 sq miles
38,000
Vaduz
German, Alemannisch

Monaco
2 sq km
0.77 sq miles
30,600
Monaco
French, Italian, Monégasque,

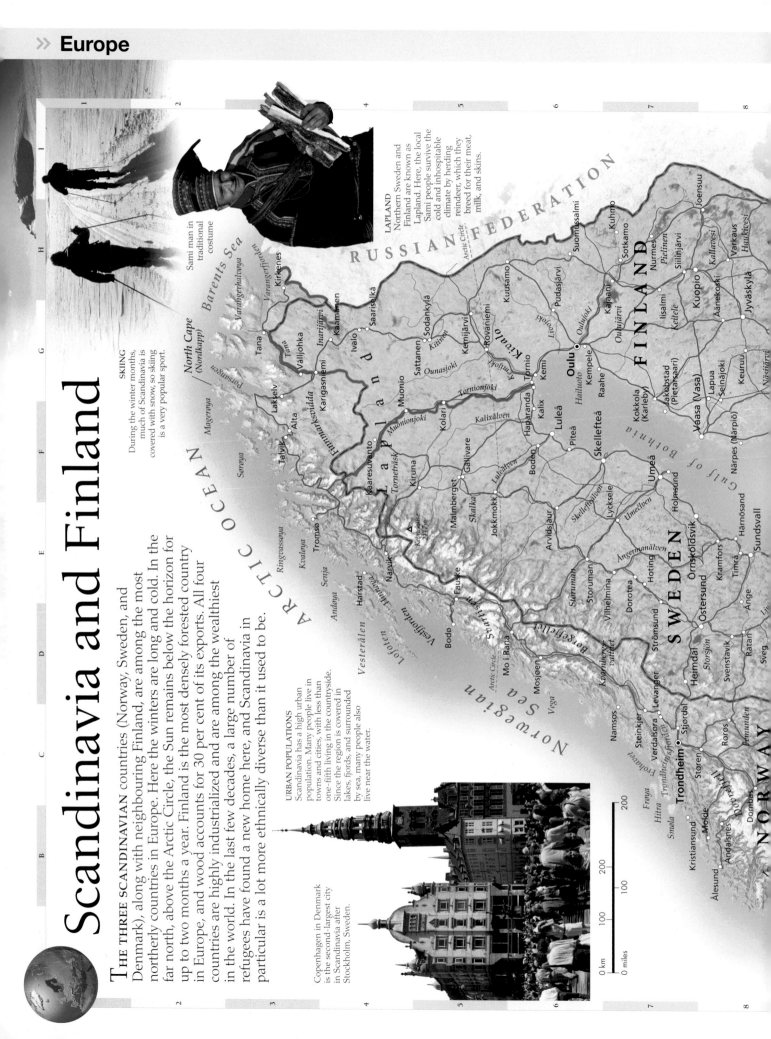

Scandinavia and Finland

THE THREE SCANDINAVIAN countries (Norway, Sweden, and Denmark), along with neighbouring Finland, are among the most northerly countries in Europe. Here the winters are long and cold. In the far north, above the Arctic Circle, the Sun remains below the horizon for up to two months a year. Finland is the most densely forested country in Europe, and wood accounts for 30 per cent of its exports. All four countries are highly industrialized and are among the wealthiest in the world. In the last few decades, a large number of refugees have found a new home here, and Scandinavia in particular is a lot more ethnically diverse than it used to be.

SKIING
During the winter months, much of Scandinavia is covered with snow, so skiing is a very popular sport.

Sami man in traditional costume

LAPLAND
Northern Sweden and Finland are known as Lapland. Here, the local Sami people survive the cold and inhospitable climate by herding reindeer, which they breed for their meat, milk, and skins.

URBAN POPULATIONS
Scandinavia has a high urban population. Many people live in towns and cities, with less than one-fifth living in the countryside. Since the region is covered in lakes, fjords, and surrounded by sea, many people also live near the water.

Copenhagen in Denmark is the second-largest city in Scandinavia after Stockholm, Sweden.

0 km 100 200
0 miles 100 200

THE SAUNA
The sauna, or steam bath, was invented in Finland about 1,000 years ago as a way of cleaning and relaxing the body. After a hot sauna, many Finns cool off by plunging into an icy pool (below) or a snowdrift.

INDUSTRIAL STRENGTH
Manufacturing is an important source of employment and wealth throughout Scandinavia and Finland. Many of the goods produced here, such as machinery, medical and technological equipment, motor vehicles (Sweden), and pharmaceuticals (Denmark), are exported all over the world. In Denmark, many people also work in agriculture, fish processing, and brewing.

NORWEGIAN FJORDS
The west coast of Norway has thousands of deep inlets, known as fjords, gouged out of the mountains by glaciers during the last ice age and then flooded by the sea. The fjords run inland between high mountains and make a favourite destination for cruise ships bringing tourists to admire the stunning scenery.

BUILDING WITH WOOD
Much of Norway and Sweden, and two-thirds of Finland, is covered by dense forests of birch, pine, spruce, and other trees. Finland has more than 16 times more forested land per person than the European average. Many people in the region work in the forestry industry, producing wood for the construction and furniture industries. This great natural resource is also used to build homes and churches, like this medieval stave church (left) in Norway.

SAVING THE ENVIRONMENT
The people of all four countries are very environmentally conscious and recycle as many household items as they can. Strict national laws protect the environment from industrial waste and pollution, although there is growing concern about the levels of pollution in the Baltic Sea.

The British Isles

For such a small group of islands, the British Isles has a very rich history. This is evident from its legacy of ancient ruins, medieval castles, dramatic cathedrals, and grand country houses. Once a leading industrial and colonial power, British monarchs ruled an empire that circled the globe. As a result, English is still widely spoken around the world. Today, many traditional industries, such as shipbuilding, mining, and engineering, have declined, and the emphasis is now on banking and insurance, as well as pharmaceuticals. The British Isles consists of two countries: the United Kingdom of Great Britain and Northern Ireland (the UK), and the Republic of Ireland.

Wales has more than 200 castles.

IRELAND
Tourists visit Ireland, attracted by its unspoiled countryside and lively cities, such as Dublin (left). Once part of Britain, Ireland gained independence in 1922. Its economy, the fastest-growing in Europe just before the global banking crisis of 2008, has since seen good recovery.

Irish horse and rider on a training run

HORSE BREEDING
Lush pastures and a mild climate have encouraged the breeding of thoroughbred racehorses in Ireland. Stud farms here raise some of the best racehorses in the world.

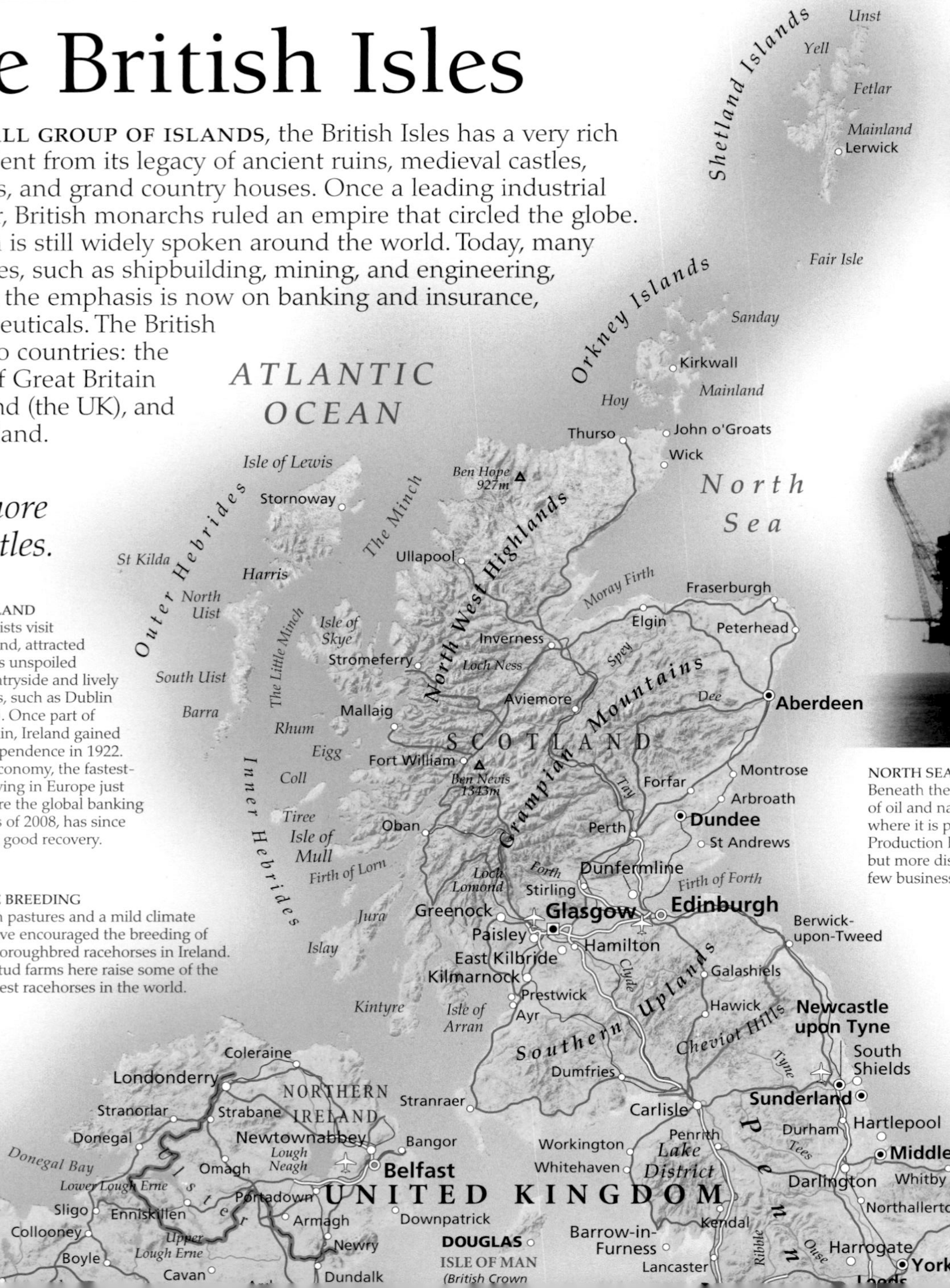

ATLANTIC OCEAN
North Sea
Shetland Islands
Unst
Yell
Fetlar
Mainland
Lerwick
Fair Isle
Orkney Islands
Sanday
Kirkwall
Mainland
Hoy
Thurso
John o'Groats
Wick
Outer Hebrides
Isle of Lewis
Stornoway
Harris
St Kilda
North Uist
South Uist
Barra
The Minch
The Little Minch
Isle of Skye
Ben Hope 927m
North West Highlands
Ullapool
Moray Firth
Fraserburgh
Elgin
Peterhead
Inverness
Loch Ness
Spey
Stromeferry
Aviemore
Grampian Mountains
Dee
Aberdeen
Mallaig
Rhum
Eigg
SCOTLAND
Fort William
Ben Nevis 1343m
Coll
Tiree
Isle of Mull
Inner Hebrides
Oban
Firth of Lorn
Montrose
Forfar
Tay
Arbroath
Dundee
Perth
St Andrews
Loch Lomond
Forth
Stirling
Dunfermline
Firth of Forth
Jura
Islay
Greenock
Glasgow
Edinburgh
Paisley
Hamilton
Berwick-upon-Tweed
East Kilbride
Clyde
Kilmarnock
Galashiels
Prestwick
Southern Uplands
Hawick
Kintyre
Isle of Arran
Ayr
Cheviot Hills
Newcastle upon Tyne
South Shields
Tyne
Coleraine
Londonderry
NORTHERN IRELAND
Dumfries
Stranraer
Carlisle
Sunderland
Stranorlar
Strabane
Durham
Hartlepool
Donegal
Newtownabbey
Bangor
Workington
Penrith
Tees
Middlesbrough
Donegal Bay
Omagh
Lough Neagh
Belfast
Whitehaven
Lake District
Lower Lough Erne
Ulster
Portadown
UNITED KINGDOM
Darlington
Whitby
Scarborough
Sligo
Enniskillen
Armagh
Downpatrick
Northallerton
Pennines
Kendal
Bridlington
Collooney
Upper Lough Erne
Newry
DOUGLAS
Barrow-in-Furness
Ribble
Ouse
Harrogate
Boyle
Isle of Man (British Crown
York
Castlebar
Cavan
Dundalk
Lancaster
Beverley

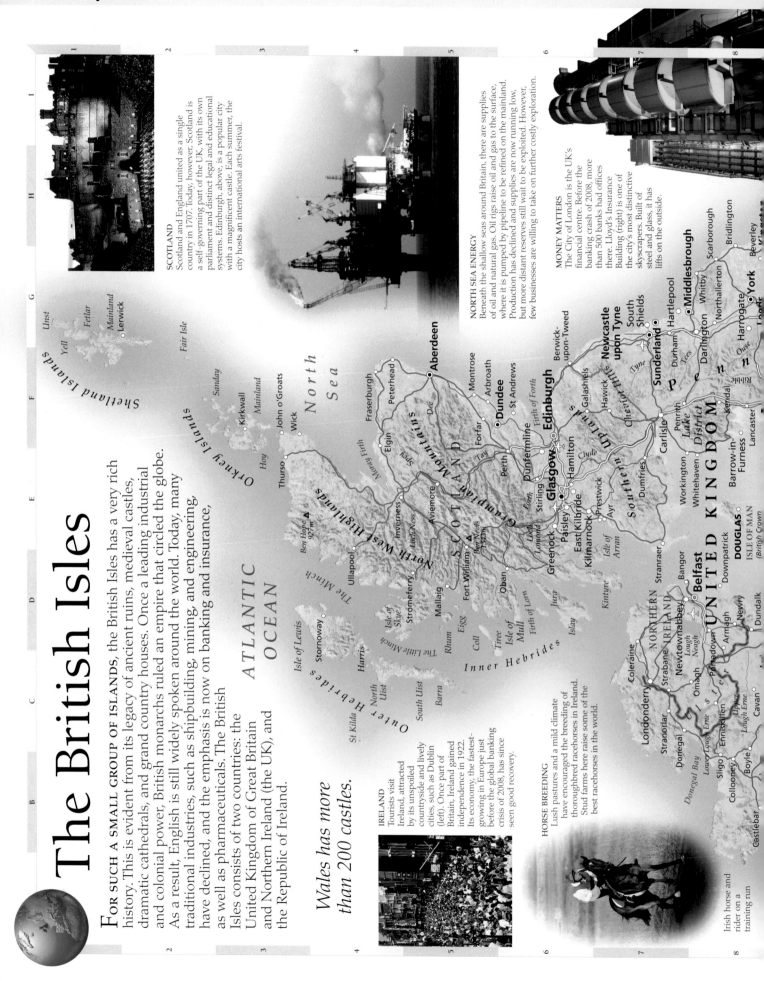

SCOTLAND
Scotland and England united as a single country in 1707. Today, however, Scotland is a self-governing part of the UK, with its own parliament and distinct legal and educational systems. Edinburgh, above, is a popular city with a magnificent castle. Each summer, the city hosts an international arts festival.

NORTH SEA ENERGY
Beneath the shallow seas around Britain, there are supplies of oil and natural gas. Oil rigs raise oil and gas to the surface, where it is pumped by pipeline to be refined on the mainland. Production has declined and supplies are now running low, but more distant reserves still wait to be exploited. However, few businesses are willing to take on further costly exploration.

MONEY MATTERS
The City of London is the UK's financial centre. Before the banking crash of 2008, more than 500 banks had offices there. Lloyd's Insurance Building (right) is one of the city's most distinctive skyscrapers. Built of steel and glass, it has lifts on the outside.

Wales playing Scotland at rugby in the Millennium Stadium, Cardiff

WALES
Wales was formally united with England in 1536, but retains its own language and traditions. Welsh is spoken widely in some parts, and public signs appear in both Welsh and English. Coal mining and steel production were important in the south, but have both declined. Rugby is the national game.

MULTICULTURAL SOCIETY
Britain once controlled a world empire with colonies in every continent. Many people – from the Indian subcontinent, Africa, and the Caribbean in particular – came here and brought their cultures with them, as well as settling into British life. Today, about one in eight British people are from an ethnic minority background.

Stonehenge in southern England was built from about 3000 BCE onwards.

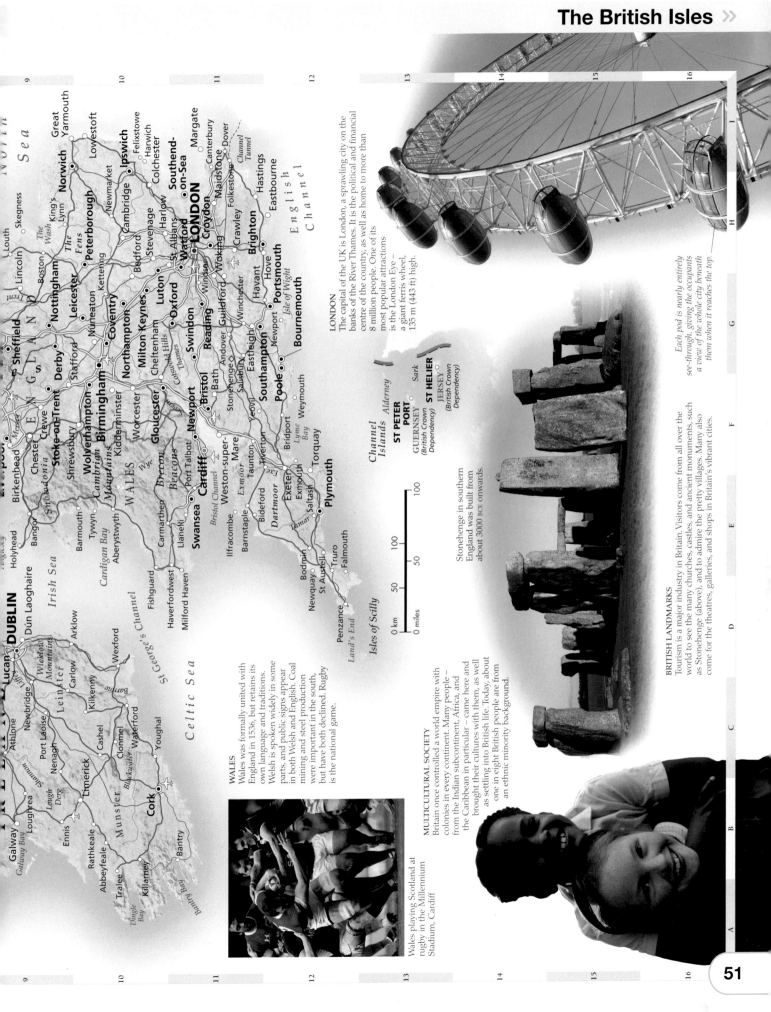

LONDON
The capital of the UK is London, a sprawling city on the banks of the River Thames. It is the political and financial centre of the country, as well as home to more than 8 million people. One of its most popular attractions is the London Eye – a giant ferris wheel, 135 m (443 ft) high.

Each pod is nearly entirely see-through, giving the occupants a view of the whole city beneath them when it reaches the top.

BRITISH LANDMARKS
Tourism is a major industry in Britain. Visitors come from all over the world to see the many churches, castles, and ancient monuments, such as Stonehenge (above), and to admire the pretty villages. Many also come for the theatres, galleries, and shops in Britain's vibrant cities.

The Low Countries

THE NETHERLANDS, BELGIUM, AND LUXEMBOURG are known as the Low Countries because the land is so flat and low-lying. In the case of the Netherlands, much of the land is below sea level – *Netherlands* is Dutch for "under lands". The three countries are among the richest in Europe and, while farming still plays an important part, they all have strong, modern economies based on manufacturing and trade. Luxembourg in particular is known as a tax haven and is a major centre for international finance. Their location at the mouth of the River Rhine and other major European rivers places the three countries at the heart of western European trade and politics – all three were founder members of the European Economic Community (now the European Union, or EU), established in 1957.

ROTTERDAM, NETHERLANDS
Every year, around 30,000 sea-going ships and 110,000 barges call at the port of Rotterdam. Lying at the mouth of the River Rhine, this port is the largest in the world and is where vast container ships from all over the world load or unload their cargoes. The smaller barges help to transport goods farther inland. With the port's advanced Vessel Traffic Service (VTS) it's possible to track ships on a radar screen up to 60 km (37 miles) off the coast and 40 km (25 miles) inland.

RECLAIMING THE LAND
Over the centuries, the Dutch have reclaimed land from the sea. They did this by building huge dykes, or dams, to keep out the sea, and then draining the surface water into canals. Windmills originally pumped out the water, but electric pumps are now used.

Tulips were introduced to the Netherlands from Turkey in 1562. Black tulips were the most valuable.

Land below sea level on main map
West Frisian Islands
(Waddeneilanden)
Schiermonnikoog
Ameland
Terschelling
Vlieland
Texel
Waddenzee
IJsselmeer
Flevoland
IJssel
NETHERLANDS
GERMANY
Eemshaven
Delfzijl
Appingedam
Loppersum
Groningen
Zuidhorn
Haren
Zuidlaren
Dokkum
Winsum
Menaldum
Leeuwarden
Harlingen
Drachten
Leek
Assen
Vlagtwedde
Borger
Sneek
Joure
Heerenveen
Wolvega
Beilen
Den Helder
Schagen
Opmeer
Emmeloord
Steenwijk
Hoogeveen
Emmen
Coevorden
Meppel
Staphorst
Alkmaar
Hoorn
Castricum
Velsen-Noord
Purmerend
Lelystad
Zwolle
Hardenberg
Den Ham
Tubbergen
Haarlem
Zaanstad
Almere
Nunspeet
Almelo
Denekamp
AMSTERDAM
Zeewolde
Rijssen
Hengelo
Noordwijk aan Zee
Amstelveen
Vaassen
Deventer
Hilversum
Baarn
Apeldoorn
Goor
Enschede
Leiden
Sassenheim

DUTCH PEOPLE
The Dutch once ruled a vast empire in Indonesia, the Caribbean, and South America. As a result, many nationalities now live here. Ethnic minorities make up about 15 per cent of the people and in some cities, the majority of primary school children have a non-Dutch background.

Dutch tulips

CROPS
Fertile soil and good irrigation have helped the Netherlands become a major exporter of agricultural products, with vegetables and tomatoes forming important crops. It is also famous for its bulbs and cut flowers, notably tulips.

0 km
25
50
75
0 miles
25
50
75
North Sea
Rotterdam
Spijkenisse
Goeree
Schouwen
Dordrecht
Werkendam
Waal
Bergse Maas
Nijmegen
Oss
Cuijk
Vlijmen
Overflakkee
Oosterhout
's-Hertogenbosch
Schijndel
Noord-Beveland
Tholen
Breda
Roosendaal
Tilburg
Oirschot
Helmond
Nieuw-Bergen
Horst
Middelburg
Goes
Vlissingen
Zuid-Beveland
Essen
Baarle-Hertog
Eindhoven
Venlo
Westerschelde
Zeebrugge
Blankenberge
Oostburg
Terneuzen
Kalmthout
Veldhoven
Someren
Kapellen
Turnhout
Bergeyk
Ostend
(Oostende)
Axel
Assenede
Beveren
Antwerp
(Antwerpen)
Lommel
Weert
Reuver
Roermond
Middelkerke
Bruges (Brugge)
Ghent
(Gent)
Sint-Niklaas
Geel
Kinrooi
Echt
Susteren
Veurne
Torhout
Aalter
Melle
Mechelen
Herselt
Beringen
Bree
Deinze
Aalst
Tremelo
Zonhoven
Roeselare
Gavere
Genk
Heerlen
Kerkrade
Ieper
Poperinge
Kortrijk
BRUSSELS
(BRUSSEL/ BRUXELLES)
Schaerbeek
Leuven
Hasselt
Geleen
Riemst
Maastricht
Vaals
Flanders
Zwevegem
Halle
Overijse
Tienen
Landen
Oupeye
Mouscron
Enghien
Wavre
Herstal
Tournai
Ath
BELGIUM
Liège
Verviers
Péruwelz
Leuze-en-Hainaut
Gembloux
Éghezée
Seraing
Hautes Fagnes
Botrange 694m
Mons
La Louvière
Namur
Huy
Jemappes
Binche
Charleroi
Erquelinnes
Malmédy
Thuin
Gerpinnes
Ciney
Walcourt
Dinant
Marche-en-Famenne
Famenne
Fagne
Ourthe
Rochefort
Weiswampach
Couvin
Hosingen
Bastogne
Our
Sûre
GERMANY
Recogne
Diekirch
Ardennes
Semois
Ettelbrück
Neufchâteau
LUXEMBOURG
FRANCE
Étalle
Arlon
Grevenmacher
Alzette
Aubange
LUXEMBOURG
Virton
Pétange
Dudelange
Esch-sur-Alzette

BELGIAN QUALITY
Belgium is renowned for its beautiful historic buildings and for its excellent food, especially chocolates. Belgians have been making top-quality chocolates for more than 100 years, and pralines, a type of filled chocolate, are a speciality. Brussels even boasts a chocolate museum.

AMSTERDAM, NETHERLANDS
The old architecture and picturesque canals make Amsterdam one of the most visited cities in Europe. Occasionally, the canals freeze over and city officials may decide it's safe for people to go skating. When they do, men and women of all ages, from very old to very young, take to the ice. Amsterdam is also home to some great museums, including the Van Gogh Museum, Rijksmuseum, and the Anne Frank House.

Cyclists have their own traffic lights – this one is green for "go".

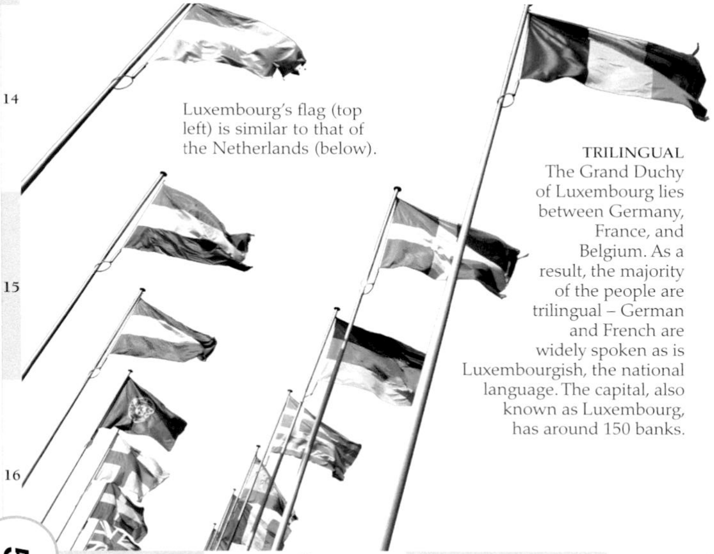

Luxembourg's flag (top left) is similar to that of the Netherlands (below).

TRILINGUAL
The Grand Duchy of Luxembourg lies between Germany, France, and Belgium. As a result, the majority of the people are trilingual – German and French are widely spoken as is Luxembourgish, the national language. The capital, also known as Luxembourg, has around 150 banks.

CYCLING
The flatness of the land makes the Netherlands ideal for cycling, and more than half a million people cycle to school or work each day. Lines of 20–100 children cycling together to school are common. Most of the roads have special cycle lanes, and bicycles are often the quickest form of transport to get around the crowded towns and cities. The use of bicycles also reduces car use and thus cuts down the amount of air pollution.

France

In direct contrast to its mainly rural landscape, France is a modern nation with most people now living in towns and cities. While industry makes up the largest section of its economy, tourism also plays a big part – France is the world's most visited country. A land of varied scenery, from gently rolling farmland in the north to a stretch of dry, warm Mediterranean coast in the south, France also shares two mountain ranges – the Pyrenees and the Alps. Each of the 22 regions within France, which includes the island of Corsica, has its own distinct identity and culture. The tiny countries of Andorra and Monaco lie next to France.

Boules, *the national game of France, is still played in village squares around the country.*

NUCLEAR POWER
Three-quarters of France's electricity is produced by nuclear power plants (above), making the country largely self-sufficient in energy and one of the main producers of nuclear power in Europe. Hydroelectric plants are also an important source of power.

TGV

HIGH-SPEED TRAVEL
France has Europe's fastest train, the TGV – *train à grande vitesse* – which travels at up to 300 kph (186 mph) during normal services. In 2007, a modified TGV even set a speed record for conventional trains of 574.8 kph (357.2 mph). The TGV network connects Paris with all the country's major cities, which makes it easier to commute or visit relatives. It also extends to Germany, Italy, Belgium, Switzerland, and through the Channel Tunnel to Britain.

STREETS OF PARIS
Tourists flock to Paris to visit its world-famous museums and art galleries, shop in its elegant stores, and soak up its vibrant atmosphere. Montmartre, which overlooks the city, is famous for its artists. Close by, in the Place du Tertre (above), visitors can have their portrait painted.

English Channel
Strait of Dover
Channel Tunnel
BELGIUM
LUX.
GERMANY
SWITZERLAND
ATLANTIC OCEAN
GUERNSEY (British Crown Dependency)
JERSEY (British Crown Dependency)
Golfe de St-Malo
Baie de la Seine
Île d'Ouessant
Iroise
Belle Île
Île d'Yeu
Dunkerque
Calais
Boulogne-sur-Mer
le Portel
Berck-Plage
St-Omer
Tourcoing
Roubaix
Lille
Douai
Valenciennes
Artois
Arras
Cambrai
Abbeville
Somme
Amiens
Albert
St-Quentin
Hirson
Charleville-Mézières
Sedan
Picardie
Dieppe
Fécamp
le Havre
Barentin
Rouen
Beauvais
Noyon
Oise
Laon
Compiègne
Cherbourg
Bayeux
Caen
St-Lô
Coutances
Lisieux
Louviers
Évreux
Seine
Senlis
Pontoise
Château-Thierry
Reims
Meuse
Thionville
Hagondange
Metz
Argenteuil
Nanterre
Versailles
Antony
PARIS
Créteil
Marne
Châlons-en-Champagne
Champagne
Lorraine
Bar-le-Duc
Alsace
Saverne
Haguenau
Schiltigheim
Strasbourg
St-Dié
Vosges
Sélestat
Colmar
Cernay
Mulhouse
St-Louis
Belfort
Audincourt
Montbéliard
Vesoul
Épinal
Moselle
Nancy
Toul
Chaumont
Troyes
Langres
Morlaix
Brest
Landerneau
Plérin
Brittany (Bretagne)
St-Brieuc
St-Malo
Granville
Avranches
Dinan
Quimper
Pontivy
Loudéac
Concarneau
Quimperlé
Lorient
Hennebont
Auray
Vannes
Rennes
Fougères
Vitré
Laval
Maine
Alençon
(Normandy) Normandie
Chartres
Île-de-France
Melun
Fontainebleau
Nemours
Sens
Yonne
Châteaubriant
Redon
la Baule-Escoublac
St-Nazaire
Nantes
Rezé
Challans
les Herbiers
la Roche-sur-Yon
les Sables-
le Mans
Sarthe
la Flèche
Trélazé
Angers
Loire
Anjou
Saumur
Cholet
Thouars
Châtellerault
Poitou
Vendôme
Touraine
Tours
Orléans
Châteaudun
Blois
Olivet
Orléanais
Montargis
Auxerre
Cosne-Cours-sur-Loire
Côte d'Or
(Burgundy) Bourgogne
Morvan
Nivernais
Vierzon
Cher
Berry
Bourges
Châteauroux
Creuse
Nevers
Dijon
Beaune
Franche-Comté
Besançon
Dôle

AVIATION INDUSTRY

The French were pioneers of aviation. They co-built Concorde and, in 1970, joined forces with German, Spanish, and UK companies to produce short- to medium-range aircraft that were both economic to run and carried up to 300 passengers. Called Airbus, these aircraft filled a vital gap in the market and changed the face of the aviation industry.

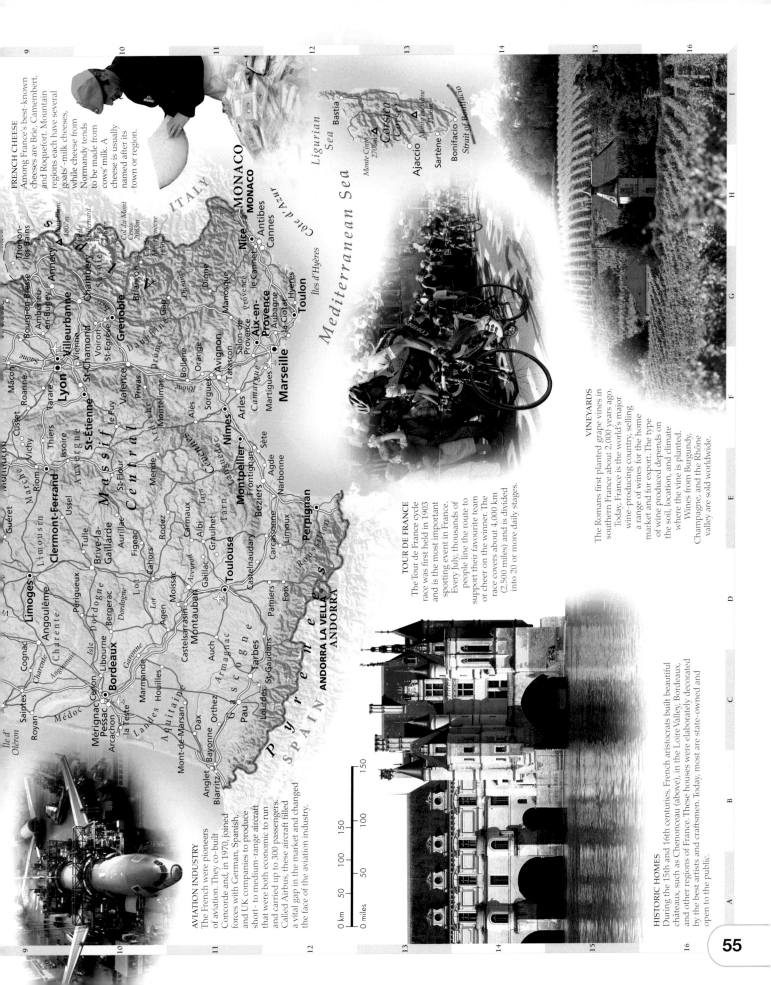

FRENCH CHEESE

Among France's best-known cheeses are Brie, Camembert, and Roquefort. Mountain regions each have several goats'-milk cheeses, while cheese from Normandy tends to be made from cows' milk. A cheese is usually named after its town or region.

HISTORIC HOMES

During the 15th and 16th centuries, French aristocrats built beautiful châteaux, such as Chenonceau (above), in the Loire Valley, Bordeaux, and other regions of France. These houses were elaborately decorated by the best artists and craftsmen. Today, most are state-owned and open to the public.

TOUR DE FRANCE

The Tour de France cycle race was first held in 1903 and is the most important sporting event in France. Every July, thousands of people line the route to support their favourite team or cheer on the winner. The race covers about 4,000 km (2,500 miles) and is divided into 20 or more daily stages.

VINEYARDS

The Romans first planted grape vines in southern France about 2,000 years ago. Today, France is the world's major wine-producing country, selling a range of wines for the home market and for export. The type of wine produced depends on the soil, location, and climate where the vine is planted. Wines from Burgundy, Champagne, and the Rhône valley are sold worldwide.

Germany and the Alpine States

LYING AT THE VERY HEART OF EUROPE, Germany is one of the world's wealthiest nations. It is also Europe's leading industrial power. To its south lie the Alpine states of Switzerland, Austria, Liechtenstein, and Slovenia. The region is famed for its beautiful Alpine scenery, mountains, and lakes. German is the main language in all but Slovenia. However, each of the five countries has its own distinct history, culture, and national identity. Indeed, since 1815, Switzerland has been recognized as a neutral nation, and has stayed out of all the wars that have affected Europe.

THE JOY OF UNIFICATION
After World War II, Germany was split, with a US-backed capitalist state in the west and a Russian-backed state in the east. Built in 1961, the Berlin Wall was 155 km (96 miles) long and was designed to stop East Germans from leaving for a better life in the West. The wall divided Berlin and separated families, friends, and a nation for 28 years. When Germany was unified (reunited) in 1990, the wall was officially demolished.

Celebrations at the Brandenburg Gate marking the 10th anniversary of the fall of the Berlin Wall

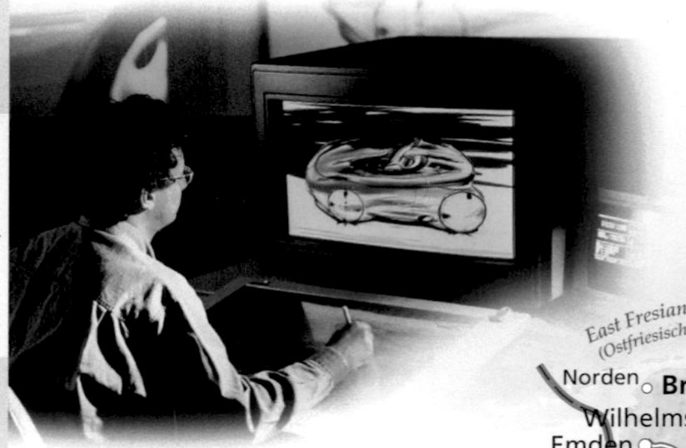

GERMAN INDUSTRY
With its coal and iron mines, the Ruhr Valley was once the powerhouse of the German economy. Today's industry ranges from engineering to high-tech goods. Quality assembly and design make Germany the fourth-largest car producer in the world.

GERMANY
DENMARK
NETHERLANDS
BELGIUM
POLAND
Baltic Sea
North Frisian Islands (Nordfriesische Inseln)
East Fresian Islands (Ostfriesische Inseln)
Helgoland Bay
Kieler Bucht
Fehmarn Belt
Fehmarn
Mecklenburger Bucht
Rügen
Pomeranian Bay
Oderhaff
Kiel Canal
Schleswig-Holstein
Westerland
Flensburg
Kappeln
Schleswig
Husum
Kiel
Rendsburg
Heide
Neumünster
Itzehoe
Cuxhaven
Puttgarden
Oldenburg
Eutin
Lübeck
Norderstedt
Hamburg
Stralsund
Bergen
Sassnitz
Greifswald
Wolgast
Anklam
Rostock
Warnemünde
Wismar
Demmin
Teterow
Malchin
Güstrow
Schwerin
Waren
Neubrandenburg
Pasewalk
Parchim
Neustrelitz
Müritz
Prenzlau
Angermünde
Eberswalde-Finow
Bad Freienwalde
Bernau
BERLIN
Frankfurt an der Oder
Potsdam
Brandenburg
Oranienburg
Neuruppin
Wittstock
Ludwigslust
Perleberg
Wittenberge
Elbe
Boizenburg
Winsen
Lüneburg
Dannenberg
Uelzen
Salzwedel
Stendal
Norden
Bremerhaven
Wilhelmshaven
Emden
Elmshorn
Stade
Rosengarten
Scheessel
Leer
Weener
Oldenburg
Bremen
Delmenhorst
Verden
Soltau
Celle
Cloppenburg
Bassum
Diepholz
Weser
Ems
Lingen
Osnabrück
Hanover (Hannover)
Peine
Wolfsburg
Braunschweig
Salzgitter
Magdeburg
Nordhorn
Rheine
Münster
Herford
Minden
Hildesheim
Seesen
Halberstadt
Schönebeck
Dessau
Bernburg
Saale
Lübbenau
Lübben
Spree
Guben
Cottbus
Ludwigsfelde
Eisenhüttenstadt
Finsterwalde
Senftenberg
Hoyerswerda
Bautzen
Görlitz
Löbau
Zittau
Rhine
Bocholt
Dülmen
Bielefeld
Gütersloh
Ahlen
Recklinghausen
Essen
Hamm
Paderborn
Northeim
Göttingen
Eisleben
Halle-Neustadt
Torgau
Duisburg
Dortmund
Warburg
Nordhausen
Halle
Leipzig
Riesa
Krefeld
Bochum
Marsberg
Kassel
Düsseldorf
Wuppertal
Solingen
Leverkusen
Olpe
Melsungen
Erfurt
Weimar
Döbeln
Saxony (Sachsen)
Dresden
Alsdorf
Cologne (Köln)
Siegen
Gotha
Jena
Hainichen
Pirna
Gera
Chemnitz
Aachen
Bonn
Marburg an der Lahn
Bad Hersfeld
Hünfeld
Saalfeld
Zwickau
Blankenheim
Schiefergebirge
Giessen
Fulda
Suhl
Plauen
Ore Mts. (Erzgebirge)
Rheinisches
Eifel
Mosel
Neuwied
Wetzlar
Hessen
Koblenz
Boppard
Coburg
Kronach
Hof
Münchberg
Lichtenfels
Marktredwitz
Wiesbaden
Frankfurt am Main
Offenbach
Mainz
Schweinfurt
Wittlich

FOOD AND DRINK
The annual Munich *Oktoberfest* is Germany's biggest beer festival. Entertainment includes parades and music.

GENEVA
Geneva lies on the shores of Lake Geneva, Europe's largest Alpine lake. This orderly city is a global centre for banking and finance. It is also a base for many international organizations, such as the Red Cross.

The Swiss speak German, French, Italian, and Romansh.

SWISS WATCHES
The Swiss invented the first wristwatch, the first quartz watch, and the first water-resistant watch. With their worldwide reputation for quality and style, timepieces make up the country's third largest export.

CZECHIA
SLOVAKIA
HUNGARY
CROATIA
FRANCE
ITALY
AUSTRIA
SWITZERLAND
SLOVENIA
LIECHTENSTEIN
VADUZ
BERN
VIENNA (WIEN)
LJUBLJANA
Neunkirchen
Saarbrücken
Heidelberg
Sinsheim
Nuremberg (Nürnberg)
Schwandorf
Neustadt an der Weinstrasse
Karlsruhe
Heilbronn
Pforzheim
Weissenburg
Regenstauf
Regensburg
Baden-Baden
Ludwigsburg
Aalen
Straubing
Deggendorf
Göppingen
Donauwörth
Ingolstadt
Passau
Hauzenberg
Kehl
Stuttgart
Heidenheim an der Brenz
Landshut
Offenburg
Reutlingen
Augsburg
Pocking
Linz
Zwettl
Hollabrunn
Mistelbach an der Zaya
Lahr
Ulm
Neu-Ulm
Munich (München)
Sankt Pölten
Tulln
Emmendingen
Rottweil
Villingen-Schwenningen
Mindelheim
Ried im Innkreis
Vöcklabruck
Wels
Steyr
Perchtoldsdorf
Traiskirchen
Freiburg im Breisgau
Bad Vöslau
Bad Krozingen
Memmingen
Stockach
Kaufbeuren
Rosenheim
Salzburg
Ebensee
Eisenstadt
Neusiedler See
Müllheim
Singen
Lake Constance
Wiener Neustadt
Lörrach
Schaffhausen
Konstanz
Kempten
Bad Ischl
Mürzzuschlag
Basel
Rhine (Rhein)
Bülach
Winterthur
Friedrichshafen
Füssen
Liezen
Leoben
Bavarian Alps
Bregenz
Zugspitze 2962m
Kitzbüheler Alpen
Fischbacher Alpen
La Chaux-de-Fonds
Jura
Biel
Aare
Zürichsee
Zürich
Sankt Gallen
Innsbruck
Schwaz
Graz
Neuchâtel
Lac de Neuchâtel
Zug
Luzern
Hohe Tauern
Judenburg
Mur
Schwyz
Grossglockner 3798m
Gurktaler Alpen
Wolfsberg
Klosters
Brenner Pass 1374m
Murska Sobota
Lausanne
Thun
Thuner See
Eiger 3970m
Vorderrhein
Chur
Lienz
Villach
Maribor
Klagenfurt
Berner Alps
Plöcken Pass 1357m
Loibl Pass 1367m
Velenje
Ptuj
Drava
Lake Geneva
Sion
Brig
St.Moritz
Jesenice
Celje
Onex
Geneva (Genève)
Monthey
Simplon Pass 2005m
Bellinzona
Tolmin
Kranj
Trbovlje
Sava
Krško
Rhône
Pennine Alps
Locarno
Lugano
Nova Gorica
Novo Mesto
Matterhorn 4478m
Lake Maggiore
Postojna
Kočevje
Great Saint Bernard Pass 2469m
Koper
Gulf of Venice
Istra
0 km 50 100
0 miles 50 100

SLOVENIA
After centuries of rule by overlords, Slovenia became independent in 1991. Although the population is only 2 million, the national culture is strong. The famous Lipizzaner show horses are named after the Slovenian farm where they were first bred.

The opera ball in Vienna

VIENNA, AUSTRIA
Vienna is a city of Baroque buildings, palaces, and famous concert halls. Grand balls with traditional waltzes are still customary. These are a reminder of when the city was the centre of the Austro-Hungarian Empire, which controlled large parts of east and central Europe.

ALPS
The Alps run from southeast France and spread eastwards through Switzerland and northern Italy into Austria and Slovenia. A popular tourist destination, the Alps are famous for dramatic scenery and winter sports.

The high and graceful stride of the Lipizzaner horses makes them excel in competitions.

Spain and Portugal

Spanish families tend to eat dinner late, at around 9 pm. So after school, children eat a snack called a merienda.

THE COUNTRIES OF SPAIN AND PORTUGAL share an area of land called the Iberian Peninsula. In the north, this land is cut off from the rest of Europe by the Pyrenees Mountains, while to the south, it is separated from Africa by the Strait of Gibraltar. The region was once ruled by Islamic people from north Africa, known as the Moors. Evidence of their culture can still be seen in buildings in the cities of Andalucía. The Moors were eventually defeated in 1492, and for a while, Portugal came under Spanish control, as did much of Europe. During the 20th century, both countries were ruled by brutal dictatorships, which were overthrown in the 1970s. They are now modern democracies and popular tourist destinations.

HARVESTING CORK
Cork is made from the outer bark of the evergreen cork oak tree. The bark is carefully stripped off, flattened, laid out in sheets, and then left to dry. The cork is used for many products, such as stoppers for wine bottles, matting, and tiles. Portugal is the world's leading exporter of cork.

LISBON
Portugal's capital city is Lisbon, which is situated at the mouth of the River Tagus on a series of steep hills and valleys. In 1755, two-thirds of the city was completely destroyed by an earthquake and tidal wave but was rebuilt with beautiful squares and public buildings. Many explorers have set sail from Lisbon in their quest to find new lands.

Trams are a feature of Lisbon streets and a popular form of transport for both the locals and tourists.

FISHING
Spain and Portugal have well-developed fishing industries with large-scale fleets and many smaller local fleets. However, overfishing along Portugal's coast and out in the north Atlantic has put many people's livelihoods at risk. Spain is still one of Europe's top fishing nations, with catches of fish, molluscs, and crustaceans reaching around 1,000 tonnes per year.

SPANISH CITIES
The majority of Spanish people live in towns and cities. Madrid is the largest Spanish city and the capital of Spain. Tourists flock to Barcelona, capital of Catalonia and a leading cultural, economic, and industrial hub. Bilbao, home to the magnificent Guggenheim Museum, is the capital of the Basque region and a busy port.

The Guggenheim, a modern-art museum in Bilbao

The Pamplona bull run is an annual fiesta that takes place in July.

FIESTAS
In Spain, many towns hold their own fiestas, or festivals, to celebrate a special event in their history or the birthday of their patron saint. These fiestas differ from one region to another. One of the most famous is held in Pamplona, where the brave run with the bulls.

Santander
Laredo
Bermeo
Zarautz
Donostia/San Sebastián
Irun
Torrelavega
Eibar
Bilbao
Tolosa
The Basque Country
(País Vasco)
Pamplona
(Iruña)
Vitoria-Gasteiz
Miranda de Ebro
Estella-Lizarra
FRANCE
Pyrenees
ANDORRA
Monte Perdido
3348m
Jaca
Burgos
Logroño
Navarra
La Seu d'Urgell
Ripoll
Figueres
Arnedo
Calahorra
Huesca
Berga
Banyoles
Manlleu
Girona (Gerona)
Lerma
La Rioja
Ejea de los Caballeros
Barbastro
Catalonia
(Cataluña)
Tudela
Ebro
Monzón
Balaguer
Vic
Palamós
Palafrugell
Blanes
Sistema Ibérico
Tarazona
Aranda de Duero
Soria
Zaragoza
Lleida
(Lérida)
Cervera
Sabadell
Arenys de Mar
Costa Brava
Fraga
Tàrrega
Terrassa
Mataró
El Burgo de Osma
Vilafranca del Penedès
Barcelona
L'Hospitalet de Llobregat
Calatayud
Valls
Sitges
Medinaceli
Aragón
Reus
El Vendrell
Tarragona
Sierra de Guadarrama
Daroca
Alcañiz
Tortosa
SPAIN
Amposta
Guadalajara
Alcalá de Henares
Sant Carles de la Ràpita
Torrejón de Ardoz
Vinaròs
Teruel
Balearic Islands
(Islas Baleares)
MADRID
Minorca
(Menorca)
Getafe
Aranjuez
Tagus
Cuenca
Javalambre
2020m
País Valenciano
Onda
Castellon de la Plana
Ciutadella
Maó
Pollença
Sa Pobla
Tarancón
Borriana
Vall d' Uxó
Palma
Manacor
Sagunto
(Sagunt)
Castilla-La Mancha
Burjassot
Golfo de Valencia
Llucmajor
Felanitx
Mota del Cuervo
Valencia
Costa del Azahar
Majorca
(Mallorca)
Campo de Criptana
Torrente
Catarroja
Socuéllamos
Sueca
Illa de Cabrera
Ibiza
(Eivissa)
Tomelloso
La Roda
Júcar
Algemesí
Cullera
Manzanares
Albacete
Xàtiva
Gandia
Oliva
Ibiza
(Eivissa)
0 km
200
400
La Solana
Almansa
Valdepeñas
Ontinyent
Alcoy
Denia
0 miles
200
400
Villanueva de los Infantes
Villena
Benidorm
Formentera
Hellín
Segura
Jumilla
Elda
Villajoyosa (La Vila Joíosa)
Monóvar
Sant Joan d'Alacant
La Carolina
Beas de Segura
Alicante (Alicant)
Moratalla
Cieza
Elche
Villacarrillo
Úbeda
Mula
Orihuela
Cazorla
Murcia
Jaén
Sistemas Béticos
Huéscar
Murcia
Costa Blanca
Totana
La Unión
Lorca
Cartagena
Baza
Granada
Guadix
Águilas
Mulhacén
3481m
Mojácar
Sierra Nevada
Mediterranean Sea
Adra
Berja
Almería
Motril

Flamenco dancing was created by the gitanos (Romani people) of Andalucía and dates back to the 15th century.

HOLY WEEK
Easter in Spain is marked by solemn celebrations, known as the Holy Week processions. These processions vary according to the region, but generally, men wear robes and hoods and carry heavy crosses to show penitence.

COASTAL RESORTS
Every year, millions of northern Europeans head south for the beaches of southern Spain and Portugal, or for the Spanish Balearic Islands. They are attracted by the warm climate as well as affordable hotels and restaurants.

REGIONAL SPAIN
There are 17 Spanish regions, each with its own distinct cultures and traditions. For example, in the south is Andalucía, with flamenco dancing and traces of Moorish influences.

Italy

The boot-shaped country of Italy stretches from the mountainous north down to the Mediterranean Sea. For much of its history, Italy consisted of city-states – such as Florence and Venice – and was united only in 1870. Regional differences in Italy are huge, as each region has its own cuisine, customs, and dialect, and is geographically quite distinct. As a result, many Italians identify themselves first by region and then by country. The largest division, however, is between the rich north and the poorer south – a rugged region with several active volcanoes and the occasional severe earthquake. The mainland of Italy includes two tiny independent states – San Marino and Vatican City.

Andrea Bocelli

HOME OF OPERA
The idea of setting drama to music originated in Italy during the 16th century. Since then, Italian composers, such as Rossini, Verdi, and Puccini, have made opera the most popular musical form in Italy. Many cities have their own opera houses.

Vatican City has a permanent population of only about 1,000 people, although more than 3,000 come to work in the city-state each day.

Carnival masks

CITY OF CANALS
The beautiful city of Venice is made up of 118 islands, 177 canals, and 400 bridges. The only way to get around is to walk or take a boat: a *vaporetto*, *motoscafo*, or *motonave*. The most distinctive boat, however, is the gondola. Each year, in the days before Ash Wednesday, Venice hosts a carnival when the city celebrates with fireworks and everyone wears spectacular masks.

COLOSSEUM
One of Rome's greatest sights is the Colosseum, which opened in 80 CE. Deadly gladiatorial combats and animal fights were staged here before crowds of up to 55,000 people.

The oval-shaped Colosseum stood at 189 m (620 ft) high.

FOOTBALL FANS
Italians are mad about football and fanatically follow the performance of teams such as Juventus, AC Milan, Inter, and Roma. Italian teams frequently win major European competitions, and the national team has won the World Cup four times – in 1934, 1938, 1982, and 2006.

Sardinia
(Sardegna)
Isola Asinara
la Maddalena
Porto Torres
Sassari
Tempio Pausania
Olbia
Alghero
Ozieri
Siniscola
Nuoro
Macomer
Punta La Marmora 1834m
Oristano
Villacidro
Iglesias
Cagliari
Carbonia
Quartu Sant' Elena
VATICAN CITY
ROME
(ROMA)
Anzio
Latina
Terracina
Gaeta
Golfo di Gaeta
Isole Ponziane
Isernia
Campobasso
San Severo
Manfredonia
Foggia
Cerignola
Barletta
Molfetta
Bari
Caserta
Campania
Benevento
Naples
(Napoli)
Vesuvius 1277m
Avellino
Torre del Greco
Salerno
Andria
Bitonto
Altamura
Puglia
Potenza
Matera
Brindisi
Taranto
Lecce
Manduria
Gallipoli
Maglie
Isola di Capri
Battipaglia
Gulf of Salerno
Agropoli
Sala Consilina
Sapri
Lauria
Appennino Lucano
Ofanto
Volturno
Adriatic Sea
Tyrrhenian Sea
Castrovillari
Golfo di Taranto
Strait of Otranto
Rossano
Cosenza
La Sila
Cirò Marino
Crotone
Amantea
Lamezia
Catanzaro
Isola Stromboli
Isole Eolie
Isola Lipari
Isola Vulcano
Ionian Sea
Trapani
Palermo
Marsala
Alcamo
Cefalù
Messina
Palmi
Siderno
Reggio di Calabria
Strait of Messina
Castelvetrano
Sicily
(Sicilia)
Mount Etna 3340m
Simeto
Catania
Agrigento
Caltanissetta
Gela
Vittoria
Ragusa
Siracusa
Modica
Pozzallo
Strait of Sicily
Isola di Pantelleria
Mediterranean Sea
Malta Channel
Gozo
MALTA
VALLETTA
Malta
Isole Pelagie
0 km 50 100
0 miles 50 100

Olive harvesters gather olives in nets

OLIVE HARVEST
Italy is a big producer of olive oil, producing around 300,000 tonnes, which is second only to Spain in Europe. The oil is produced by first pressing the fruits of the olive tree between steel or stone rollers, then squeezing oil from the pulp using a press. Olive trees flourish in the fertile soils and the mild, frost-free climate of southern Italy.

VATICAN CITY
This tiny state in Rome is the centre of the Roman Catholic Church and home to the Pope. As well as St Peter's Basilica and the surrounding buildings and gardens, the Vatican boasts Michelangelo's Sistine Chapel. The state has its own flag, postage stamps, and coins.

Swiss guards, in their red, yellow, and blue striped costumes, stand at the gates into Vatican City.

HOME LIFE
Family life is important in Italy, and most people live at home until they marry. This is partly due to lack of cheap housing. Lunch (*pranzo*) is often the main meal of the day.

RENAISSANCE ITALY
Florence (below) sits either side of the River Arno. During the 15th century, a new movement in art and architecture, known as the Renaissance, or rebirth, began in Italy. Painters and sculptors, such as Leonardo da Vinci, Michelangelo, and Raphael, created beautiful works of art using improved techniques of perspective and realism. Many of these can still be seen in the galleries and churches of Florence.

Central Europe

FOUR COUNTRIES LIE at the heart of central Europe – Poland, Czechia (until 2016, the Czech Republic), Slovakia, and Hungary. The region is composed of wide plains broken by gentle hills and the Carpathian mountain range in the south. In the late 1980s, these countries broke away from decades of communist rule and, as new democracies, began to modernize. EU-members since 2004, they have seen a rise in living standards, despite the global economic crisis of 2008 hitting their growing economies.

FAMILY FARMS
Poland has one of the largest agricultural sectors in Europe, with more than 12 per cent of the workforce employed on the land. Most farms are still small, family-run businesses, growing grains, sugar beet, and potatoes. Large numbers of pigs and other animals are also kept.

TRADITIONAL TRADES
The countries of central Europe are heavily industrialized. Vast coal mines, steel works (above), and engineering works dominate the urban landscape. Although some of these sites are old and poorly equipped, these countries are trying to update machinery and introduce measures to improve standards of environmental pollution.

GOLDEN PRAGUE
Prague, the capital of Czechia, is one of Europe's most charming and beautiful cities. Unlike many other central European cities, it escaped serious damage in both World Wars, and contains many fine historic buildings, soaring church spires, and grand squares.

Part of Prague's colourful history is preserved in buildings around the Old Town Square.

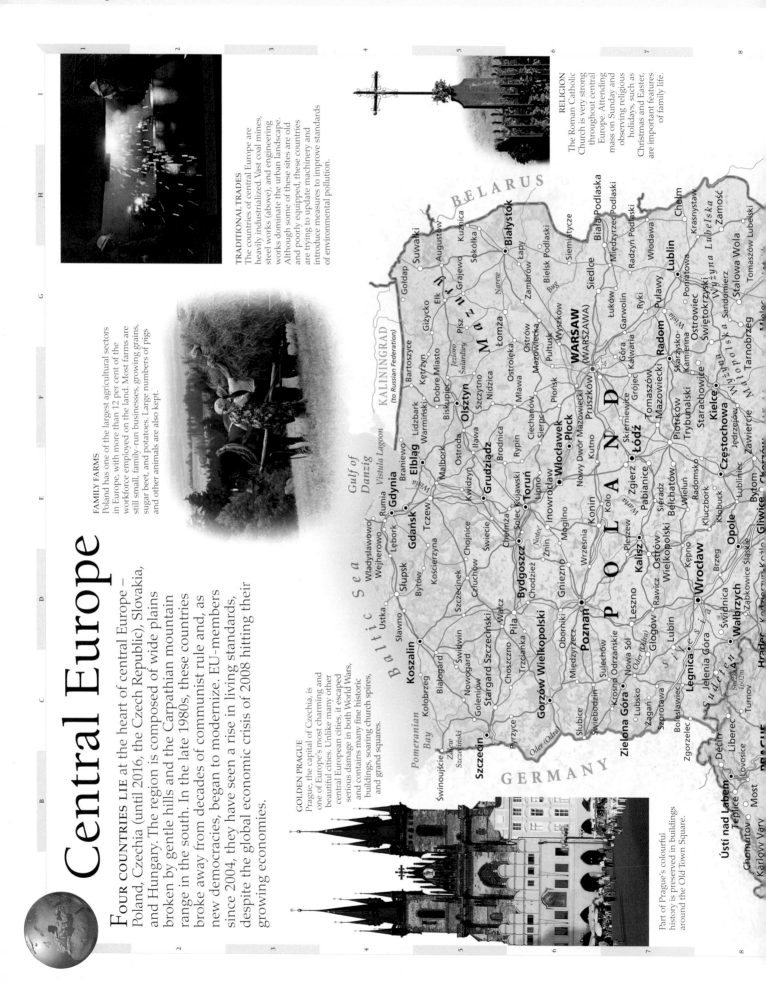

RELIGION
The Roman Catholic Church is very strong throughout central Europe. Attending mass on Sunday and observing religious holidays, such as Christmas and Easter, are important features of family life.

Budapest was once two cities – Buda on the right bank of the River Danube, and Pest on the left bank.

FOLK CULTURE
Traditional folk culture is still preserved in Slovakia, and is seen as an essential part of regional identity. Throughout the year, especially during the summer months, folk festivals are held in many towns. The people dress up in their colourful regional folk costumes, play traditional instruments, and sing and dance.

INDUSTRIAL LIFE
Czechia is central Europe's most industrialized country, with a large car manufacturing sector. It is renowned for its centuries-old glass industry and also produces some of the world's best-known beers. Pilsner lager, for example, originated in the town of Plzen, while Budweiser beer has been brewed at České Budějovice for more than a century.

HOT SPRINGS
A land of fertile plains, Hungary is also famous for its numerous hot springs. In the capital city of Budapest, there are more than 100 hot springs. The warm waters rise naturally from the ground, and spas and baths are centred on these springs. They are as popular today as they were centuries ago, when the Romans used the hot springs on the Buda side of the city.

Széchenyi baths in Budapest has outdoor pools open all year.

LANDSCAPE OF SLOVAKIA
Slovakia is divided between a fertile, lowland south and a more rugged, mountainous north. The country is far more rural than its industrial neighbour, Czechia. Most Slovaks live in small towns and mountain villages. The Tatra Mountains in the north are popular with skiers and hikers, who bring in much-needed tourist income.

Southeast Europe

UNTIL 1991, CROATIA, Bosnia and Herzegovina, Serbia, Montenegro, and Macedonia were all part of Yugoslavia. Ethnic tensions between the Serbs and other peoples in Yugoslavia caused a series of bloody wars that broke up the country. Peace was eventually restored in 1999, but all five countries have suffered intense economic problems as a result. So, too, has Albania since its communist government collapsed. The six nations do, however, have huge potential, with considerable agricultural and mineral resources. In the north, the River Danube is an important trading route for both Croatia and Serbia, while Croatia has a flourishing tourist industry along its beautiful Adriatic coast.

THE ADRIATIC
The long Adriatic coastline of Croatia is one of the most beautiful in Europe. The wooded hillsides, pretty beaches, such as Markarska (right), islands, and historic towns such as Dubrovnik attract tourists from all over Europe. The archipelago is also popular for sailing holidays.

Janica Kostelić

SPORTING ACHIEVEMENT
Croatia is a great sporting nation. Former skier Janica Kostelić has won four Olympic gold medals (three in 2002 and one in 2006), making her one of the most successful female Alpine skiers of all time. Other popular sports are football (soccer), tennis, and basketball.

The Dalmatian dog is named after the coastal region of Dalmatia in Croatia, its first known home.

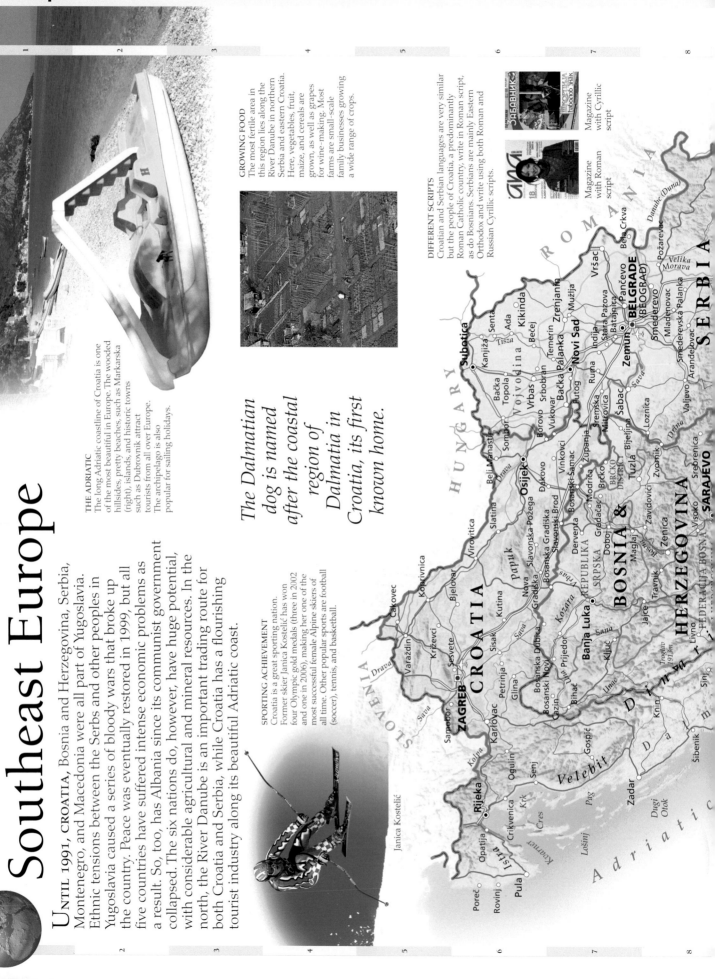

GROWING FOOD
The most fertile area in this region lies along the River Danube in northern Serbia and eastern Croatia. Here, vegetables, fruit, maize, and cereals are grown, as well as grapes for wine-making. Most farms are small-scale family businesses growing a wide range of crops.

DIFFERENT SCRIPTS
Croatian and Serbian languages are very similar but the people of Croatia, a predominantly Roman Catholic country, write in Roman script, as do Bosnians. Serbians are mainly Eastern Orthodox and write using both Roman and Russian Cyrillic scripts.

Magazine with Roman script

Magazine with Cyrillic script

DUBROVNIK
The medieval walled city of Dubrovnik, at the very southern tip of Croatia on the Adriatic Sea, is one of the architectural gems of Europe. In 1991, Serb troops shelled the city, causing immense damage. The city was restored after the end of the war. Other historic cities damaged during the fighting, notably Sarajevo and Mostar, in Bosnia and Herzegovina, have also been restored.

Vis
Hvar
Korčula
Mljet
Mostar
Ploče
Metković
Dubrovnik
Trebinje
Kotor
Cetinje
PODGORICA
Nikšić
Pljevlja
Prijepolje
Sjenica
Bijelo Polje
Novi Pazar
MONTENEGRO
Berane
North Albanian Alps
Lake Scutari
Bar
Shkodër
Bajram Curri
Gjakovë/Đakovica
Lumi i Drinit
Kukës
Lezhë
Laç
Krujë
Peshkopi
Burrel
Durrës
TIRANA (TIRANË)
Kavajë
Lumi i Shkubinit
Elbasan
Lushnjë
Fier
Kuçovë
Berat
Vlorë
ALBANIA
Lumi i Devollit
Lumi i Osumit
Lumi i Vjosës
Tepelenë
Gjirokastër
Sarandë
Konispol
Corfu (Kérkyra)
Strait of Otranto
Black Drin
Lake Ohrid
Pogradec
Korçë
Debar
Struga
Ohrid
Kičevo
Gostivar
Tetovo
SKOPJE
Bitola
Lake Prespa
Prilep
MACEDONIA
Veles
Štip
Kočani
Bregalnica
Radoviš
Kavadarci
Strumica
Crna Reka
Vardar
Gevgelija
Kumanovo
Ibar
Kopaonik
Mitrovicë/Mitrovica
Pejë/Peć
Gjeravicë/Đeravica 2,658m
Fushë Kosovë/Kosovo Polje
KOSOVO (disputed)
PRISTINA (PRISHTINË)
Rahovec
Prizren
Ferizaj/Uroševac
Gjilan/Gnjilane
Preševo
Vushtrri/Vučitrn
Podujevë/Podujevo
Kruševac
Aleksinac
Prokuplje
Niš
Leskovac
Južna Morava
Vranje
Bujanovac
Surdulica
Vlasotince
Pirot
Knjaževac
Zaječar
Balkan Mountains
BULGARIA
GREECE
0 km 50 100
0 miles 50 100

Lake Prespa

GREAT LAKES
Macedonia contains two huge lakes – Ohrid and Prespa. The latter has clear water, fed by underground streams, and is a popular tourist spot. Both lakes have substantial fish stocks, especially of trout and eel, which are used to make local dishes.

Eel

LIFE IN ALBANIA
Albania is one of the poorest countries in Europe. Most people are ethnic Albanian, with a sizeable Greek minority in the south of the country. Loyalty to one's family or clan is more important than national identity, and married sons often live with their parents and look after them in old age.

An Albanian family

APOLLONIA
About 13 km (8 miles) outside the city of Fier, Albania, lie the ruins of an ancient city called Apollonia. Founded in 588 BCE by Greeks from Corinth, it is one of 30 cities named after the Greek god Apollo. Austrian archaeologists began excavating the site during World War I, and French archaeologists continued the digging in the 1930s. However, much of the city still remains buried in the surrounding hills.

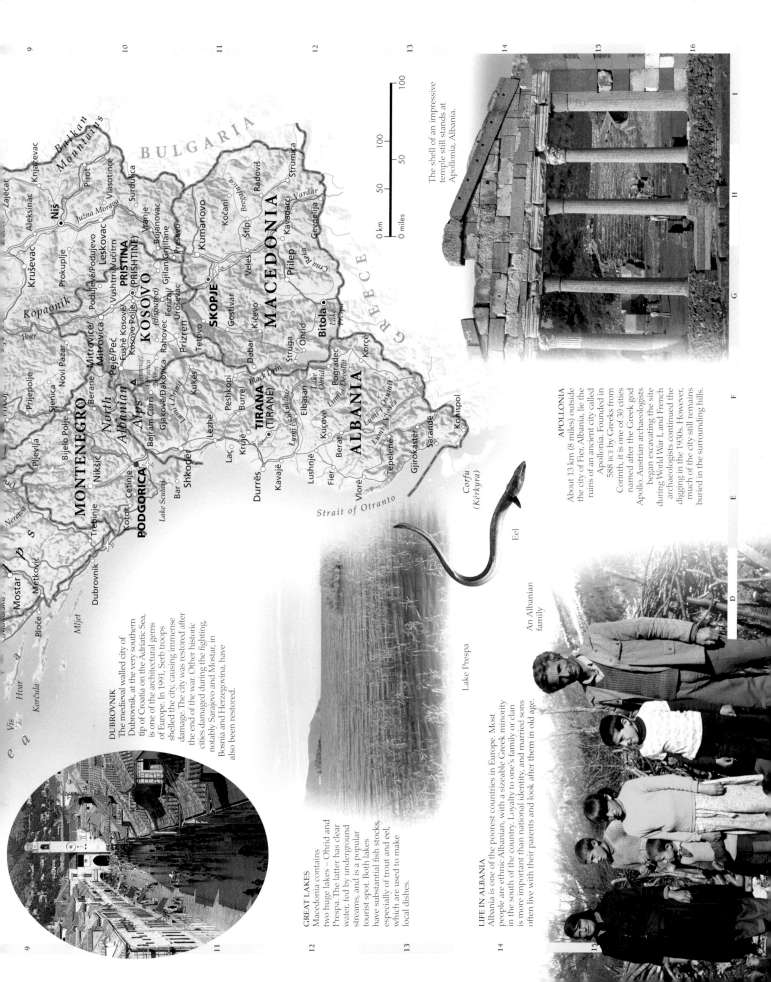

The shell of an impressive temple still stands at Apollonia, Albania.

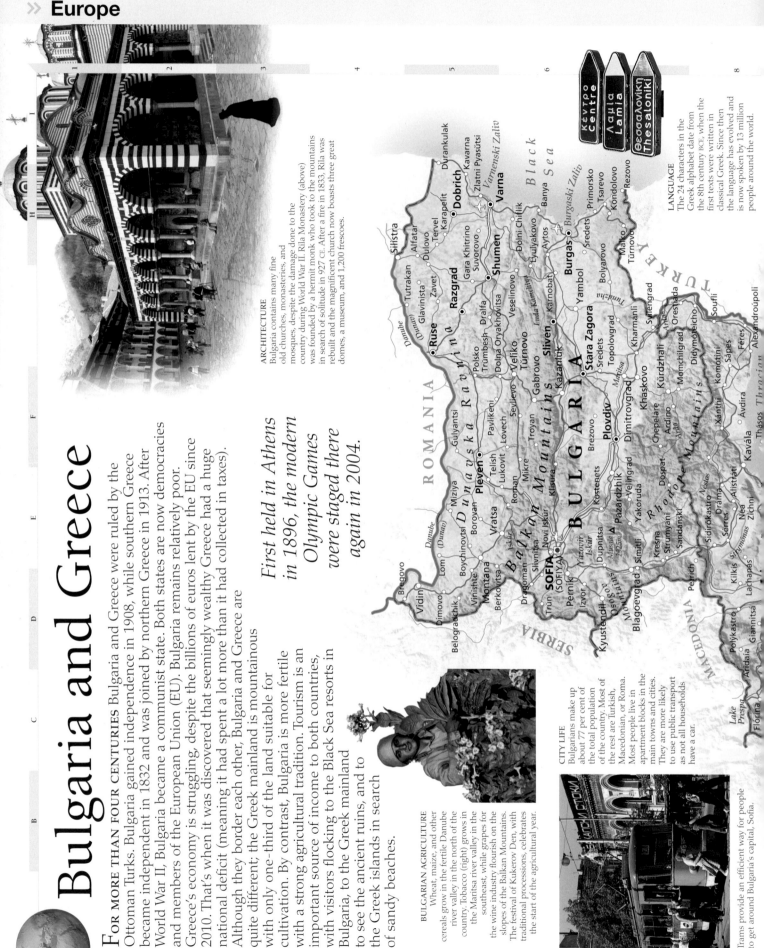

Bulgaria and Greece

For more than four centuries Bulgaria and Greece were ruled by the Ottoman Turks. Bulgaria gained independence in 1908, while southern Greece became independent in 1832 and was joined by northern Greece in 1913. After World War II, Bulgaria became a communist state. Both states are now democracies and members of the European Union (EU). Bulgaria remains relatively poor. Greece's economy is struggling, despite the billions of euros lent by the EU since 2010. That's when it was discovered that seemingly wealthy Greece had a huge national deficit (meaning it had spent a lot more than it had collected in taxes). Although they border each other, Bulgaria and Greece are quite different; the Greek mainland is mountainous with only one-third of the land suitable for cultivation. By contrast, Bulgaria is more fertile with a strong agricultural tradition. Tourism is an important source of income to both countries, with visitors flocking to the Black Sea resorts in Bulgaria, to the Greek mainland to see the ancient ruins, and to the Greek islands in search of sandy beaches.

First held in Athens in 1896, the modern Olympic Games were staged there again in 2004.

ARCHITECTURE
Bulgaria contains many fine old churches, monasteries, and mosques, despite the damage done to the country during World War II. Rila Monastery (above) was founded by a hermit monk who took to the mountains in search of solitude in 927 CE. After a fire in 1833, Rila was rebuilt and the magnificent church now boasts three great domes, a museum, and 1,200 frescoes.

BULGARIAN AGRICULTURE
Wheat, maize, and other cereals grow in the fertile Danube river valley in the north of the country. Tobacco (right) grows in the Maritsa river valley in the southeast, while grapes for the wine industry flourish on the slopes of the Balkan Mountains. The festival of Kukerov Den, with traditional processions, celebrates the start of the agricultural year.

СТОКИ

Trams provide an efficient way for people to get around Bulgaria's capital, Sofia.

CITY LIFE
Bulgarians make up about 77 per cent of the total population of the country. Most of the rest are Turkish, Macedonian, or Roma. Most people live in apartment blocks in the main towns and cities. They are more likely to use public transport as not all households have a car.

ROMANIA
SERBIA
MACEDONIA
TURKEY
BULGARIA
Black Sea
Danube (Dunav)
Dunavska Ravnina
Balkan Mountains
Rhodope Mountains
Osogov Mountains
Musala 2925m
Varnenski Zaliv
Burgaski Zaliv
Lake Prespa
Bregovo
Vidin
Dimovo
Belogradchik
Lom
Boychinovtsi
Miziya
Gulyantsi
Vinishte
Montana
Berkovitsa
Borovan
Vratsa
Pleven
Telish
Lukovit
Lovech
Pavlikeni
Iskur
Roman
Dragoman
Slivnitsa
Novi Iskur
SOFIA (SOFIYA)
Trun
Pernik
Izvor
Yazovir Iskur
Kyustendil
Dupnitsa
Blagoevgrad
Simitli
Kresna
Strumyani
Sandanski
Petrich
Mikre
Troyan
Klisura
Sevlievo
Gabrovo
Veliko Turnovo
Kazanluk
Kostenets
Pazardzhik
Velingrad
Yakoruda
Dospat
Brezovo
Plovdiv
Dimitrovgrad
Maritsa
Stara Zagora
Sredets
Topolovgrad
Kharmanli
Khaskovo
Chepelare
Ardino
Arda
Kurdzhali
Momchilgrad
Svilengrad
Orestiada
Didymoteicho
Soufli
Tutrakan
Glavinista
Ruse
Zavet
Silistra
Alfatar
Dulovo
Tervel
Karapelit
Durankulak
Razgrad
Polsko Trumbesh
Dralfa
Dolna Oryakhovitsa
Gara Khitrino
Suvorovo
Shumen
Dobrich
Kavarna
Zlatni Pyasutsi
Varna
Veselinovo
Dolni Chiflik
Luda Kamchiya
Lyulyakovo
Aytos
Banya
Sliven
Karnobat
Yambol
Burgas
Sredets
Primorsko
Tsarevo
Kondolovo
Rezovo
Bolyarovo
Tundzha
Malko Turnovo
Sidirokastro
Nestos
Drama
Serres
Strymonas
Alistrati
Nea Zichni
Xanthi
Komotini
Sapes
Feres
Alexandroupoli
Kavala
Avdira
Thasos
Kilkis
Lachanas
Polykastro
Aridaia
Giannitsa
Florina

Κέντρο Centre
Λαμία Lamia
Θεσσαλονίκη Thesaloniki

LANGUAGE
The 24 characters in the Greek alphabet date from the 8th century BCE, when the first texts were written in classical Greek. Since then the language has evolved and is now spoken by 13 million people around the world.

GREEK ISLANDS
More than 2,000 islands lie off the mainland of Greece. The Cyclades and Dodecanese in the Aegean Sea are often rocky and arid, while the Ionian Islands, such as Zákynthos (below), are more fertile. Tourists often travel from one island to another by ferry or hovercraft.

CORINTH CANAL
The Corinth Canal was built to provide a shortcut for ships travelling between the Aegean and Ionian Seas. Dug through solid limestone, the steep-sided canal was begun in 1882 by the French and completed in 1893 by the Greeks.

EARTHQUAKES
The idyllic landscape of the Greek Islands, such as Santorini (left), can be rocked by earthquakes. This is because the islands and mainland of Greece, as well as Bulgaria, sit on a plate boundary. There is now a Greek Seismic Code that outlines regulations on all new buildings.

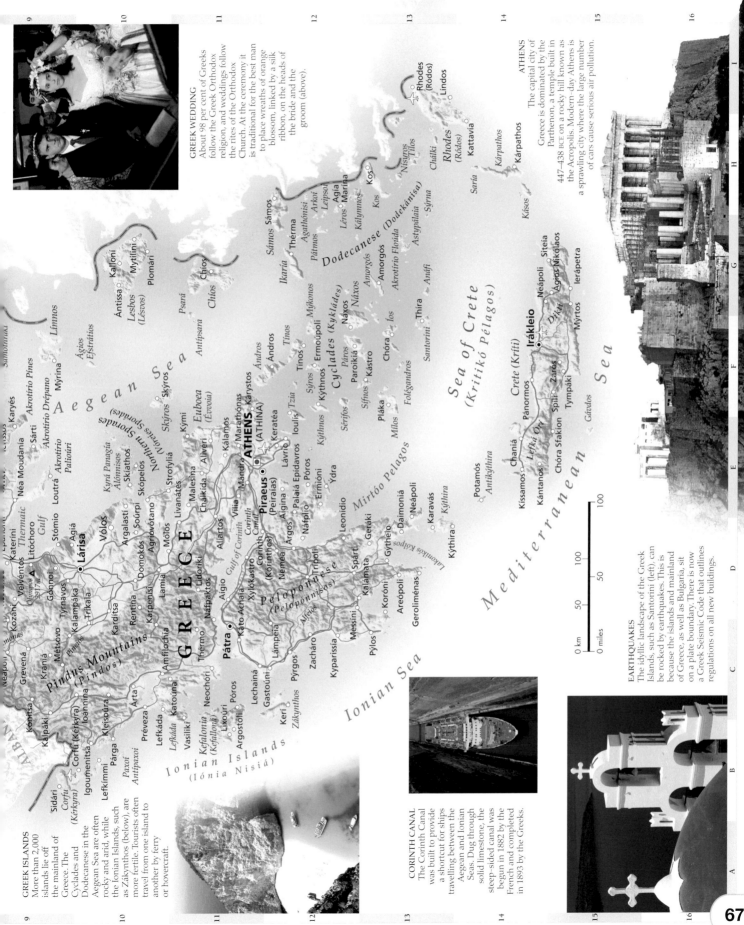

GREEK WEDDING
About 98 per cent of Greeks follow the Greek Orthodox religion, and weddings follow the rites of the Orthodox Church. At the ceremony it is traditional for the best man to place wreaths of orange blossom, linked by a silk ribbon, on the heads of the bride and the groom (above).

ATHENS
The capital city of Greece is dominated by the Parthenon, a temple built in 447–438 BCE on a rocky hill known as the Acropolis. Modern-day Athens is a sprawling city where the large number of cars cause serious air pollution.

Ukraine, Moldova, & Romania

THROUGHOUT MUCH OF THE LAST CENTURY, Ukraine and Moldova formed part of the Soviet Union (USSR), while Romania was ruled for 20 years by the communist dictator Nicolae Ceausescu. In 1989, Ceausescu was overthrown, while Ukraine and Moldova became independent in 1991. Today, the three countries are still struggling to fully transform themselves into modern democracies, although Romania joined the EU in 2007. Outdated technology, dependency on gas and oil from their powerful neighbour Russia, and economic and environmental problems have slowed their progress. It is also a region of ethnic tensions, highlighted in 2014 when Russia annexed Ukraine's Crimean peninsula, where a large part of the population consists of Russians left behind after the USSR break-up.

CITY LIFE
Romania has many cities and towns with a mix of old and new buildings. Sibiu (left) was founded in the 12th century and, at one time, had 19 guilds – each representing a different craft – within its city walls. Much remains from this colourful history, especially in the painted buildings of the old town.

FOLK CUSTOMS
Despite years of communist rule, folk customs thrived in the rural areas of Romania and Ukraine. In Ukraine, singers perform *dumas*, historical epics that tell of slavery under the Turks. One of the traditional instruments is a bandura (left), a stringed instrument that sounds like a harpsichord.

DRACULA'S CASTLE
Situated in Transylvania, Bran Castle is a favourite tourist destination. This is where author Bram Stoker's fictional blood-drinking Count Dracula lived. The story is probably based on a 15th-century Romanian prince, Vlad Dracula, who reigned for less than 10 years but caused more than 50,000 deaths.

The word Transylvania *means "land beyond the forests".*

EASTER BREAD
In Romania, Easter is celebrated with a meal of roast lamb served with a bread called *cozonac*. This is made by pounding nuts, raisins, and even cocoa, into the dough.

INDUSTRY IN THE UKRAINE
Ukraine is the world's tenth largest steel producer, and also has a big vehicle and space industry. Most of the heavy industry, however, is situated in the east, an area badly affected by Ukrainian-Russian tensions, and exports have been severely damaged since the fall-out with Russia.

HOLIDAYS BY THE SEA
In the days of the Russian empire, aristocracy and artists flocked to the Black Sea resorts of the Crimea, especially Yalta; the famous authors Leo Tolstoy and Anton Chekhov holidayed here. During the Soviet era, it was the nation's top holiday destination. After 1991, it began attracting foreign visitors, but tourism has declined since Russia annexed Crimea in 2014.

PEOPLE OF ROMANIA
Romanians speak Romanian – a language closely related to French, Italian, and Spanish. The country also has sizeable Hungarian and Roma minorities, which have both been discriminated against in recent years. Most Hungarian speakers live in the region of Romania known as Transylvania.

Children of the Maramures region of Transylvania.

RICH SOILS OF MOLDOVA
Moldova consists of partially wooded plains intercut with rivers and streams. About 75 per cent of the land is rich in chernozem (black) soil, which is very fertile. Wine and sunflower production are important here. Fruit and vegetables, such as pumpkins (left), also grow well.

Baltic States & Belarus

THE THREE BALTIC STATES, Estonia, Latvia, and Lithuania, all share a stretch of coast on the Baltic Sea lined with sandy beaches. Belarus lies between Poland, Ukraine, and the Russian Federation. Following independence from the Soviet Union in 1991, all these countries faced problems such as price rises, food shortages, and pollution. However, the Baltic States have reformed into hi-tech societies and economies and are EU members since 2004. Belarus has kept close links with Russia and has been the slowest to reform. This mainly rural country has stayed isolated from the rest of Europe and, with few natural resources, remains one of its poorest nations.

SINGING REVOLUTION
Estonia is known for its classical music tradition – most notably its choirs. This love of music was most powerful when people raised their voices during the Singing Revolution in 1988 (right), part of their move towards independence.

The Estonian flag waved at a pre-independence rally in 1988

TALLINN OLD TOWN
With its colourful buildings, turreted walls, and gabled roofs, Tallinn is one of the best-preserved capital cities in Europe. All the winding, cobbled streets lead to the Town Hall Square (left).

Baltic Sea
Gulf of Finland
Gulf of Riga
Narva Bay
Väinameri
ESTONIA
LATVIA
LITHUANIA
RUSSIAN FEDERATION
POLAND
KALININGRAD
(to Russian Federation)
TALLINN
RIGA
VILNIUS
Tartu
Pärnu
Narva
Kohtla-Järve
Klaipėda
Kaunas
Šiauliai
Panevėžys
Daugavpils
Liepāja
Jelgava
Jūrmala
Ventspils
Kaliningrad
Navapolatsk/Novopolotsk
Polatsk/Polotsk
Saaremaa
Hiiumaa
Lake Peipus
Lake Pskov
Suur Munamägi 318m
Gaiziņa Kalns 311m
Western Dvina
Neman
Neris
Curonian Lagoon
Kurzeme
Žemaičių Aukštumas

From the early days of public broadband usage, Estonia has been one of Europe's most connected countries.

AMBER
Two-thirds of the world's amber, the fossilized resin of pine trees, is washed up from the sea bed along the Baltic coast. Amber is used to make jewellery, among other things.

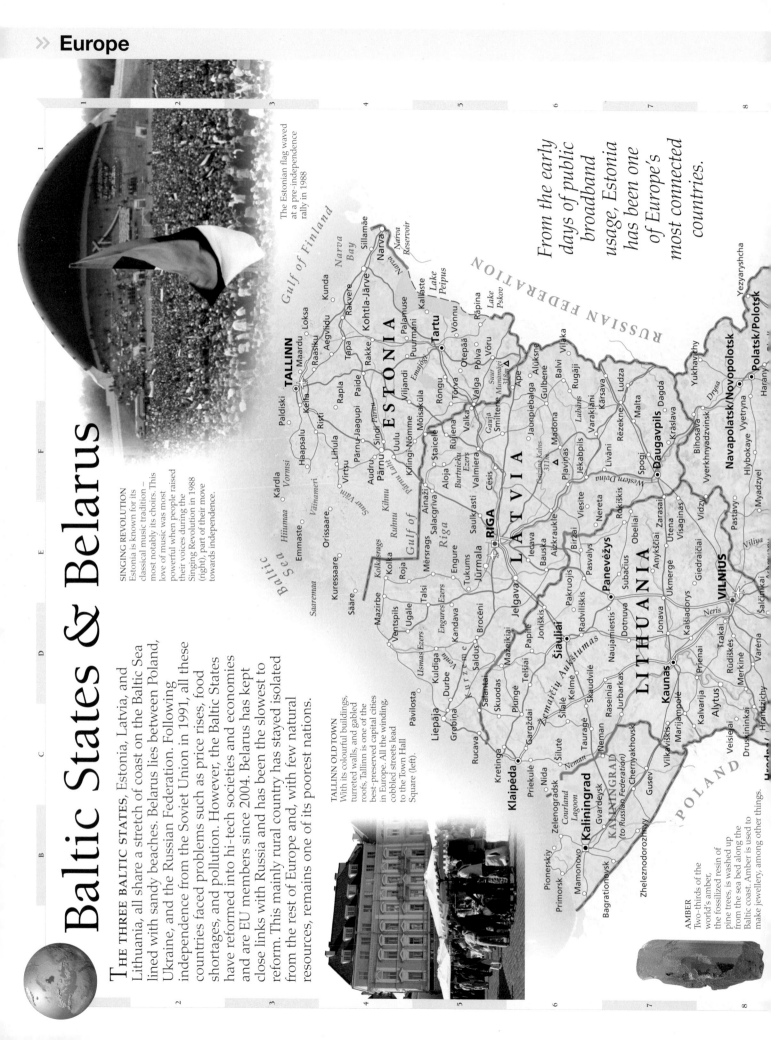

TEXTILES
Lithuania has a strong textile industry, with clothes, bed linen, curtains, and towels made for export. Estonia and Latvia are also famous for their linen products, many beautifully hand-crafted.

BELARUS
POLAND
UKRAINE
RUSSIAN FEDERATION
MINSK
Brest
Zhabinka
Kobryn
Damachava
Makrany
Pruzhany
Ruzhany
Novy Dvor
Vawkavysk
Masty
Shchuchyn
Orlya
Zel'va
Navahrudak
Slonim
Ivatsevichy
Haradzyets
Drahichyn
Ivanava
Pinsk
Abrova
Hantsavichy
Lyakhavichy
Lyusina
Byelaruskaya Hrada
Baranavichy/Baranovichi
Stowbtsy
Nyasvizh
Rudzyensk
Mar"ina Horka
Kapyl'
Shyshchytsy
Slutsk
Syemyezhava
Salihorsk
Starobin
Bastyn'
Luninyets
Yasyel'da
Pripet Marshes
Mikashevichy
Zhytkavichy
Kaptsevichy
Tonyezh
Pyetrykaw
Simanichy
Lyel'chytsy
Milashavichy
Yel'sk
Dabryn'
Narowlya
Mazyr
Pripet
Ptsich
Shyichy
Kalinkavichy
Rechytsa
Homyel'/Gomel'
Khoyniki
Loyew
Byval'ki
Dnieper
(Dnyapro/Dnepr)
Krasnaye
Plyeshchanitsy
Minskaya Wzvyshsha
Zhodzina
Barysaw/Borisov
Byarezina
Chervyen'
Pukhavichy
Tal'ka
Asipovichy
Staryya Darohi
Brozha
Shchadryn
Aktsyabrski
Svyetlahorsk/Svetlogorsk
Yalizava
Chachevichy
Babruysk/Bobruysk
Abidavichy
Dashkawka
Rahachow
Zhlobin
Buda-Kashalyova
Uvaravichy
Kastsyukowka
Dobrush
Tsyerakhowka
Chashniki
Vitsyebsk/Vitebsk
Lyozna
Bahushewsk
Krupki
Talachyn
Kruhlaye
Orsha
Dnieper
Sava
Shklow
Byalynichy
Horki
Mahilyow/Mogilev
Harbavichy
Chavusy
Khodasy
Cherykaw
Krychaw
Slawharad
Klimavichy
Myerkulavichy
Kastsyukovichy
Baron'ki
Bug

0 km	50	100
0 miles	50	100

MINSK
The capital of Belarus, Minsk, was destroyed during World War II and then rebuilt in a starkly modern style. Minsk is the country's economic centre: Cars, lorries and tractors, electrical household goods and equipment are all produced here. Farm produce (above) is also sold in the markets.

FARMING
The fertile soils and flat landscapes make this region good for farming. The Baltic States, particulary Latvia (left), have large dairy farms. Belarus is a major producer of flax, which is used to make linen and other products. Potatoes (used to make vodka), sugar beet, and other root crops are also grown here.

GYMNASTICS
The former Soviet Union worked its young athletes and gymnasts extremely hard in order to win Olympic medals and thus national glory. Many of the most famous gymnasts of the era came from Belarus, notably Olga Korbut and Svetlana Boginskaya (right), who won three gold, one silver, and one bronze Olympic medals.

LITHUANIAN COSTUME
In some Lithuanian villages people wear traditional folk costume for festive occasions. Women's clothing is generally colourful (left) and might include a white linen shirt, a skirt, and an apron. The decoration and style of the costume shows which region of Lithuania the wearer comes from.

Ferns thriving by a lake in a Latvian forest

FORESTS AND LAKES
All four countries are low-lying with many moors, bogs, unspoiled lakes, and fir and pine forests. Forestry is an important industry, especially in Estonia and Latvia, providing wood pulp for paper making, and timber for furniture and houses.

European Russia

Separated from Asian Russia (see pp.78–79) by the Ural Mountains, European Russia takes up about one-third of the European landmass. The climate and landscape range from cold desert and frozen tundra in the north to the warm coast of the Black Sea in the southwest. Forests and grassy steppes cover vast areas, and Europe's two largest lakes, the Ladoga and the Onega, lie here. Life for most Russians changed considerably after the collapse of communism in 1991, since when the country has been through enormous economic and political changes. More than 110 million people – three-quarters of the total Russian population – live in European Russia, most of them in cities. The huge capital, Moscow, is famous for its onion-domed churches and the medieval Kremlin, residence of the Russian president.

The Church of the Saviour on Spilled Blood marks the spot where Tsar Alexander II was murdered in 1881.

ST PETERSBURG
Once Russia's capital, St Petersburg was built in the 18th century by Tsar Peter the Great as a "Window on the West". Today, it is a popular tourist destination, full of grand palaces and extravagant architecture (left). The city spreads over some 40 islands, linked by a network of canals and rivers.

Sleeping Beauty is performed here by dancers from the Kirov Ballet.

BALLET
Russia is famous for its ballet companies, such as the Bolshoi Ballet of Moscow and the Kirov Ballet of St Petersburg. Most of the ballets performed are classics, such as *Swan Lake* or *Sleeping Beauty*. Developed in Europe in the 19th century, ballet became a popular form of entertainment in the 20th century.

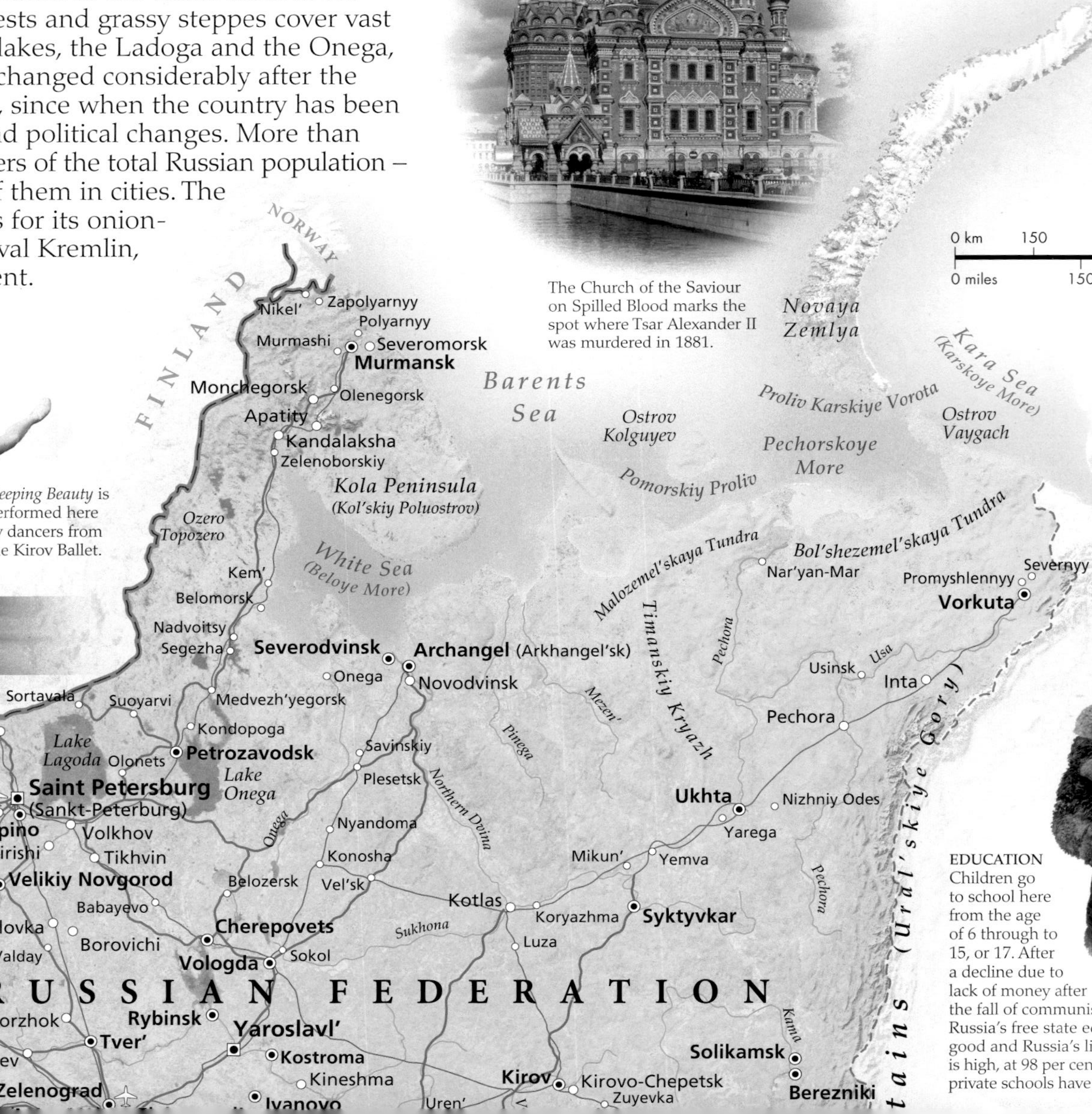
0 km 150 300
0 miles 150 300
NORWAY
FINLAND
ESTONIA
LATVIA
Barents Sea
White Sea (Beloye More)
Kola Peninsula (Kol'skiy Poluostrov)
Novaya Zemlya
Kara Sea (Karskoye More)
Proliv Karskiye Vorota
Ostrov Vaygach
Pechorskoye More
Ostrov Kolguyev
Pomorskiy Proliv
Malozemel'skaya Tundra
Bol'shezemel'skaya Tundra
Timanskiy Kryazh
Gulf of Finland
Lake Lagoda
Lake Onega
Ozero Topozero
RUSSIAN FEDERATION
(Ural'skiye Gory)
Nikel'
Zapolyarnyy
Polyarnyy
Murmashi
Severomorsk
Murmansk
Monchegorsk
Olenegorsk
Apatity
Kandalaksha
Zelenoborskiy
Kem'
Belomorsk
Nadvoitsy
Segezha
Severodvinsk
Archangel (Arkhangel'sk)
Onega
Novodvinsk
Medvezh'yegorsk
Sortavala
Suoyarvi
Vyborg
Kondopoga
Petrozavodsk
Olonets
Savinskiy
Plesetsk
Petrodvorets
Saint Petersburg (Sankt-Peterburg)
Gatchina
Kolpino
Volkhov
Tikhvin
Luga
Kirishi
Pskov
Sol'tsy
Velikiy Novgorod
Ostrov
Porkhov
Opochka
Uglovka
Babayevo
Borovichi
Valday
Velikiye Luki
Zapadnaya Dvina
Torzhok
Rzhev
Smolensk
Zelenograd
Tver'
Rybinsk
Yaroslavl'
Kostroma
Kineshma
Ivanovo
Nyandoma
Konosha
Belozersk
Vel'sk
Cherepovets
Sokol
Vologda
Kotlas
Koryazhma
Luza
Syktyvkar
Mikun'
Yemva
Ukhta
Yarega
Nizhniy Odes
Pechora
Usinsk
Inta
Nar'yan-Mar
Promyshlennyy
Severnyy
Vorkuta
Kirov
Kirovo-Chepetsk
Zuyevka
Uren'
Solikamsk
Berezniki
Northern Dvina
Pinega
Mezen'
Sukhona
Pechora
Usa
Kama

EDUCATION
Children go to school here from the age of 6 through to 15, or 17. After a decline due to lack of money after the fall of communism, these days Russia's free state education is good and Russia's literacy rate is high, at 98 per cent. Lately more private schools have opened, too.

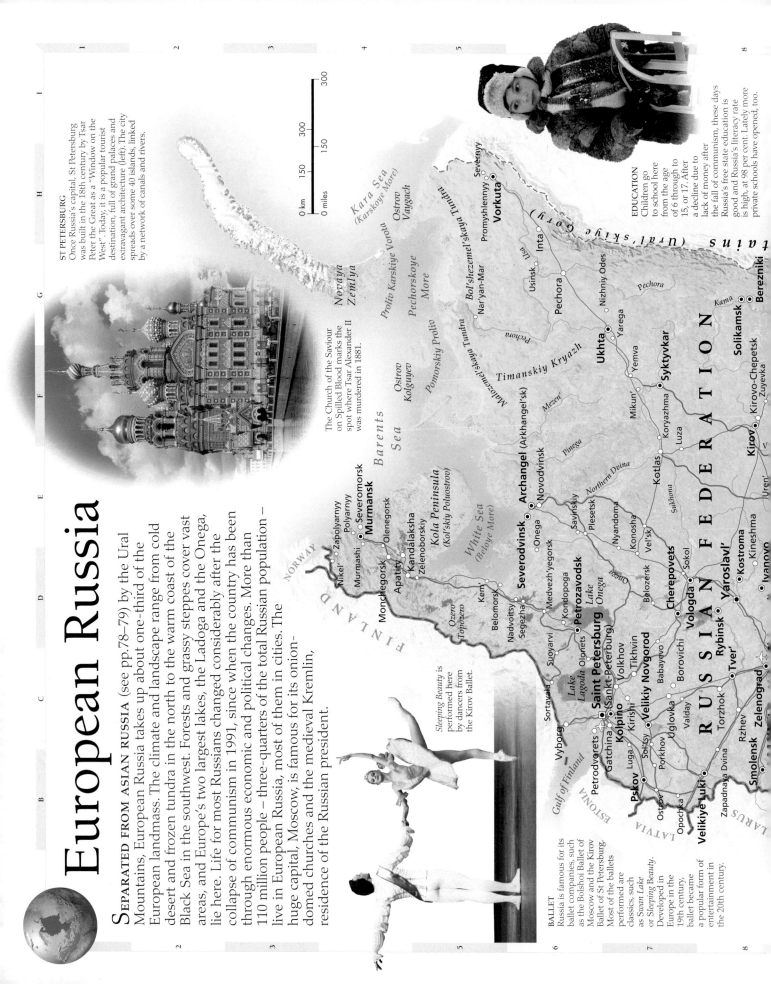

Industrial smog casts a haze over Moscow.

POLLUTION
The communists invested heavily in industry, but their outdated methods of production are still affecting the environment. Rivers such as the Volga are badly polluted, and many cities are covered in a permanent and poisonous smog. Chest infections and other diseases related to air pollution are common.

RURAL LIFE
Rural life became extremely tough after the collapse of large, state-run farms in the 1990s, and many people lived in poverty. Since then, private-owned, small-scale farms have become more common and productive. Grains – mainly wheat and barley – and sunflower oil are the top agricultural exports.

THE TATARS
Russia's largest ethnic minority, the Tatars (below), are an Islamic people descended from the Mongols. Their largest population lives in the Tatarstan Republic, midway between Moscow and the Urals.

Icons, common in the Russian Orthodox Church, are religious images painted on wooden panels.

The title tsar, or czar, once used for Russian rulers, means "emperor" and comes from the ancient Roman title "Caesar".

MOSCOW METRO
Not many underground railways can claim to be tourist attractions, but Moscow's metro can. Built in the 1930s, many of its stations are decorated with beautiful chandeliers, mosaics, paintings, and sculptures. One of the busiest, most efficient metros in the world, it is used by more than 7 million people daily.

THE RUSSIAN CHURCH
The main religion in Russia is the Russian Orthodox Church. Under communism, all religion was banned, and churches and monasteries were left to decay. Today, many of these historic buildings have been restored, and many Russians attend church services regularly.

ASIA

The vast continent of Asia is dominated by two giant nations – China and India, each with more than a billion people and a rich and colourful history. Both are being transformed by rapid economic growth, and so are many other Asian countries, listed below in order of size. Yet in some regions of central Asia life has barely changed in a thousand years.

China
9,596,960 sq km
3,705,407 sq miles
1,373,541,000
Beijing
Mandarin, Wu, Cantonese, Hsiang, Min, Hakka, Kan

Iran
1,648,195 sq km
636,368 sq miles
82,801,600
Tehran
Farsi, Azeri, Luri, Gilaki, Mazandarani, Kurdish, Turkmen, Arabic, Balochi

Afghanistan
652,230 sq km
251,826 sq miles
33,332,000
Kabul
Pashto, Tajik, Dari, Farsi, Uzbek, Turkmen

Iraq
438,317 sq km
169,234 sq miles
38,146,000
Baghdad
Arabic, Kurdish, Turkic languages, Armenian, Assyrian

Philippines
300,000 sq km
115,830 sq miles
102,624,000
Manila
Filipino, English, Tagalog, Cebuano, Ilocano, Hiligaynon, many other local languages

Nepal
147,181 sq km
56,827 sq miles
29,034,000
Kathmandu
Nepali, Maithili, Bhojpuri

India
3,287,263 sq km
1,269,212 sq miles
1,266,884,000
New Delhi
Hindi, English, Urdu, Bengali, Marathi, Telugu, Tamil, Bihari, Gujarati, Kannada.

Mongolia
1,564,116 sq km
603,905 sq miles
3,031,000
Ulaanbaatar
Khalkha Mongolian, Kazakh, Chinese, Russian

Yemen
527,968 sq km
203,848 sq miles
27,393,000
Sanaak
Arabic

Japan
377,915 sq km
145,913 sq miles
126,702,000
Tokyo
Japanese, Korean, Chinese

Laos
236,800 sq km
91,428 sq miles
7,019,000
Vientiane
Lao, Mon-Khmer, Yao, Vietnamese, Chinese, French

Bangladesh
143,998 sq km
55,598 sq miles
156,187,000
Dhaka
Bengali, Urdu, Chakma, Marma (Magh), Garo, Khasi, Santhali, Tripura, Mru

Kazakhstan
2,724,900sq km
1,052,084 sq miles
18,360,000
Astana
Kazakh, Russian, Ukrainian, German, Uzbek, Tatar, Uyghur

Pakistan
796,095 sq km
307,372 sq miles
201,956,000
Islamabad
Punjabi, Sindhi, Pashtu, Urdu, Balochi, Brahui

Thailand
513,120 sq km
198,116 sq miles
68,201,000
Bangkok
Thai, Chinese, Malay, Khmer, Mon, Karen, Miao

Vietnam
331,210 sq km
127,880 sq miles
95,261,000
Hanoi
Vietnamese, Chinese, Thai, Khmer, Muong, Nung, Miao, Yao, Jarai

Kyrgyzstan
199,951 sq km
77,201 sq miles
5,728,000
Bishkek
Kyrgyz, Russian, Uzbek, Tatar, Ukrainian

Tajikistan
143,100 sq km
55,251 sq miles
8,331,000
Dushanbe
Tajik, Uzbek, Russian

Saudi Arabia
2,149,690 sq km
829,995 sq miles
28,160,000
Riyadh
Arabic

Turkey
783,562 sq km
302,533 sq miles
80,275,000
Ankara
Turkish, Kurdish, Arabic, Circassian, Armenian, Greek, Georgian, Ladino (Judaeo-Spanish)

Turkmenistan
488,100 sq km
188,455 sq miles
5,291,000
Ashgabat
Turkmen, Uzbek, Russian, Kazakh, Tatar

Malaysia
329,847 sq km
127,354 sq miles
30,950,000
Kuala Lumpur
Bahasa Malaysia, Malay, Chinese, Tamil, English

Syria
185,180 sq km
71,498 sq miles
17,185,000
Damascus
Arabic, French, Kurdish, Armenian, Circassian, Turkic languages, Assyrian, Aramaic

North Korea
120,538 sq km
46,540 sq miles
25,115,000
Pyongyang
Korean

Indonesia
1,904,569 sq km
735,354 sq miles
258,316,000
Jakarta
Javanese, Sundanese

Myanmar (Burma)
676,578 sq km
261,227 sq miles
56,890,000
Nay Pyi Taw
Burmese, Shan, Karen

Uzbekistan
447,400 sq km
172,741 sq miles
29,474,000
Tashkent
Uzbek, Russian, Tajik

Oman
309,500 sq km
119,498 sq miles
3,355,000
Muscat
Arabic, Balochi, Farsi, Hindi

Cambodia
181,035 sq km
69,898 sq miles
15,957,000
Phnom Penh
Khmer, French, Chinese

South Korea
99,720 sq km
38,502 sq miles
50,924,000
Seoul
Korean

Jordan
89,342 sq km
34,495 sq miles
8,185,000
Amman
Arabic

Sri Lanka
65,610 sq km
25,332 sq miles
22,235,000
Colombo
Sinhala, Tamil, Sinhala-Tamil, English

Azerbaijan
86,600 sq km
33,436 sq miles
9,873,000
Baku
Azerbaijani, Russian

Bhutan
38,394 sq km
14,824 sq miles
750,100
Thimphu
Dzongkha, Nepali, Assamese

Israel
20,770 sq km
8,019 sq miles
8,175,000
Jerusalem
Hebrew, Arabic, Yiddish, German, Russian, Polish, Romanian, Persian

Qatar
11,586 sq km
4,473 sq miles
2,258,000
Doha
Arabic

United Arab Emirates
83,600 sq km
32,278 sq miles
5,927,000
Abu Dhabi
Arabic, Farsi, Indian and Pakistani languages, English

Taiwan
35,980 sq km
13,892 sq miles
23,465,000
Taipei
Amoy Chinese, Mandarin Chinese, Hakka Chinese

Kuwait
17,818 sq km
6,880 sq miles
2,833,000
Kuwait City
Arabic, English

Lebanon
10,400 sq km
4,015 sq miles
6,238,000
Beirut
Arabic, French, Armenian, Assyrian

Bahrain
741 sq km
286 sq miles
1,379,000
Manama
Arabic

Seychelles
455 sq km
176 sq miles
93,200
Victoria
French Creole, English, French

Georgia
69,700 sq km
26,911 sq miles
4,928,000
T'bilisi
Georgian, Russian, Azeri

Armenia
29,743 sq km
11,484 sq miles
3,051,000
Yerevan
Armenian, Azeri, Russian

East Timor
14,874 sq km
5,743 sq miles
1,261,000
Dili
Tetum (Portuguese/

Brunei
5,765 sq km
2,226 sq miles
436,600
Bandar Seri Begawan
Malay, English, Chinese

Singapore
697 sq km
269 sq miles
5,782,000
Singapore
Mandarin, Malay, Tamil

Maldives
298 sq km
115 sq miles
393,000
Malé
Dhivehi (Maldivian)

Turkey and the Caucasus

TURKEY LIES IN BOTH ASIA and Europe – separated by the Bosphorus – and was once part of the powerful Ottoman Empire. Although the population is 99 per cent Muslim, modern Turkey is a country with no official religion. Western Turkey is relatively industrialized, with a tourist industry along the Mediterranean coast that brings in considerable income. Many farmers and herders in the centre and east, however, struggle to make a living in the arid environment. To the northeast lie the Caucasus countries of Georgia, Azerbaijan, and Armenia. Once part of the USSR, they are now independent.

ISTANBUL
The different faces of Turkey can be seen in its former capital, Istanbul, which lies on both sides of the Bosphorus waterway. Churches, mosques, and ancient buildings in both European and Islamic styles sit side by side with modern shops and offices. Bridges link the two parts of the city. In 1923, Ankara became the new capital.

TURKISH FOOD
Turkey is self-sufficient in food and grows specialized crops such as aubergines, peppers, figs, and dates. A typical Turkish meal might consist of spiced lamb, often grilled on a skewer with onion and tomato to make a *shish kebab*. This would be served with rice or cracked wheat.

EPHESUS
Tourism is one of Turkey's major industries. As well as beach resorts, the country has many ancient sites. One of these is the old Greek city of Ephesus, which lies 56 km (35 miles) south of modern-day Izmir on the Aegean coast. The city was famous for its Temple of Artemis, which was considered one of the seven wonders of the world.

Visitors to Ephesus admiring the remains of the Library of Celsus

FATHER OF THE TURKS
Mustafa Kemal Atatürk (1881–1938), founder of the modern Turkish state, became its first president in 1923. He introduced many reforms, including more equality for women and better education for all. He also declared that Islam was no longer to be the official religion.

OIL FROM AZERBAIJAN
Many years ago, caravans of camels carried vessels loaded with oil from Baku to nearby countries. By the end of the 19th century, the city was known as the "black gold" capital of the world. Today, Azerbaijan produces and exports oil as well as natural gas.

Mount Ararat in Turkey is said to be the resting place of Noah's ark after the flood described in the Bible.

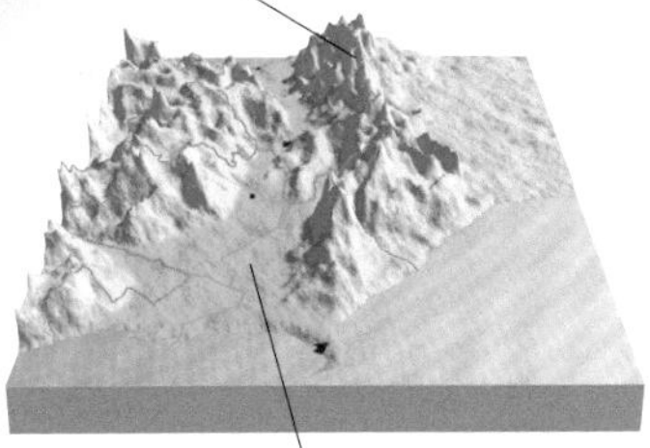

Caucasus Mountains block cold air from the north.

Vines and fruit grow in the valleys.

CAUCASUS
The towering Caucasus Mountains protect Armenia, Georgia, and Azerbaijan from the cold northerly winds. As a result, farmers can take advantage of this mild climate to grow citrus fruit, tobacco, and tea. Walnuts and hazelnuts are valuable export crops.

CARPET MARKET
Turkey is world-famous for its knotted-pile carpets, known as kilims, woven by skilled craftworkers. Each region of Turkey produces carpets with different designs and colours. Every worker incorporates into the designs symbols that tell the maker's own family history or origins.

Turkish carpets, made in centres such as Malatya and Kayseri

PEOPLE OF TURKEY
The Turks, who make up about 70 per cent of the population of 80 million, are a diverse group with a shared sense of national identity. The largest minority in Turkey – about 15 million people – are the Kurds (below), who speak their own language but have no homeland. They live in eastern Turkey, as well as in neighbouring Iraq and Iran.

Russia and Kazakhstan

THE RUSSIAN FEDERATION is the biggest country in the world, almost twice as big as either the USA or China. It extends halfway around the world, crosses two continents, and spans 11 time zones. The vast region of Siberia alone is larger than Canada. Kazakhstan lies to its south and is a large but sparsely populated country. From 1917 to 1991, both countries were part of the Union of Soviet Socialist Republics (USSR), the world's first communist state. When the USSR collapsed, Russia, Kazakhstan, and the 13 other member republics gained independence. Today, Russia and Kazakhstan are both ruled by elected presidents. Both countries have a lot of fertile land, huge mineral deposits, and many other natural resources. However, Russia still has a very low life expectancy rate compared to other industrialized countries.

0 km 400 800
0 miles 400 800
Franz Josef Land
North Cape (Nordkapp)
Barents Sea
ARCTIC
FINLAND
Gulf of Finland
LAT.
EST.
Murmansk
Kandalaksha
Kola Peninsula
White Sea
Saint Petersburg (Sankt-Peterburg)
Lake Lagoda
Petrozavodsk
Lake Onega
Pskov
Velikiy Novgorod
Severodvinsk
Arkhangel'sk
Novaya Zemlya
Kara Sea (Karskoye More)
Ostrov Kolguyev
Ostrov Belyy
Dikson
BELARUS
Smolensk
Cherepovets
Vel'sk
Severnaya Dvina
Pechora
Nar'yan-Mar
Yamal Peninsula
MOSCOW (MOSKVA)
Tver'
Vologda
Bryansk
Yaroslavl'
Kotlas
Ukhta
Vorkuta
Obskaya Guba
Talnakh
Tula
Kineshma
Syktyvkar
Salekhard
Noril'sk
UKRAINE
Belgorod
Ryazan'
Vladimir
Nizhniy Novgorod
Ob'
Nadym
Igarka
Voronezh
Tambov
Kirov
Glazov
Solikamsk
Nyagan'
Penza
Kazan'
Izhevsk
Perm'
Ural Mountains
Serov
West Siberian Plain
Taz
Yenisey
Black Sea
Rostov-na-Donu
Ul'yanovsk
Saratov
Khanty-Mansiysk
Krasnodar
Tol'yatti
Naberezhnyye Chelny
Yekaterinburg
Sochi
Volgograd
Samara
Surgut
Nizhnevartovsk
Stavropol'
Volga
Sterlitamak
Ufa
Tyumen'
Tobol'sk
Elbrus 5642m
Ural'sk
Ural
Chelyabinsk
RUSSIA
Orenburg
Tobol
Ishim
Irtysh
Caucasus
Nal'chik
Astrakhan'
Magnitogorsk
GEORGIA
Vladikavkaz
Atyrau
Orsk
Kostanay
Petropavlovsk
Groznyy
Aktobe (Aktyubinsk)
Alga
Rudnyy
Omsk
Tomsk
Makhachkala
Kokshetau
Fort-Shevchenko
Emba
Atbasar
Shchuchinsk
Novosibirsk
Krasnoyarsk
Aktau
Chelkar
Kulunda Steppe
Kemerovo
AZERBAIJAN
Caspian Sea
Zhanaozen
KAZAKHSTAN
ASTANA
Pavlodar
Barnaul
Ustyurt Plateau
Aral Sea
Aral'sk
Temirtau
Novokuznetsk
Abakan
Novokazalinsk
Saran'
Karagandy
Semey
Syr Darya
Zhezkazgan
Kazakh Uplands
Ridder
TURKMENISTAN
UZBEKISTAN
Zhosaly
Kyzylorda
Shar
Zyryanovsk
Ust'-Kamenogorsk
Gora Belukha 4506m
Balkhash
Ayaguz
Ozero Zaysan
Altai Mountains
Kyzyl Kum
Turkistan
Kentau
Lake Balkhash
Karatau
Arys'
Shu
Taldykorgan
Shymkent
Taraz
Tekeli
Kirghiz Range
CHINA
Almaty (Alma-Ata)
KYRGYZSTAN

Lake Baikal is up to 1,940 m (6,365 ft) deep and contains more than 20 per cent of the world's freshwater supply.

Kazakh man hunting with a trained golden eagle

KAZAKH CULTURE

The majority of people in Kazakhstan are Kazakh Muslims. They were once a nomadic people who travelled around on horseback, herding their sheep. Although about half of the Kazakhs live in rural areas, retaining a strong loyalty to their clans and families, the city of Almaty and the new, modern capital of Astana are growing quickly, due to wealth generated by oil and gas.

Coal miners in Siberia

NATURAL WEALTH

Siberia contains around a quarter of the world's natural gas reserves and has vast deposits of oil, as well as abundant minerals such as coal and precious metals including gold. However, many of these resources are inaccessible or in remote places, and the extreme winters make it difficult to extract them.

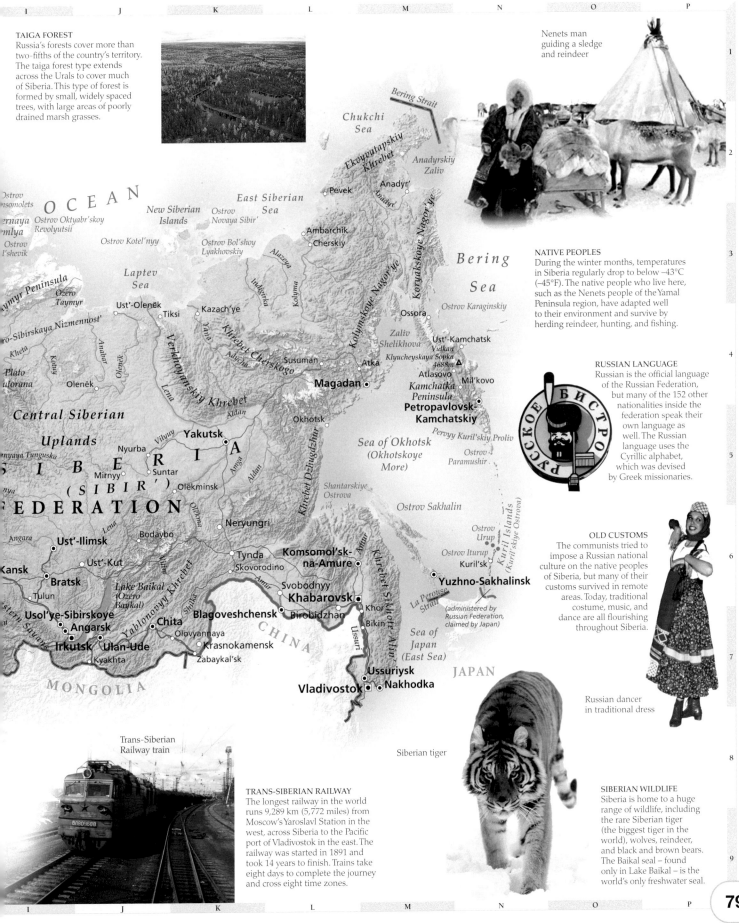

TAIGA FOREST
Russia's forests cover more than two-fifths of the country's territory. The taiga forest type extends across the Urals to cover much of Siberia. This type of forest is formed by small, widely spaced trees, with large areas of poorly drained marsh grasses.

Nenets man guiding a sledge and reindeer

NATIVE PEOPLES
During the winter months, temperatures in Siberia regularly drop to below –43°C (–45°F). The native people who live here, such as the Nenets people of the Yamal Peninsula region, have adapted well to their environment and survive by herding reindeer, hunting, and fishing.

RUSSIAN LANGUAGE
Russian is the official language of the Russian Federation, but many of the 152 other nationalities inside the federation speak their own language as well. The Russian language uses the Cyrillic alphabet, which was devised by Greek missionaries.

OLD CUSTOMS
The communists tried to impose a Russian national culture on the native peoples of Siberia, but many of their customs survived in remote areas. Today, traditional costume, music, and dance are all flourishing throughout Siberia.

Russian dancer in traditional dress

Siberian tiger

Trans-Siberian Railway train

TRANS-SIBERIAN RAILWAY
The longest railway in the world runs 9,289 km (5,772 miles) from Moscow's Yaroslavl Station in the west, across Siberia to the Pacific port of Vladivostok in the east. The railway was started in 1891 and took 14 years to finish. Trains take eight days to complete the journey and cross eight time zones.

SIBERIAN WILDLIFE
Siberia is home to a huge range of wildlife, including the rare Siberian tiger (the biggest tiger in the world), wolves, reindeer, and black and brown bears. The Baikal seal – found only in Lake Baikal – is the world's only freshwater seal.

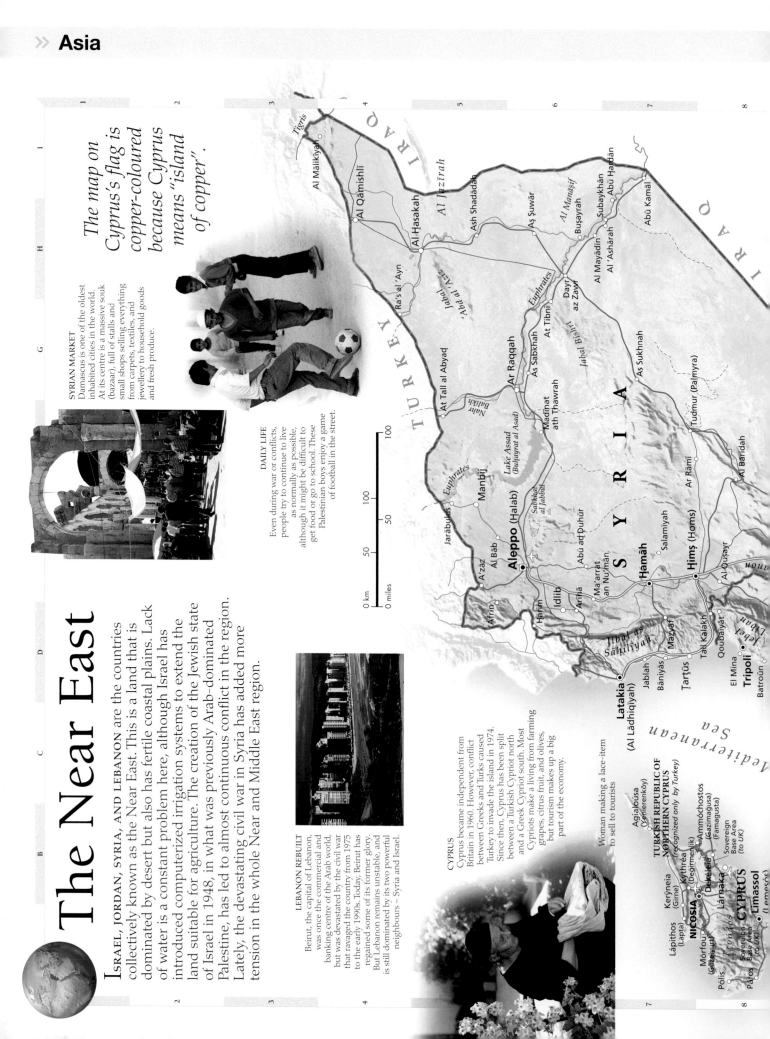

The Near East

ISRAEL, JORDAN, SYRIA, AND LEBANON are the countries collectively known as the Near East. This is a land that is dominated by desert but also has fertile coastal plains. Lack of water is a constant problem here, although Israel has introduced computerized irrigation systems to extend the land suitable for agriculture. The creation of the Jewish state of Israel in 1948, in what was previously Arab-dominated Palestine, has led to almost continuous conflict in the region. Lately, the devastating civil war in Syria has added more tension in the whole Near and Middle East region.

SYRIAN MARKET
Damascus is one of the oldest inhabited cities in the world. At its centre is a massive souk (bazaar), full of stalls and small shops selling everything from carpets, textiles, and jewellery to household goods and fresh produce.

The map on Cyprus's flag is copper-coloured because Cyprus means "island of copper".

DAILY LIFE
Even during war or conflicts, people try to continue to live as normally as possible, although it might be difficult to get food or go to school. These Palestinian boys enjoy a game of football in the street.

LEBANON REBUILT
Beirut, the capital of Lebanon, was once the commercial and banking centre of the Arab world, but was devastated by the civil war that ravaged the country from 1975 to the early 1990s. Today, Beirut has regained some of its former glory. But Lebanon remains unstable, and is still dominated by its two powerful neighbours – Syria and Israel.

Woman making a lace-item to sell to tourists

CYPRUS
Cyprus became independent from Britain in 1960. However, conflict between Greeks and Turks caused Turkey to invade the island in 1974. Since then, Cyprus has been split between a Turkish Cypriot north and a Greek Cypriot south. Most Cypriots make a living from farming grapes, citrus fruit, and olives, but tourism makes up a big part of the economy.

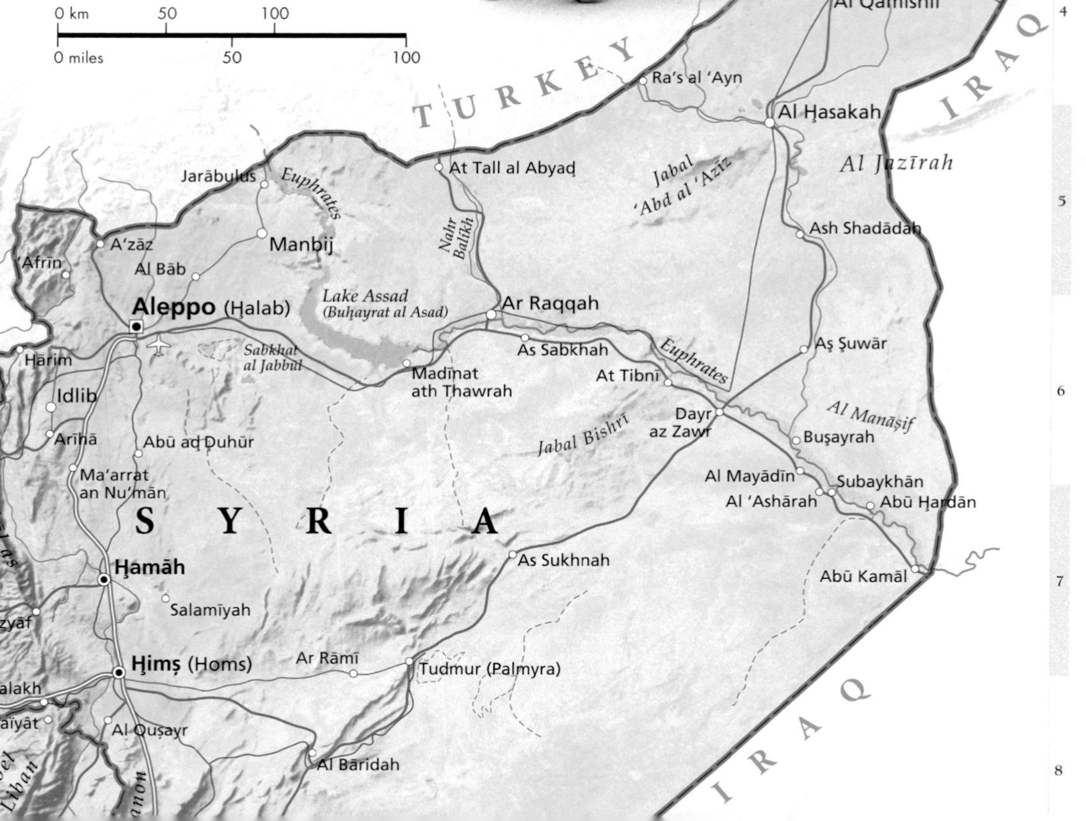

0 km 50 100
0 miles 50 100
TURKEY
IRAQ
SYRIA
Tigris
Al Mālikīyah
Al Qāmishlī
Ra's al 'Ayn
Al Ḩasakah
Al Jazīrah
Jabal 'Abd al 'Azīz
At Tall al Abyaḑ
Ash Shadādah
Jarābulus
Euphrates
Manbij
A'zāz
Nahr Balīkh
Afrīn
Al Bāb
Lake Assad
(Buḩayrat al Asad)
Aleppo (Ḩalab)
Ar Raqqah
Sabkhat al Jabbūl
As Sabkhah
Aş Şuwār
Ḩārim
Madīnat ath Thawrah
At Tibnī
Idlib
Arīḩā
Abū aḑ Ḑuhūr
Dayr az Zawr
Al Manāşif
Buşayrah
Jabal Bishrī
Ma'arrat an Nu'mān
Al Mayādīn
Al 'Ashārah
Subaykhān
Abū Ḩardān
Latakia
(Al Lādhiqīyah)
Jibāl as Sāḩilīyah
Ḩamāh
As Sukhnah
Abū Kamāl
Jablah
Salamīyah
Bāniyās
Mazyāf
Ţarţūs
Ḩimş (Homs)
Ar Rāmī
Tudmur (Palmyra)
Tall Kalakh
Qoubaïyât
Al Quşayr
El Mina
Tripoli
Jebel Liban
Al Bāridah
Batroûn
Mediterranean Sea
Agialoúsa
(Yenierenköy)
TURKISH REPUBLIC OF NORTHERN CYPRUS
(recognized only by Turkey)
Lápithos
(Lapta)
Kerýneia
(Girne)
Kythréa
(Değirmenlik)
NICOSIA
Ammóchostos
(Gazimağusa)
(Famagusta)
Mórfou
(Güzelyurt)
Dekéleia
Lárnaka
Sovereign Base Area
(to UK)
Pólis
Troódos
CYPRUS
Páfos
Limassol
(Lemesós)

LAND OF REFUGEES
The frequent wars between Israel and its Arab neighbours, and conflicts in the Gaza Strip and West Bank, led to a huge number of Palestinian refugees fleeing Israel to seek shelter in neighbouring countries. In addition, from 2011, the civil war in Syria added almost 5 million of new refugees ending up in Jordan, Lebanon, Turkey, and Iraq. While some refugees are permanently settled, the majority live in huge, poorly equipped camps with only basic facilities and little chance of work or education.

Refugees living in crowded conditions near Amman, Jordan

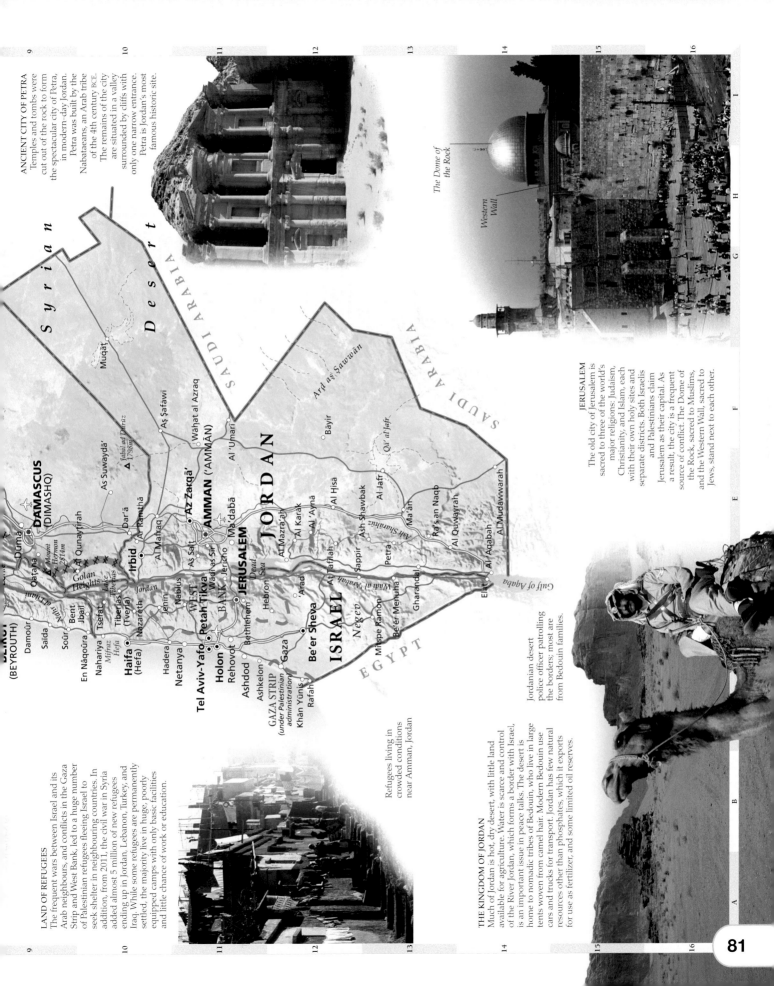

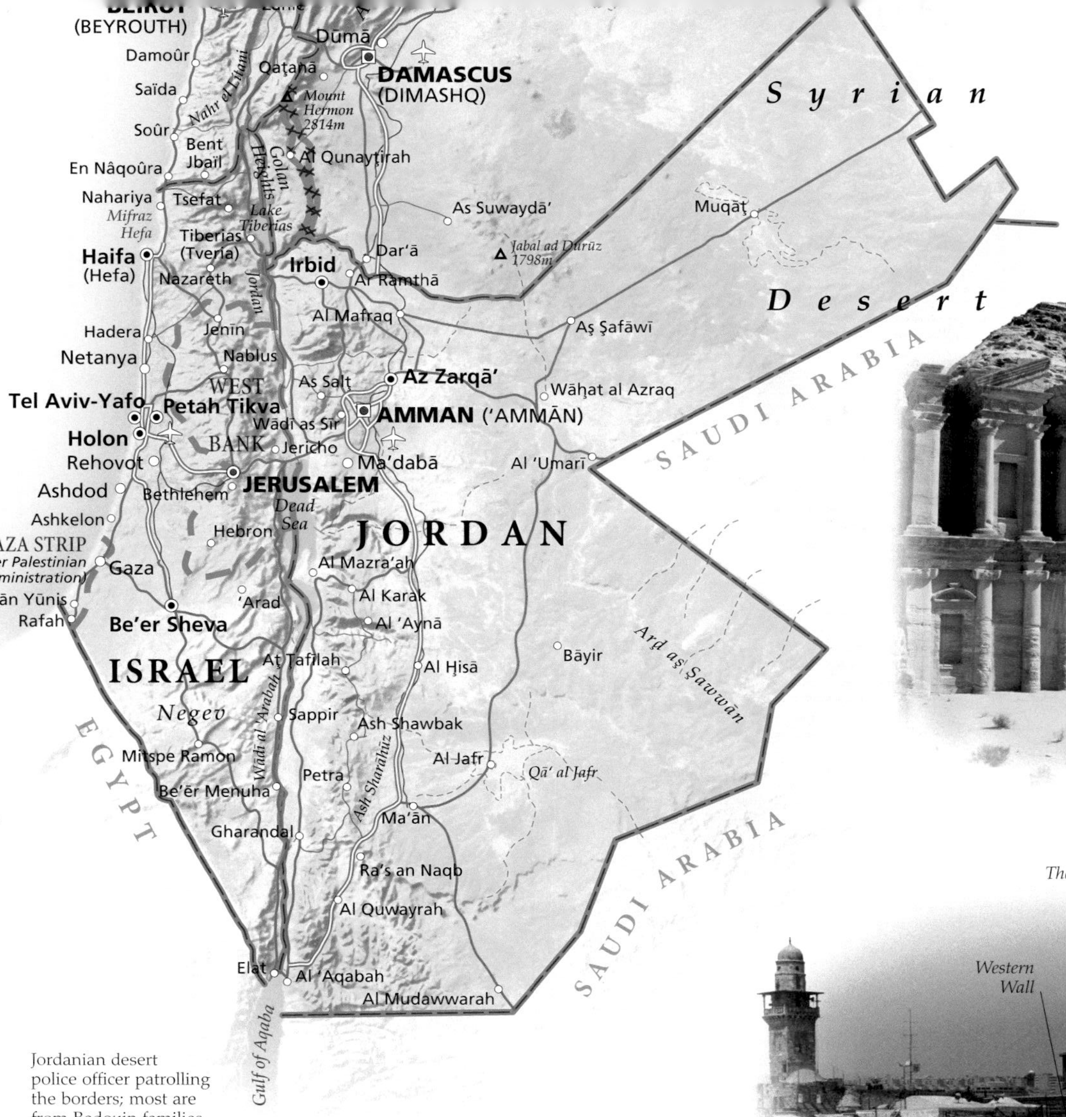

ANCIENT CITY OF PETRA
Temples and tombs were cut out of the rock to form the spectacular city of Petra, in modern-day Jordan. Petra was built by the Nabataeans, an Arab tribe of the 4th century BCE. The remains of the city are situated in a valley surrounded by cliffs with only one narrow entrance. Petra is Jordan's most famous historic site.

THE KINGDOM OF JORDAN
Much of Jordan is hot, dry desert, with little land available for agriculture. Water is scarce and control of the River Jordan, which forms a border with Israel, is an important issue in peace talks. The desert is home to nomadic tribes of Bedouin, who live in large tents woven from camel hair. Modern Bedouin use cars and trucks for transport. Jordan has few natural resources other than phosphates, which it exports for use as fertilizer, and some limited oil reserves.

Jordanian desert police officer patrolling the borders; most are from Bedouin families.

JERUSALEM
The old city of Jerusalem is sacred to three of the world's major religions: Judaism, Christianity, and Islam, each with their own holy sites and separate districts. Both Israelis and Palestinians claim Jerusalem as their capital. As a result, the city is a frequent source of conflict. The Dome of the Rock, sacred to Muslims, and the Western Wall, sacred to Jews, stand next to each other.

The Middle East

The middle east is home to the world's oldest civilizations, which grew up in the Tigris and Euphrates river valleys of present-day Iraq more than 6,000 years ago. The world's first towns and cities were built here. Since then, many powerful empires have dominated the region, all leaving a wealth of buildings and monuments behind them. Today, the Middle East is at the centre of the Islamic world. The population of every country is Arab and speaks Arabic, except Iran, where half the population are Farsi-speaking Persians.

DESERT WARS
Most international boundaries in the Middle East were drawn by the former European colonial powers, and have often caused conflict. Iraq and Iran fought a bitter eight-year war along their common border from 1980. Since then, further conflicts between Iraq and international forces, as well as against the so-called "Islamic State" terrorist organization, have caused much suffering here.

OIL PRODUCTION
The Middle East is the world's major oil producer – Saudi Arabia alone produces more than 12 per cent of the world's supply. Oil has brought great wealth to the region, in particular to Saudi Arabia and the Gulf States.

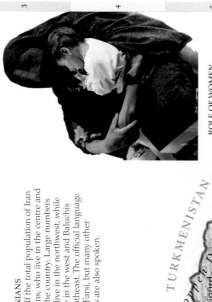

The Persian language is written in Arabic script

THE IRANIANS
About half the total population of Iran are Persians, who live in the centre and north of the country. Large numbers of Azeris live in the northwest, while Kurds live in the west and Baluchis in the southeast. The official language of Iran is Farsi, but many other languages are also spoken.

ROLE OF WOMEN
Family life is important throughout the Muslim world. The role of women varies from country to country – traditionally, women stay at home and look after the family, but some now work. In public, many cover their head with a hijab, or whole body with a burqa.

Red Sea
Arabian Peninsula
SAUDI ARABIA
Ar Rub' al Khālī (Empty Quarter)
YEMEN
OMAN
UNITED ARAB EMIRATES
QATAR
BAHRAIN
MANAMA (AL MANĀMAH)
DOHA (AD DAWḤAH)
ABU DHABI (ABŪ ẒABY)
Dubai (Dubayy)
Sharjah (Ash Shāriqah)
MUSCAT (MASQAṬ)
RIYADH (AR RIYĀḌ)
Medina (Al Madīnah)
Mecca (Makkah)
Jedda (Jiddah)
Aṭ Ṭā'if
Abhā
Najrān
SANA (ṢAN'Ā')
Aden ('Adan)
Hodeida (Al Hudaydah)
Ta'izz
Al Mukallā
Ṣalālah
Gulf of Aden
Gulf of Oman
Arabian Sea
Bab el Mandeb
Tropic of Cancer
Socotra (Suquṭrā) (to Yemen)
0 km 150 300
0 miles 150 300

ISLAM
The Islamic religion began in the 7th century in the holy cities of Mecca and Medina in Saudi Arabia. Minarets, the tall thin towers of mosques, dominate the skyline of every town and city in the region. From these, devout Muslims are summoned to pray five times a day. Muslims are also required to make a Hajj, or pilgrimage, to Mecca (above) at least once in their lifetime.

The Qur'an, the book of sacred writings of Islam

Saudi Arabia is the only country in the world to be named after its royal family – the house of Al Saud.

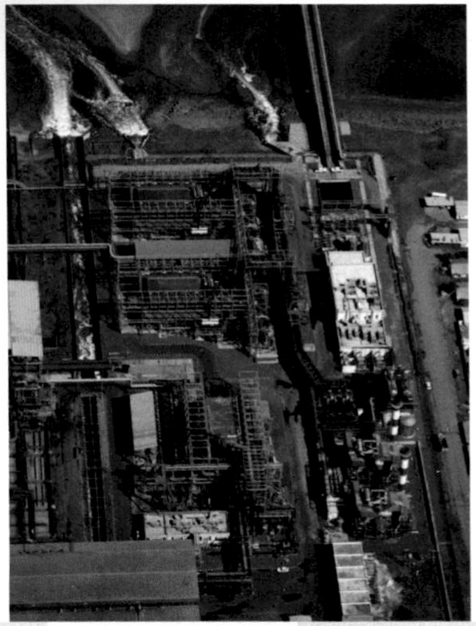

WATER
Much of the Middle East is covered with a hot desert. Water is scarce although there are some oases where animals can be watered and crops irrigated. On the coastline, desalination plants, such as this one in Oman, remove salt from seawater to make it suitable for domestic consumption and agriculture.

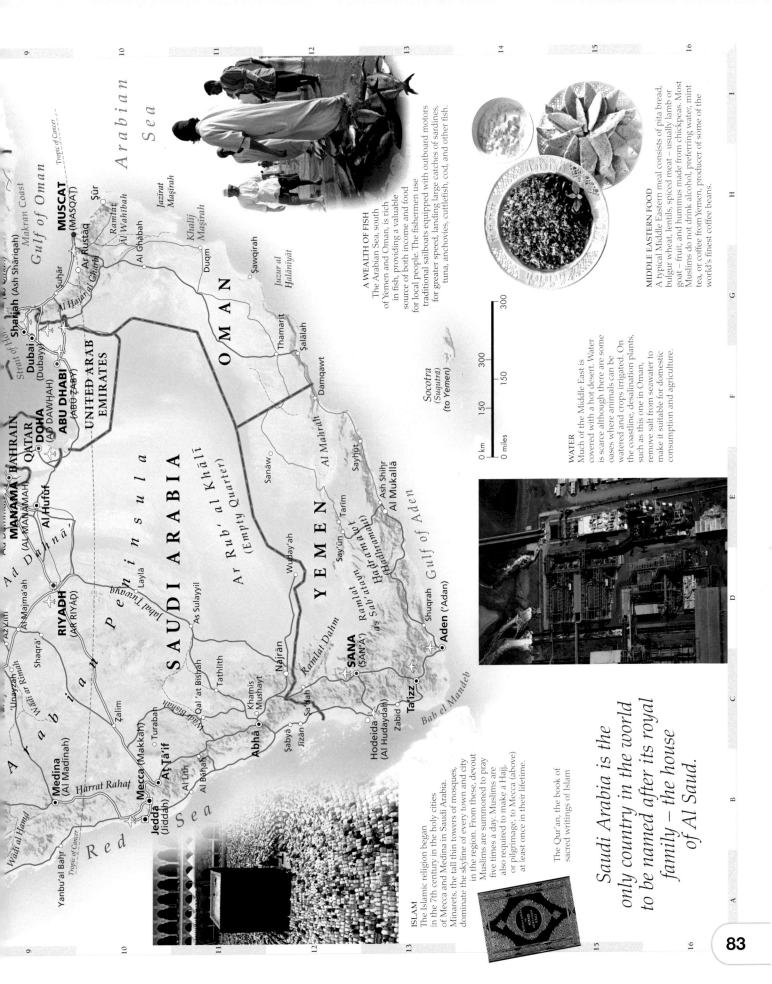

A WEALTH OF FISH
The Arabian Sea, south of Yemen and Oman, is rich in fish, providing a valuable source of both income and food for local people. The fishermen use traditional sailboats equipped with outboard motors for greater speed, landing large catches of sardines, tuna, anchovies, cuttlefish, cod, and other fish.

MIDDLE EASTERN FOOD
A typical Middle Eastern meal consists of pita bread, bulgur wheat, lentils, spiced meat – usually lamb or goat – fruit, and hummus made from chickpeas. Most Muslims do not drink alcohol, preferring water, mint tea, or coffee from Yemen, producer of some of the world's finest coffee beans.

Central Asia

THE FIVE CENTRAL ASIAN NATIONS rise up from hot deserts in the west and south to cold, high mountain ranges in the east. The area has oil, gas, and mineral reserves, as well as other natural resources, but water is often scarce and agriculture is limited. The four northern nations were once part of the Soviet Union and are now independent nations. Afghanistan is a landlocked country and three-quarters of its land is inaccessible terrain. It was invaded by the Soviet Union in 1979, prompting a continuous series of civil wars. The 2001 invasion by American and other Western forces overthrew the fundamentalist Islamic regime and led to democratic presidential elections, but Afghanistan is still unstable. Wrecked by more than 30 years of warfare, it is one of the poorest and most deprived nations on Earth.

One of the world's largest gold mines is at Muruntau in the Kyzyl Kum desert in Uzbekistan.

FESTIVALS IN AFGHANISTAN
Despite the horrors of recent years, the Afghans still celebrate important Islamic festivals, notably Eid ul-Fitr, which marks the end of the holy month of Ramadan. People visit friends and family and eat a festive meal together. The art of storytelling still flourishes in Afghanistan, as does the *attan*, the national dance.

An Afghan man carries bread with which to break the Ramadan fast.

Children in Kabul, Afghanistan, made homeless by war

LIFE EXPECTANCY
As a result of war, drought, and poverty, people in Afghanistan can expect to live an average of only 51 years, one of the lowest life expectancy rates in the world. Infant mortality is extremely high. Health services have almost completely collapsed and few trained doctors and nurses are available to help the sick. Many children have been orphaned or made homeless, and few have been able to go to school.

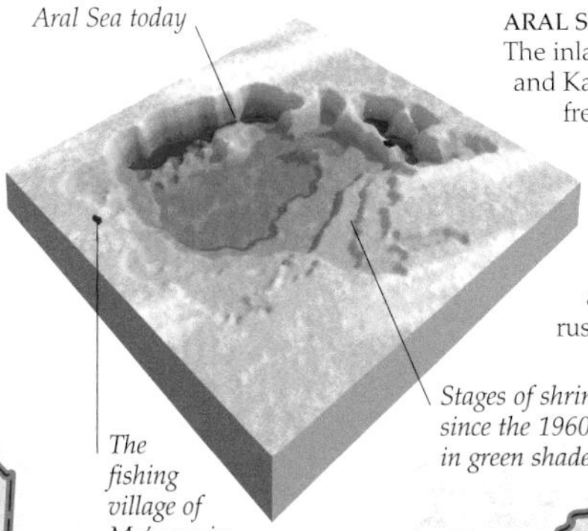

ARAL SEA ENVIRONMENTAL DISASTER
The inland Aral Sea, between Uzbekistan and Kazakhstan, was once a vast, thriving freshwater lake full of fish. Over the years, the rivers flowing into it were diverted or drained to provide irrigation for crops. The sea has now shrunk to less than one-tenth of its original size, reducing the numbers of fish, and leaving former fishing villages and rusting ships stranded inland.

A man in front of his home, called a yurt, in western Pamir, Tajikistan

MOUNTAIN LIFE
The two small eastern republics of Kyrgyzstan and Tajikistan are both very mountainous and are subject to earthquakes and landslides. Only about six per cent of Tajikistan can be used for growing crops, whereas Kyrgyzstan is more fertile.

LOCAL WEALTH
Uzbekistan, Turkmenistan, and Kyrgyzstan all grow considerable crops of cotton – Uzbekistan is the world's sixth largest producer – as well as fruit and vegetables. The three countries are also rich in mineral deposits, such as gold, mercury, sulphur, and uranium, and have reserves of coal, oil, and natural gas.

Harvesting cotton in Uzbekistan

THE TAJIKS
The majority of people of Tajikistan are Iranian in origin and speak Tajik, which is related to Farsi. The minority Uzbeks are made up mainly of descendents of Turkic-speaking (related to Turkish) nomads. This division has led to ethnic tension between the two groups. Civil war between the government and Islamic rebels in the east of the country during the 1990s led to an exodus of Uzbeks and Russians, who had moved into the country when it was part of the Soviet Union.

Tajik horsemen in Pamir, Tajikistan

Tilla-Kari, a 17th-century Islamic religious school in Samarqand, Uzbekistan

THE SILK ROAD
The Silk Road is the ancient trading route that brought silks and other fine goods from China through central Asia and the Middle East to Europe. Many cities were built along its route, including Buxoro (Bukhara, Uzbekistan), an important place of pilgrimage for Muslims, and Samarqand, which contains some of the finest Islamic architecture in the world. Many of these cities are now UNESCO-designated World Heritage Sites.

Indian Subcontinent

SEPARATED FROM the rest of Asia by the Himalayas, the Indian subcontinent is home to more than one-fifth of the world's population – almost 1.7 billion people. They have a long and complex history, form many different ethnic groups, speak a wide variety of languages, and worship many different gods. While some people in these countries are wealthy, many others live in poverty. Tensions between and within countries in this region have sometimes erupted in warfare. The Indian subcontinent is often affected by natural disasters, notably cyclones in the Bay of Bengal, and earthquakes and floods in Pakistan. However, India, the most heavily populated nation and once prone to famine, is now more than self-sufficient in food. All but Nepal and Bhutan were once ruled by the British, whose legacy can be seen in the common language of English, in some architecture, the vast railway system, and in sport – most notably cricket.

MONSOON
From May/June to September, warm, moist southerly winds sweep up from the Indian Ocean and the Bay of Bengal across the subcontinent. Once these winds meet dry land, moisture falls as monsoon rainfall. Although this irrigates the land and replenishes the water supply, it can also cause severe flooding.

FAMILY LIFE IN PAKISTAN
Pakistanis have strong ties to their extended families, and often many generations live and work together in family-run businesses. Smaller family units, however, are becoming more common in urban areas. Although some women hold prominent positions in public and commercial life, such as Benazir Bhutto who was prime minister twice before she was assassinated in December 2007, most women do not work outside the home.

AFGHANISTAN
IRAN
PAKISTAN
Hindu Kush
Khyber Pass 1080m
Peshāwar
Mingāora
Mardān
ISLĀMĀBĀD
Wāh
Rāwalpindi
Jhelum
Potwar Plateau
Sargodha
Gujrāt
Gujrānw
Lahore
Amri
Chaman
Toba Kākar Range
Quetta
Faisalābād
Multān
Dera Ghāzi Khān
Sibi
Okāra
Chandīga
Bathinda
Chāgai Hills
Kālat
Baluchistān
Bahāwalpur
Jacobābād
Shikārpur
Lārkāna
Sukkur
Khairpur
Rahīmyār Khān
Central Makrān Range
Turbat
Gwādar
Pasni
Kirthar Range
Indus
Thar Desert
Bīkāner
NEW DE
Jaisalmer
Jodhpur
Jaipur
Nawābshāh
Hyderābād
Mīrpur Khās
Karāchi
Sind
Sujāwal
Mouths of the Indus
Pāli
Beāwar
Rājasthān
Udaipur
Kota
Rann of Kachchh
Pālanpur
Tropic of Cancer
Gulf of Kachchh
Gāndhīdhām
Gujarāt
Ahmadābād
Godhra
Ratlām
Jāmnagar
Rājkot
Indore
Vadodara
Porbandar
Bhāvnagar
Sātpura Ra
Bhusāwal
Sūrat
Gulf of Khambhāt
Damān
Manmād
Nāshik
Aurangā
Kalyān
Mumbai (Bombay)
Pune
Mahārāshtra
Nānd
Bārāmati
Solāpur
Arabian Sea
Western Ghats
Kolhāpur
Karnātaka
Belgaum
Panaji
Gadag
Hubli
Dāvang
Shimoga
Udupi
Mangalore
Bangalo
Mysore
Kāsaragod
Kannur (Cannanore)
Kozhikode (Calicut)
Kerala
Coimbatore
Ernākulam
Kochi (Cochin)
Kollam (Quilon)
Thiruvananthapuram (Trivandrum)
0 km 150 300
0 miles 150 300

SRI LANKA
In 1983, civil war erupted in Sri Lanka between the Buddhist majority Sinhalese, who dominate the government, and the Hindu minority Tamils, who wanted to establish their own independent state in the north of the island. The civil war, which ended in 2009 when the government defeated the Tamil Tigers, has cost many lives and disrupted the island's economy. Yet Sri Lanka still has one of the highest literacy rates in the world and high levels of health care.

School child, Sri Lanka

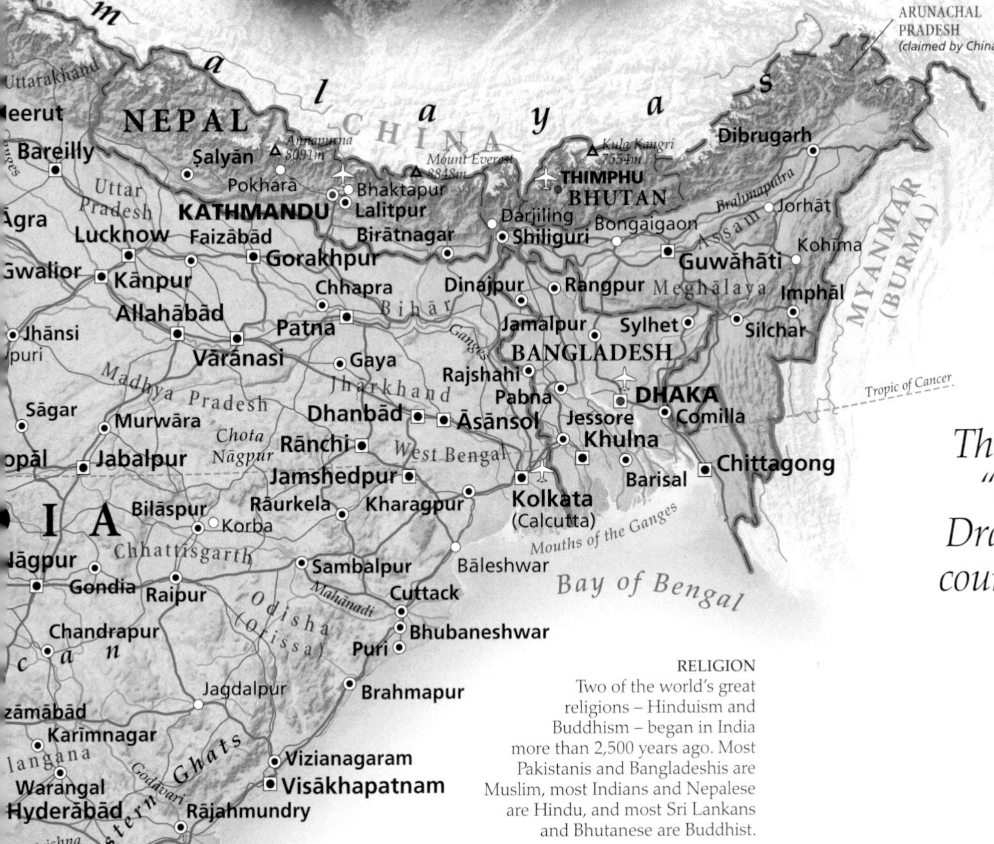
A "line of control" was agreed between India and Pakistan (1972)
AKSAI CHIN (administered by China, claimed by India)
DEMCHOK/ DEMQOG (administered by China, claimed by India)
ARUNACHAL PRADESH (claimed by China)
H i m a l a y a s
NEPAL
CHINA
BHUTAN
BANGLADESH
MYANMAR (BURMA)
Uttarakhand
Meerut
Bareilly
Salyān
Annapurna 8091m
Mount Everest 8848m
Kula Kangri 7554m
Pokhara
Bhaktapur
KATHMANDU
Lalitpur
Uttar Pradesh
Agra
Lucknow
Faizābād
Gorakhpur
Birātnagar
Darjiling
Shiliguri
THIMPHU
Bongaigaon
Brahmaputra
Assam
Dibrugarh
Jorhāt
Kohima
Guwāhāti
Meghālaya
Imphāl
Gwalior
Kānpur
Chhapra
Dinajpur
Rangpur
Allahābād
Bihār
Patna
Jamalpur
Sylhet
Silchar
Jhānsi
Vārānasi
Gaya
Ganges
Rajshahi
Jhārkhand
Pabna
DHAKA
Tropic of Cancer
Madhya Pradesh
Sāgar
Murwāra
Dhanbād
Āsānsol
Jessore
Comilla
Chota Nāgpur
Rānchi
West Bengal
Khulna
Bhopāl
Jabalpur
Jamshedpur
Barisal
Chittagong
Kolkata (Calcutta)
Bilāspur
Korba
Rāurkela
Kharagpur
INDIA
Mouths of the Ganges
Nāgpur
Chhattisgarh
Sambalpur
Bāleshwar
Gondia
Raipur
Mahānadi
Cuttack
Bay of Bengal
Odisha (Orissa)
Chandrapur
Bhubaneshwar
Puri
Deccan
Jagdalpur
Brahmapur
Nizāmābād
Karīmnagar
Telangana
Vizianagaram
Godavari
Eastern Ghats
Warangal
Visākhapatnam
Hyderābād
Rājahmundry
Krishna
Vijayawāda
Kurnool
Andhra Pradesh
Chīrāla
Ongole
Kāvali
Nellore
Cuddapah
Chennai (Madras)
Vellore
Kānchīpuram
Salem
Pondicherry
Tiruchchirāppalli
Palk Strait
Madurai
Jaffna
Mannar
SRI LANKA
Tuticorin
Trincomalee
Gulf of Mannar
Puttalam
Batticaloa
Negombo
Kandy
COLOMBO
SRI JAYEWARDENAPURA KOTTE
Kalutara
Galle
Matara
INDIAN OCEAN
North Andaman
Middle Andaman
Port Blair
South Andaman
Andaman Islands (to India)
Little Andaman
Car Nicobar
Nicobar Islands (to India)
Andaman Sea
Katchall Island
Little Nicobar
Great Nicobar
Indira Point

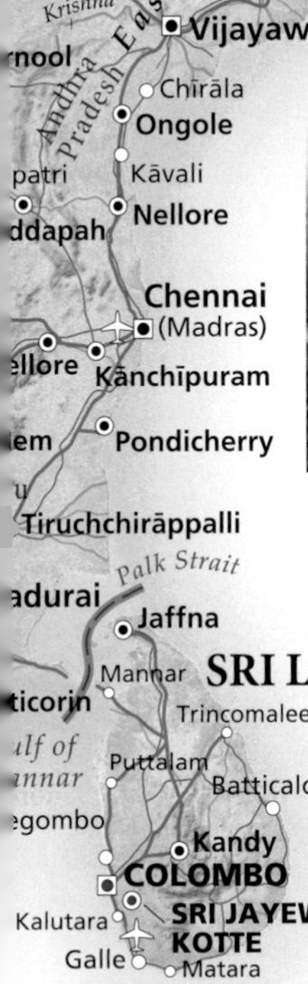

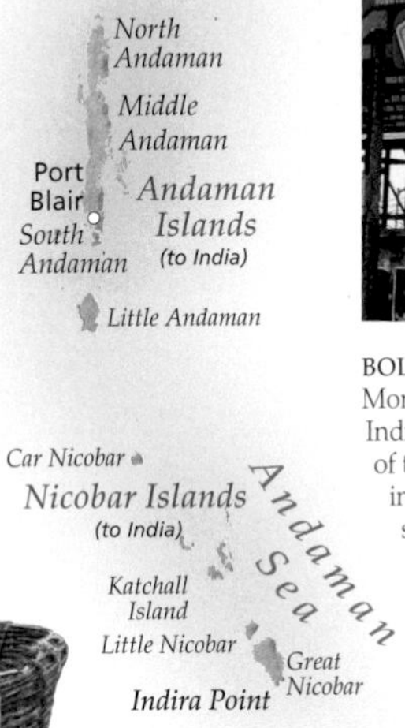

THE HIMALAYAS
The highest chain of mountains in the world, the Himalayas have eight peaks that are more than 8,000 m (26,247 ft) high. Everest, the world's highest mountain at 8,848 m (29,029 ft), is on the border of Nepal and Tibet. Mountaineers come from far and wide to scale these massive peaks.

Bhutanese people

BHUTAN
Hidden away in the Himalayas, the people of Bhutan are devoutly Buddhist and have little contact with the outside world. A minority of the population are Nepalese Hindus who came to the country in the first half of the last century. Most Bhutanese live in the fertile river valleys of the centre and south of the country. Traditional dress – the *kira* for women and the *gho* for men – is widely worn.

The name Bhutan means "Land of the Thunder Dragon" in Dzongkha, the country's official language.

RELIGION
Two of the world's great religions – Hinduism and Buddhism – began in India more than 2,500 years ago. Most Pakistanis and Bangladeshis are Muslim, most Indians and Nepalese are Hindu, and most Sri Lankans and Bhutanese are Buddhist.

Hindus bathe in the River Ganges, which is considered sacred.

PYAAR KA PUNCHNAMA
COME FALL OUT OF LOVE
LOVE BREATHES ITS LAST MAY 20

BOLLYWOOD
More films are produced in Mumbai (Bombay), India – more than 1,000 a year – than in the whole of the USA, turning "Bollywood", as it is known, into a major cultural centre. Famous for their song and dance routines and glamorous stars, Bollywood films generally had historical and social themes. Today, these have expanded to include more contemporary stories as the films have found a fan base in the large Indian diaspora across the world.

TEA IN SRI LANKA
Sri Lanka is the world's largest exporter of tea. The plantations are located mainly in the centre of the island and employ women to pick the delicate, green shoots of the bushes.

Western China and Mongolia

CHINA IS A LAND of great geographical diversity and amazing landscapes. More than 90 per cent of the population are Han Chinese – descendents of people who settled here more than 5,000 years ago. This region includes western China, Mongolia, and Tibet. Mongolia gained its independence from China in 1911 and is now an independent democracy. Tibet is currently governed by China. Compared with eastern China, this region is sparsely populated and characterized by vast deserts, remote mountains, and extreme temperatures.

DESERT LANDS
The cold, rocky Gobi Desert (right) stretches for more than 1,000,000 sq km (380,000 sq miles) through Mongolia and northeast China. Many dinosaur bones and eggs have been found here, making it one of the richest dinosaur fossil regions in the world.

THE MONGOLIANS
Most of the people living in Mongolia are Khalkh Mongols. About 70 per cent of Mongols now live in urban areas, but some still lead traditional lives as nomadic herders. They live in large felt tents, called *yurts*. Smoke from the central iron stove escapes through a chimney in the roof.

In traditional Mongolian khoomi *singing, men are able to sing several notes at once.*

B
C
D
E
F
G
H
2
3
4
5
6
7
8
9
A
B
G
H
Hövsgöl Nuur
Uus Nuur
Ulaangom
Ölgiy
Altay Mountains
KAZAKHSTAN
Altay
Har Us Nuur
Hyargas Nuur
Halban
Mörö
Hovd
Har Nuur
Hangayn Nuruu
Tsetser
Ulungur Hu
MO
Karamay
Altay
Bayanhon
Gurbantünggüt Shamo
Borohoro Shan
Kuytun
Shihezi
Yining
Fukang
Jimsar
Ürümqi
Qitai
Aj Bogd Uul 3802m
Tien Shan
Jengish Chokusu/Tömür Feng 7443m
Turpan
Turpan Pendi
Hami
Atas Bogd 2695m
KYRGYZSTAN
Bosten Hu
Korla
Kuruktag
Xingxingxia
G
Kashi
Tarim He
Tarim Basin
GANSU
TAJIKISTAN
Yengisar
XINJIANG
Shache
Laojunmiao
Yecheng
Takla Makan Desert
Ruoqiang
Qilian Shan
Pishan
(claimed by India)
Moyu
Altun Shan
Danghe Nanshan
Hotan
Qira
C H I N
Qaidam Pendi
PAKISTAN
Karakoram Range
K2 8611m
Kunlun Shan
Golmud
Dulan
AKSAI CHIN
Burhan Budai Shan
INDIA
Indus
AKSAI CHIN (administered by China, claimed by India)
Plateau of Tibet (Qingzang Gaoyuan)
QINGHAI
Rutog
Tongtian He
Bayan Har Shan
DEMCHOK/DÊMQOG (administered by China, claimed by India)
TIBET
Gar Xincun
Yushu
Mekong
Zanda
Tanggula Shan
Gozhê
Siling Co
Amdo
Tangra Yumco
Gyaring Co
Nam Co
Nagqu
Qamdo
Ngangzê Co
Damxung
Salween
Brahmaputra
Nyainqêntanglha Shan
Maizhokunggar
Hengduan Shan
Lhazê
Xigazê
Lhasa
NEPAL
Gonggar
Gyangzê
Himalayas
ARUNACHAL PRADESH (claimed by China)
Mount Everest 8848m
BHUTAN
INDIA
MYANMAR (BURMA)

CHINESE WRITING
The Chinese alphabet is not made up of letters. Instead, separate symbols stand for individual words or parts of words. There are more than 50,000 characters in the Chinese language. The same symbols are used everywhere in China, and no matter what Chinese language or dialect people speak, they can all read the same script.

兒童百科全書

Chinese symbols, whose strokes have to be written in a certain order

MONASTERIES IN MONGOLIA
Under communism, Mongolians were forbidden to practise their traditional Buddhist faith, which was viewed as superstitious and unscientific. Since the democratic government was set up in 1990, some monasteries have reopened. Many people, however, no longer follow any religion.

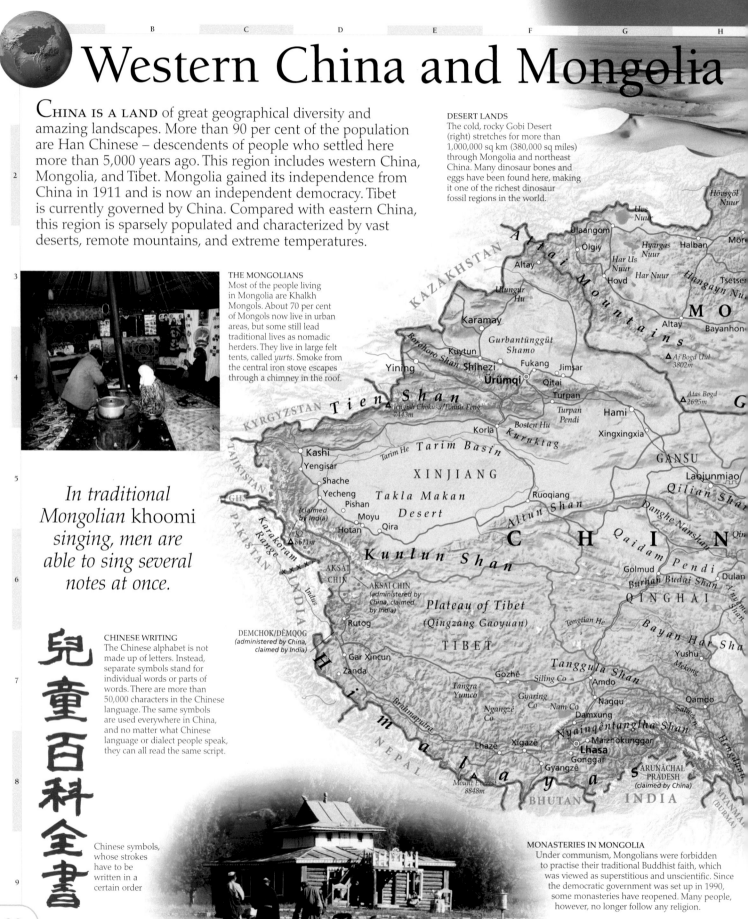

I
J
K
L
M
N
O
P
0 km 200 400
0 miles 200 400
RUSS. FED.
RUSSIAN FEDERATION
Mohe
Tahe
Amur (Heilong Jiang)
Argun (Ergun He)
Ergun
Jagdaqi
Great Khingan Range (Da Hinggan Ling)
Fuyuan
Yichun
Bei'an
Hegang
Nancha
Jiamusi
HEILONGJIANG
Manzhouli
Yakeshi
Hulun Nur
Hulun Buir (Hailar)
Qiqihar
Tonghe
Jixi
Lake Khanka
Sühbaatar
Selenga
Darhan
Onon Gol
Choybalsan
Harbin
Shangzhi
Mudanjiang
Erdenet
ULAN BATOR (ULAANBAATAR)
Menengiyn Tal
Manchuria
Öndörhaan
Songyuan
Hulingol
Dzuunmod
Kerulen
Baruun-Urt
Changchun
Jilin
Yanji
JILIN
Sea of Japan (East Sea)
OLIA
Xi Ujimqin Qi
Tongliao
Siping
Liaoyuan
Saynshand
Xilinhot
Baishan
INNER MONGOLIA (Nei Mongol Zizhiqu)
LIAONING
Liao He
NORTH KOREA
Erenhot
Gobi Desert
Dalandzadgad
Altayn Nuruu
Chifeng (Ulanhad)
HEBEI
Ulan Qab (Jining)
Lang Shan
Hohhot
Baotou
Yellow River (Huang He)
SHANXI
Yabrai Shan
Wuhai (Haibowan)
Mu Us Shadi
Tengger Shamo
Yinchuan
Great Wall of China
NINGXIA
Tongxin
Xining
Lanzhou
Pingliang
GANSU
Tianshui
SHAANXI
Lugu
Zhugqu
Wenxian
SICHUAN
1
2
3
4
5
6
7
8
9

FESTIVAL OF NAADAM
Each July, people all over Mongolia celebrate the sports festival of Naadam. Three sports – wrestling (above), archery, and horse riding – are the focus of the festivities. The skills needed to take part in these activities are those that would have helped people survive the traditional nomadic lifestyle.

GREAT WALL OF CHINA
About 2,200 years ago, approximately 300,000 slaves began to build China's enormous Great Wall. Originally built to protect China's northern borders, it is the longest human-made structure ever built and stretches from central Asia to the Yellow Sea, a distance of 6,400 km (3,980 miles).

PEOPLE OF TIBET
Most Tibetans live in the valleys of the Tibetan plateau, high in the Himalayas and surrounded by the world's tallest mountains. Tibetans have their own language and culture. Recently, many Han Chinese have settled in this region.

Tibetan village children

TRADITIONAL MEDICINE
As well as modern medicine, many Chinese still use alternative remedies. Traditional medicine is based on the belief that health is achieved by balancing a person's mind and body – their yin and yang. Any imbalance is treated with medicines made from dried plant materials (left). Some animals, including Asiatic bears, are now endangered due to the demand for parts used in traditional medicine.

Buddhist prayer flags

BUDDHIST TIBET
Many Tibetans are devout Buddhists. Their religious leader, the Dalai Lama, used to live in Lhasa. In 1951, however, Tibet became part of China and the government restricted the people's religious freedom and lifestyle. This has resulted in tension between the Tibetans and the Chinese government. The Dalai Lama now lives in exile in India.

Eastern China and Korea

CHINA HAS A LARGE population of almost 1.4 billion, with two-thirds living in eastern China. For thousands of years, powerful emperors ruled China. During this period, Chinese civilization was very advanced, but much of the population lived in poverty. In 1949, after a communist revolution, the People's Republic of China was established. Food, education, and health care became available to more people, but there was also a loss of freedom. Today, Chinese people have more freedom, but the government still has tight control over their lives. The Korean peninsula is divided politically into north and south, and political tensions continue to exist between the two governments. Since 1949, Taiwan has been in dispute with China over who governs the mountainous island of Taiwan.

NEW YEAR CELEBRATIONS
Chinese New Year, also known as the Spring Festival, is the country's most important festival. It is usually held in January or February. Good-luck messages decorate buildings and there are feasts, fireworks, fairs, and processions. People wear red clothes for good luck and give gifts of coins to symbolize wealth.

Chinese New Year parade

HONG KONG
For 100 years, Hong Kong was a British colony. Then, in 1997, it was returned to China. These small islands are some of the most densely populated parts of the world. Most people live and work in high-rise buildings. It has a prosperous economy at the heart of global finance and the people there have one of the world's highest life expectancies.

Skyline of Hong Kong with a Chinese junk in the foreground

SMALL FAMILIES
China's population grows by millions each year. In 1979, to try to control the rising population, the government brought in policies to stop parents from having more than one child. As a result, many Chinese children do not have brothers and sisters, but this might change as a two-child policy was introduced in 2016.

PADDY FIELDS
Rice forms the basis of most Chinese meals. It grows in paddy fields in the southeast of the country. During the growing season, fields are flooded so farmers can grow more rice more quickly. In the drier regions, wheat is grown and used to make noodles, buns, and dumplings. Rice or wheat is combined with local vegetables, meats, and spices to create regional dishes.

Bayan Har Shan
QINGHAI
GANSU
NINGXIA
Tongchuan
Xianyang
Baoji
Xi'an
Hanzhong
SHAANXI
Hongyuan
Guangyuan
Yalong Jiang
SICHUAN
Mianyang
Wanyuan
TIBET
Luhuo
Nanchong
Sichuan Pendi
Chengdu
Wanzhou
Litang
Ya'an
C H I
Leshan
Neijiang
Chongqing
CHONGQING
Hengduan Shan
Jinsha Jiang
Zigong
Xichang
Yangtze (Chang Jiang)
Tongzi
Zhongdian
Zunyi
Huaihua
Zhoatong
GUIZHOU
Panzhihua
Guiyang
Anshun
Kaili
Dali
Guanling
Duyun
MYANMAR (BURMA)
Salween
Baoshan
Kunming
Dushan
YUNNAN
Xingxi
Yuxi
Wuliang Shan
Liuzhou
Kaiyuan
Bose
Tropic of Cancer
Wenshan
GUANGXI
Mekong
Gejiu
Nanning
Jinghong
VIETNAM
Qinzhou
Beihai
LAOS
0 km 150 300
0 miles 150 300
Gulf of Tonkin
Danzhou
Dongfang
HAINAN

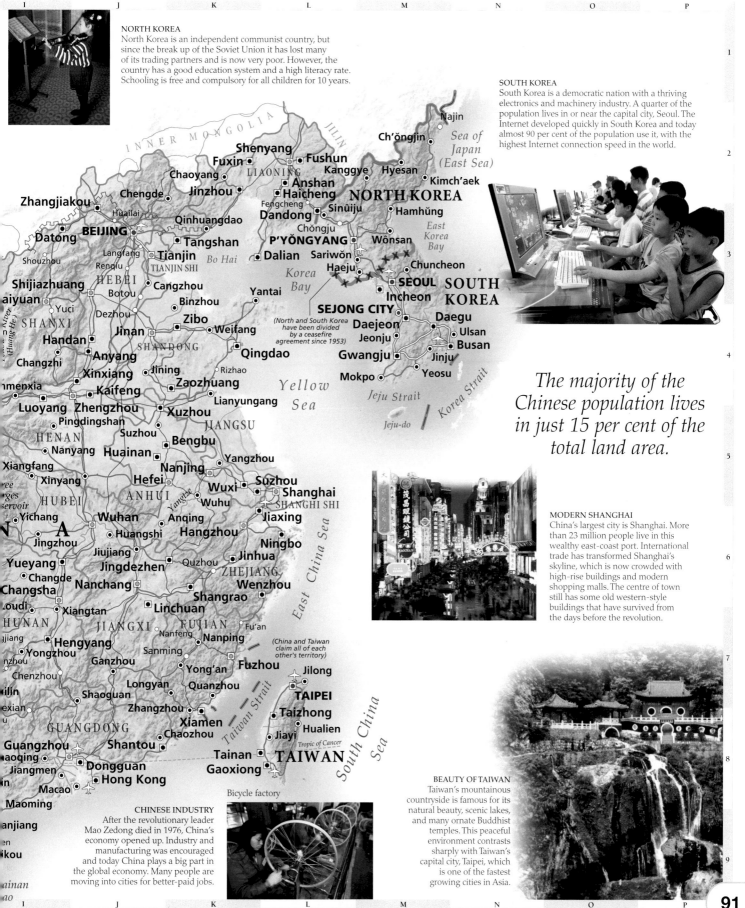

NORTH KOREA
North Korea is an independent communist country, but since the break up of the Soviet Union it has lost many of its trading partners and is now very poor. However, the country has a good education system and a high literacy rate. Schooling is free and compulsory for all children for 10 years.

SOUTH KOREA
South Korea is a democratic nation with a thriving electronics and machinery industry. A quarter of the population lives in or near the capital city, Seoul. The Internet developed quickly in South Korea and today almost 90 per cent of the population use it, with the highest Internet connection speed in the world.

The majority of the Chinese population lives in just 15 per cent of the total land area.

MODERN SHANGHAI
China's largest city is Shanghai. More than 23 million people live in this wealthy east-coast port. International trade has transformed Shanghai's skyline, which is now crowded with high-rise buildings and modern shopping malls. The centre of town still has some old western-style buildings that have survived from the days before the revolution.

BEAUTY OF TAIWAN
Taiwan's mountainous countryside is famous for its natural beauty, scenic lakes, and many ornate Buddhist temples. This peaceful environment contrasts sharply with Taiwan's capital city, Taipei, which is one of the fastest growing cities in Asia.

Bicycle factory

CHINESE INDUSTRY
After the revolutionary leader Mao Zedong died in 1976, China's economy opened up. Industry and manufacturing was encouraged and today China plays a big part in the global economy. Many people are moving into cities for better-paid jobs.

Japan

Japan is situated in the north Pacific Ocean off the coast of the Asian continent. It is made up of four main islands and more than 3,000 smaller ones. The Japanese people have a distinctive culture based on traditions built up over thousands of years. They have their own language and script. School children all learn to read and write both in the traditional script and using letters. Social rules in Japan are strict, and respect and politeness are considered very important. Most people bow when greeting one another, for example. Japan is a very modern country, however, with one of the world's most technologically advanced societies. Its economy is based on the development and production of cutting-edge electronics and vehicles, and most families have the latest consumer goods.

EARTHQUAKES
The islands of Japan are situated in an area where four of Earth's tectonic plates meet. This causes frequent earthquakes. Japanese school children are taught how to keep safe during an earthquake by sheltering in a doorway or under a table.

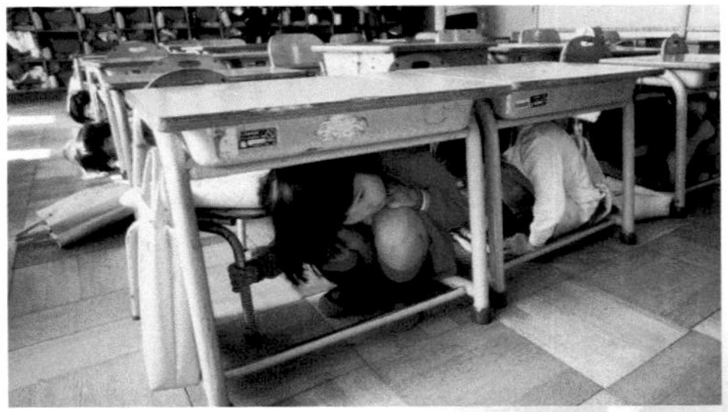

OVERCROWDING
Most of the country's 127 million people live in cities in the flatter, coastal areas. Tokyo and Osaka are very crowded, and homes here are usually very small and are designed to make the most of the limited space.

La Pérouse Strait
Sea of Okhotsk
Ostrov Kunashir
Kuril Islands
Ostrov Shikotan
(Kuril Islands administered by Russian Federation, claimed by Japan)
Rebun-tō
Rishiri-tō
Wakkanai
Nakagawa
Monbetsu
Nayoro
Shibetsu
Shirataki
Abashiri
Shari
Kitami
Bekkai
Nemuro
Asahi-dake 2290m
Asahikawa
Akkeshi
Hokkaidō
Kushiro
Takikawa
Shintoku
Ishikari-wan
Obihiro
Otaru
Ebetsu
Sapporo
Horoshiri-dake 2052m
Chitose
Hiroo
Iwanai
Tomakomai
Noboribetsu
Muroran
Setana
Uchiura-wan
Okushiri-tō
Esashi
Hakodate
Mutsu
Fukushima
Mutsu -wan
Tsugaru-kaikyō
Aomori
Towada
Goshogawara
Hachinohe
Kuroishi
Kuji
Hirosaki
Fudi
Ōdate
Iwate
Miyako
Noshiro
Gojōme
Morioka
Akita
Hanamaki
Honjō
Yokote
Kesennuma
Yuzawa
Shizugawa
Sakata
Shinjō
Ishinomaki
Tsuruoka
Furukawa
0 km 100 200
0 miles 100 200

RELIGIONS OF JAPAN
Many Japanese people follow a mix of the Shinto and Buddhist religions, attending wedding blessings in Shinto shrines and funerals in Buddhist temples. Buddhism originated in India and arrived in Japan in the 6th century, whereas the Shinto faith is native to Japan. Respect for nature is especially important in the Shinto religion. Many natural locations, such as Mount Fuji, are considered sacred.

Mount Fuji, a dormant volcano

Japanese Temple

Traditional and modern dresses

FASHION IN JAPAN
On ordinary days, Japanese people usually wear western-style clothes. Most children have a school uniform. On festival days, such as Children's Day, many people prefer to wear the traditional kimono. Women's kimonos are often made of colourful silk, decorated with beautiful designs.

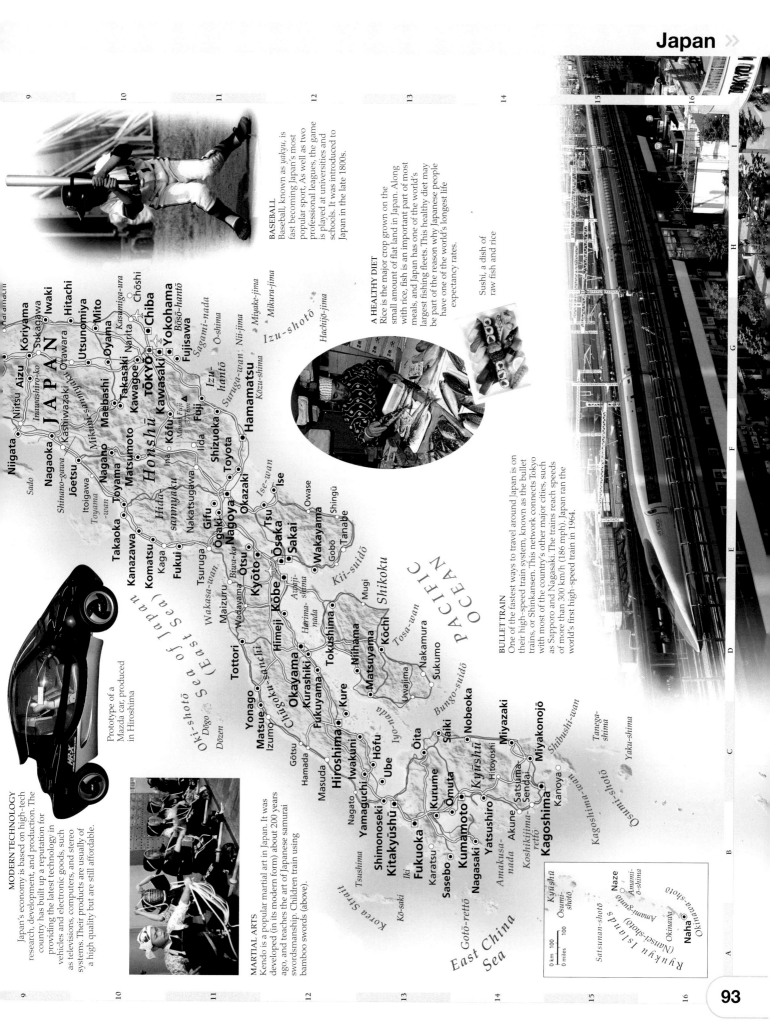

MODERN TECHNOLOGY
Japan's economy is based on high-tech research, development, and production. The country has built up a reputation for providing the latest technology in vehicles and electronic goods, such as televisions, computers, and stereo systems. Their products are usually of a high quality but are still affordable.

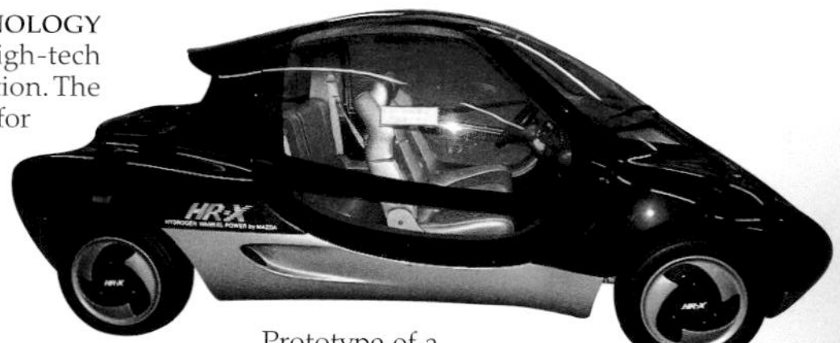

Prototype of a Mazda car, produced in Hiroshima

MARTIAL ARTS
Kendo is a popular martial art in Japan. It was developed (in its modern form) about 200 years ago, and teaches the art of Japanese samurai swordsmanship. Children train using bamboo swords (above).

BASEBALL
Baseball, known as *yakyu*, is fast becoming Japan's most popular sport. As well as two professional leagues, the game is played at universities and schools. It was introduced to Japan in the late 1800s.

A HEALTHY DIET
Rice is the major crop grown on the small amount of flat land in Japan. Along with rice, fish is an important part of most meals, and Japan has one of the world's largest fishing fleets. This healthy diet may be part of the reason why Japanese people have one of the world's longest life expectancy rates.

Sushi, a dish of raw fish and rice

BULLET TRAIN
One of the fastest ways to travel around Japan is on their high-speed train system, known as the bullet trains, or Shinkansen. This network connects Tokyo with most of the country's other major cities, such as Sapporo and Nagasaki. The trains reach speeds of more than 300 km/h (186 mph). Japan ran the world's first high-speed train in 1964.

Mainland SE Asia

THE PENINSULA of Southeast Asia lies directly to the south of India and China, between the Pacific and Indian Oceans. It is made up of Myanmar (Burma), Thailand, Vietnam, Cambodia, and Laos. Over thousands of years, the influence of people from nearby India, China, and Arabian countries has helped to give this region a diverse mix of cultures and religions. Much of the land here is mountainous, with half the region covered in forest. Most people live in coastal or lowland regions, where they can grow crops such as rice, raise cattle, and catch fish. In recent years, the electronics industry has also become an important part of southeast Asian economies, especially in Thailand.

ORPHANS IN CAMBODIA
A high number of Cambodian children live in orphanages, some because they have lost their parents, others due to poverty.

Cambodian orphanage

GROWING RICE
Rice is the most important crop in Southeast Asia. It grows well in wet lowland areas, such as the Mekong River delta in Vietnam, where the plants can be grown in paddy fields. Most rice is planted and harvested by women.

RURAL LIVING
Most people in Southeast Asia live in rural areas rather than cities, and farming is the most common occupation. The steep, mountainous regions are often unsuitable for growing crops or raising cattle, however, and many farming communities are based in the fertile river valleys and deltas. There are more than 200 villages on and around this lake (right) in Myanmar.

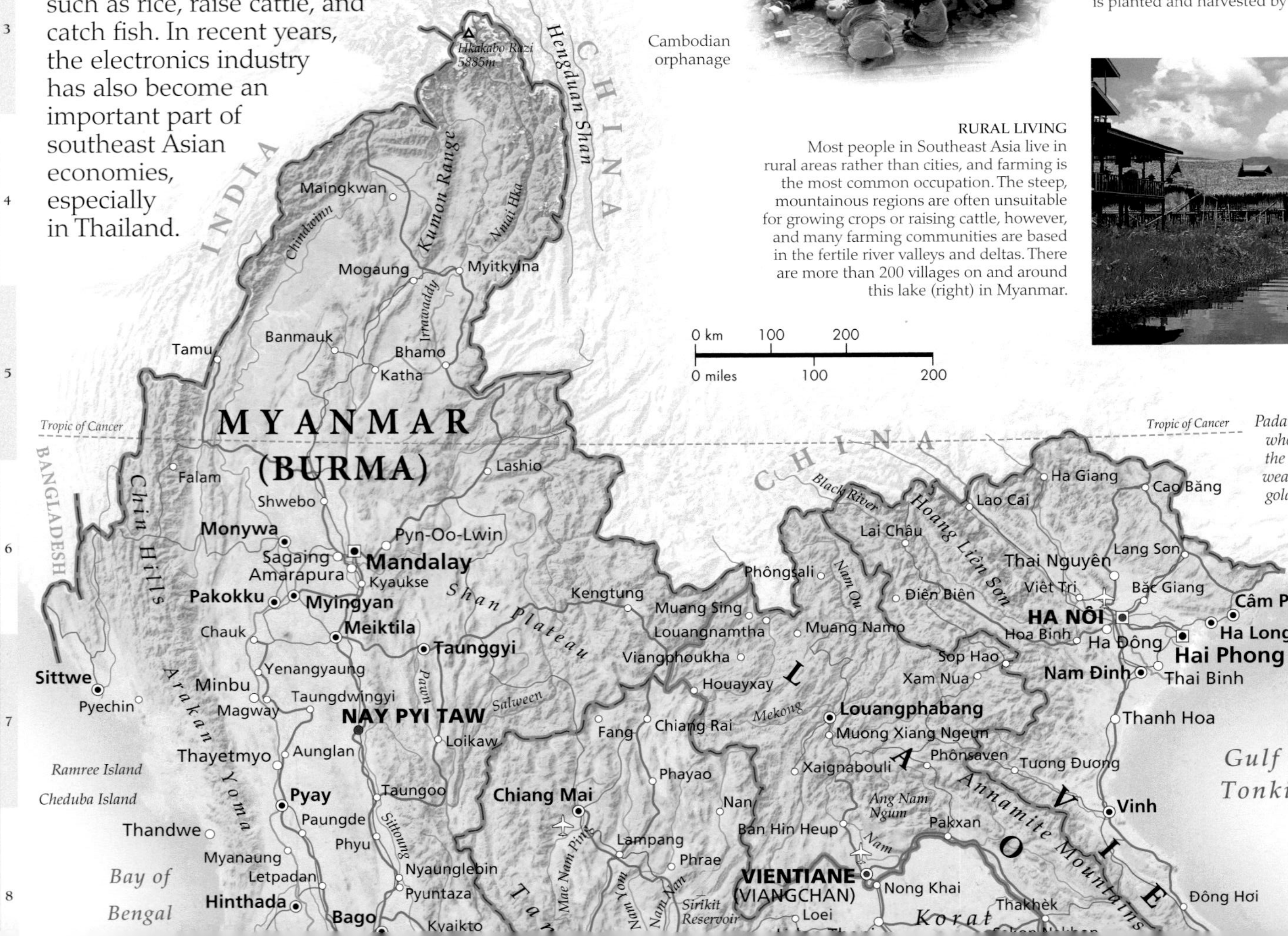

B
C
D
E
F
G
I
1
2
3
4
5
6
7
8
INDIA
CHINA
Hkakabo Razi 5885m
Hengduan Shan
Maingkwan
Kumon Range
Nmai Hka
Chindwinn
Mogaung
Myitkyina
Irrawaddy
Banmauk
Bhamo
Katha
Tamu
0 km 100 200
0 miles 100 200
Tropic of Cancer
BANGLADESH
MYANMAR (BURMA)
Lashio
Falam
Chin Hills
Shwebo
Monywa
Sagaing
Amarapura
Pyn-Oo-Lwin
Mandalay
Kyaukse
Pakokku
Myingyan
Shan Plateau
Chauk
Meiktila
Taunggyi
Kengtung
Muang Sing
Louangnamtha
Viangphoukha
Houayxay
Phôngsali
Nam Ou
Muang Namo
Black River
Lai Châu
Hoang Liên Son
Điện Biên
Lao Cai
Ha Giang
Cao Băng
Lang Sơn
Thai Nguyên
Viêt Tri
Băc Giang
HA NÔI
Hoa Binh
Ha Đông
Câm Pha
Ha Long
Hai Phong
Thai Binh
Nam Đinh
Sop Hao
Xam Nua
Thanh Hoa
Sittwe
Pyechin
Arakan Yoma
Minbu
Magway
Yenangyaung
Taungdwingyi
NAY PYI TAW
Salween
Pawn
Loikaw
Thayetmyo
Aunglan
Ramree Island
Cheduba Island
Pyay
Paungde
Taungoo
Sittoung
Phyu
Thandwe
Myanaung
Letpadan
Hinthada
Bago
Nyaunglebin
Pyuntaza
Kyaikto
Bay of Bengal
Fang
Chiang Rai
Mekong
Louangphabang
Muong Xiang Ngeum
Phônsaven
Tuong Đuong
Phayao
Chiang Mai
Mae Nam Ping
Lampang
Nam Yom
Nam Nan
Phrae
Nan
Sirikit Reservoir
Xaignabouli
LAOS
Ang Nam Ngum
Ban Hin Heup
Pakxan
VIENTIANE (VIANGCHAN)
Nong Khai
Loei
Thakhek
Annamite Mountains
VIETNAM
Vinh
Gulf of Tonkin
Đông Hơi
Korat

Padaung women, who are part of the Karen tribe, wear distinctive gold neck rings.

KAREN TRIBE
There are 600,000 tribespeople living in the northeastern hills of Thailand. The Karen are the largest hill tribe. They originated from Myanmar, but moved into Thailand to escape political unrest.

FLOATING MARKET
The capital of Thailand, Bangkok, is a busy, crowded city with more than 9 million inhabitants. The city was built on an island in the river, and has many canals. Boats, known as sampans, (above) act as floating markets from which traders sell fresh fruit and vegetables.

A new type of gibbon, named after Star Wars' Luke Skywalker, was discovered in the mountains between Myanmar and China in 2017.

THAI BEACHES
Tourism is a major industry for Thailand. Popular destinations include the country's lively capital, Bangkok, and the beautiful island beach resorts (below). Phuket, Thailand's largest island, is often referred to as the "Pearl of the South".

ANGKOR
The impressive temple complex of Angkor in Cambodia attracts visitors interested in its history and architecture. This combination of temples and palaces was built in 1113 CE by the Khmer king Suryavarman II. The buildings, such as Angkor Wat, below, are made of stone and brick and are decorated with relief sculptures showing mythical scenes of Hindu gods and great royal processions. The complex was uncovered in 1861 by French naturalist Henri Mouhot, following stories of a "lost city" in the jungle.

Angkor Wat

MONASTIC LIFE
The main religion in mainland Southeast Asia is Buddhism. Nearly all Thai villages have their own temple, or wat, which is the centre of village life. Most young men spend some time in a monastery, where they have few possessions and spend much of their time in meditation.

Maritime SE Asia

TO THE SOUTH OF THE ASIAN mainland lies maritime Southeast Asia. It includes Malaysia, Indonesia, East Timor, Singapore, and the Philippines. Part of Malaysia is connected to the mainland, but the rest of the region is made up of more than 20,000 islands that stretch across the Pacific and Indian Oceans. Lying near the Equator, the climate is mostly hot, wet, and humid. Most of the larger islands are mountainous and covered in dense forest, and many people live in villages near rivers or on the coast. Like the rest of Southeast Asia, the population is made up of people from many different cultural backgrounds speaking hundreds of different languages. The most common religion is Islam, except in the Philippines, where most people are Roman Catholic.

GREAT APES
The orangutans are great apes that live only in Borneo and the northern corner of Sumatra. They spend most of their time in the trees, even building tree-top nests in which to sleep. Sadly, the orangutan is endangered because of deforestation.

Ubadiah Mosque, Malaysia

PEOPLE OF MALAYSIA
Ethnic Malaysians make up 50 per cent of the population and are known as bumiputera, meaning "sons of the soil". Most Malaysians are Muslim. Ethnic Chinese form 23 per cent of the population.

Sultan of Brunei

THE SULTAN OF BRUNEI
Brunei is ruled by a sultan who lives in the world's largest palace. The sultan is one of the wealthiest men in the world.

Andaman Sea
THAILAND
South China Sea
Strait of Malacca
Banda Aceh
Sigli
Langsa
Meulaboh
Medan
Pulau Simeulue
Tebingtinggi
Pematangsiantar
Kepulauan Banyak
Sibolga
Danau Toba
Pulau Nias
Panyabungan
Equator
George Town
Butterworth
Pulau Pinang
Taiping
Ipoh
Kota Bharu
Kuala Terengganu
Dungun
Kuala Lipis
Cukai
Kuantan
Klang
KUALA LUMPUR
PUTRAJAYA
Seremban
Melaka
Muar
Keluang
Batu Pahat
Johor Bahru
SINGAPORE
Kepulauan Natuna
M A L A Y S I A
Kota Kinabalu
BANDAR SERI BEGAWAN
BRUNEI
Miri
Bintulu
Banjaran Tamabo
Selat Serasan
Sibu
Batang Rajang
Sarawak
Kuching
Sri Aman
Singkawang
Sidas
Pontianak
Sungai Kapuas
Pegunungan Muller
Borneo
Kalimantan
Sungai Barito
Sampit
Kandangan
Banjarmasin
Balikpapan
Pekanbaru
Solok
Rengat
Kepulauan Lingga
Padang
Pulau Siberut
Kepulauan Mentawai
Batang Hari
Kualatungkal
Jambi
Pangkalpinang
Bangka
Selat Karimata
Sungaipenuh
Sumatra (Sumatera)
Palembang
Pegunungan Barisan
Lahat
Bengkulu
INDIAN OCEAN
I N D
Pulau Belitung
Kotabumi
Bandar Lampung
Cirebon
JAKARTA
Serang
Bogor
Sukabumi
Bandung
Selat Sunda
Tasikmalaya
Cilacap
Magelang
Yogyakarta
Surakarta
Tegal
Pekalongan
Semarang
Kudus
Java (Jawa)
Java Sea
Pulau Madura
Surabaya
Probolinggo
Jember
Malang
Kediri
Madiun
Mataram

SINGAPORE
As the financial and industrial centre of Southeast Asia, Singapore is one of the wealthiest countries in this region. It has a thriving high-tech industry and a high standard of living. There are strictly enforced laws forbidding littering and other small crimes. The death penalty is imposed for drug smuggling. The government also controls the press and restricts the Internet.

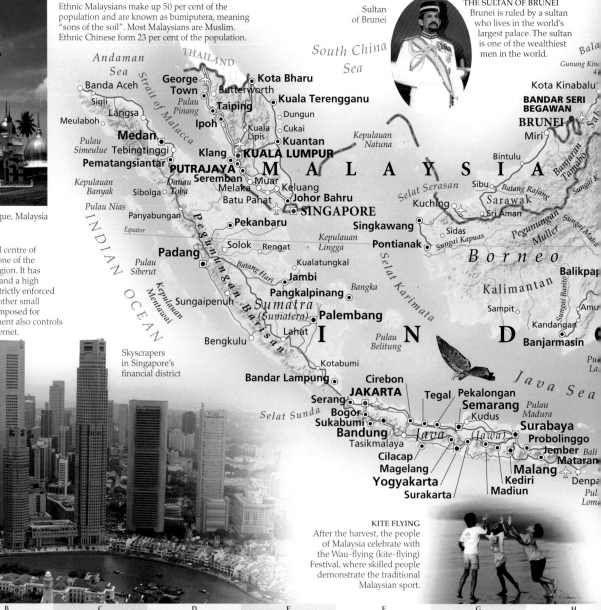

Skyscrapers in Singapore's financial district

KITE FLYING
After the harvest, the people of Malaysia celebrate with the Wau-flying (kite-flying) Festival, where skilled people demonstrate the traditional Malaysian sport.

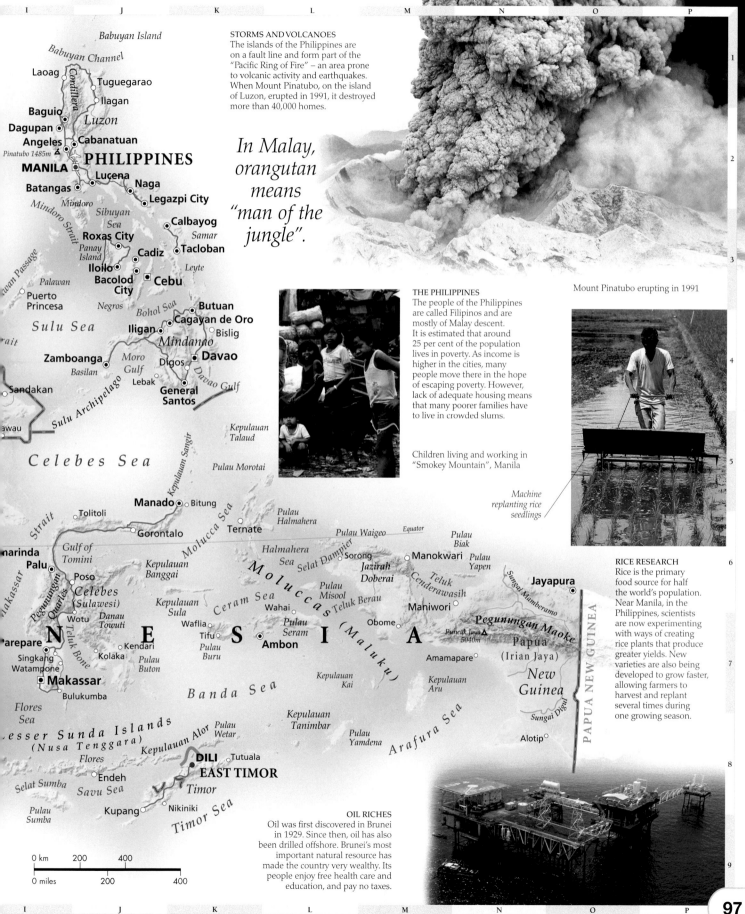

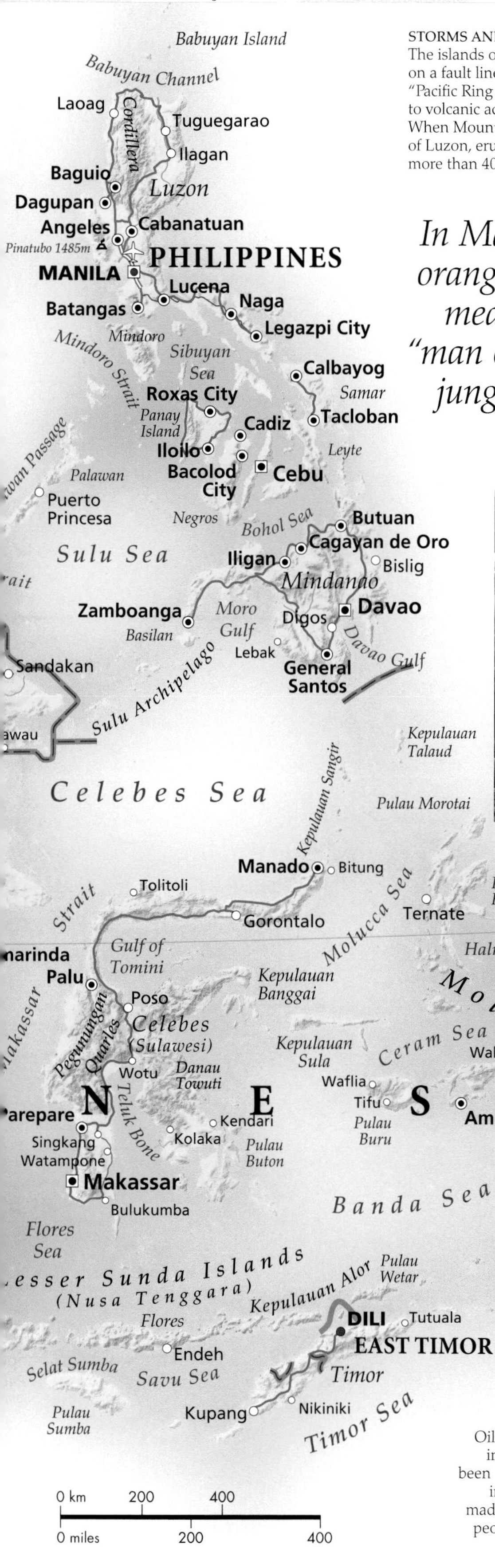
I J K L M N O P
1 2 3 4 5 6 7 8 9
Babuyan Island
Babuyan Channel
Laoag
Tuguegarao
Cordillera
Ilagan
Baguio
Luzon
Dagupan
Angeles
Cabanatuan
Pinatubo 1485m
PHILIPPINES
MANILA
Lucena
Batangas
Naga
Legazpi City
Mindoro
Mindoro Strait
Sibuyan Sea
Calbayog
Samar
Roxas City
Panay Island
Cadiz
Tacloban
Iloilo
Leyte
Bacolod City
Cebu
Palawan
Puerto Princesa
Negros
Bohol Sea
Butuan
Cagayan de Oro
Sulu Sea
Iligan
Bislig
Mindanao
Zamboanga
Moro Gulf
Digos
Davao
Basilan
Davao Gulf
Sandakan
Lebak
General Santos
Sulu Archipelago
Kepulauan Talaud
Celebes Sea
Kepulauan Sangir
Pulau Morotai
Manado
Bitung
Tolitoli
Strait
Gorontalo
Molucca Sea
Ternate
Pulau Halmahera
Pulau Waigeo
Equator
Pulau Biak
Gulf of Tomini
Halmahera Sea
Selat Dampier
Sorong
Manokwari
Pulau Yapen
Palu
Kepulauan Banggai
Jazirah Doberai
Teluk Cenderawasih
Sungai Mamberamo
Jayapura
Poso
Moluccas (Maluku)
Pulau Misool
Pegunungan Quarles
Celebes (Sulawesi)
Kepulauan Sula
Ceram Sea
Teluk Berau
Maniwori
Wahai
Wotu
Danau Towuti
Waflia
Pulau Seram
Obome
Pegunungan Maoke
Puncak Jaya 5040m
Teluk Bone
Tifu
Ambon
Papua (Irian Jaya)
Parepare
Kendari
Pulau Buru
Singkang
Kolaka
Pulau Buton
Amamapare
Watampone
Makassar
Kepulauan Kai
Kepulauan Aru
New Guinea
Bulukumba
Banda Sea
Flores Sea
Kepulauan Tanimbar
Sungai Digul
PAPUA NEW GUINEA
Lesser Sunda Islands (Nusa Tenggara)
Pulau Wetar
Kepulauan Alor
Pulau Yamdena
Arafura Sea
Alotip
Flores
DILI
Tutuala
EAST TIMOR
Endeh
Selat Sumba
Savu Sea
Timor
Pulau Sumba
Kupang
Nikiniki
Timor Sea
0 km 200 400
0 miles 200 400

STORMS AND VOLCANOES
The islands of the Philippines are on a fault line and form part of the "Pacific Ring of Fire" – an area prone to volcanic activity and earthquakes. When Mount Pinatubo, on the island of Luzon, erupted in 1991, it destroyed more than 40,000 homes.

In Malay, orangutan means "man of the jungle".

Mount Pinatubo erupting in 1991

Children living and working in "Smokey Mountain", Manila

THE PHILIPPINES
The people of the Philippines are called Filipinos and are mostly of Malay descent. It is estimated that around 25 per cent of the population lives in poverty. As income is higher in the cities, many people move there in the hope of escaping poverty. However, lack of adequate housing means that many poorer families have to live in crowded slums.

Machine replanting rice seedlings

RICE RESEARCH
Rice is the primary food source for half the world's population. Near Manila, in the Philippines, scientists are now experimenting with ways of creating rice plants that produce greater yields. New varieties are also being developed to grow faster, allowing farmers to harvest and replant several times during one growing season.

OIL RICHES
Oil was first discovered in Brunei in 1929. Since then, oil has also been drilled offshore. Brunei's most important natural resource has made the country very wealthy. Its people enjoy free health care and education, and pay no taxes.

Indian Ocean

THE THIRD LARGEST ocean in the world, the Indian Ocean is bounded by Africa, Asia, Australasia, and the Southern Ocean. The ocean contains some 5,000 islands. Madagascar and Sri Lanka are large, but most of the islands are small and ringed by coral reefs. The people of the Maldives have very mixed origins, incorporating Indian, Sinhalese, Arab, and African heritage, while two-thirds of those living on Mauritius are Indian immigrants and their descendents. Altogether, about one-fifth of the world's population live on this ocean's warm shores. Those along the northern coasts are often threatened by monsoon rain and tropical storms, which can cause severe flooding.

THE MALDIVES
The Maldives is a low-lying archipelago of 1,190 small, coral islands, of which 200 are inhabited. The main industries are fishing – still carried out by traditional pole and line methods to conserve stocks – and tourism. Holiday resorts are on separate islands to those inhabited by the locals, so as not to disturb the Maldive peoples' traditional Muslim lifestyles.

CORAL ISLANDS
Coral is a living organism formed in warm water by tiny sea creatures known as polyps. These creatures build limestone skeletons around themselves, which accumulate over thousands of years. As sea levels change, this coral can be exposed as low-lying islands or submerged as reefs.

Market on the largest Seychelles island, Mahé

THE SEYCHELLES
The Seychelles consists of around 155 islands – some are coral islands while others are mountainous and made of granite. Most Seychellois people are Creoles – people of mixed African, Asian, and European ancestry. There are also small Chinese and Indian communities.

ENVIRONMENT
Beautiful shells are for sale on this beach in South Africa. If the trader only collects empty shells, no harm is done, but in many parts of the world, dealers hunt live shellfish, sea turtles, and rare species of starfish and sea urchins. Nations such as the Maldives take great care to protect their environment.

LIMITED TOURISM
The tropical climate, sandy beaches, beautiful coral reefs, and abundant marine life make both the Seychelles and the Maldives ideal tourist destinations. These same features also make them extremely attractive to scuba divers. However, the fragile environment of both island nations means that they have deliberately tried to make them exclusive, attracting only limited numbers of wealthy visitors, instead of pursuing mass tourism.

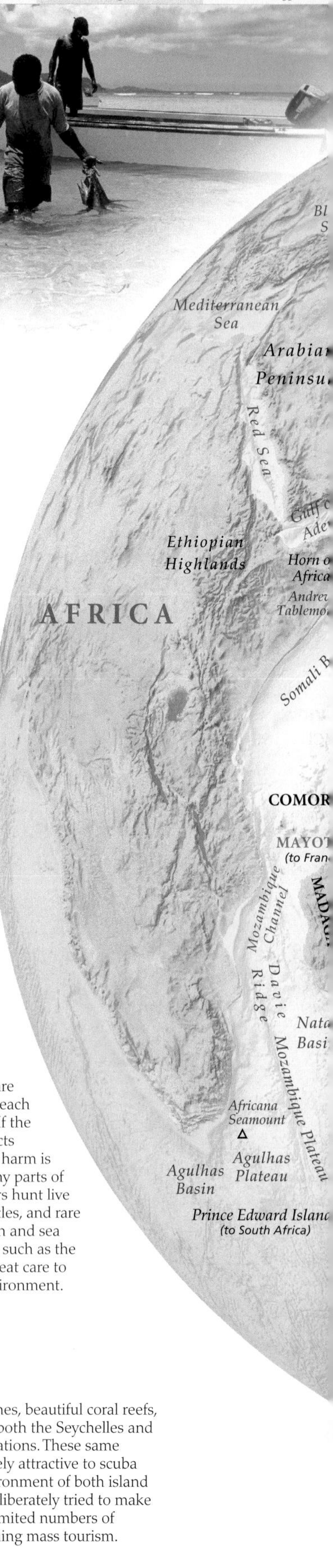
Mediterranean Sea
Red Sea
Ethiopian Highlands
AFRICA
COMOR
MAYOT
Mozambique Channel
Davie Ridge
Mozambique Plateau
Africana Seamount
Agulhas Plateau
Agulhas Basin
Prince Edward Islanc
(to South Africa)

I
J
K
L
M
N
O
P
1
2
3
4
5
6
7
8
Aral Sea
Caspian Sea
Tien Shan
Gobi
ASIA
Himalayas
Iranian Plateau
Yellow Sea
Gulf of Oman
Indus Fan
Murray Ridge
Owen Fracture Zone
Arabian Sea
Arabian Basin
Lakshadweep Islands (to India)
Ganges Fan
Bay of Bengal
Andaman Islands (to India)
SRI LANKA
Nicobar Islands (to India)
PACIFIC OCEAN
Gulf of Thailand
Andaman Sea
South China Sea
Carlsberg Ridge
MALDIVES
MALE'
Chagos-Laccadive Plateau
Chagos Trench
Ceylon Plain
Mid-Indian Ridge
Mid-Indian Basin
Ninetyeast Ridge
Kepulauan Mentawai
Sumatra
Borneo
East Indies
VICTORIA
BRITISH INDIAN OCEAN TERRITORY (to UK)
Cocos Basin
Investigator Ridge
Java Sea
Celebes
Java
Java Trench
CHRISTMAS ISLAND (to Australia)
COCOS ISLANDS (to Australia)
INDIAN OCEAN
North Australian Basin
Argo Fracture Zone
Egeria Fracture Zone
Wharton Basin
Exmouth Plateau
MAURITIUS
RÉUNION (to France)
Cuvier Plateau
Southwest Indian Ridge
East Indiaman Ridge
AUSTRALASIA & OCEANIA
Broken Ridge
Perth Basin
Naturaliste Plateau
Diamantina Fracture Zone
Crozet Basin
Amsterdam Island
St Paul Island
Southeast Indian Ridge
FRENCH SOUTHERN & ANTARCTIC LANDS (to France)
Crozet Islands
Kerguelen Plateau
Kerguelen
HEARD & MCDONALD ISLANDS (to Australia)
Lena Tablemount
Banzare Seamounts
South Indian Basin
Enderby Plain
SOUTHERN OCEAN
ANTARCTICA

SALT FROM THE SEA

Salt is essential for life and has been traded here for centuries. People around the Indian Ocean make salt by flooding large, flat areas with sea water. As the water evaporates in the sun, salt crystals are left behind. These are then collected, drained, and cleaned.

18
A

Collecting salt in the Maldives

MANGROVES

A lot of the coast in the tropical part of the Indian Ocean is fringed with mangrove forests. These amazing trees live in brackish water and have long roots that trap sediment and protect the coast from erosion. Without these trees, settlements and land along the coast are in danger of being damaged by high tides and strong storms.

The moutia dance of the Seychelles was brought to the islands by African slaves in the 1700s.

INTERNATIONAL SEAWAYS

The Indian Ocean contains some of the busiest and most important shipping routes in the world. Smaller ships sail to and from the Mediterranean Sea and the ports of Europe and America through the Red Sea and Suez Canal, while larger freighters and oil tankers from the Persian Gulf sail around the Cape of Good Hope at the southern tip of Africa.

WILHELMSEN LINES

Norwegian freighter

AUSTRALASIA & OCEANIA

Unknown to the outside world before the 17th century, Australia is a still a sparsely inhabited land where most people live in cities. At its heart is a great arid desert, in stark contrast to the islands of Oceania where all life revolves around the glittering ocean. The 3,000 named islands are grouped into nations, listed below in order of land area.

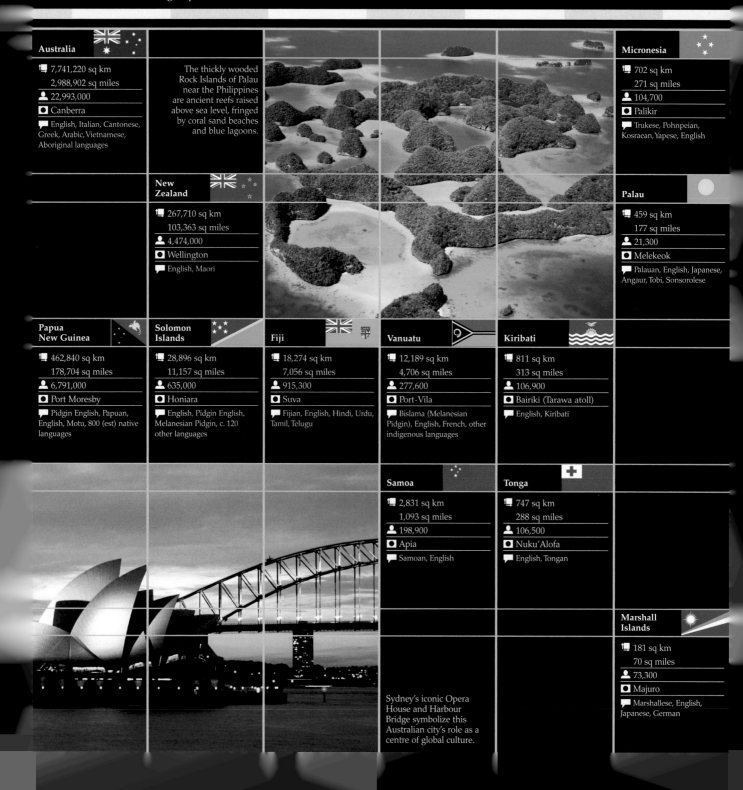

Australia

- 7,741,220 sq km
  2,988,902 sq miles
- 22,993,000
- Canberra
- English, Italian, Cantonese, Greek, Arabic, Vietnamese, Aboriginal languages

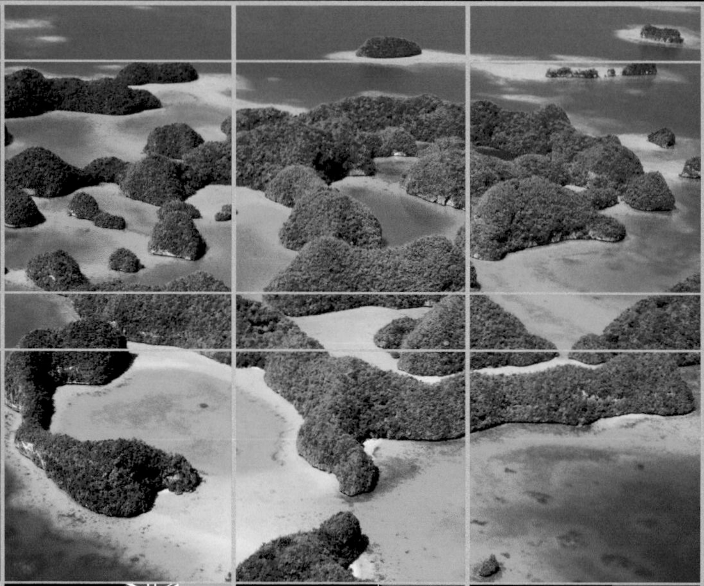

The thickly wooded Rock Islands of Palau near the Philippines are ancient reefs raised above sea level, fringed by coral sand beaches and blue lagoons.

Micronesia

- 702 sq km
  271 sq miles
- 104,700
- Palikir
- Trukese, Pohnpeian, Kosraean, Yapese, English

New Zealand

- 267,710 sq km
  103,363 sq miles
- 4,474,000
- Wellington
- English, Maori

Palau

- 459 sq km
  177 sq miles
- 21,300
- Melekeok
- Palauan, English, Japanese, Angaur, Tobi, Sonsorolese

Papua New Guinea

- 462,840 sq km
  178,704 sq miles
- 6,791,000
- Port Moresby
- Pidgin English, Papuan, English, Motu, 800 (est) native languages

Solomon Islands

- 28,896 sq km
  11,157 sq miles
- 635,000
- Honiara
- English, Pidgin English, Melanesian Pidgin, c. 120 other languages

Fiji

- 18,274 sq km
  7,056 sq miles
- 915,300
- Suva
- Fijian, English, Hindi, Urdu, Tamil, Telugu

Vanuatu

- 12,189 sq km
  4,706 sq miles
- 277,600
- Port-Vila
- Bislama (Melanesian Pidgin), English, French, other indigenous languages

Kiribati

- 811 sq km
  313 sq miles
- 106,900
- Bairiki (Tarawa atoll)
- English, Kiribati

Samoa

- 2,831 sq km
  1,093 sq miles
- 198,900
- Apia
- Samoan, English

Tonga

- 747 sq km
  288 sq miles
- 106,500
- Nuku'Alofa
- English, Tongan

Sydney's iconic Opera House and Harbour Bridge symbolize this Australian city's role as a centre of global culture.

Marshall Islands

- 181 sq km
  70 sq miles
- 73,300
- Majuro
- Marshallese, English, Japanese, German

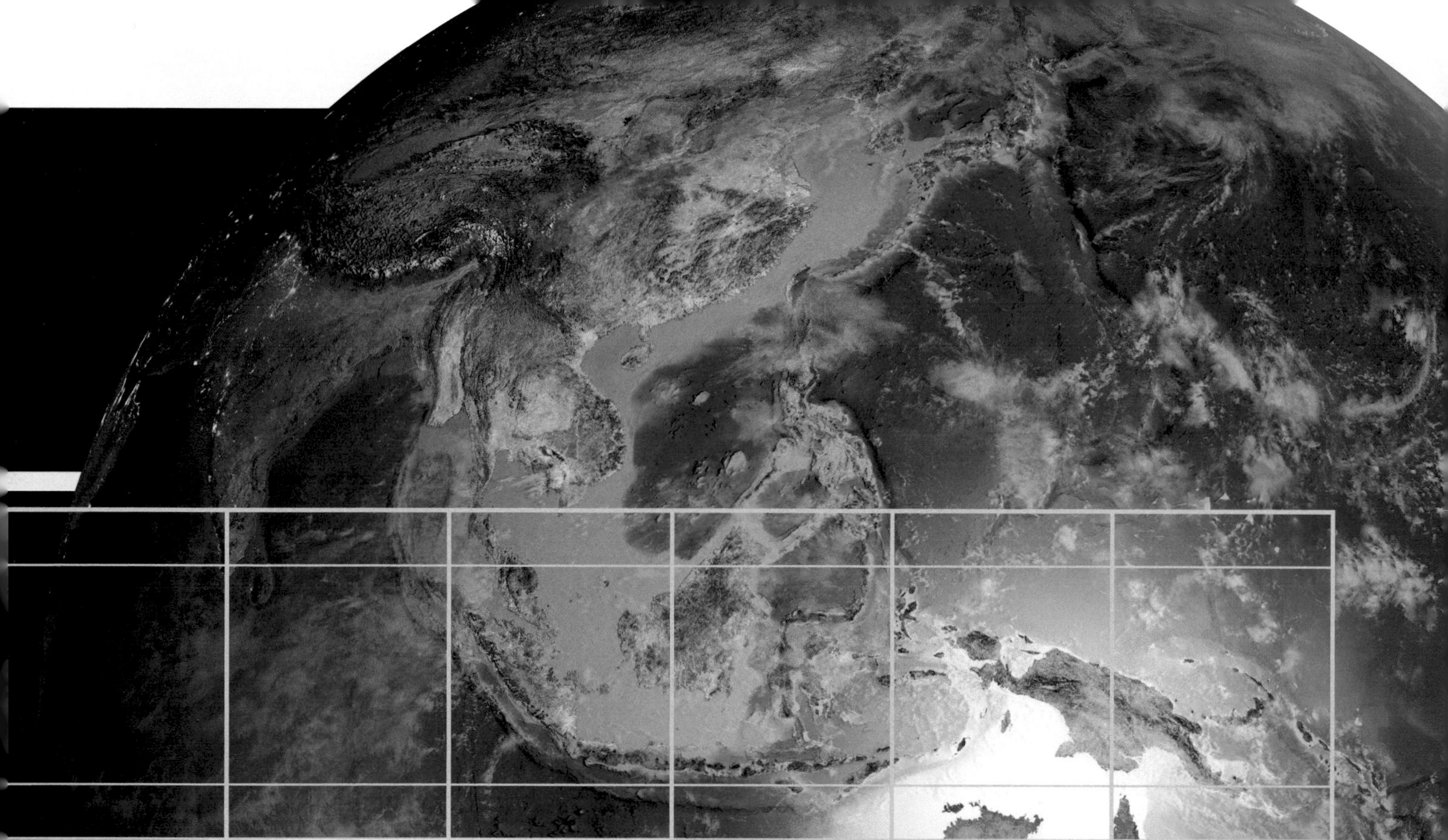

The ancestors of today's Pacific Islanders reached their islands by crossing the ocean in giant canoes. Many islanders still rely on the sea for a living.

Tuvalu

- 26 sq km
  10 sq miles
- 11,000
- Fongafale (Funafuti Atol)
- Tuvaluan, Kiribati, English

Nauru

- 21 sq km
  8 sq miles
- 9,600
- None
- Nauruan, Kiribati, Chinese, Tuvaluan, English

The colourfully named Champagne Pool is one of many hot springs in Rotorua, New Zealand – one of the most volcanically active countries in the world.

SW Pacific

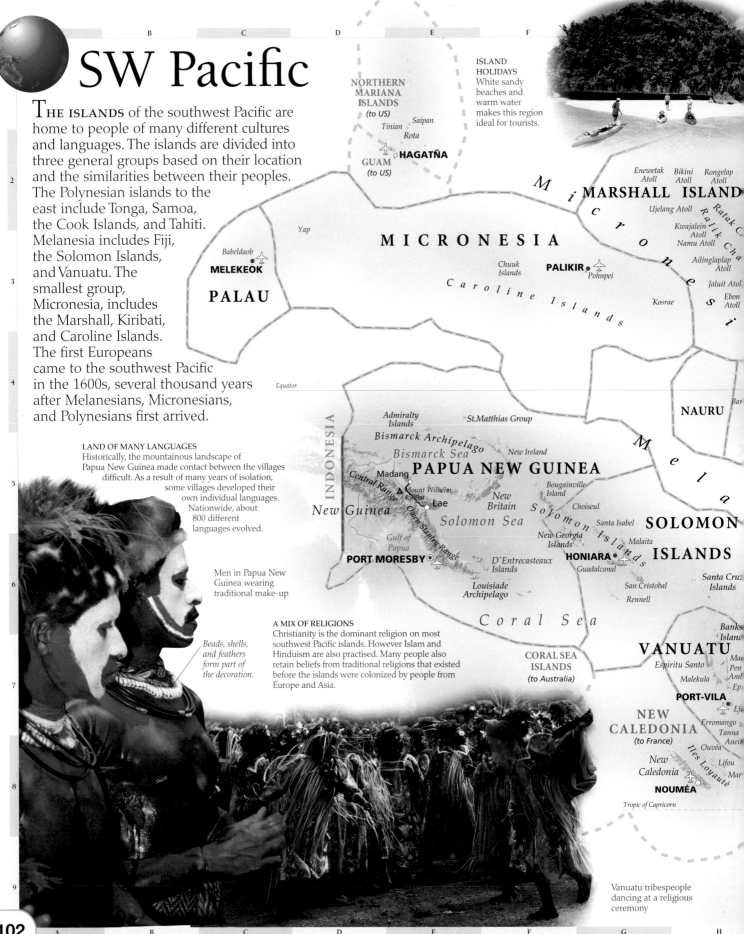

THE ISLANDS of the southwest Pacific are home to people of many different cultures and languages. The islands are divided into three general groups based on their location and the similarities between their peoples. The Polynesian islands to the east include Tonga, Samoa, the Cook Islands, and Tahiti. Melanesia includes Fiji, the Solomon Islands, and Vanuatu. The smallest group, Micronesia, includes the Marshall, Kiribati, and Caroline Islands. The first Europeans came to the southwest Pacific in the 1600s, several thousand years after Melanesians, Micronesians, and Polynesians first arrived.

ISLAND HOLIDAYS
White sandy beaches and warm water makes this region ideal for tourists.

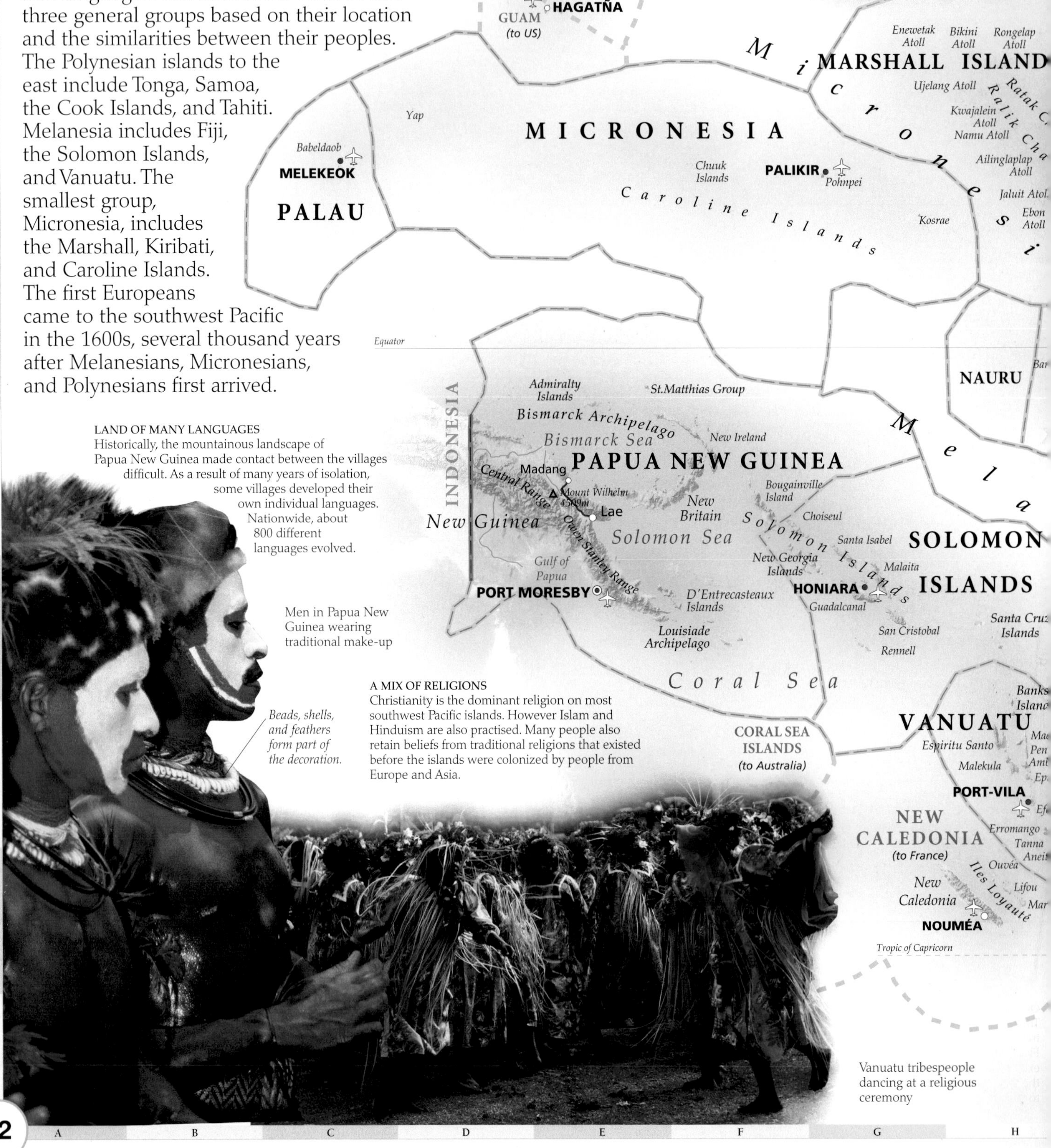
NORTHERN MARIANA ISLANDS
(to US)
Tinian
Saipan
Rota
HAGATÑA
GUAM
(to US)
Micronesia
MARSHALL ISLAND
Enewetak Atoll
Bikini Atoll
Rongelap Atoll
Ujelang Atoll
Kwajalein Atoll
Namu Atoll
Ailinglaplap Atoll
Jaluit Atol
Ebon Atoll
Ratak C
Ralik Cha
Yap
MICRONESIA
Babeldaob
MELEKEOK
PALAU
Chuuk Islands
PALIKIR
Pohnpei
Kosrae
Caroline Islands
Equator
NAURU
INDONESIA
Admiralty Islands
St.Matthias Group
Bismarck Archipelago
Bismarck Sea
New Ireland
Melanesia
Madang
PAPUA NEW GUINEA
Central Range
Mount Wilhelm 4,509m
Lae
New Britain
Bougainville Island
Choiseul
New Guinea
Owen Stanley Range
Solomon Sea
Solomon Islands
Santa Isabel
SOLOMON ISLANDS
Gulf of Papua
New Georgia Islands
Malaita
PORT MORESBY
HONIARA
D'Entrecasteaux Islands
Guadalcanal
Santa Cruz Islands
San Cristobal
Louisiade Archipelago
Rennell
Coral Sea
Banks Island
CORAL SEA ISLANDS
(to Australia)
VANUATU
Espiritu Santo
Malekula
PORT-VILA
NEW CALEDONIA
(to France)
Erromango
Tanna
Ouvéa
Iles Loyauté
Lifou
New Caledonia
NOUMÉA
Tropic of Capricorn

LAND OF MANY LANGUAGES
Historically, the mountainous landscape of Papua New Guinea made contact between the villages difficult. As a result of many years of isolation, some villages developed their own individual languages. Nationwide, about 800 different languages evolved.

Men in Papua New Guinea wearing traditional make-up

Beads, shells, and feathers form part of the decoration.

A MIX OF RELIGIONS
Christianity is the dominant religion on most southwest Pacific islands. However Islam and Hinduism are also practised. Many people also retain beliefs from traditional religions that existed before the islands were colonized by people from Europe and Asia.

Vanuatu tribespeople dancing at a religious ceremony

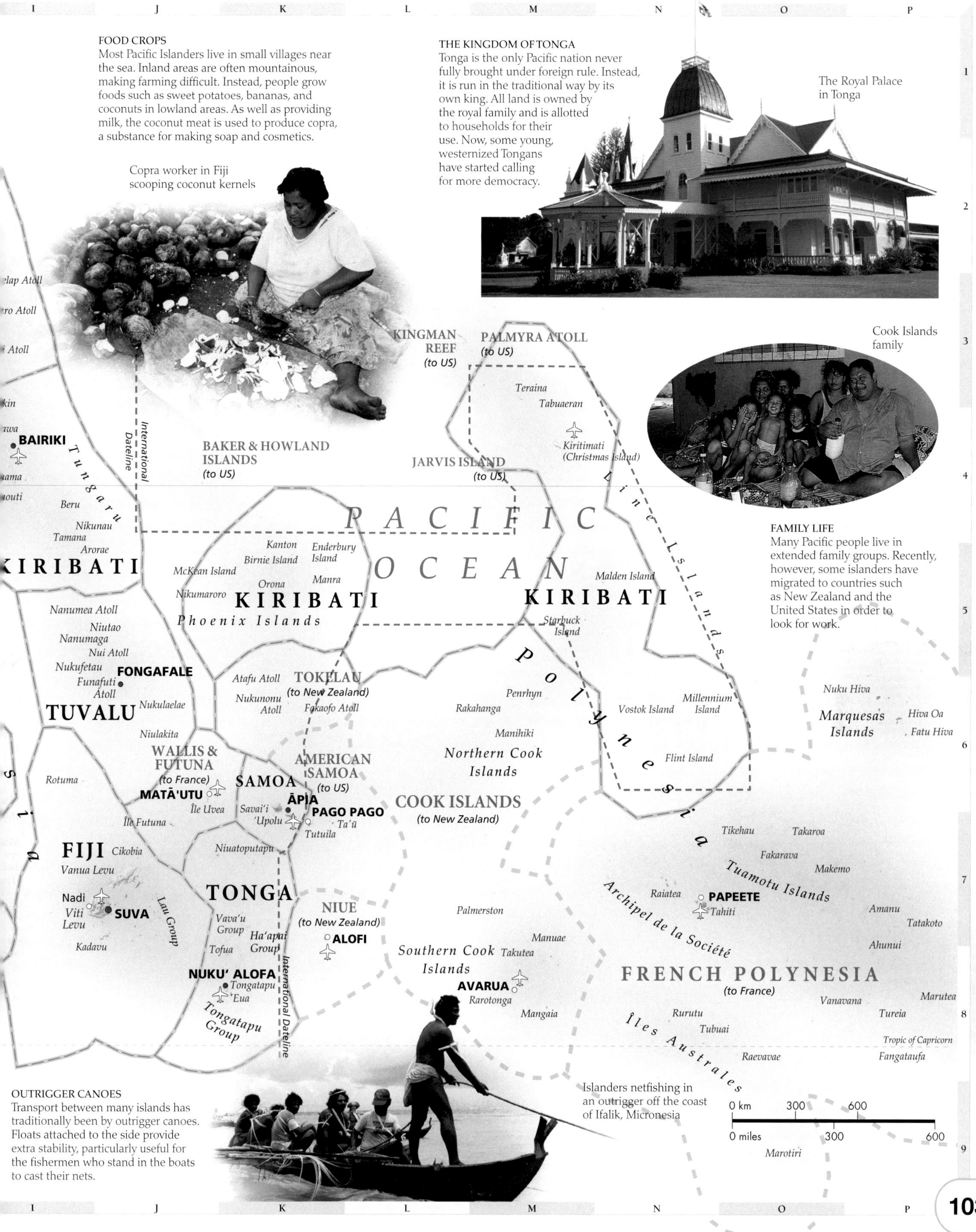
I
J
K
L
M
N
O
P
1
2
3
4
5
6
7
8
9
PACIFIC OCEAN
KINGMAN REEF (to US)
PALMYRA ATOLL (to US)
Teraina
Tabuaeran
Kiritimati (Christmas Island)
BAKER & HOWLAND ISLANDS (to US)
JARVIS ISLAND (to US)
BAIRIKI
Tungaru
Beru
Nikunau
Tamana
Arorae
KIRIBATI
International Dateline
Kanton
Enderbury Island
Birnie Island
McKean Island
Orona
Manra
Nikumaroro
KIRIBATI
Phoenix Islands
Malden Island
KIRIBATI
Line Islands
Starbuck Island
Nanumea Atoll
Niutao
Nanumaga
Nui Atoll
Nukufetau
FONGAFALE
Funafuti Atoll
TUVALU
Nukulaelae
Niulakita
Atafu Atoll
TOKELAU (to New Zealand)
Nukunonu Atoll
Fakaofo Atoll
Penrhyn
Rakahanga
Manihiki
Vostok Island
Millennium Island
Flint Island
Nuku Hiva
Marquesas Islands
Hiva Oa
Fatu Hiva
Polynesia
WALLIS & FUTUNA (to France)
MATĀ'UTU
Île Uvea
Île Futuna
Rotuma
SAMOA
Savai'i
'Upolu
ĀPIA
AMERICAN SAMOA (to US)
PAGO PAGO
Ta'ū
Tutuila
Northern Cook Islands
COOK ISLANDS (to New Zealand)
Tikehau
Takaroa
Fakarava
Makemo
Tuamotu Islands
FIJI
Cikobia
Vanua Levu
Nadi
Viti Levu
SUVA
Kadavu
Lau Group
Niuatoputapu
TONGA
Vava'u Group
Ha'apai Group
Tofua
NUKU' ALOFA
Tongatapu
'Eua
Tongatapu Group
International Dateline
NIUE (to New Zealand)
ALOFI
Palmerston
Manuae
Takutea
Southern Cook Islands
AVARUA
Rarotonga
Mangaia
Raiatea
PAPEETE
Tahiti
Archipel de la Société
Amanu
Tatakoto
Ahunui
FRENCH POLYNESIA (to France)
Vanavana
Marutea
Tureia
Rurutu
Tubuai
Îles Australes
Raevavae
Tropic of Capricorn
Fangataufa
0 km 300 600
0 miles 300 600
Marotiri

FOOD CROPS

Most Pacific Islanders live in small villages near the sea. Inland areas are often mountainous, making farming difficult. Instead, people grow foods such as sweet potatoes, bananas, and coconuts in lowland areas. As well as providing milk, the coconut meat is used to produce copra, a substance for making soap and cosmetics.

Copra worker in Fiji scooping coconut kernels

THE KINGDOM OF TONGA

Tonga is the only Pacific nation never fully brought under foreign rule. Instead, it is run in the traditional way by its own king. All land is owned by the royal family and is allotted to households for their use. Now, some young, westernized Tongans have started calling for more democracy.

The Royal Palace in Tonga

Cook Islands family

FAMILY LIFE

Many Pacific people live in extended family groups. Recently, however, some islanders have migrated to countries such as New Zealand and the United States in order to look for work.

OUTRIGGER CANOES

Transport between many islands has traditionally been by outrigger canoes. Floats attached to the side provide extra stability, particularly useful for the fishermen who stand in the boats to cast their nets.

Islanders netfishing in an outrigger off the coast of Ifalik, Micronesia

Australia

A HUGE, GENERALLY FLAT COUNTRY, Australia has relatively few inhabitants. This is mainly because most of the land is hot, semi-arid desert – known as the outback – unsuitable for towns or farms. In places where there is some vegetation, or the land has been irrigated, sheep and cattle are grazed. Wheat is grown in the fertile south. The first people to live here were the Aboriginals, who arrived from Asia at least 50,000 years ago. Today, most Australians are descendants of European immigrants, with a more recent addition of Asians.

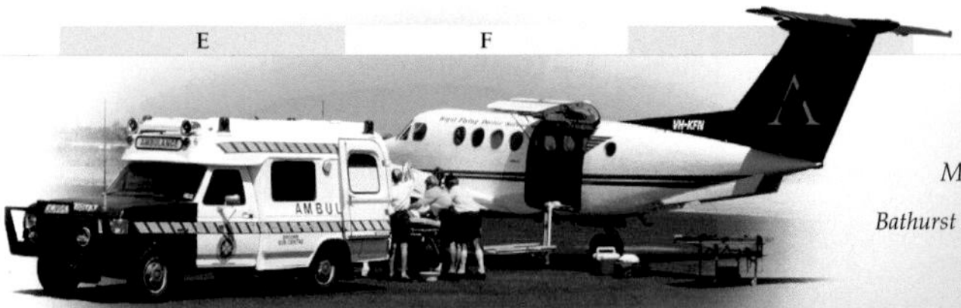
AMBU

FLYING DOCTOR
For anyone living in the remote Australian outback, the nearest doctor can be many hours away. When emergency help is needed, the Royal Flying Doctor Services can get to the scene to treat a patient or fly them to hospital.

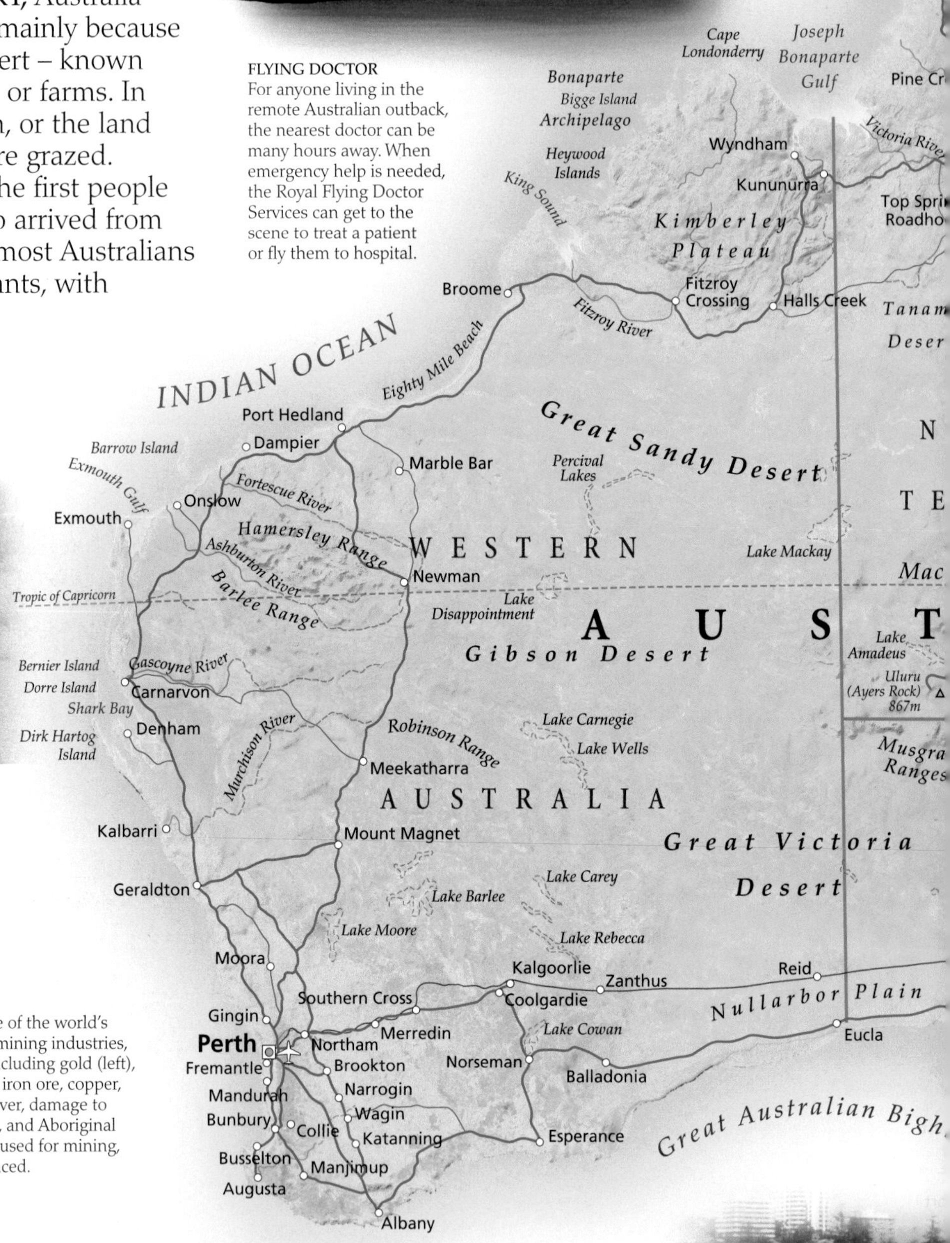
B
C
D
E
F
H
Melville Island
Bathurst Island
Darwin
Cape Londonderry
Joseph Bonaparte Gulf
Pine Cr
Bonaparte Archipelago
Bigge Island
Heywood Islands
King Sound
Wyndham
Kununurra
Victoria River
Top Spri
Roadho
Kimberley Plateau
Broome
Fitzroy Crossing
Halls Creek
Fitzroy River
Tanam
Deser
INDIAN OCEAN
Eighty Mile Beach
Port Hedland
Dampier
Barrow Island
Exmouth Gulf
Marble Bar
Percival Lakes
Great Sandy Desert
N
Onslow
Fortescue River
Exmouth
Hamersley Range
Ashburton River
WESTERN
T E
Lake Mackay
Newman
Mac
Tropic of Capricorn
Barlee Range
Lake Disappointment
A U S T
Lake Amadeus
Gibson Desert
Uluru (Ayers Rock) 867m
Bernier Island
Dorre Island
Gascoyne River
Carnarvon
Shark Bay
Dirk Hartog Island
Denham
Murchison River
Robinson Range
Lake Carnegie
Lake Wells
Meekatharra
Musgra Ranges
AUSTRALIA
Kalbarri
Mount Magnet
Great Victoria Desert
Geraldton
Lake Carey
Lake Barlee
Lake Moore
Lake Rebecca
Moora
Kalgoorlie
Reid
Zanthus
Southern Cross
Coolgardie
Nullarbor Plain
Gingin
Merredin
Lake Cowan
Eucla
Perth
Northam
Fremantle
Brookton
Norseman
Balladonia
Mandurah
Narrogin
Bunbury
Wagin
Collie
Katanning
Esperance
Great Australian Bight
Busselton
Manjimup
Augusta
Albany
2
3
4
5
6
7
8
9
0 km 200 400
0 miles 200 400

AUSTRALIAN ABORIGINALS
The original inhabitants of Australia had an intimate understanding of their environment. This connection to the land, and its plants and animals, affects every aspect of their culture. When Europeans started arriving in the late 18th century, only the Aboriginals in remote areas escaped contact with the diseases they brought. Today, Aboriginals rarely live off the land, but work in factories or farms.

MINING
Australia has one of the world's most important mining industries, with resources including gold (left), coal, natural gas, iron ore, copper, and opals. However, damage to the environment, and Aboriginal claims over land used for mining, still need to be faced.

AUSTRALIAN FOOTBALL
A popular sport here is Australian Rules Football. One of the rules is that players can kick or punch the ball but they must not throw it. Many Australians either play the game themselves or support their favourite team. As the name implies, the game originated in Australia, but it now has leagues in other countries, such as Great Britain and the USA.

OUTDOOR SPORTS
A warm climate, with easy access to beaches and wilderness areas, has made outdoor activities an important part of modern Australian life. Water sports, such as swimming, sailing, and surfing, are especially popular. Because of the danger of exposure to strong sunlight, people are told to cover up and always use sunscreen.

I
J
K
L
M
N
O
P
1
2
3
4
5
6
7
8
9
Arafura Sea
Torres Strait
Badu Island
Moa Island
Prince of Wales Island
Cape York
Endeavour Strait
South Goulburn Island
Wessel Islands
Gulf of Carpentaria
Arnhem Land
Groote Eylandt
Cape York Peninsula
Princess Charlotte Bay
Sir Edward Pellew Group
Great Barrier Reef
Great Dividing Range
Daly Waters
Wellesley Islands
Mornington Island
Mitchell River
Cooktown
Port Douglas
Cairns
Atherton
Innisfail
Tully
Hinchinbrook Island
Coral Sea
Barkly Tableland
Gilbert River
Normanton
Burketown
Gregory Range
Flinders River
Townsville
Bowen
Whitsunday Group
Charters Towers
Cloncurry
Mount Isa
Selwyn Range
Hughenden
Bloomsbury
Mackay
Winton
QUEENSLAND
Alice Springs
Longreach
Barcaldine
Clermont
Marlborough
Yeppoon
Emerald
Rockhampton
Tropic of Capricorn
Curtis Island
Gladstone
Cooper Creek
Springsure
Blackall
Biloela
Fraser Island
Simpson Desert
Windorah
Bundaberg
Augathella
Gayndah
Maryborough
Charleville
Mitchell
Murgon
Gympie
Roma
Miles
Caloundra
Dalby
SOUTH AUSTRALIA
Brisbane
Ipswich
Coober Pedy
Lake Eyre North
-15m
Lake Blanche
Grey Range
Cunnamulla
St. George
Moonie
Toowoomba
Bollon
Goondiwindi
Warwick
Surfers Paradise
Murwillumbah
Stanthorpe
Lake Eyre South
Marree
Lake Callabonna
Warrego River
Moree
Lismore
Tarcoola
Lake Torrens
Flinders Ranges
Lake Frome
Barrier Range
Barwon River
Bourke
Walgett
Narrabri
Armidale
Grafton
Coffs Harbour
Lake Everard
Lake Gairdner
Port Augusta
Broken Hill
Wilcannia
Cobar
Nyngan
Gunnedah
Tamworth
Port Macquarie
NEW SOUTH WALES
Dubbo
Taree
Whyalla
Peterborough
Ivanhoe
Muswellbrook
Eyre Peninsula
Port Pirie
Crystal Brook
Darling River
Lachlan River
Parkes
Orange
Newcastle
Gosford
Spencer Gulf
Murray River
Mildura
Bathurst
Parramatta
Sydney
Elizabeth
Gawler
Murrumbidgee River
Cootamundra
Wollongong
Port Lincoln
Adelaide
Hay
Investigator Strait
Tailem Bend
Ouyen
Wagga Wagga
Goulburn
CANBERRA
Deniliquin
Mount Kosciuszko 2229m
AUSTRALIAN CAPITAL TERRITORY
Kangaroo Island
Keith
Albury
Shepparton
Wodonga
Cooma
Horsham
Bendigo
Wangaratta
Australian Alps
Naracoorte
VICTORIA
Bega
Tasman Sea
Mount Gambier
Sunbury
Ballarat
Melbourne
Portland
Moe
Sale
Warrnambool
Geelong
Traralgon
South East Point
King Island
Bass Strait
Flinders Island
Hunter Island
Banks Strait
Cape Barren Island
Marrawah
Burnie
Devonport
Launceston
TASMANIA
Maria Island
Hobart

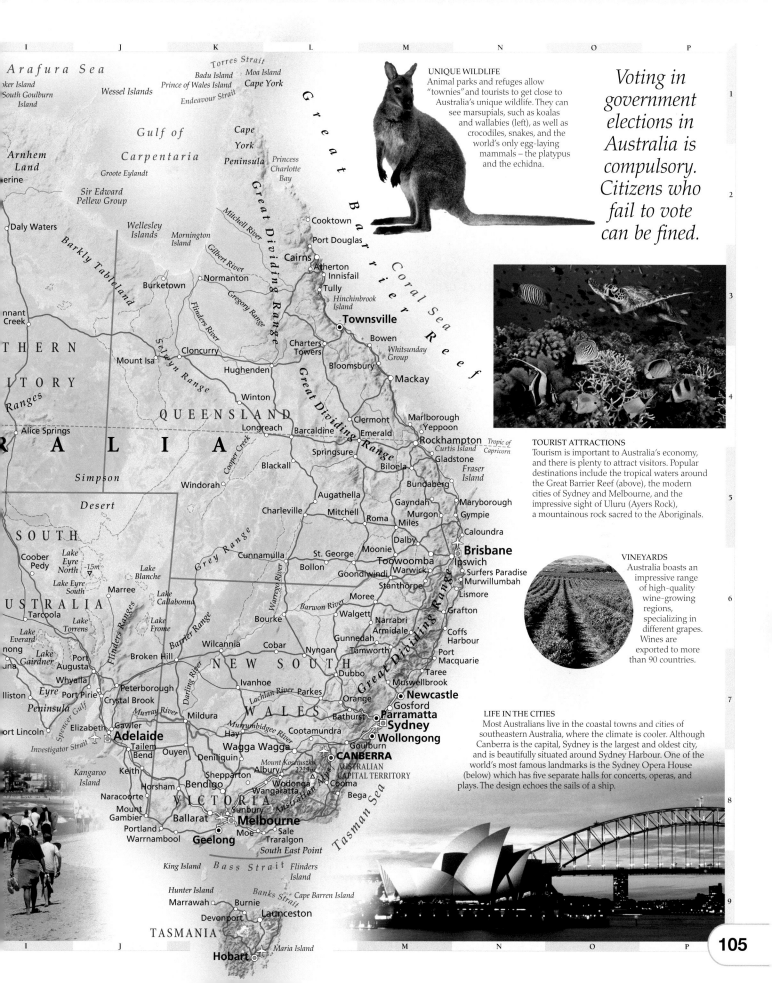

UNIQUE WILDLIFE
Animal parks and refuges allow "townies" and tourists to get close to Australia's unique wildlife. They can see marsupials, such as koalas and wallabies (left), as well as crocodiles, snakes, and the world's only egg-laying mammals – the platypus and the echidna.

Voting in government elections in Australia is compulsory. Citizens who fail to vote can be fined.

TOURIST ATTRACTIONS
Tourism is important to Australia's economy, and there is plenty to attract visitors. Popular destinations include the tropical waters around the Great Barrier Reef (above), the modern cities of Sydney and Melbourne, and the impressive sight of Uluru (Ayers Rock), a mountainous rock sacred to the Aboriginals.

VINEYARDS
Australia boasts an impressive range of high-quality wine-growing regions, specializing in different grapes. Wines are exported to more than 90 countries.

LIFE IN THE CITIES
Most Australians live in the coastal towns and cities of southeastern Australia, where the climate is cooler. Although Canberra is the capital, Sydney is the largest and oldest city, and is beautifully situated around Sydney Harbour. One of the world's most famous landmarks is the Sydney Opera House (below) which has five separate halls for concerts, operas, and plays. The design echoes the sails of a ship.

New Zealand

MADE UP OF TWO MAIN ISLANDS and several smaller ones, New Zealand is one of the most isolated countries in the world. Located in the southern Pacific, the country has a mild climate, with warm summers and cool, wet winters. Both main islands have mountains, short, swift-flowing rivers, forests, and fertile farmland. Until the Europeans arrived, most of the landscape was covered in dense forest, known as native bush. Today, although forests remain, much has been cleared for farming. Most New Zealanders live on North Island, which is warmer and less mountainous. Although New Zealanders are of mainly British descent, the Maoris – a people of Polynesian origin – were the first to arrive about 1,000 years ago. Today, non-Maori Polynesians and Asians are adding to the ethnic mix. The country has a liberal, clean, green image and a high standard of living.

AUCKLAND
With its safe harbour and nearby scenic islands, Auckland is known as the "city of sails". It boasts more pleasure boats per person than anywhere else in the world. The water that separates the bigger islands is home to dolphins, families of blue penguins, and the occasional whale.

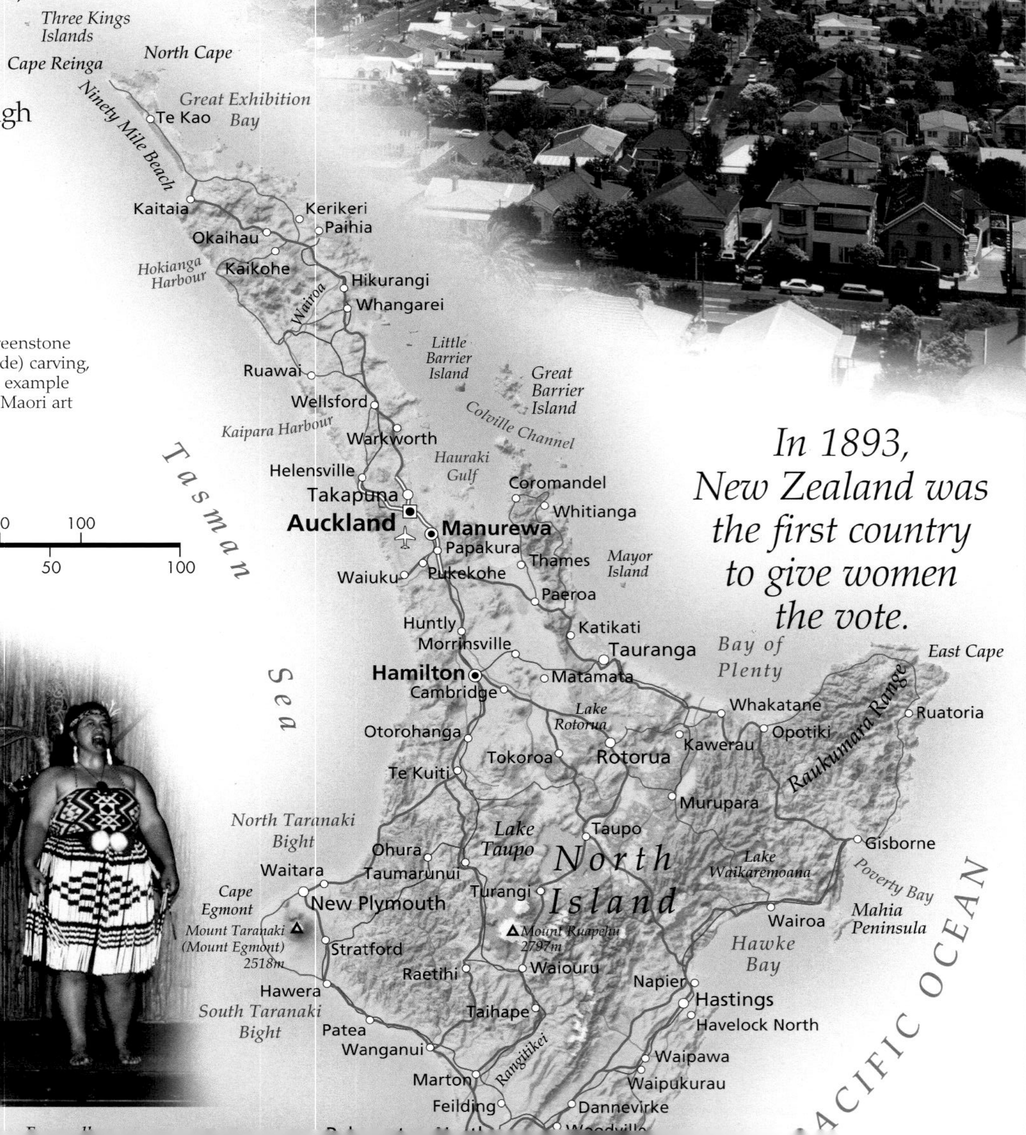
Three Kings Islands
Cape Reinga
North Cape
Ninety Mile Beach
Te Kao
Great Exhibition Bay
Kaitaia
Kerikeri
Paihia
Okaihau
Kaikohe
Hokianga Harbour
Wairoa
Hikurangi
Whangarei
Little Barrier Island
Great Barrier Island
Ruawai
Wellsford
Kaipara Harbour
Colville Channel
Warkworth
Hauraki Gulf
Helensville
Coromandel
Whitianga
Takapuna
Auckland
Manurewa
Papakura
Thames
Mayor Island
Waiuku
Pukekohe
Paeroa
Tasman Sea
Huntly
Katikati
Morrinsville
Tauranga
Bay of Plenty
East Cape
Hamilton
Matamata
Cambridge
Lake Rotorua
Whakatane
Ruatoria
Otorohanga
Kawerau
Opotiki
Raukumara Range
Tokoroa
Rotorua
Te Kuiti
Murupara
North Taranaki Bight
Lake Taupo
Taupo
Gisborne
Ohura
North Island
Waitara
Taumarunui
Lake Waikaremoana
Poverty Bay
Cape Egmont
Turangi
New Plymouth
Wairoa
Mahia Peninsula
Mount Taranaki (Mount Egmont) 2518m
Mount Ruapehu 2797m
Hawke Bay
Stratford
Raetihi
Waiouru
Hawera
Napier
Hastings
South Taranaki Bight
Taihape
Havelock North
Patea
Wanganui
Rangitikei
Waipawa
Marton
Waipukurau
Feilding
Dannevirke
PACIFIC OCEAN
0 km 50 100
0 miles 50 100

In 1893, New Zealand was the first country to give women the vote.

MAORI CULTURE
Maoris make up almost 14 per cent of the population, with most living on North Island. Before the coming of the *Pakeha* (white man), Maori history was passed on orally to succeeding generations. This included many legends and *waiata* (songs). Their carvings in wood (left) and stone (right) were another way they recorded and remembered events. In recent years, interest in Maori culture has increased, and school children are now taught the Maori language.

Greenstone (jade) carving, an example of Maori art

FILM INDUSTRY
New Zealand has a well-established film industry. Today, thanks to the acclaimed films based on J.R.R. Tolkien's trilogy *The Lord of the Rings* (above) and *The Hobbit*, the country has become increasingly popular with international studios for location work. The country offers an unusually wide range of scenery as well as technical experts.

NEW ZEALAND
South Island
Southern Alps
WELLINGTON
Porirua
Lower Hutt
Masterton
Cape Palliser
Cook Strait
Picton
Nelson
Motueka
Bay
Richmond
Richmond Range
Wairau
Blenheim
Seddon
Cape Campbell
Clarence
Kaikoura
Karamea Bight
Mount Owen 1875m
Seddonville
Westport
Cape Foulwind
Reefton
Springs Junction
Runanga
Greymouth
Lake Brunner
Hurunui
Hanmer Springs
Hokitika
Ross
Otira
Arthur's Pass 920m
Waipara
Pegasus Bay
Abut Head
Whataroa
Rakaia
Oxford
Rangiora
Kaiapoi
Christchurch
Lyttelton
Fox Glacier
Darfield
Aoraki (Mt Cook) 3744m
Mount Cook
Canterbury Plains
Lake Ellesmere
Banks Peninsula
Haast
Mayfield
Ashburton
Hinds
Canterbury Bight
Lake Pukaki
Fairlie
Geraldine
Temuka
Timaru
Milford Sound
Lake Wanaka
Wanaka
Lake Hawea
Waitaki
Studholme
Waimate
George Sound
Caswell Sound
Lake Te Anau
Lake Wakatipu
Queenstown
Livingstone Mts
Cromwell
Alexandra
Oamaru
Eyre Mts
Hampden
Clutha
Taieri
Fiordland
Te Anau
Lumsden
Resolution Island
Lake Manapouri
Mataura
Dunedin
Mosgiel
West Cape
Waiau
Otago Peninsula
Lake Hauroko
Winton
Gore
Milton
Riverton
Balclutha
Ta Waewae Bay
Invercargill
Tokanui
Foveaux Strait
Toetoes Bay
Codfish Island
Halfmoon Bay
Ruapuke Island
Stewart Island
Muttonbird Islands
South West Cape

Flightless Kiwi bird

AN AGRICULTURAL NATION
Agriculture is of prime importance, and accounts for more than half of national export earnings. Orchards produce a vast range of fruit from apples (above) to kiwi fruit (below). Cereals and other crops, such as sunflowers, add colour and variety to the landscape. Traditional sheep and cattle farming has expanded to include deer, goats, and even ostriches.

UNIQUE WILDLIFE
New Zealand has many unique and endangered animal species, especially birds. There were no mammal predators before humans introduced them, so many animal species have few means of defence, and some birds such as the kiwi cannot fly. Conservation schemes are now in place to protect endangered species.

GREEN ENERGY
Most of the country's electricity comes from hydroelectric power. It is generated by river water gushing through turbines inside dams at power stations. New Zealand also has geothermal energy, using heat from inside Earth.

Lady Knox geyser, North Island

VOLCANIC ACTIVITY
A fault line runs through New Zealand, where two major tectonic plates meet. It has caused devastating earthquakes, but has also helped to create breathtaking scenery. This includes South Island's Southern Alps, and many smaller volcanic mountains, hot springs, and geysers on North Island.

ADVENTURE SPORTS PARADISE
New Zealand offers a huge range of adventure sports and outdoor activities, from white-water rafting (below) to bungee jumping. The latter originated in Queenstown on South Island. The town is billed as the country's top adventure tourism destination because its surrounding lakes, mountains, and rivers, and its mostly dry climate, are ideal for outdoor pursuits.

Pacific Ocean

THE LARGEST OCEAN ON EARTH, the Pacific covers one-third of Earth's surface. The island nations of Japan, Indonesia, Australia, New Zealand, and many others are completely surrounded by this enormous ocean, which stretches from the Arctic in the north to the Southern Ocean in the south. The Pacific is also the world's deepest ocean – its greatest known depth is in the Mariana Trench, off Guam, which plunges steeply for 11,033 m (36,198 ft). Within the Pacific, there are many smaller seas that lie near land. These include the Tasman Sea, the South China Sea, and the Bering Sea. There are more than 30,000 islands in the Pacific. Most are too small or barren to be inhabited, but others are home to people of many different cultures and religions. The native island peoples fall into three main groups – Polynesians, Melanesians, and Micronesians. Although the word *pacific* means "peaceful", strong currents, tropical storms, and tsunamis can all make this ocean far from peaceful.

Hawaiian conch shells, once blown to sound a warning

HAWAII
This chain of eight volcanic islands and 124 islets forms the 50th state of the United States of America, and was admitted to the union in 1959. The dramatic landscape and palm-fringed beaches make Hawaii a popular destination for tourists. Today, native Hawaiians are a minority in their own land.

Marine iguana on black volcanic rocks, Galápagos Islands

GALÁPAGOS ISLANDS
When British naturalist Charles Darwin (1809–1882) went to the Galápagos Islands, he found many unusual animals. He also noticed differences between animals of the same species living elsewhere. This led him to believe that, over time, animals adapt, or evolve, to suit their habitats.

TSUNAMI
Earthquakes beneath the sea may cause giant waves called tsunamis. These can travel great distances across the ocean, building into a huge wall of water as they approach the coast. They can leave immense damage in their wake.

Black smoker chimney

Large red tube worms

DEEP-SEA VENTS
Underwater exploration has revealed some amazing places deep in the Pacific. Large vents, formed by solidified minerals, act as chimneys for super-hot steam and gas that stream up from the sea bed. These vents are known as black smokers. Scientists have found a host of new creatures living in this hostile environment.

SURFING
The Hawaiian sport of surfing ranks as the oldest sport in the USA. It was first practised by the nobility as a form of religious ceremony until the 1820s when missionaries, who thought it immoral, tried to ban it. Today, surfing is one of the most popular watersports and can be seen all over the world, from Australia to the UK.

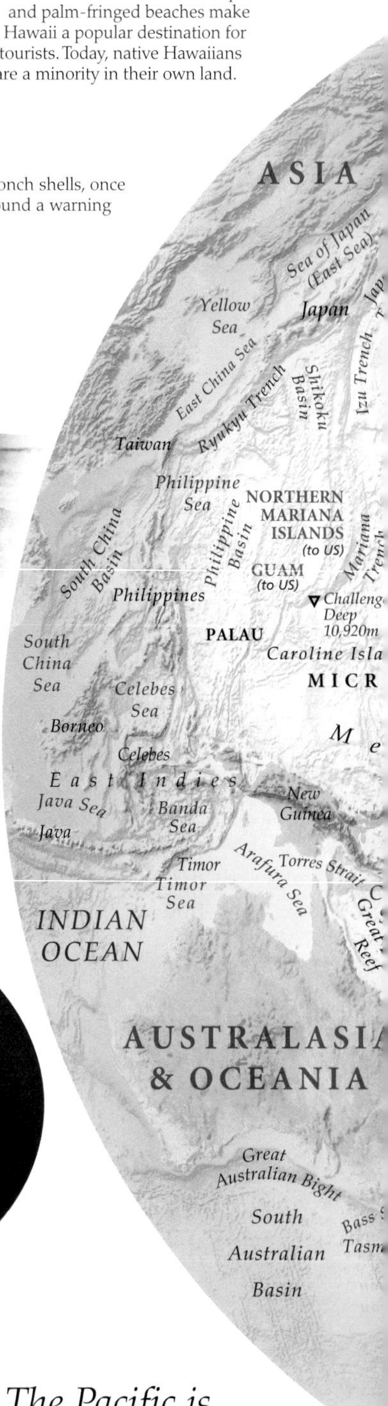
ASIA
Sea of Japan (East Sea)
Yellow Sea
Japan
East China Sea
Ryukyu Trench
Shikoku Basin
Izu Trench
Taiwan
Philippine Sea
NORTHERN MARIANA ISLANDS (to US)
GUAM (to US)
Mariana Trench
Philippine Basin
South China Basin
Philippines
Challenger Deep 10,920m
PALAU
South China Sea
Caroline Isla
MICR
Celebes Sea
Borneo
Celebes
East Indies
Java Sea
Banda Sea
Java
New Guinea
Timor
Timor Sea
Arafura Sea
Torres Strait
Great Reef
INDIAN OCEAN
AUSTRALASIA & OCEANIA
Great Australian Bight
South Australian Basin

The Pacific is larger than Earth's entire land surface.

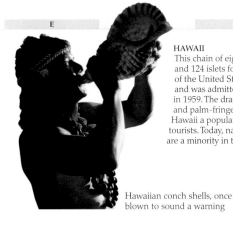

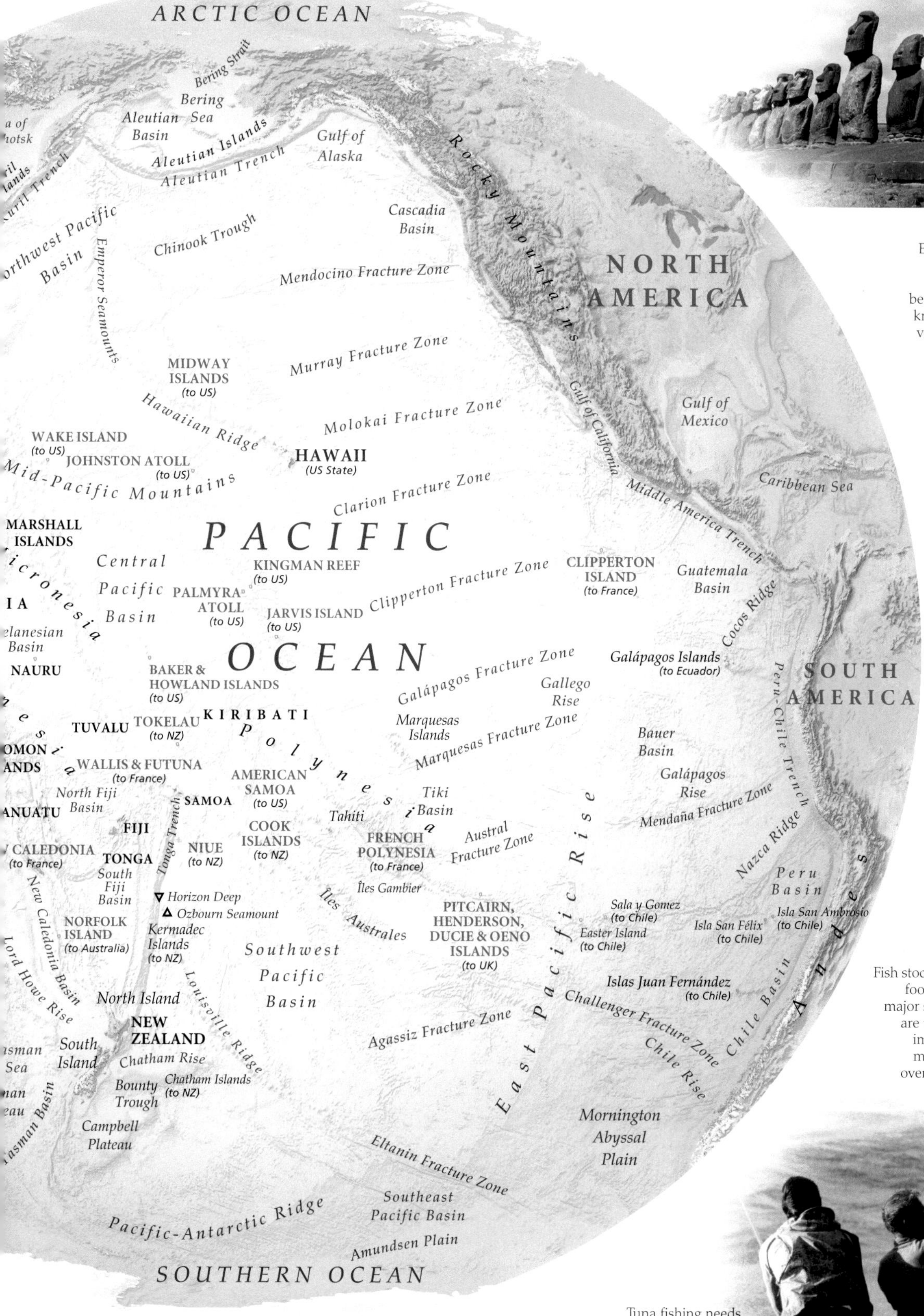
I J K L M N O P
ARCTIC OCEAN
Bering Strait
Bering Sea
Aleutian Basin
Aleutian Islands
Aleutian Trench
Gulf of Alaska
Rocky Mountains
Cascadia Basin
Chinook Trough
Northwest Pacific Basin
Emperor Seamounts
Mendocino Fracture Zone
NORTH AMERICA
Murray Fracture Zone
MIDWAY ISLANDS (to US)
Hawaiian Ridge
Molokai Fracture Zone
Gulf of California
Gulf of Mexico
WAKE ISLAND (to US)
JOHNSTON ATOLL (to US)
HAWAII (US State)
Mid-Pacific Mountains
Clarion Fracture Zone
Middle America Trench
Caribbean Sea
MARSHALL ISLANDS
PACIFIC OCEAN
Micronesia
Central Pacific Basin
KINGMAN REEF (to US)
PALMYRA ATOLL (to US)
JARVIS ISLAND (to US)
Clipperton Fracture Zone
CLIPPERTON ISLAND (to France)
Guatemala Basin
Cocos Ridge
Melanesian Basin
NAURU
BAKER & HOWLAND ISLANDS (to US)
Galápagos Fracture Zone
Galápagos Islands (to Ecuador)
Gallego Rise
SOUTH AMERICA
Peru-Chile Trench
TUVALU
TOKELAU (to NZ)
KIRIBATI
Polynesia
Marquesas Islands
Marquesas Fracture Zone
Bauer Basin
WALLIS & FUTUNA (to France)
AMERICAN SAMOA (to US)
SAMOA
North Fiji Basin
Tiki Basin
Galápagos Rise
Tahiti
Mendaña Fracture Zone
FIJI
COOK ISLANDS (to NZ)
NIUE (to NZ)
TONGA
Tonga Trench
FRENCH POLYNESIA (to France)
Austral Fracture Zone
Nazca Ridge
NEW CALEDONIA (to France)
South Fiji Basin
Horizon Deep
Ozbourn Seamount
Îles Gambier
Îles Australes
PITCAIRN, HENDERSON, DUCIE & OENO ISLANDS (to UK)
Sala y Gomez (to Chile)
Easter Island (to Chile)
Isla San Félix (to Chile)
Isla San Ambrosio (to Chile)
Peru Basin
Andes
New Caledonia Basin
NORFOLK ISLAND (to Australia)
Kermadec Islands (to NZ)
Southwest Pacific Basin
East Pacific Rise
Islas Juan Fernández (to Chile)
Lord Howe Rise
Louisville Ridge
North Island
NEW ZEALAND
South Island
Challenger Fracture Zone
Chile Basin
Agassiz Fracture Zone
Chile Rise
Chatham Rise
Chatham Islands (to NZ)
Bounty Trough
Campbell Plateau
Tasman Sea
Tasman Basin
Mornington Abyssal Plain
Eltanin Fracture Zone
Southeast Pacific Basin
Pacific-Antarctic Ridge
Amundsen Plain
SOUTHERN OCEAN
I J K L M
3 5 6 7 8

EASTER ISLAND
Easter Island, or Rapa Nui, in the Pacific lies more than 3,218 km (2,000 miles) from the nearest populated land. It is best known for the gigantic stone figures, known as Moai, which were carved from volcanic rock and erected facing the sea. It is thought that the people who built the statues were of Peruvian descent.

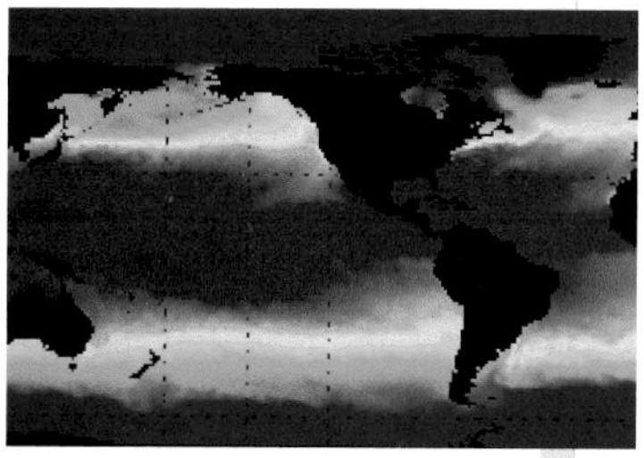

EL NIÑO
Every few years, winds off the South American coast weaken, causing an unusually warm ocean current, known as El Niño. This kills off plankton that provide food for fish such as anchovies. Scientists use heat-sensitive cameras to map ocean temperatures and keep track of El Niño. The warmest waters are shown in orange/red (above).

SOUTH PACIFIC FISH
Fish stocks in the south Pacific are an important food source for the island countries and a major source of employment. Migratory tuna are the most important fish. However, it is important that the industry is effectively managed to avoid the constant threat of overfishing and the collapse of fish stocks.

Tuna fishing needs to be carefully monitored.

Antarctica

THE FROZEN CONTINENT OF ANTARCTICA is covered by a vast icecap, many thousands of years old, and surrounded by the freezing seas of the Southern Ocean. It is the only continent with no permanent inhabitants – the only people who come here are scientists or tourists. Although the land is rich in oil and minerals, mining is prohibited under the laws of the Antarctic Treaty. This treaty, agreed by 53 countries, made Antarctica a "continent for science" to be used for peaceful purposes only.

DAY TRIPPERS
Tourists visit Antarctica in summer. There are no resorts, so visitors generally stay on small cruise ships. When they come ashore, people have to wear insulated clothing and goggles to protect their eyes from glare off the ice.

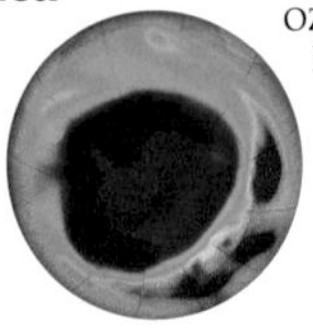

OZONE HOLE
High in the atmosphere, ozone (a gas) forms a natural shield that protects us from the Sun's ultraviolet rays. Scientists at both poles have found holes in the ozone layer, caused by chemicals known as CFCs, once used in aerosols, fridges, and plastic packaging.

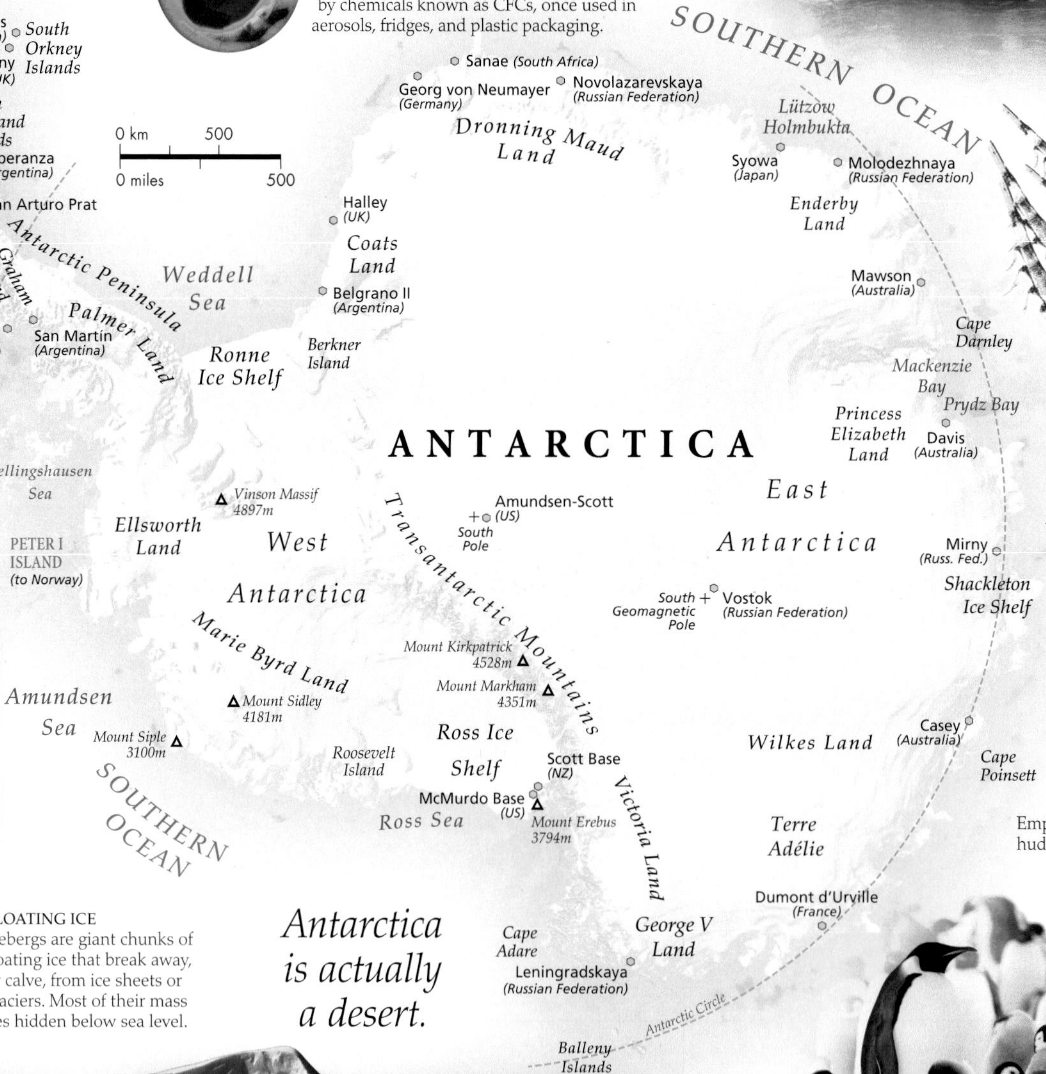

SOUTHERN OCEAN
Orcadas (Argentina)
South Orkney Islands
Signy (UK)
South Shetland Islands
Drake Passage
Esperanza (Argentina)
Capitán Arturo Prat (Chile)
Antarctic Peninsula
Graham Land
Palmer (US)
Palmer Land
Rothera (UK)
San Martin (Argentina)
0 km 500
0 miles 500
Sanae (South Africa)
Georg von Neumayer (Germany)
Novolazarevskaya (Russian Federation)
Dronning Maud Land
Lützow Holmbukta
Syowa (Japan)
Molodezhnaya (Russian Federation)
Enderby Land
Halley (UK)
Coats Land
Weddell Sea
Belgrano II (Argentina)
Mawson (Australia)
Cape Darnley
Mackenzie Bay
Prydz Bay
Ronne Ice Shelf
Berkner Island
Princess Elizabeth Land
Davis (Australia)
ANTARCTICA
Bellingshausen Sea
Vinson Massif 4897m
Amundsen-Scott (US)
South Pole
East Antarctica
PETER I ISLAND (to Norway)
Ellsworth Land
West Antarctica
Transantarctic Mountains
Mirny (Russ. Fed.)
Shackleton Ice Shelf
South Geomagnetic Pole
Vostok (Russian Federation)
Marie Byrd Land
Mount Kirkpatrick 4528m
Mount Markham 4351m
Amundsen Sea
Mount Sidley 4181m
Mount Siple 3100m
Ross Ice Shelf
Roosevelt Island
Scott Base (NZ)
Wilkes Land
Casey (Australia)
Cape Poinsett
SOUTHERN OCEAN
McMurdo Base (US)
Ross Sea
Mount Erebus 3794m
Victoria Land
Terre Adélie
Dumont d'Urville (France)
Cape Adare
George V Land
Leningradskaya (Russian Federation)
Antarctic Circle
Balleny Islands

KRILL
Tiny, shrimp-like creatures, krill are the primary food source for a great number of Antarctic animals. These include whales, seals, penguins, squid, and fish.

RESEARCH
The only people who stay in Antarctica are scientists. They come to study the climate, weather, and geology. By taking ice samples, for example, they can learn about changes in the world's climate over the years.

Scientist checking an ice core

Antarctica is actually a desert.

FLOATING ICE
Icebergs are giant chunks of floating ice that break away, or calve, from ice sheets or glaciers. Most of their mass lies hidden below sea level.

Emperor penguins huddling for warmth

PENGUINS
Penguins walk awkwardly on land, but can swim swiftly to catch fish. Waterproof feathers and a thick layer of fat help keep them warm.

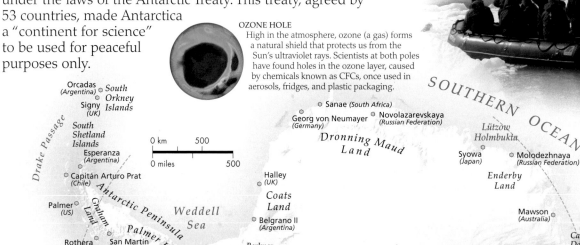

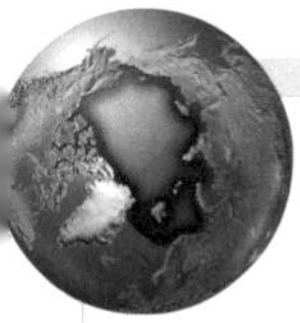

Arctic Ocean

THE SMALLEST OF THE WORLD'S oceans, the Arctic is almost entirely surrounded by the northern edges of North America, Europe, and Asia. For most of the year, its waters are covered by a thick sheet of ice, although warmer currents from the Pacific and Atlantic melt the ice along the continental coasts for a short time in summer. Despite the harsh conditions, the region is home to a range of wildlife, such as reindeer, musk ox, foxes, and wolves. Some people, including the Inuit of Canada and the Sami of northern Scandinavia, have also adapted to this tough environment.

LONG DAYS
Seasons at the poles are extreme. Polar summers are short but there can be sunshine for 24 hours a "day" as the Sun never dips below the horizon (above). This is because Earth rotates at an angle to the Sun.

B
C
D
E
F
G
H
1
2
3
4
5
6
7
8
9
A
Bering Strait
Arctic Circle
Chukchi Sea
Ostrov Vrangelya
East Siberian Sea
Beaufort Sea
Amundsen Gulf
Novosibirskiye Ostrova
RUSSIAN FEDERATION
Banks Island
Victoria Island
Laptev Sea
Melville Island
ARCTIC
CANADA
Queen Elizabeth Islands
Severnaya Zemlya
North Pole
OCEAN
Lancaster Sound
Ellesmere Island
Nares Strait
North Geomagnetic Pole
Lincoln Sea
Franz Josef Land
Kara Sea
Knud Rasmussen Land
Kap Morris Jesup
Baffin Bay
Wandel Sea
Kong Frederik VIII Land
SVALBARD (to Norway)
Spitsbergen
LONGYEARBYEN
0 km 250 500
0 miles 250 500
GREENLAND (to Denmark)
Greenland Sea
Bjørnøya (to Norway)
Barents Sea
NUUK
Arctic Circle
Norwegian Sea
Kong Christian IX Land
JAN MAYEN (to Norway)
Denmark Strait
ICELAND
REYKJAVÍK

ALASKAN OIL
Reserves of oil and gas in the Beaufort Sea, off the coast of Alaska, have attracted interest. However, the introduction of ships and oil platforms brings problems. In a bid to protect the area, several environmental organizations are actively working to prevent drilling for more oil in this area.

Walruses breed off the Arctic coasts.

NORTHERN LIGHTS
In midwinter, the north polar skies are sometimes lit up by dramatic curtains of red and green light. Known as the northern lights, these special effects are caused by disturbances in the upper atmosphere. The same happens near Antarctica, where the effect is called the southern lights.

ARCTIC SURVIVORS
Polar bears live along the Arctic coasts of Canada, Greenland, and Russia. They hunt seals and fish at points where the sea ice melts. With so much Arctic ice having melted away in recent years, the polar bear's habitat is slowly disappearing. An insulating layer of fat, called blubber, helps the bears survive the cold. Their white fur also provides essential camouflage on the ice.

Gazetteer

HOW TO USE THE GAZETTEER

This gazetteer is a selection of the names in *Children's Illustrated World Atlas*, and helps you find places on the maps. For example, to find the city of Lisbon in Portugal, look up its name in the gazetteer. The entry reads:

Lisbon *Capital* Portugal 58 E6

The first number, 58, tells you that Lisbon appears on the map on page 58. The second number, E6, shows that it is in square E6. Turn to page 58. Trace down from the letter E along the top of the grid (or up from the letter E on the bottom of the grid), and then across from the number 6 on the side of the grid. You will find Lisbon in the area where the letter and number meet.

A

Aachen *Town* Germany 56 B7
Aalborg *Town* Denmark 49 B11
Aalen *Town* Germany 57 E9
Aalst *Town* Belgium 53 D11
Aalter *Town* Belgium 53 C10
Äänekoski *Town* Finland 48 G8
Aarhus *Town* Denmark 49 C12
Aba *Town* Nigeria 41 L8
Aba *Town* Democratic Republic of the Congo 42 I8
Ābādān *Town* Iran 82 E7
Abakan *Town* Russian Federation 78 H7
Abbeville *Town* France 54 E5
Abéché *Town* Chad 42 F6
Abengourou *Town* Côte d'Ivoire 41 I8
Aberdeen *Town* South Dakota, USA 12 G4
Aberdeen *Town* Maryland, USA 9 H8
Aberdeen *Town* Scotland, UK 50 F5
Aberystwyth *Town* Wales, UK 51 E10
Abhā *Town* Saudi Arabia 83 C11
Abidjan *Town* Côte d'Ivoire 40 H8
Abilene *Town* Texas, USA 17 K5
Åbo *see* Turku
Abomey *Town* Benin 41 J7
Abrantes *Town* Portugal 58 F6
Abu Dhabi *Capital* United Arab Emirates 83 F9
Abu Hamed *Town* Sudan 38 E6
Abuja *Capital* Nigeria 41 L7
Abū Kamāl *Town* Syria 80 I7
Abū Ẓaby *see* Abu Dhabi
Acapulco *Town* Mexico 19 J9
Acarigua *Town* Venezuela 26 D5
Accra *Capital* Ghana 41 I8
Aconcagua, Cerro *Mountain* Argentina 30 D7
A Coruña *Town* Spain 58 E2
Adamawa Highlands *Mountain range* Cameroon 42 D8
'Adan *see* Aden
Adana *Town* Turkey 76 G6
Adapazari *Town* Turkey 76 E4
Ad Dahnā' *Desert* Saudi Arabia 83 E9
Ad Dakhla *Town* Western Sahara 36 C7
Ad Dammān *Town* Saudi Arabia 83 E9
Ad Dawḩah *see* Doha
Addis Ababa *Capital* Ethiopia 39 F9
Adelaide *Town* South Australia, Australia 105 J7
Aden *Town* Yemen 83 D13
Aden, Gulf of Indian Ocean 83 E13
Adirondack Mountains New York, USA 8 H4
Ādīs Ābeba *see* Addis Ababa
Adiyaman *Town* Turkey 76 H6
Adrar *Town* Algeria 36 G6
Aegean Sea Greece 67 F9
Afghanistan *Country* 84 H7
Afmadow *Town* Somalia 39 G11
Afyon *Town* Turkey 76 E5
Agadez *Town* Niger 41 L4
Agadir *Town* Morocco 36 E5
Agen *Town* France 55 D10
Agialoúsa *Town* Cyprus 80 B7
Āgra *Town* India 87 I3
Ağri *Town* Turkey 77 K4
Agrigento *Town* Sicily, Italy 61 E13
Agropoli *Town* Italy 61 F10
Aguachica *Town* Colombia 26 C5
Agua Prieta *Town* Mexico 18 F3
Aguascalientes *Town* Mexico 19 I7
Aguaytía *Town* Peru 27 B10
Aguilas *Town* Spain 59 J8
Aguililla *Town* Mexico 19 I8
Ahaggar *Mountain range* Algeria 37 I7
Ahlen *Town* Germany 56 C7
Ahmadābād *Town* India 86 G4
Ahuachapán *Town* El Salvador 20 E5
Ahvāz *Town* Iran 82 E7
Aiken *Town* South Carolina, USA 11 J4
Ailigandí *Town* Panama 21 N7
'Aïn Ben Tili *Town* Mauritania 40 G2
Aiquile *Town* Bolivia 27 E12
Aïr, Massif de l' *Mountain range* Niger 41 L4
Aix-en-Provence *Town* France 55 G11
Aizu *Town* Japan 93 G9
Ajaccio *Town* France 55 I13
Ajo *Town* Arizona, USA 16 E5
Akchâr *Desert* Mauritania 40 E3
Akhalts'ikhe *Town* Georgia 77 K3
Akhisar *Town* Turkey 76 C5
Akhtubinsk *Town* Russian Federation 73 D11
Akita *Town* Japan 92 F8
Akjoujt *Town* Mauritania 40 E3
Akkeshi *Town* Japan 92 H5
Akron *Town* Ohio, USA 13 M6
Akrotírion *Town* Cyprus 80 A8
Aksai Chin *Administrative region* China 88 D6
Aksaray *Town* Turkey 76 F5
Akşehir *Town* Turkey 76 E5
Aktau *Town* Kazakhstan 78 D6
Aktobe *Town* Kazakhstan 78 E6
Aktsyabrski *Town* Belarus 71 F11
Akula *Town* Democratic Republic of the Congo 43 F9
Akune *Town* Japan 93 B14
Alabama *State* USA 10 G5
Alabama River Alabama, USA 10 G6
Al 'Amārah *Town* Iraq 82 D7
Alamo *Town* Nevada, USA 14 H7
Alamogordo *Town* New Mexico, USA 16 H5
Åland *Island group* Finland 49 F9
Alanya *Town* Turkey 76 E7
Al 'Aqabah *Town* Jordan 81 D14
Alaşehir *Town* Turkey 76 D5
Alaska *Province* Canada 4 E5
Alaska, Gulf of Alaska, USA 4 E6
Alaska Range *Mountain Range* Alaska, USA 4 E5
Albacete *Town* Spain 59 J6
Alba Iulia *Town* Romania 68 E6
Albania *Country* 65 F12
Albany *River* Ontario, Canada 6 F5
Albany *Town* Western Australia, Australia 104 E7
Albany *Town* Georgia, USA 10 H6
Albany *Town* New York, USA 9 I5
Al Bāridah *Town* Syria 80 F8
Al Başrah *Town* Iraq 82 D7
Alberta *Province* Canada 4 H7
Albert, Lake Democratic Republic of the Congo 43 I9
Albuquerque *Town* New Mexico, USA 16 H4
Alcañiz *Town* Spain 59 K5
Alcoy *Town* Spain 59 K7
Alderney *Island* Channel Islands, UK 51 G13
Aleksin *Town* Russian Federation 73 C9
Alençon *Town* France 54 D7
Alenquer *Town* Brazil 29 I2
Aleppo *Town* Syria 80 E6montserrat
Alessandria *Town* Italy 60 C5
Aleutian Islands *Island Group* Alaska, USA 4 B5
Alexander Archipelago *Island* British Colombia, Canada 4 E7
Alexandria *Town* Louisiana, USA 10 E6
Alexandria *Town* Egypt 38 D4
Alexandria *Town* Romania 68 F7
Alexandroúpoli *Town* Greece 66 G8
Alga *Town* Kazakhstan 78 E6
Algarve *Region* Spain 58 E8
Algeciras *Town* Spain 58 G9
Alger *see* Algiers
Algeria *Country* 36 H5
Al Ghābah *Town* Oman 83 G10
Al Ghurdaqah *see* Hurghada
Algiers *Capital* Algeria 36 H3
Algona *Town* Iowa, USA 12 H5
Al Ḩ,asakah *Town* Syria 80 H5
Al Ḩillah *Town* Iraq 82 D7
Al Hudaydah *see* Hodeida
Al Hufūf *Town* Saudi Arabia 83 E9
Alíartos *Town* Greece 67 E11
Alicante *Town* Spain 59 L7
Alice Springs *Town* Northern Territory, Australia 105 I4
Aliquippa *Town* Pennsylvania, USA 8 E7
Al Ismā'īlīya *Town* Egypt 38 E4
Al Jafr *Town* Jordan 81 E13
Al Jaghbūb *Town* Libya 37 N5
Al Jahrā' *Town* Kuwait 82 D8
Al Jawf *Town* Saudi Arabia 82 B8
Al Jazīrah *Physical region* Syria/Iraq 80 I5
Al Karak *Town* Jordan 81 E12
Al Khārijah *Town* Egypt 38 D5
Al Khums *Town* Libya 37 K4
Alkmaar *Town* Netherlands 52 E7
Al Kufrah *Town* Libya 37 N7
Al Kūt *Town* Iraq 82 D7
Al Kuwayt *see* Kuwait
Allahābād *Town* India 87 I4
Allegheny Plateau Pennsylvania/New York, USA 8 F6
Allentown *Town* Pennsylvania, USA 9 H7
Al Līth *Town* Saudi Arabia 83 B11
Alma-Ata *see* Almaty
Al Madīnah *see* Medina
Al Mafraq *Town* Jordan 81 E10
Al Majma'ah *Town* Saudi Arabia 83 D9
Al Mālikīyah *Town* Syria 80 I4
Al Manāmah *see* Manama
Almansa *Town* Spain 59 K7
Al Marj *Town* Libya 37 M4
Almaty *Town* Kazakhstan 78 G8
Al Mawşil *see* Mosul
Al Mayādīn *Town* Syria 80 H6
Almelo *Town* Netherlands 52 G8
Almere *Town* Netherlands 52 F8
Almería *Town* Spain 59 J8
Al'met'yevsk *Town* Russian Federation 73 F9
Al Minyā *Town* Egypt 38 D4
Almirante *Town* Panama 21 K8
Al Mukallā *Town* Yemen 83 E13
Alofi *Capital* Niue 103 K7
Alotip *Town* Indonesia 97 N8
Alpena *Town* Michigan, USA 13 L4
Alpine *Town* Texas, USA 17 I7
Alps *Mountain range* Central Europe 57 D12
Al Qāmishlī *Town* Syria 80 I4
Al Qunayţirah *Town* Syria 81 D9
Altai Mountains *Mountain range* Mongolia/Russian Federation 88 F4
Altamaha River Georgia, USA 11 I5
Altamira *Town* Brazil 29 J2
Altamura *Town* Italy 61 H10
Altar, Desierto de *Desert* Mexico 18 D2
Altay *Town* China 88 F3
Altay *Town* Mongolia 88 H3
Altin Köprü *Town* Iraq 82 C6
Altiplano *Physical region* Bolivia 27 E13
Altoona *Town* Pennsylvania, USA 9 F7
Altun Ha *Ancient site* Belize 20 F2
Altun Shan *Mountain range* China 88 G5
Al 'Umarī *Town* Jordan 81 F11
Al 'Uwaynāt *Town* Libya 37 J6
Alupka *Town* Ukraine 69 K7
Alva *Town* Okahoma, USA 17 L3
Al Wajh *Town* Saudi Arabia 83 A9
Alwar *Town* India 86 H3
Al Wari'ah *Town* Saudi Arabia 82 D8
Alytus *Town* Lithuania 70 D8
Amamapare *Town* Indonesia 97 N7
Amantea *Town* Italy 61 G12
Amarapura *Town* Myanmar 94 B6
Amarillo *Town* Texas, USA 17 J4
Amazon *River* Brazil 29 J2
Amazon Basin Brazil 28 G3
Ambanja *Town* Madagascar 45 M4
Ambarchik *Town* Russian Federation 78 L3
Ambato *Town* Ecuador 26 A8
Amboasary *Town* Madagascar 45 L7
Ambon *Town* Indonesia 97 K7
American Samoa *Dependent territory* USA, Pacific Ocean 103 K6
Amersfoort *Town* Netherlands 52 F8
Amfilochía *Town* Greece 67 C10
Amherst *Town* Nova Scotia, Canada 7 K7
Amiens *Town* France 54 E6
Amman *Capital* Jordan 81 E11
'Ammān *see* Amman
Ammóchostos *Town* Cyprus 80 B8
Āmol *Town* Iran 82 F5
Amos *Town* Québec, Canada 6 H6
Amritsar *Town* India 86 H2
Amstelveen *Town* Netherlands 52 F8
Amsterdam *Capital* Netherlands 52 E8
Am Timan *Town* Chad 42 F6
Amundsen Gulf Canada 4 H4
Amundsen-Scott *Research station* Antarctica 110 E6
Amundsen Sea Southern Ocean 110 B7
Amuntai *Town* Indonesia 96 H7
Amur *River* China 89 L2
Amyderýa *River* Uzbekistan 84 G4
Anadyr' *Town* Russian Federation 78 M2
Anamur *Town* Turkey 76 F7
Anápolis *Town* Brazil 29 K5
Anatolia *Plateau* Turkey 76 E6
Anchorage *Town* Alaska, Canada 4 E5
Ancona *Town* Italy 60 F7
Andalucía *Region* Spain 58 H8
Andaman Islands *Island group* India 87 M8
Andaman Sea Indian Ocean 87 M8
Anderson *Town* Indiana, USA 13 K6
Andes *Mountain range* South America 26–27, 30–31
Andijon *Town* Uzbekistan 85 K4
Andkhvoy *Town* Afghanistan 84 H5
Andorra *Country* 55 D12
Andorra la Vella *Capital* Andorra 55 D12
Andreanof Islands *Island Group* Alaska, USA 4 A4
Andrews *Town* Texas, USA 17 J5
Andria *Town* Italy 61 H10
Andros Island The Bahamas 22 F2
Andros Town *Town* The Bahamas 22 F2
Angarsk *Town* Russian Federation 79 I7
Angeles *Town* Philippines 97 I2
Angel Falls *Waterfall* Venezuela 26 F6
Ångermanälven *River* Sweden 48 E7
Angers *Town* France 54 C7
Angkor Wat *Ancient site* Cambodia 95 F10
Anglesey *Island* Wales, UK 51 E9
Angola *Country* 44 E3
Angola Basin *Undersea feature* Atlantic Ocean 33 M6
Angoulême *Town* France 55 D9
Angren *Town* Uzbekistan 85 J3
Anguilla *Dependent territory* UK, Atlantic Ocean 23 N5
Anhui *Administrative region* China 91 J5
Ankara *Capital* Turkey 76 F4
Annaba *Town* Algeria 37 I3
An Nafūd *Desert* Saudi Arabia 82 B8
'Annah *Town* Iraq 82 C6
An Najaf *Town* Iraq 82 C7
Annamite Mountains *Mountain range* Laos 94 F8
Annapolis *Town* Maryland, USA 8 G8
Ann Arbor *Town* Michigan, USA 13 L5

An Nāşirīyah *Town* Iraq 82 D7
Annecy *Town* France 55 G9
Anniston *Town* Alabama, USA 10 H4
Anqing *Town* China 91 J6
Anshan *Town* China 91 L2
Anshun *Town* China 90 G7
Antakya *Town* Turkey 76 H7
Antalya *Town* Turkey 76 E6
Antananarivo *Capital* Madagascar 45 M5
Antarctica 110
Antarctic Peninsula Antarctica 110 B4
Antibes *Town* France 55 H11
Anticosti, Île d' *Island* Québec, Canada 7 K5
Antigua *Island* Antigua & Barbuda 23 N6
Antigua & Barbuda *Country* 23 N5
Anti-Lebanon *Mountain range* Syria 81 E9
Antofagasta *Town* Chile 30 D5
Antony *Town* France 54 E7
Antsiranana *Town* Madagascar 45 M3
Antwerp *Town* Belgium 53 E10
Antwerpen *see* Antwerp
Anyang *Town* China 91 J4
Anzio *Town* Italy 61 E9
Aomori *Town* Japan 92 F7
Aoraki *Mountain* New Zealand 107 C11
Aosta *Town* Italy 60 B4
Aozou *Town* Chad 42 E3
Apatity *Town* Russian Federation 72 D5
Apeldoorn *Town* Netherlands 52 F8
Apennines *Mountain range* Italy 60 C8
Āpia *Capital* Samoa 103 K7
Apoera *Town* Suriname 26 G6
Appalachian Mountains USA 8 H4
Appingedam *Town* Netherlands 52 G6
Appleton *Town* Wisconsin, USA 13 J4
Apuseni, Munpii *Mountain range* Romania 68 E5
Āqchah *Town* Afghanistan 85 I5
Aquidauana *Town* Brazil 29 I6
Arabian Peninsula Saudi Arabia 82 B8
Arabian Sea Indian Ocean 83 H10
Aracaju *Town* Brazil 29 N4
Araçuai *Town* Brazil 29 L6
'Arad *Town* Israel 81 D12
Arad *Town* Romania 68 D6
Arafura Sea Australia 105 I1
Araguaia, Rio *River* Brazil 29 J5
Araguaína *Town* Brazil 29 K3
Araguari *Town* Brazil 29 K6
Arāk *Town* Iran 82 E6
Arakan Yoma *Mountain range* Myanmar 94 B7
Aral Sea Uzbekistan/Kazakhstan 84 G1
Aral'sk *Town* Kazakhstan 78 E7
Aranda de Duero *Town* Spain 59 I4
'Ar'ar *Town* Saudi Arabia 82 C7
Ararat, Mount Turkey 77 L4
Arbīl *Town* Iraq 82 D6
Archangel *Town* Russian Federation 72 E6
Arco *Town* Italy 60 D5
Arctic Ocean 111 M5
Ardabīl *Town* Iran 82 E5
Ardakān *Town* Iran 82 F7
Ardennes *Physical region* Belgium 53 F13
Arequipa *Town* Peru 27 D12
Arezzo *Town* Italy 60 E7
Argalastí *Town* Greece 67 E10
Argenteuil *Town* France 54 E6
Argentina *Country* 31 E9
Argentine Basin *Undersea feature* Atlantic Ocean 33 J8
Argo *Town* Sudan 38 D6
Arica *Town* Chile 30 C3
Arizona *State* USA 16 E4
Arkansas *State* USA 10 E3
Arkansas City *Town* Kansas, USA 12 G8
Arkhangel'sk *see* Archangel
Arklow *Town* Ireland 51 D9
Arles *Town* France 55 F11
Arlington *Town* Texas, USA 17 M5
Arlington *Town* Virginia, USA 11 K2
Arlon *Town* Belgium 53 F13
Armenia *Country* 77 L4
Armenia *Town* Colombia 26 B6
Armstrong *Town* Ontario, Canada 6 E5
Arnaía *Town* Greece 67 E9
Arnhem *Town* Netherlands 53 F9
Arnhem Land *Region* Australia 105 I2
Ar Ramādī *Town* Iraq 82 C6
Arran, Isle of *Island* Scotland, UK 50 E7
Ar Raqqah *Town* Syria 80 G6
Arras *Town* France 54 F5
Ar Rawḑatayn *Town* Kuwait 82 D8
Arriaga *Town* Mexico 19 M9
Ar Riyāḑ *see* Riyadh
Ar Rub' al Khālī *Desert* Saudi Arabia 83 E11
Ar Rustāq *Town* Oman 83 G9
Ar Rut'bah *Town* Iraq 82 B6
Artashat *Town* Armenia 77 L4
Artemisa *Town* Cuba 22 D3
Artvin *Town* Turkey 77 J3
Arua *Town* Uganda 39 E10
Aruba *Dependent territory* Netherlands, Atlantic Ocean 23 J8
Arusha *Town* Tanzania 39 F12
Arvidsjaur *Town* Sweden 48 E6
Arys' *Town* Kazakhstan 78 F7
Asadābād *Town* Afghanistan 85 K7
Asahikawa *Town* Japan 92 G5
Asamankese *Town* Ghana 41 I8
Āsānsol *Town* India 87 K4
Ascension Island *Dependent territory* UK, Atlantic Ocean 33 K5
Ascoli Piceno *Town* Italy 60 F8
Aseb *Town* Eritrea 38 G8
Ashdod *Town* Israel 81 C11
Asheville *Town* North Carolina, USA 11 I4
Ashgabat *Capital* Turkmenistan 84 F5
Ashkelon *Town* Israel 81 C11
Ashmyany *Town* Belarus 70 E8
Ash Shadādah *Town* Syria 80 H5
Ash Shiḩr *Town* Yemen 83 E13
Asipovichy *Town* Belarus 71 F10
Asmara *Capital* Eritrea 38 F7
As Sabkhah *Town* Syria 80 G6
Assad, Lake Syria 80 F6
Aş Şafāwī *Town* Jordan 81 F10
As Salv *Town* Jordan 81 D11
Assam *Region* India 87 L3
Assamakka *Town* Niger 41 K4
As Samāwah *Town* Iraq 82 D7
Assen *Town* Netherlands 52 G6
Assu *Town* Brazil 29 M3
As Sukhnah *Town* Syria 80 G7
As Sulaymānīyah *Town* Iran 82 D6
As Sulayyil *Town* Saudi Arabia 83 D11
Aş Şuwār *Town* Syria 80 H6
As Suwaydā' *Town* Syria 81 E10
Astana *Capital* Kazakhstan 78 F6
Asti *Town* Italy 60 C5
Astrakhan' *Town* Russian Federation 73 D12
Asunción *Capital* Paraguay 30 G4
Aswān *Town* Egypt 38 E5
Asyūţ *Town* Egypt 38 E5
Atacama Desert Chile 30 D6
Atbara *Town* Sudan 38 E7
Atbasar *Town* Kazakhstan 78 F6
Ath *Town* Belgium 53 D11
Athabasca, Lake Saskatchewan, Canada 5 I7
Athens *Capital* Greece 67 E11
Athens *Town* Georgia, USA 11 I4
Athína *see* Athens
Athlone *Town* Ireland 51 C9
Ati *Town* Chad 42 E6
Atka *Town* Russian Federation 78 L4
Atka *Town* Alaska, USA 4 B5
Atlanta *Town* Georgia, USA 10 H4
Atlantic City *Town* New Jersey, USA 9 I8
Atlantic Ocean 32–33
Atlas Mountains *Mountain range* Morocco/Algeria 36 F4
Atsumi *Town* Japan 92 F8
Aţ Ţafīlah *Town* Jordan 81 E12
Aţ Ţā'if *Town* Saudi Arabia 83 B10
At Tall al Abyaḑ *Town* Syria 80 F5
Aţ Ţanf *Town* Syria 81 G9
Attawapiskat *Town* Ontario, Canada 6 G5
Atyrau *Town* Kazakhstan 78 E6
Auch *Town* France 55 D11
Auckland *Town* New Zealand 106 F5
Augsburg *Town* Germany 57 E10
Augusta *Town* Georgia, USA 11 I5
Augusta *Town* Maine, USA 9 K3
Aurangābād *Town* India 86 H5
Aurillac *Town* France 55 E10
Aurora *Town* Colorado, USA 15 L6
Aurora *Town* Illinois, USA 13 J6
Austin *Town* Texas, USA 17 L7
Australes, Îles *Island chain* French Polynesia 103 N8
Australia *Country* 105 L5
Australian Capital Territory *Territory* Australia 105 L8
Austria *Country* 57 G11
Ausuituq *see* Grise Fiord
Auxerre *Town* France 54 F7
Avarua *Capital* Cook Islands 103 M8
Aveiro *Town* Portugal 58 E5
Avellino *Town* Italy 61 F10
Avezzano *Town* Italy 61 F9
Aviemore *Town* Scotland, UK 50 E5
Avignon *Town* France 55 F11
Ávila *Town* Spain 58 H5
Avilés *Town* Spain 58 G2
Avon *Town* New York, USA 8 F5
Āwash *Town* Ethiopia 39 G9
Awbārī *Town* Libya 37 K6
Axel Heiberg Island Nunavut, Canada 5 I2
Ayacucho *Town* Peru 27 C11
Ayaguz *Town* Kazakhstan 78 G7
Ayaviri *Town* Peru 27 D11
Aydin *Town* Turkey 76 C6
Ayers Rock *see* Uluru
Ayorou *Town* Niger 41 J5
Ayutthaya *Town* Thailand 95 D10
Ayvalik *Town* Turkey 76 C5
Azaouâd *Desert* Mali 41 I4
A'zāz *Town* Syria 80 E5
Azerbaijan *Country* 77 M4
Azores *Island group* Portugal 32 H5
Azov, Sea of Black Sea 69 L6
Azuaga *Town* Spain 58 G7
Azul *Town* Argentina 31 G9
Az Zaqazīg *Town* Egypt 38 E4
Az Zarqā' *Town* Jordan 81 E11
Az Zāwiyah *Town* Libya 37 K4

B

Baalbek *Town* Lebanon 80 E8
Baardheere *Town* Somalia 39 G11
Baarn *Town* Netherlands 52 E8
Babayevo *Town* Russian Federation 72 C7
Babruysk *Town* Belarus 71 F10 *see also* Bobruysk
Babuyan Channel *Strait* Philippines 97 J1
Bacabal *Town* Brazil 29 L3
Bacău *Town* Romania 68 G6
Bačka Palanka *Town* Serbia 64 G7
Bac Liêu *Town* Vietnam 95 G12
Bacolod City *Town* Philippines 97 J3
Badajoz *Town* Spain 58 F6
Baden-Baden *Town* Germany 57 C9
Bad Hersfeld *Town* Germany 56 D7
Badlands *Region* North Dakota, USA 12 E3
Bafatá *Town* Guinea-Bissau 40 E6
Baffin Bay Nunavut, Canada 5 K3
Baffin Island Nunavut, Canada 5 K4
Bafoussam *Town* Cameroon 42 C8
Bafra *Town* Turkey 76 G3
Bagé *Town* Brazil 29 J9
Baghdad *Capital* Iraq 82 D6
Baghlān *Town* Afghanistan 85 J6
Bago *Town* Myanmar 94 B8
Bagrationovsk *Town* Kaliningrad 70 B7
Baguio *Town* Philippines 97 I2
Bahamas, The *Country* 22 G3
Baharly *Town* Turkmenistan 84 F4
Bahāwalpur *Town* Pakistan 86 G3
Bahía Blanca *Town* Argentina 31 F9
Bahir Dar *Town* Ethiopia 38 F8
Bahrain *Country* 83 F9
Bahushewsk *Town* Belarus 71 G9
Baia Mare *Town* Romania 68 E5
Baikal, Lake Russian Federation 79 J6
Bailén *Town* Spain 59 I7
Ba Illi *Town* Chad 42 E6
Bairiki *Capital* Kiribati 103 I4
Baishan *Town* China 89 M4
Baja *Town* Hungary 63 E12
Baja California *Peninsula* Mexico 18 D4
Bajram Curri *Town* Albania 65 F10
Baker *Town* Oregon, USA 14 H3
Baker & Howland Islands *Dependent territory* USA, Pacific Ocean 103 J4
Baker Lake *Town* Nunavut, Canada 5 J6
Bakersfield *Town* California, USA 14 G7
Bākhtarān *Town* Iran 82 D6
Baki *see* Baku
Baku *Capital* Azerbaijan 77 N3
Balakovo *Town* Russian Federation 73 E10
Balashov *Town* Russian Federation 73 D10
Balaton *Lake* Hungary 63 D12
Balclutha *Town* New Zealand 107 C13
Baleares, Islas *see* Balearic Islands
Balearic Islands *Island group* Spain 59 M5
Bāleshwar *Town* India 87 K5
Bali *Island* Indonesia 96 H8
Balikesir *Town* Turkey 76 C4
Balikpapan *Town* Indonesia 96 H6
Balkanabat *Town* Turkmenistan 84 D4
Balkan Mountains *Mountain range* Bulgaria 66 D6
Balkh *Town* Afghanistan 85 I6
Balkhash *Town* Kazakhstan 78 G7
Balkhash, Lake Kazakhstan 78 G7
Ballarat *Town* Victoria, Australia 105 K8
Balsas *Town* Brazil 29 L3
Balsas, Río *River* Mexico 19 J8
Bălpi *Town* Moldova 68 H5
Baltic Sea Northern Europe 49 D12
Baltimore *Town* Maryland, USA 9 G8
Balykchy *Town* Kyrgyzstan 85 M3
Bam *Town* Iran 82 G8
Bamako *Capital* Mali 40 G6
Bambari *Town* Central African Republic 42 F8
Bamberg *Town* Germany 56 E8
Bamenda *Town* Cameroon 42 C8
Banda Aceh *Town* Indonesia 96 C4
Bandarbeyla *Town* Somalia 39 I9
Bandar-e 'Abbās *Town* Iran 82 G8
Bandar-e Būshehr *Town* Iran 82 E8
Bandar-e Khamīr *Town* Iran 82 G8
Bandar Lampung *Town* Indonesia 96 E7
Bandar Seri Begawan *Capital* Brunei 96 H5
Banda Sea Indonesia 97 K7
Bandirma *Town* Turkey 76 C4
Bandundu *Town* Democratic Republic of the Congo 43 E11
Bandung *Town* Indonesia 96 F8
Bangalore *Town* India 86 H7
Banghāzī *see* Benghazi
Bangkok *Capital* Thailand 95 D10
Bangladesh *Country* 87 K4
Bangor *Town* Maine, USA 9 L3
Bangor *Town* Wales, UK 51 E9
Bangui *Capital* Central African Republic 42 E8
Ban Hua Hin *Town* Thailand 95 D10
Bāniyās *Town* Syria 80 D7
Banja Luka *Town* Bosnia & Herzegovina 64 D7
Banjarmasin *Town* Indonesia 96 H7
Banjul *Capital* Gambia 40 E5
Banks Peninsula New Zealand 107 E11
Banská Bystrica *Town* Slovakia 63 E10
Bantry *Town* Ireland 51 B11
Baoji *Town* China 90 H5
Baoshan *Town* China 90 E7
Baotou *Town* China 89 J5
Ba'qūbah *Town* Iraq 82 D6
Bar *Town* Montenegro 65 E11
Bārāmati *Town* India 86 H6
Baranavichy *Town* Belarus 71 D10 *see also* Baranovichi
Baranovichi *Town* Belarus 71 D10 *see also* Baranavichy
Barbados *Country* 23 P7
Barbuda *Island* Antigua & Barbuda 23 N5
Barcelona *Town* Venezuela 26 E5
Barcelona *Town* Spain 59 M4
Bareilly *Town* India 87 I3
Barents Sea Arctic Ocean 111 N8
Bar Harbor *Town* Maine, USA 9 L3
Bari *Town* Italy 61 H10
Barillas *Town* Guatemala 20 D3
Barinas *Town* Venezuela 26 D5
Barisal *Town* Bangladesh 87 L4

Barisan, Pegunungan *Mountain range* Indonesia 96 D7
Barkly Tableland *Plateau* Northern Territory, Australia 105 J3
Bârlad *Town* Romania 68 G6
Barlee Range *Mountain range* Western Australia, Australia 104 E4
Barletta *Town* Italy 61 H10
Barnaul *Town* Russian Federation 78 H6
Barnstaple *Town* England, UK 51 E11
Baron'ki *Town* Belarus 71 H11
Barquisimeto *Town* Venezuela 26 D5
Barrancabermeja *Town* Colombia 26 C5
Barranquilla *Town* Colombia 26 B4
Barreiras *Town* Brazil 29 L4
Barreiro *Town* Portugal 58 E7
Barrow-in-Furness *Town* England, UK 50 F8
Barstow *Town* California, USA 14 H8
Bartlesville *Town* Okahoma, USA 17 M3
Bartoszyce *Town* Poland 62 F5
Barysaw *Town* Belarus 71 F9 *see also* Borisov
Basarabeasca *Town* Moldova 68 H6
Basel *Town* Switzerland 57 C11
Basque Country, The *Region* Spain 59 I3
Basra *see* Al Başrah
Bassano del Grappa *Town* Italy 60 E5
Basse-Terre *Island* Guadeloupe 23 N6
Basse-Terre *Capital* Guadeloupe 23 N6
Basseterre *Capital* Saint Kitts & Nevis 23 N6
Bassikounou *Town* Mauritania 40 H5
Bass Strait Australia 105 K9
Bata *Town* Equatorial Guinea 43 C9
Batangas *Town* Philippines 97 I2
Bătdâmbâng *Town* Cambodia 95 E10
Bath *Town* England, UK 51 F11
Bath *Town* Maine, USA 8 K4
Bathinda *Town* India 86 H2
Bathurst *Town* New South Wales, Australia 105 L7
Batman *Town* Turkey 77 J6
Batna *Town* Algeria 37 I3
Baton Rouge *Town* Louisiana, USA 10 E6
Batticaloa *Town* Sri Lanka 87 J9
Batumi *Town* Georgia 77 J3
Batu Pahat *Town* Malaysia 96 E5
Bauchi *Town* Nigeria 41 L6
Bauska *Town* Latvia 70 E6
Bavaria *Region* Germany 57 E10
Bayamo *Town* Cuba 22 G4
Bayan Har Shan *Mountain range* China 88 H7
Bay City *Town* Michigan, USA 13 L5
Baydhabo *Town* Somalia 39 H10
Bayeux *Town* France 54 D6
Bāyir *Town* Jordan 81 F12
Baykal, Ozero *see* Lake Baikal
Bayreuth *Town* Germany 56 E8
Baytown *Town* Texas, USA 17 N7
Beaufort Sea Arctic Ocean 11 L4
Beaumont *Town* Texas, USA 17 N6
Beauvais *Town* France 54 E6
Beāwar *Town* India 86 H3
Béchar *Town* Algeria 36 G5
Bedford *Town* England, UK 51 H10
Bedford *Town* Pennsylvania, USA 8 F8
Be'er Sheva *Town* Israel 81 D12
Bei'an *Town* China 89 M2
Beihai *Town* China 90 H9
Beijing *Capital* China 91 J3
Beilen *Town* Netherlands 52 G7
Beira *Town* Mozambique 45 J5
Beirut *Capital* Lebanon 81 D9
Beja *Town* Portugal 58 F7
Békéscsaba *Town* Hungary 63 G12
Bekobod *Town* Uzbekistan 85 J4
Belarus *Country* 71 E9
Bełchatów *Town* Poland 62 E7
Belcher Islands *Island group* Canada 6 G3
Beledweyne *Town* Somalia 39 H10
Belém *Town* Brazil 29 K2
Belén *Town* Nicaragua 20 H6
Belfast *Town* Northern Ireland, UK 50 D7
Belfield *Town* North Dakota, USA 12 E3
Belfort *Town* France 54 H8
Belgaum *Town* India 86 G6
Belgium *Country* 53 D11
Belgorod *Town* Russian Federation 73 B10
Belgrade *Capital* Serbia 64 G7
Belgrano II *Research station* Antarctica 110 D4
Belize *Country* 20 F2
Belize City *Town* Belize 20 F2
Belle Isle, Strait of Québec, Canada 7 M5
Bellevue *Town* Washington, USA 14 G2
Bellingham *Town* Washington, USA 14 G1
Bello *Town* Colombia 26 C6
Bellville *Town* South Africa 44 F9
Belmopan *Capital* Belize 20 F2
Belogradchik *Town* Bulgaria 66 D5
Belo Horizonte *Town* Brazil 29 L6
Belomorsk *Town* Russian Federation 72 D6
Beloretsk *Town* Russian Federation 73 G10
Bemaraha *Mountain range* Madagascar 45 L5
Benavente *Town* Spain 58 G4
Bend *Town* Oregon, USA 14 G3
Bendigo *Town* Victoria, Australia 105 K8
Benevento *Town* Italy 61 F10
Bengal, Bay of Indian Ocean 87 L5
Bengbu *Town* China 91 J5
Benghazi *Town* Libya 37 M4
Bengkulu *Town* Indonesia 96 E7
Benguela *Town* Angola 44 D3
Benidorm *Town* Spain 59 K7
Beni-Mellal *Town* Morocco 36 F4
Benin *Country* 41 J7
Benin, Bight of *Coastal feature* Nigeria 41 J8
Benin City *Town* Nigeria 41 K8
Beni Suef *Town* Egypt 38 D4
Ben Nevis *Mountain* Scotland, UK 50 E5
Benson *Town* Arizona, USA 16 F6
Bent Jbaïl *Town* Lebanon 81 D10
Benton *Town* Arkansas, USA 10 E4
Benue *River* Nigeria 41 L7
Benue *River* Nigeria 41 L7
Beograd *see* Belgrade
Berat *Town* Albania 65 F12
Berbera *Town* Somalia 39 H9
Berbérati *Town* Cameroon 42 D8
Berdyans'k *Town* Ukraine 69 L6
Berdychiv *Town* Ukraine 68 H3
Berezhany *Town* Ukraine 68 F3
Berezniki *Town* Russian Federation 72 G8
Bergamo *Town* Italy 60 D5
Bergen *Town* Norway 49 A9
Bergen *Town* Germany 56 F4
Bergerac *Town* France 55 D10
Bering Sea Russian Federation 79 N3
Bering Strait Russian Federation/USA 79 M2
Berkeley *Town* California, USA 14 F6
Berlin *Capital* Germany 56 G6
Berlin *Town* New Hampshire, USA 9 J3
Bermuda *Dependent territory* UK, Atlantic Ocean 32 H3
Bern *Capital* Switzerland 57 C11
Berner Alps *Mountain range* Switzerland 57 C12
Bertoua *Town* Cameroon 42 D8
Besançon *Town* France 54 G8
Betafo *Town* Madagascar 45 M5
Bethlehem *Town* Israel 81 D11
Béticos, Sistemas *Mountain range* Spain 59 I8
Bétou *Town* Congo 43 E9
Beveren *Town* Belgium 53 D10
Beyrouth *see* Beirut
Béziers *Town* France 55 E11
Bhaktapur *Town* Nepal 87 J3
Bhāvnagar *Town* India 86 G5
Bhopāl *Town* India 86 H4
Bhubaneshwar *Town* India 87 K5
Bhusāwal *Town* India 86 H5
Bhutan *Country* 87 L3
Biała Podlaska *Town* Poland 62 H7
Białystok *Town* Poland 62 H6
Biarritz *Town* France 55 B11
Bicaz *Town* Romania 68 G5
Biel *Town* Switzerland 57 C11
Bielefeld *Town* Germany 56 D6
Bielsko-Biała *Town* Poland 63 E9
Biên Hoa *Town* Vietnam 95 G11
Bié, Planalto do *Plateau* Angola 44 F3
Bighorn Mountains Wyoming, USA 15 K3
Bighorn River Montana, USA 15 K3
Bignona *Town* Senegal 40 E5
Big Sioux River South Dakota, USA 12 G4
Bihać *Town* Bosnia & Herzegovina 64 C7
Bijelo Polje *Town* Montenegro 65 F9
Bīkāner *Town* India 86 G3
Bikin *Town* Russian Federation 78 M7
Bikini Atoll Marshall Islands 102 H2
Bilāspur *Town* India 87 J5
Biläsuvar *Town* Azerbaijan 77 N4
Bila Tserkva *Town* Ukraine 69 I3
Bilauktaung Range *Mountain range* Thailand 95 D11
Bilbao *Town* Spain 59 I3
Billings *Town* Montana, USA 15 J3
Bilma, Grand Erg de *Desert* Niger 41 M4
Biloxi *Town* Mississippi, USA 10 F6
Binghamton *Town* New York, USA 8 G6
Bingöl *Town* Turkey 77 J5
Bintulu *Town* Malaysia 96 G5
Binzhou *Town* China 91 K4
Birāk *Town* Libya 37 K6
Birao *Town* Central African Republic 42 G7
Birātnagar *Town* Nepal 87 K3
Bīrjand *Town* Iran 82 H6
Birkenfeld *Town* Germany 57 C9
Birkenhead *Town* England, UK 51 F9
Birmingham *Town* England, UK 50 G10
Birmingham *Town* Alabama, USA 10 G5
Birnin Konni *Town* Niger 41 K5
Birobidzhan *Town* Russian Federation 79 L7
Birsk *Town* Russian Federation 73 G9
Biržai *Town* Lithuania 70 E6
Biscay, Bay of Atlantic Ocean 33 L2
Bishkek *Capital* Kyrgyzstan 85 L2
Biskra *Town* Algeria 37 I4
Bislig *Town* Philippines 97 K4
Bismarck *Town* North Dakota, USA 12 F3
Bismarck Archipelago *Island chain* Papua New Guinea 102 E5
Bismarck Sea Pacific Ocean 102 E5
Bissau *Capital* Guinea-Bissau 40 E6
Bistripa *Town* Romania 68 F5
Bitlis *Town* Turkey 77 K5
Bitola *Town* Macedonia 65 G12
Bitonto *Town* Italy 61 H10
Bitterroot Range *Mountain range* Idaho, USA 15 I2
Bitung *Town* Indonesia 97 K6
Bizerte *Town* Tunisia 37 J3
Bjørnøya Norway 111 N8
Black Forest *Region* Germany 57 C10
Black Hills *Mountain range* South Dakota, USA 12 E4
Blackpool *Town* England, UK 50 F8
Black Range *Mountain range* New Mexico, USA 16 G5
Black Rock Desert Nevada, USA 14 G5
Black Sea Asia/Europe 69 I6
Black Sea Lowland Ukraine 69 J6
Black Volta *River* Ghana 41 I6
Blagoevgrad *Town* Bulgaria 66 E7
Blagoveshchensk *Town* Russian Federation 79 L7
Blanca, Bahía *Bay* Argentina 31 F10
Blanca, Costa *Coastal region* Spain 59 K7
Blanes *Town* Spain 59 M4
Blantyre *Town* Malawi 45 J4
Blida *Town* Algeria 36 H3
Bloemfontein *Capital* South Africa 44 H7
Bloomfield *Town* New Mexico, USA 16 G3
Bloomington *Town* Indiana, USA 12 H4
Bloomington *Town* Minnesota, USA 13 K7
Bloomsbury *Town* Queensland, Australia 105 M4
Bluefields *Town* Nicaragua 21 J6
Blue Nile *River* Sudan 38 E8
Blumenau *Town* Brazil 29 K8
Bo *Town* Sierra Leone 40 F7
Boa Vista *Town* Brazil 28 H1
Bobo-Dioulasso *Town* Burkina Faso 40 H6
Bobruysk *Town* Belarus 71 F10 *see also* Babruysk
Bocay *Town* Nicaragua 20 H4
Bocholt *Town* Germany 56 C6
Bochum *Town* Germany 56 C7
Bodaybo *Town* Russian Federation 78 J6
Boden *Town* Sweden 48 F6
Bodrum *Town* Turkey 76 C6
Bogale *Town* Myanmar 95 B9
Bogor *Town* Indonesia 96 F8
Bogotá *Capital* Colombia 26 C6
Bo Hai *Gulf* China 91 K3
Bohemia *Region* Czechia 63 B9
Bohemian Forest *Region* Germany 57 F10
Bohol Sea Philippines 97 J4
Boise *Town* Idaho, USA 14 H4
Boise City *Town* Okahoma, USA 17 J3
Bojnūrd *Town* Iran 82 G5
Boké *Town* Guinea 40 E6
Bolesławiec *Town* Poland 62 C7
Bolgatanga *Town* Ghana 41 I6
Bolivia *Country* 27 E11
Bologna *Town* Italy 60 E6
Bolton *Town* England, UK 51 F9
Bolu *Town* Turkey 76 E4
Bolzano *Town* Italy 60 E4
Boma *Town* Democratic Republic of the Congo 43 D11
Bombay *see* Mumbai
Bonaire *Dependent territory* Netherlands, Atlantic Ocean 23 K8
Bonaparte Archipelago *Island group* Australia 104 F2
Bondoukou *Town* Côte d'Ivoire 41 I7
Bone, Teluk *Bay* Indonesia 97 I7
Bongaigaon *Town* India 87 L3
Bongo, Massif des *Mountain range* Central African Republic 42 G7
Bonifacio *Town* Corsica, France 55 I13
Bonifacio, Strait of Mediterranean Sea 61 B9
Bonn *Town* Germany 56 C8
Boppard *Town* Germany 56 C8
Borås *Town* Sweden 49 D11
Bordeaux *Town* France 55 D10
Bordj Omar Driss *Town* Algeria 37 I6
Børgefjellet *Mountain range* Norway 48 D6
Borgholm *Town* Sweden 49 E11
Borisoglebsk *Town* Russian Federation 73 D10
Borisov *Town* Belarus 71 F9 *see also* Barysaw
Borneo *Island* Indonesia 96 G6
Bornholm *Island* Denmark 49 D13
Borovan *Town* Bulgaria 66 E5
Borovichi *Town* Russian Federation 72 C7
Boryslav *Town* Ukraine 68 E3
Bose *Town* China 90 H8
Bosnia & Herzegovina *Country* 64 D8
Bosporus *River* Turkey 76 D3
Bossembélé *Town* Central African Republic 42 E8
Bossier City *Town* Louisiana, USA 10 D5
Boston *Town* Massachusetts, USA 9 K5
Bothnia, Gulf of Finland 48 F7
Botoşani *Town* Romania 68 G5
Botou *Town* China 91 J3
Botswana *Country* 44 G6
Bouar *Town* Central African Republic 42 E8
Bou Craa *Town* Western Sahara 36 D6
Bougouni *Town* Mali 40 G6
Boujdour *Town* Western Sahara 36 C6
Boulder *Town* Colorado, USA 15 K5
Boulogne-sur-Mer *Town* France 54 E5
Boundiali *Town* Côte d'Ivoire 40 H7
Bourges *Town* France 54 E8
Bourke *Town* New South Wales, Australia 105 L6
Bournemouth *Town* England, UK 51 G12
Bouvet Island *Dependent territory* Norway, Atlantic Ocean 33 L8
Boysun *Town* Uzbekistan 85 I5
Bozeman *Town* Montana, USA 15 J3
Brades *Capital* Montserrat 23 N6
Bradford *Town* England, UK 50 G8
Brahmapur *Town* India 87 K5
Brahmaputra *River* Asia 87 L3
Brăila *Town* Romania 68 G7
Brampton *Town* Ontario, Canada 6 G8
Brandenburg *Town* Germany 56 F6
Brasília *Capital* Brazil 29 K5
Braşov *Town* Romania 68 F6
Bratislava *Capital* Slovakia 63 D10
Bratsk *Town* Russian Federation 79 I6
Braunschweig *Town* Germany 56 E6
Brava, Costa *Coastal region* Spain 59 N4
Brawley *Town* California, USA 14 H8
Brazil *Country* 28 G4
Brazzaville *Capital* Congo 43 D11
Brecon Beacons *Hills* Wales, UK 51 F10

Breda *Town* Netherlands 53 E9
Bregovo *Town* Bulgaria 66 D5
Brčko District *Administrative region* Bosnia & Herzegovina 64 E7
Bremen *Town* Germany 56 D5
Bremerhaven *Town* Germany 56 D5
Brenner Pass Italy/Austria 60 E4
Brescia *Town* Italy 60 D5
Brest *Town* Belarus 71 B10
Brest *Town* France 54 A6
Brezovo *Town* Bulgaria 66 F6
Bria *Town* Central African Republic 42 F8
Briançon *Town* France 55 G10
Bridgeport *Town* Connecticut, USA 9 I6
Bridgetown *Capital* Barbados 23 P7
Bridlington *Town* England, UK 50 H8
Brig *Town* Switzerland 57 C12
Brighton *Town* England, UK 51 H11
Brindisi *Town* Italy 61 I10
Brisbane *Town* Queensland, Australia 105 M6
Bristol *Town* England, UK 51 F11
Bristol Channel Wales/England, UK 51 E11
British Columbia *Province* Canada 4 G7
British Indian Ocean Territory *Dependent territory UK*, Indian Ocean 99 J5
British Virgin Islands *Dependent territory* UK, Atlantic Ocean 23 M5
Brittany *Region* France 54 B6
Brive-la-Gaillarde *Town* France 55 D10
Brno *Town* Czechia 63 D9
Broken Arrow *Town* Okahoma, USA 17 M3
Brookhaven *Town* Mississippi, USA 10 F6
Brooks Range *Mountain Range* Alaska, USA 4 F4
Broome *Town* Western Australia, Australia 104 F3
Brownfield *Town* Texas, USA 17 J5
Brownwood *Town* Texas, USA 17 L6
Brownsville *Town* Texas, USA 17 M9
Bruges *Town* Belgium 53 C10
Brugge *see* Bruges
Brunei *Country* 96 H5
Brussel *see* Brussels
Brussels *Capital* Belgium 53 D11
Bruxelles *see* Brussels
Bryan *Town* Texas, USA 17 M6
Bryansk *Town* Russian Federation 73 B9
Bucaramanga *Town* Colombia 26 C5
Bucharest *Capital* Romania 68 F7
București *see* Bucharest
Budapest *Capital* Hungary 63 E11
Buenaventura *Town* Colombia 26 B6
Buena Vista *Town* Bolivia 27 E12
Buenos Aires *Capital* Argentina 30 G8
Buffalo *Town* New York, USA 8 F5
Buffalo *Town* South Dakota, USA 12 E3
Bug *River* Poland 62 G6
Buguruslan *Town* Russian Federation 73 F10
Buḩayrat al Asad *see* Lake Assad
Bujanovac *Town* Serbia 65 G10
Bujumbura *Capital* Burundi 39 D12
Bukavu *Town* Democratic Republic of the Congo 43 H10
Bukoba *Town* Tanzania 39 E11
Bulawayo *Town* Zimbabwe 44 H5
Bulgaria *Country* 66 F6
Bumba *Town* Democratic Republic of the Congo 43 G9
Bungo-suidō *Strait* Japan 93 D13
Bünyan *Town* Turkey 76 G5
Buraydah *Town* Saudi Arabia 83 C9
Burdur *Town* Turkey 76 D6
Burgas *Town* Bulgaria 66 H6
Burgos *Town* Spain 59 I3
Burgundy *Region* France 54 F8
Buriram *Town* Thailand 95 E9
Burketown *Town* Queensland, Australia 105 J3
Burkina Faso *Country* 41 I6
Burlington *Town* New York, USA 9 I4
Burma *see* Myanmar
Burns *Town* Oregon, USA 14 G4
Burnsville *Town* Minnesota, USA 12 H4
Bursa *Town* Turkey 76 D4
Burundi *Country* 39 D12
Busan *Town* South Korea 91 M4
Buta *Town* Democratic Republic of the Congo 43 G9
Butterworth *Town* Malaysia 96 D4
Butuan *Town* Philippines 97 K4
Buxoro *Town* Uzbekistan 84 H4
Buynaksk *Town* Russian Federation 73 D14
Büyükağri Daği *see* Ararat, Mount
Buzău *Town* Romania 68 G7
Buzuluk *Town* Russian Federation 73 F10
Byahoml' *Town* Belarus 71 F9
Byalynichy *Town* Belarus 71 G10
Bydgoszcz *Town* Poland 62 E6
Byelaruskaya Hrada *Ridge* Belarus 71 D9
Bytom *Town* Poland 62 E8
Bytča *Town* Slovakia 63 E9

C

Cabanatuan *Town* Philippines 97 J2
Cabimas *Town* Venezuela 26 D5
Cabinda *Town* Angola 44 D1
Cabinda *Province* Angola 44 D1
Caborca *Town* Mexico 18 E3
Cabot Strait Canada 7 L6
Cáceres *Town* Spain 58 G6
Cachimbo *Town* Brazil 29 I4
Cachimbo, Serra do *Mountain range* Brazil 29 I4
Cadiz *Town* Philippines 97 J3
Cádiz *Town* Spain 58 G9
Cadiz, Gulf of Spain 58 F8
Caen *Town* France 54 D6
Cagayan de Oro *Town* Philippines 97 K4
Cagliari *Town* Sardinia, Italy 61 B11
Caguas *Town* Puerto Rico 23 L5
Caicos Passage *Strait* The Bahamas 23 I3
Cairns *Town* Queensland, Australia 105 L3
Cairo *Capital* Egypt 38 E4
Cajamarca *Town* Peru 27 B9
Čakovec *Town* Croatia 64 D5
Calabar *Town* Nigeria 41 L8
Calafat *Town* Romania 68 E7
Calais *Town* France 54 E5
Calais *Town* Maine, USA 9 L2
Calama *Town* Chile 30 D4
Călărași *Town* Romania 68 G7
Calatayud *Town* Spain 59 J4
Calbayog *Town* Philippines 97 J3
Calcutta *see* Kolkata
Calgary *Town* Alberta, Canada 4 H8
Cali *Town* Colombia 26 B6
Calicut *Town* India 86 H8 *see also* Kozhikode
California *State* USA 14 H7
California, Gulf of Mexico 18 E4
Callao *Town* Peru 27 B11
Caltanissetta *Town* Sicily, Italy 61 E13
Caluula *Town* Somalia 38 I8
Camacupa *Town* Angola 44 E3
Camagüey *Town* Cuba 22 F4
Camaná *Town* Peru 27 C12
Ca Mau *Town* Vietnam 95 F12
Cambodia *Country* 95 F10
Cambrai *Town* France 54 F5
Cambrian Mountains Wales, UK 51 F10
Cambridge *Town* England, UK 51 H10
Cambridge *Town* Maryland, USA 8 H9
Cambridge *Town* Ohio, USA 13 M6
Cambridge Bay *Town* Nunavut, Canada 5 I5
Camden *Town* Maine, USA 9 K4
Cameroon *Country* 42 C8
Camopi *Town* French Guiana 26 I7
Campeche *Town* Mexico 19 N7
Campeche, Bay of Mexico 19 M7
Cẩm Pha *Town* Vietnam 94 G6
Câmpina *Town* Romania 68 F7
Campina Grande *Town* Brazil 29 N4
Campinas *Town* Brazil 29 K7
Campobasso *Town* Italy 61 F9
Campo Grande *Town* Brazil 29 I6
Campos dos Goytacazes *Town* Brazil 29 L7
Câmpulung *Town* Romania 68 E6
Cam Ranh *Town* Vietnam 95 H11
Çanakkale *Town* Turkey 76 C4
Çanakkale Boğazi *see* Dardanelles
Canada *Country* 4 G8
Canary Islands *Island group* Spain, Atlantic Ocean 33 K3
Canaveral, Cape *Coastal feature* Florida, USA 11 J7
Canavieiras *Town* Brazil 29 M5
Canberra *Capital* Australia 105 L8
Cancún *Town* Mexico 19 P6
Cangzhou *Town* China 91 J3
Caniapiscau, Réservoir de *Reservoir* Québec, Canada 7 I4
Çankiri *Town* Turkey 76 F4
Cannanore *Town* India 86 H8 *see also* Kannur
Cannes *Town* France 55 H12
Canoas *Town* Brazil 29 J8
Canon City *Town* Colorado, USA 15 K6
Cantábrica, Cordillera *Mountain range* Spain 58 G3
Canterbury *Town* England, UK 51 I11
Cần Thơ *Town* Vietnam 95 G12
Canton *Town* Ohio, USA 13 M6
Canyon *Town* Texas, USA 17 J4
Cape Basin *Undersea feature* Atlantic Ocean 33 M7
Cape Breton Island Nova Scotia, Canada 7 L7
Cape Charles *Town* Virginia, USA 11 L2
Cape Coast *Town* Ghana 41 I8
Cape Horn *Coastal feature* Chile 31 E15
Cape Town *Capital* South Africa 44 F9
Cape Verde *Country* 33 K4
Cape Verde Basin *Undersea feature* Atlantic Ocean 33 J4
Cape York Peninsula Queensland, Australia 105 K2
Cap-Haïtien *Town* Haiti 23 I5
Capitán Arturo Prat *Research station* Antarctica 110 B4
Caprivi Strip *Physical region* Namibia 44 G4
Caracaraí *Town* Brazil 28 H1
Caracas *Capital* Venezuela 26 E4
Caravelas *Town* Brazil 29 M6
Carbonia *Town* Sardinia, Italy 61 B11
Cárdenas *Town* Cuba 22 E3
Cardiff *Town* Wales, UK 51 F11
Carei *Town* Romania 68 E5
Caribbean Sea Atlantic Ocean 32 H4
Carlisle *Town* England, UK 50 F7
Carlisle *Town* Pennsylvania, USA 8 G7
Carlow *Town* Ireland 51 D9
Carlsbad *Town* New Mexico, USA 17 I5
Carmarthen *Town* Wales, UK 51 E10
Carmelita *Town* Guatemala 20 E2
Carmen *Town* Mexico 19 N7
Carnarvon *Town* Western Australia, Australia 104 D5
Carolina *Town* Brazil 29 K3
Caroline Islands *Island group* Micronesia 102 F3
Carpathian Mountains *Mountain range* Poland/Slovakia/Romania 68 F5
Carpentaria, Gulf of Australia 105 J2
Carpi *Town* Italy 60 D6
Carrara *Town* Italy 60 D6
Carson City *Town* Nevada, USA 14 G6
Cartagena *Town* Colombia 26 B5
Cartagena *Town* Spain 59 K8
Carthage *Ancient site* Tunisia 37 J3
Cartwright *Town* Newfoundland & Labrador, Canada 7 L4
Carúpano *Town* Venezuela 26 F4
Caruthersville *Town* Missouri, USA 13 J8
Cary *Town* North Carolina, USA 11 K3
Casablanca *Town* Morocco 36 E4
Cascade Range *Mountain Range* Oregon/Washington, USA 14 F4
Caserta *Town* Italy 61 F10
Casey *Research station* Antarctica 110 G7
Casper *Town* Wyoming, USA 15 K4
Caspian Depression *Lowland* Russian Federation 73 D12
Caspian Sea Asia 73 D13
Casteggio *Town* Italy 60 C5
Castellon de la Plana *Town* Spain 59 K5
Castelvetrano *Town* Sicily, Italy 61 D13
Castlebar *Town* Ireland 50 B8
Castricum *Town* Netherlands 52 E7
Castries *Capital* St. Lucia 23 O7
Castrovillari *Town* Italy 61 G11
Catacamas *Town* Honduras 20 H4
Catalonia *Region* Spain 59 L4
Cataluña *see* Catalonia
Catania *Town* Sicily, Italy 61 G13
Catanzaro *Town* Italy 61 H12
Catskill Mountains New York, USA 8 H5
Caucasia *Town* Colombia 26 B5
Caucasus *Mountain range* Asia/Europe 77 J2
Caviana de Fora, Ilha *Island* Brazil 29 K2
Cayenne *Capital* French Guiana 26 I6
Cayes *Town* Haiti 22 H5
Cayman Islands *Dependent territory* UK, Atlantic Ocean 22 E5
Cebu *Town* Philippines 97 J3
Cecina *Town* Italy 60 D7
Cedar City *Town* Utah, USA 15 I6
Cedar Falls *Town* Iowa, USA 12 H5
Cedar Rapids *Town* Iowa, USA 13 I5
Cefalù *Town* Sicily, Italy 61 E12
Celebes *Island* Indonesia 97 J7
Celebes Sea Pacific Ocean 97 I5
Celje *Town* Slovenia 57 H12
Celldömölk *Town* Hungary 63 D11
Celle *Town* Germany 56 E6
Celtic Sea Atlantic Ocean 51 C11
Cenderawasih, Teluk *Bay* Indonesia 97 M6
Central African Republic *Country* 42 G8
Central, Cordillera *Mountain range* Colombia 26 B7
Central, Cordillera *Mountain range* Dominican Republic 23 J5
Central, Cordillera *Mountain range* Panama 21 K8
Central Pacific Basin *Undersea feature* Pacific Ocean 109 J5
Central, Planalto *Physical region* Brazil 29 K5
Central Range *Mountain range* Papua New Guinea 102 E5
Central Siberian Uplands *Plateau* Russian Federation 79 I5
Central, Sistema *Mountain range* Spain 58 H5
Central Valley California, USA 14 G5
Ceram Sea Pacific Ocean 97 K7
Cerignola *Town* Italy 61 G10
Cerro de Pasco *Town* Peru 27 B10
Cesena *Town* Italy 60 E6
České Budějovice *Town* Czechia 63 B9
Český Krumlov *Town* Czechia 63 B10
Ceuta *Town* Spain 58 H9
Cévennes *Mountain range* France 55 F11
Ceyhan *Town* Turkey 76 G6
Ceylanpinar *Town* Turkey 77 J6
Chachapoyas *Town* Peru 27 B9
Chad *Country* 42 E5
Chad, Lake Chad 42 D5
Chāgai Hills *Mountain range* Pakistan 86 E2
Chaillu, Massif du *Mountain range* Gabon 43 C10
Chakhānsūr *Town* Afghanistan 84 G8
Chalatenango *Town* El Salvador 20 F4
Chalkidikí *Peninsula* Greece 67 E9
Challans *Town* France 54 C8
Challenger Deep *Undersea feature* Pacific Ocean 108 H4
Châlons-en-Champagne *Town* France 54 G6
Chalon-sur-Saône *Town* France 54 G8
Chaman *Town* Pakistan 86 F2
Chambéry *Town* France 55 G10
Champagne *Region* France 54 F7
Champaign *Town* Illinois, USA 13 J6
Champlain, Lake New York, USA 9 I4
Champotón *Town* Mexico 19 N7
Chañaral *Town* Chile 30 C5
Chandīgarh *Town* India 86 H2
Chandrapur *Town* India 87 I5
Changchun *Town* China 89 M3
Changde *Town* China 91 I6
Chang Jiang *see* Yangtze
Changsha *Town* China 91 I6
Changzhi *Town* China 91 I4
Channel Islands *Island group* UK 51 G13
Channel Tunnel UK/France 51 I11
Chantada *Town* Spain 58 F3
Chanthaburi *Town* Thailand 95 E10
Chaoyang *Town* China 91 K2
Chaozhou *Town* China 91 J8
Chapayevsk *Town* Russian Federation 73 E10

Chārīkār *Town* Afghanistan 85 J6
Charity *Town* Guyana 26 G5
Charleroi *Town* Belgium 53 E12
Charlesbourg *Town* Québec, Canada 7 I7
Charleston *Town* West Virginia, USA 11 I2
Charleston *Town* South Carolina, USA 11 J5
Charleville-Mézières *Town* France 54 G6
Charlotte *Town* North Carolina, USA 11 J4
Charlotte Amalie *Capital* Virgin Islands 23 M5
Charlottetown *Town* Prince Edward Island, Canada 7 L6
Charters Towers *Town* Queensland, Australia 105 L3
Châteaubriant *Town* France 54 D7
Châteauroux *Town* France 54 E8
Châtellerault *Town* France 54 D8
Chatham Islands *Island group* New Zealand 109 J8
Chattahoochee River Alabama/Georgia, USA 10 H5
Chattanooga *Town* Tennessee, USA 10 H4
Chatyr-Tash *Town* Kyrgyzstan 85 M4
Châu Đôc *Town* Cambodia 95 F11
Chauk *Town* Myanmar 94 B7
Chaykovskiy *Town* Russian Federation 73 F9
Cheb *Town* Czechia 62 A8
Cheboksary *Town* Russian Federation 73 E9
Chech, Erg *Desert* Algeria 36 F7
Chefchaouen *Town* Morocco 36 F4
Chelkar *Town* Kazakhstan 78 E6
Chełm *Town* Poland 62 H7
Chelsea *Town* Vermont, USA 9 J4
Cheltenham *Town* England, UK 51 G10
Chelyabinsk *Town* Russian Federation 78 F5
Chemnitz *Town* Germany 56 F7
Chengde *Town* China 91 J2
Chengdu *Town* China 90 G6
Chennai *Town* India 87 I7
Chenzhou *Town* China 91 I7
Chepelare *Town* Bulgaria 66 F7
Cherepovets *Town* Russian Federation 72 D7
Cherkasy *Town* Ukraine 69 J4
Cherkessk *Town* Russian Federation 73 C11
Chernihiv *Town* Ukraine 69 I2
Chernivtsi *Town* Ukraine 68 G4
Chernyakhovsk *Town* Kaliningrad 70 C7
Cherry Hill *Town* New Jersey, USA 8 H8
Cherskiy *Town* Russian Federation 78 L3
Cherskogo, Khrebet *Mountain range* Russian Federation 79 K4
Cherykaw *Town* Belarus 71 G11
Chesapeake Bay *Coastal feature* USA 8 G9
Chester *Town* England, UK 51 F9
Chetumal *Town* Mexico 19 O7
Cheviot Hills Scotland, UK 50 F7
Cheyenne *Town* Wyoming, USA 15 L5
Chhapra *Town* India 87 J3
Chiang Mai *Town* Thailand 94 D8
Chiang Rai *Town* Thailand 94 D7
Chiba *Town* Japan 93 G10
Chibougamau *Town* Québec, Canada 6 H6
Chicago *Town* Illinois, USA 13 J6
Chichén-Itzá *Ancient site* Mexico 19 O6
Chickasha *Town* Oklahoma, USA 17 L4
Chiclayo *Town* Peru 27 A9
Chicoutimi *Town* Québec, Canada 7 I6
Chieti *Town* Italy 60 F8
Chifeng *Town* China 89 L4
Chihuahua *Town* Mexico 18 G4
Childress *Town* Texas, USA 17 K4
Chile *Country* 30 D6
Chillán *Town* Chile 31 C9
Chilpancingo *Town* Mexico 19 K8
Chimán *Town* Panama 21 N8
Chimbote *Town* Peru 27 B10
Chimoio *Town* Mozambique 45 I5
China *Country* 88 H6/91 J6
Chinandega *Town* Nicaragua 20 G5
Chingola *Town* Zambia 44 H3
Chin Hills *Mountain range* Myanmar 94 A6
Chioggia *Town* Italy 60 E5
Chíos *Town* Greece 67 G11
Chipata *Town* Zambia 45 I3
Chiquián *Town* Peru 27 B10
Chīrāla *Town* India 87 I7
Chirchiq *Town* Uzbekistan 85 J3
Chirripó Grande, Cerro *Mountain* Costa Rica 21 J8
Chişinău *Capital* Moldova 68 H6
Chita *Town* Russian Federation 79 J7
Chitato *Town* Angola 44 F2
Chitose *Town* Japan 92 F5
Chittagong *Town* Bangladesh 87 L4
Chitungwiza *Town* Zimbabwe 45 I5
Chlef *Town* Algeria 36 H3
Choele Choel *Town* Argentina 31 E10
Ch'ok'ē *Mountain range* Ethiopia 38 F8
Cholet *Town* France 54 D8
Choluteca *Town* Honduras 20 G5
Chomutov *Town* Czechia 62 B8
Chon Buri *Town* Thailand 95 D10
Ch'ŏngjin *Town* North Korea 91 M2
Chŏngju *Town* North Korea 91 L3
Chongqing *Town* China 90 H6
Chŏnju *Town* South Korea 91 M4
Chóra Sfakíon *Town* Greece 67 E14
Chornomors'ke *Town* Ukraine 69 J7
Chorzów *Town* Poland 62 E8
Chōshi *Town* Japan 93 H10
Choûm *Town* Mauritania 40 F3
Choybalsan *Town* Mongolia 89 K3
Christchurch *Town* New Zealand 107 E11
Christmas Island *Dependent territory* Australia, Indian Ocean 99 L5
Chukchi Sea Arctic Ocean 111 M3
Chula Vista *Town* California, USA 14 G9
Chulucanas *Town* Peru 27 B9
Chuncheon *Town* South Korea 91 M3
Churchill *Town* Manitoba, Canada 5 J7
Chusovoy *Town* Russian Federation 72 G8
Chuy *Town* Uruguay 30 H8
Ciechanów *Town* Poland 62 F6
Ciego de Ávila *Town* Cuba 22 F4
Cienfuegos *Town* Cuba 22 E3
Cilacap *Town* Indonesia 96 F8
Cincinnati *Town* Ohio, USA 13 L7
Cirebon *Town* Indonesia 96 F7
Cirò Marino *Town* Italy 61 H12
Citrus Heights *Town* California, USA 14 G6
Ciudad Bolívar *Town* Venezuela 26 F5
Ciudad Camargo *Town* Mexico 18 H4
Ciudad del Este *Town* Paraguay 30 H5
Ciudad Guayana *Town* Venezuela 26 F5
Ciudad Guzmán *Town* Mexico 19 I8
Ciudad Hidalgo *Town* Mexico 19 N9
Ciudad Juárez *Town* Mexico 18 G2
Ciudad Lerdo *Town* Mexico 19 I5
Ciudad Madero *Town* Mexico 19 K6
Ciudad Mante *Town* Mexico 19 K6
Ciudad Obregón *Town* Mexico 18 F5
Ciudad Ojeda *Town* Colombia 26 C5
Ciudad Real *Town* Spain 59 I6
Ciudad-Rodrigo *Town* Spain 58 G5
Ciudad Valles *Town* Mexico 19 K6
Ciudad Victoria *Town* Mexico 19 K6
Civitanova Marche *Town* Italy 60 F7
Civitavecchia *Town* Italy 60 D8
Clarence Town *Town* The Bahamas 22 H3
Clarksburg *Town* West Virginia, USA 11 J1
Clarksville *Town* Tennessee, USA 10 G3
Clearwater *Town* Florida, USA 11 I7
Clermont-Ferrand *Town* France 55 E9
Cleveland *Town* Ohio, USA 13 M6
Clinton *Town* Mississippi, USA 10 F5
Clipperton Island *Dependent territory* France, Pacific Ocean 109 M4
Cloppenburg *Town* Germany 56 C6
Clovis *Town* New Mexico, USA 17 I4
Cluj-Napoca *Town* Romania 68 E5
Clyde *River* Scotland, UK 50 F6
Coari *Town* Brazil 28 H3
Coast Mountains Alaska/ British Colombia 4 F7
Coast Ranges *Mountain Range* California/ Oregon, USA 14 F3
Coatzacoalcos *Town* Mexico 19 M8
Cobán *Town* Guatemala 20 E3
Cobija *Town* Bolivia 27 D10
Coburg *Town* Germany 56 E8
Cochabamba *Town* Bolivia 27 E12
Cochin *Town* India 86 H8 *see also* Kochi
Cochrane *Town* Chile 31 C12
Cochrane *Town* Ontario, Canada 6 G6
Cockburn Town *Capital* Turks & Caicos Islands 23 I4
Coconino Plateau Arizona, USA 16 E3
Cocos Islands *Dependent territory* Australia, Indian Ocean 99 K5
Cod, Cape *Coastal feature* Massachusetts, USA 9 K5
Cognac *Town* France 55 D9
Coihaique *Town* Chile 31 C12
Coimbatore *Town* Sri Lanka 86 H8
Coimbra *Town* Portugal 58 E5
Colby *Town* Kansas, USA 12 E7
Colchester *Town* England, UK 51 I10
Colima *Town* Mexico 19 I8
College Station *Town* Texas, USA 17 M6
Colmar *Town* France 54 H7
Cologne *Town* Germany 56 C7
Colombia *Country* 26 C7
Colombo *Capital* Sri Lanka 87 I9
Colón *Town* Panama 21 M7
Colorado *State* USA 15 K6
Colorado City *Town* Texas, USA 17 K5
Colorado Plateau Arizona, USA 16 F3
Colorado, Río *River* Argentina 31 E9
Colorado River Mexico/USA 15 J6
Colorado Springs *Town* Colorado, USA 15 L6
Columbia *Town* Tennessee, USA 10 H3
Columbia *Town* South Carolina, USA 11 J4
Columbia *Town* Maryland, USA 8 G8
Columbia *Town* Missouri, USA 13 I7
Columbia Plateau Idaho/Oregon, USA 14 H4
Columbia River Oregon/Washington, USA 14 G3
Columbus *Town* Ohio, USA 13 L7
Columbus *Town* Nebraska, USA 12 G6
Columbus *Town* Georgia, USA 10 H5
Comacchio *Town* Italy 60 E6
Comayagua *Town* Honduras 20 G4
Comilla *Town* Bangladesh 87 L4
Comitán *Town* Mexico 19 N9
Como *Town* Italy 60 C4
Comodoro Rivadavia *Town* Argentina 31 E12
Como, Lake Italy 60 D4
Comoros *Country* 45 L3
Conakry *Capital* Guinea 40 E7
Concarneau *Town* France 54 B7
Concepción *Town* Chile 31 C9
Concepción *Town* Paraguay 30 G5
Conchos, Río *River* Mexico 18 H4
Concord *Town* New Hampshire, USA 9 J5
Concordia *Town* Argentina 30 G7
Congo *Country* 43 E9
Congo *River* Democratic Republic of the Congo/Congo 43 G9
Congo Basin *Drainage basin* Central Africa 43 F10
Congo, Democratic Republic of the *Country* 43 G10
Connaught *Cultural region* Ireland 50 B8
Connecticut *State* USA 9 J6
Connecticut River USA 9 J5
Consolación del Sur *Town* Cuba 22 D3
Constanpa *Town* Romania 68 H7
Constantine *Town* Algeria 37 I3
Coober Pedy *Town* South Australia, Australia 105 I6
Cookeville *Town* Tennessee, USA 10 H3
Cook Islands *Dependent territory* New Zealand, Pacific Ocean 103 M7
Cook, Mount *see* Aoraki
Cook Strait New Zealand 107 F9
Cooktown *Town* Queensland, Australia 105 L2
Cooma *Town* New South Wales, Australia 105 L8
Coon Rapids *Town* Minnesota, USA 12 H4
Coos Bay *Town* Oregon, USA 14 F4
Copán *Ancient site* Honduras 20 F4
Copenhagen *Capital* Denmark 49 C12
Copiapó *Town* Chile 30 C6
Coquimbo *Town* Chile 30 C7
Coral Sea Pacific Ocean 102 F6
Coral Sea Islands *Dependent territory* Australia, Coral Sea 102 F7
Corcovado, Golfo *Gulf* Chile 31 C11
Cordele *Town* Georgia, USA 11 I5
Córdoba *Town* Spain 58 H7
Córdoba *Town* Argentina 30 E7
Córdoba *Town* Mexico 19 L8
Corfu *Island* Greece 67 B9
Corfu *Town* Greece 67 B9
Corinth *Town* Mississippi, USA 10 G4
Corinth *Town* Greece 67 D11
Corinth Canal Greece 67 E11
Cork *Town* Ireland 51 B10
Çorlu *Town* Turkey 76 C3
Corner Brook *Town* Québec, Canada 7 L5
Coro *Town* Venezuela 26 D4
Coromandel *Town* New Zealand 106 G5
Corozal *Town* Belize 20 F1
Corpus Christi *Town* Texas, USA 17 M8
Corrientes *Town* Argentina 30 G6
Corse *see* Corsica
Corsica *Island* France 55 I13
Cortés *Town* Costa Rica 21 J8
Cortina d'Ampezzo *Town* Italy 60 F4
Çorum *Town* Turkey 76 G4
Corvallis *Town* Oregon, USA 14 F3
Cosenza *Town* Italy 61 G12
Costa Rica *Country* 21 J7
Côte d'Ivoire *Country* 40 G7
Cotonou *Town* Benin 41 J8
Cotswold Hills England, UK 51 G10
Cottbus *Town* Germany 56 G7
Council Bluffs *Town* Iowa, USA 12 G6
Couvin *Town* Belgium 53 E13
Coventry *Town* England, UK 51 G10
Craiova *Town* Romania 68 E7
Crawley *Town* England, UK 51 H11
Cremona *Town* Italy 60 D5
Crescent City *Town* California, USA 14 F4
Crestview *Town* Florida, USA 10 G6
Crete *Island* Greece 67 F14
Crete, Sea of Greece 67 F13
Créteil *Town* France 54 E6
Crewe *Town* England, UK 51 F9
Crimea *Peninsula* Ukraine 69 K7
Cristuru Secuiesc *Town* Romania 68 F6
Croatia *Country* 64 C6
Crookston *Town* Minnesota, USA 12 G2
Crotone *Town* Italy 61 H12
Croydon *Town* England, UK 51 H11
Crozet Islands *Island group* Indian Ocean 99 I7
Cuauhtémoc *Town* Mexico 18 G4
Cuautla *Town* Mexico 19 K8
Cuba *Country* 22 F4
Cúcuta *Town* Colombia 26 C5
Cuddapah *Town* India 87 I7
Cuenca *Town* Ecuador 26 A8
Cuernavaca *Town* Mexico 19 K8
Cuiabá *Town* Brazil 29 I5
Cuito *River* Angola 44 F4
Cukai *Town* Malaysia 96 E5
Culiacán *Town* Mexico 18 G6
Cullera *Town* Spain 59 K6
Cumaná *Town* Venezuela 26 E5
Cumberland *Town* Maryland, USA 8 F8
Cumberland Plateau Tennessee, USA 10 H3
Cuneo *Town* Italy 60 B6
Curaçao *Dependent territory* Netherlands, Atlantic Ocean 23 K8
Curicó *Town* Chile 30 C8
Curitiba *Town* Brazil 29 K7
Cusco *Town* Peru 27 D11
Cuttack *Town* India 87 K5
Cuxhaven *Town* Germany 56 D5
Cyclades *Island group* Greece 67 F12
Cyprus *Country* 80 A8
Cyrenaica *Cultural region* Libya 37 M4
Czechia *Country* 63 C9
Czech Republic *see* Czechia
Częstochowa *Town* Poland 62 E8
Człuchów *Town* Poland 62 D5

D

Dabeiba *Town* Colombia 26 B5
Daegu *Town* South Korea 91 M4
Daejeon *Town* South Korea 91 M4
Dagupan *Town* Philippines 97 I2
Dakar *Capital* Senegal 40 D5
Dalain Hob *Town* China 89 I5

F

G

Junín *Town* Argentina 30 F8
Jura *Mountain range* Switzerland 57 C11
Jūrmala *Town* Latvia 70 E5
Juruá, Rio *River* Brazil 28 G3
Jutiapa *Town* Guatemala 20 E4
Juticalpa *Town* Honduras 20 H4
Jutland *Peninsula* Denmark 49 B12
Jwaneng *Town* Botswana 44 G6
Jylland *see* Jutland
Jyväskylä *Town* Finland 48 G8

K

K2 *Mountain* Pakistan/China 86 H1
Kabale *Town* Uganda 39 D11
Kabinda *Town* Democratic Republic of the Congo 43 G11
Kabul *Capital* Afghanistan 85 J7
Kabwe *Town* Zambia 44 H4
Kachchh, Rann of *Salt marsh* India 86 G4
Kadoma *Town* Zimbabwe 44 H4
Kaduna *Town* Nigeria 41 L6
Kadzhi-Say *Town* Kyrgyzstan 85 M3
Kaga *Town* Japan 93 E10
Kagoshima *Town* Japan 93 C14
Kahramanmaraş *Town* Turkey 76 H6
Kaifeng *Town* China 91 J4
Kaikoura *Town* New Zealand 107 F10
Kaili *Town* China 90 H7
Kairouan *Town* Tunisia 37 J3
Kaiserslautern *Town* Germany 57 C9
Kaiyuan *Town* China 90 F8
Kajaani *Town* Finland 48 H7
Kalahari Desert Namibia 44 F6
Kalamariá *Town* Greece 66 E8
Kalámata *Town* Greece 67 D12
Kalamazoo *Town* Michigan, USA 13 K5
Kalasin *Town* Thailand 95 F9
Kālat *Town* Pakistan 86 F2
Kalbarri *Town* Western Australia, Australia 104 D5
Kalemie *Town* Democratic Republic of the Congo 43 I11
Kalgoorlie *Town* Western Australia, Australia 104 F6
Kalima *Town* Democratic Republic of the Congo 43 H10
Kalimantan *Region* Indonesia 96 G6
Kaliningrad *Administrative region* Russian Federation 70 B7
Kaliningrad *Town* Kaliningrad 70 B6
Kalisz *Town* Poland 62 E7
Kalmar *Town* Sweden 49 E12
Kaluga *Town* Russian Federation 73 C9
Kalyān *Town* India 86 G5
Kamarang *Town* Guyana 26 F6
Kamchatka Peninsula Russian Federation 79 M4
Kamensk-Shakhtinskiy *Town* Russian Federation 73 C11
Kamina *Town* Democratic Republic of the Congo 43 G12
Kamloops *Town* British Colombia, Canada 4 G8
Kampala *Capital* Uganda 39 E11
Kâmpóng Cham *Town* Cambodia 95 G11
Kâmpóng Thum *Town* Cambodia 95 F10
Kam"yanets'-Podil's'kyy *Town* Ukraine 68 G4
Kamyshin *Town* Russian Federation 73 D11
Kananga *Town* Democratic Republic of the Congo 43 F11
Kanash *Town* Russian Federation 73 E9
Kanazawa *Town* Japan 93 E10
Kānchīpuram *Town* India 87 I7
Kandahār *Town* Afghanistan 84 H8
Kandalaksha *Town* Russian Federation 72 D5
Kandi *Town* Benin 41 J6
Kandy *Town* Sri Lanka 87 I9
Kanggye *Town* North Korea 91 M2
Kanjiža *Town* Serbia 64 G6
Kankan *Town* Guinea 40 G6
Kannur *Town* India 86 H8 *see also* Cannanore
Kano *Town* Nigeria 41 L6
Kanoya *Town* Japan 93 C14
Kānpur *Town* India 87 I3
Kansas *State* USA 12 F7
Kansas City *Town* Kansas, USA 12 H7
Kansas River Kansas, USA 12 G7
Kansk *Town* Russian Federation 79 I6
Kaolack *Town* Senegal 40 E5
Kaoma *Town* Zambia 44 G4
Kaposvár *Town* Hungary 63 E12
Kara-Balta *Town* Kyrgyzstan 85 L3
Karabük *Town* Turkey 76 F3
Karāchi *Town* Pakistan 86 F4
Karagandy *Town* Kazakhstan 78 G7
Karakol *Town* Kyrgyzstan 85 M3
Karakoram Range *Mountain range* Pakistan/India 86 H1
Karaman *Town* Turkey 76 F6
Karamay *Town* China 88 F4
Kara Sea Arctic Ocean 111 O6
Karatau *Town* Kazakhstan 78 F7
Karatsu *Town* Japan 93 B13
Karbalā' *Town* Iraq 82 C7
Kardítsa *Town* Greece 67 D10
Kärdla *Town* Estonia 70 F3
Kargi *Town* Turkey 76 G3
Karibib *Town* Namibia 44 E6
Karigasniemi *Town* Finland 48 G4
Karimata, Selat *Strait* Indonesia 96 F7
Karīmnagar *Town* India 87 I6
Karin *Town* Somalia 38 H8
Karlovac *Town* Croatia 64 C6
Karlovy Vary *Town* Czechia 62 B8
Karlskrona *Town* Sweden 49 D12
Karlsruhe *Town* Germany 57 C9
Karlstad *Town* Sweden 49 D10
Karnāl *Town* India 86 H3
Karnobat *Town* Bulgaria 66 H6
Kars *Town* Turkey 77 K4
Kárystos *Town* Greece 67 F11
Kaş *Town* Turkey 76 D7
Kasai *River* Democratic Republic of the Congo 43 E11
Kāsaragod *Town* India 86 H7
Kāshān *Town* Iran 82 E6
Kashi *Town* China 88 D5
Kashiwazaki *Town* Japan 93 F9
Kasongo *Town* Democratic Republic of the Congo 43 H11
Kasongo-Lunda *Town* Democratic Republic of the Congo 43 E11
Kaspiysk *Town* Russian Federation 73 D14
Kassala *Town* Sudan 38 F7
Kassel *Town* Germany 56 D7
Kasserine *Town* Tunisia 37 J4
Kastamonu *Town* Turkey 76 F3
Kasulu *Town* Tanzania 39 D12
Katahdin, Mount Maine, USA 9 L2
Katha *Town* Myanmar 94 C5
Katherine *Town* Northern Territory, Australia 105 I2
Kathmandu *Capital* Nepal 87 J3
Katikati *Town* New Zealand 106 G6
Katiola *Town* Côte d'Ivoire 40 H7
Katowice *Town* Poland 62 E8
Katsina *Town* Nigeria 41 L6
Kattaqo'rg'on *Town* Uzbekistan 85 I4
Kattegat *Sea* Denmark/Sweden 49 C12
Kaunas *Town* Lithuania 70 D7
Kavála *Town* Greece 66 F8
Kāvali *Town* India 87 I7
Kavarna *Town* Bulgaria 66 I5
Kawagoe *Town* Japan 93 G10
Kawasaki *Town* Japan 93 G10
Kayan *Town* Myanmar 94 C8
Kayseri *Town* Turkey 76 G5
Kazach'ye *Town* Russian Federation 78 K4
Kazakhstan *Country* 78 E6
Kazakh Uplands Kazakhstan 78 F7
Kazan' *Town* Russian Federation 73 E9
Kazanlŭk *Town* Bulgaria 66 F6
Kāzerūn *Town* Iran 82 F8
Kecskemét *Town* Hungary 63 F11
Kediri *Town* Indonesia 96 G8
Kędzierzyn-Koźle *Town* Poland 62 E8
Keith *Town* South Australia, Australia 105 J8
Kěk-Art *Town* Kyrgyzstan 85 L4
Kelowna *Town* British Colombia, Canada 4 G9
Kelso *Town* Washington, USA 14 F3
Keluang *Town* Malaysia 96 E5
Kemah *Town* Turkey 76 H5
Kemerovo *Town* Russian Federation 78 H6
Kemi *Town* Finland 48 G6
Kemijärvi *Town* Finland 48 G5
Kempten *Town* Germany 57 E10
Kendal *Town* England, UK 50 F8
Kengtung *Town* Myanmar 94 D6
Kénitra *Town* Morocco 36 F4
Kenora *Town* Ontario, Canada 6 D5
Kenosha *Town* Wisconsin, USA 13 J5
Kentau *Town* Kazakhstan 78 F7
Kentucky *State* USA 10 G3
Kenya *Country* 39 F11
Kerch *Town* Ukraine 69 L7
Kerkrade *Town* Netherlands 53 F11
Kérkyra *see* Corfu
Kermadec Islands *Island group* New Zealand 109 J7
Kermān *Town* Iran 82 G7
Kesennuma *Town* Japan 92 G8
Kettering *Town* Ohio, USA 13 L7
Key Largo *Town* Florida, USA 11 J9
Key West *Town* Florida, USA 11 J9
Khabarovsk *Town* Russian Federation 78 D4
Khairpur *Town* Pakistan 86 G3
Khanthabouli *Town* Laos 95 F9
Khanty-Mansiysk *Town* Russian Federation 78 G5
Khān Yūnis *Town* Israel 81 C12
Kharagpur *Town* India 87 K4
Kharkiv *Town* Ukraine 69 L3
Khartoum *Capital* Sudan 38 E7
Khasavyurt *Town* Russian Federation 73 D14
Khaskovo *Town* Bulgaria 66 F7
Khaydarkan *Town* Kyrgyzstan 85 K4
Kherson *Town* Ukraine 69 J6
Khmel'nyts'kyy *Town* Ukraine 68 G3
Khon Kaen *Town* Thailand 95 E9
Khōst *Town* Afghanistan 85 J7
Khouribga *Town* Morocco 36 E4
Khujand *Town* Tajikistan 85 J4
Khulna *Town* Bangladesh 87 L4
Khust *Town* Ukraine 68 E4
Khvoy *Town* Iran 82 D5
Khyber Pass Afghanistan/Pakistan 86 G1
Kidderminster *Town* England, UK 51 F10
Kiel *Town* Germany 56 E4
Kielce *Town* Poland 62 F8
Kiev *Capital* Ukraine 69 I3
Kigali *Capital* Rwanda 39 D12
Kigoma *Town* Tanzania 39 D12
Kii-suidō *Bay* Japan 93 E12
Kikinda *Town* Serbia 64 G6
Kikwit *Town* Democratic Republic of the Congo 43 E11
Kilis *Town* Turkey 76 H7
Killarney *Town* Ireland 51 B10
Killeen *Town* Texas, USA 17 L6
Kilmarnock *Town* Scotland, UK 50 E6
Kimberley *Town* South Africa 44 G7
Kimberley Plateau Western Australia, Australia 104 G3
Kimch'aek *Town* North Korea 91 M2
Kindia *Town* Guinea 40 F6
Kineshma *Town* Russian Federation 72 D8
Kingman Reef *Dependent territory* USA, Pacific Ocean 103 L3
Kingston *Capital* Jamaica 22 G6
Kingston *Town* Ontario, Canada 6 H8
Kingston upon Hull *Town* England, UK 50 H6
Kingstown *Capital* St Vincent & The Grenadines 23 O8
Kinshasa *Capital* Democratic Republic of the Congo 43 D11
Kipushi *Town* Democratic Republic of the Congo 43 H13
Kirghiz Range *Mountain range* Kyrgyzstan 85 K3
Kiribati *Country* 103 L5
Kirikhan *Town* Turkey 76 H7
Kirikkale *Town* Turkey 76 F4
Kirishi *Town* Russian Federation 72 C7
Kirkenes *Town* Norway 48 H3
Kirkland Lake *Town* Ontario, Canada 6 G6
Kirklareli *Town* Turkey 76 C3
Kirkūk *Town* Iraq 82 D6
Kirkwall *Town* Scotland,UK 50 F3
Kirov *Town* Russian Federation 72 F8
Kirovo-Chepetsk *Town* Russian Federation 72 F8
Kirovohrad *Town* Ukraine 69 J4
Kiruna *Town* Sweden 48 F5
Kisangani *Town* Democratic Republic of the Congo 43 H9
Kislovodsk *Town* Russian Federation 73 C11
Kismaayo *Town* Somalia 39 G11
Kissidougou *Town* Guinea 40 G7
Kissimmee, Lake Florida, USA 11 J7
Kisumu *Town* Kenya 39 E11
Kitakyūshū *Town* Japan 93 B13
Kitami *Town* Japan 92 G4
Kitchener *Town* Ontario, Canada 6 G8
Kitwe *Town* Zambia 44 H3
Kivalo *Ridge* Finland 48 G6
Kivertsi *Town* Ukraine 68 G2
Kivu, Lake Democratic Republic of the Congo 43 H10
Kladno *Town* Czechia 62 B8
Klagenfurt *Town* Austria 57 G11
Klaipėda *Town* Lithuania 70 C6
Klamath Falls *Town* Oregon, USA 14 F4
Klang *Town* Malaysia 96 D5
Klarälven *River* Sweden 49 D9
Klerksdorp *Town* South Africa 44 H7
Klintsy *Town* Russian Federation 73 B9
Ključ *Town* Bosnia & Herzegovina 64 D7
Klosters *Town* Switzerland 57 D11
Kluczbork *Town* Poland 62 E8
Knin *Town* Croatia 64 C8
Knoxville *Town* Tennessee, USA 11 I3
Kōbe *Town* Japan 93 E12
København *see* Copenhagen
Koblenz *Town* Germany 56 C8
Kočani *Town* Macedonia 65 H11
Kočevje *Town* Slovenia 57 H12
Kochi *Town* India 86 H8 *see also* Cochin
Kōchi *Town* Japan 93 D13
Kodiak *Town* Alaska, USA 4 D6
Kōfu *Town* Japan 93 F10
Kohīma *Town* India 87 M3
Kohtla-Järve *Town* Estonia 70 H4
Koko *Town* Nigeria 41 K6
Kokshetau *Town* Kazakhstan 78 F6
Kola Peninsula Russian Federation 72 E5
Kolari *Town* Finland 48 F5
Kolda *Town* Senegal 40 E5
Kolhāpur *Town* India 86 G6
Kolkatta *Town* India 87 K4
Kollam *Town* India 86 H9 *see also* Quilon
Köln *see* Cologne
Kołobrzeg *Town* Poland 62 C5
Kolomna *Town* Russian Federation 73 C9
Kolpino *Town* Russian Federation 72 C7
Kol'skiy Poluostrov *see* Kola Peninsula
Kolwezi *Town* Democratic Republic of the Congo 43 G13
Komatsu *Town* Japan 93 E10
Komsomol'sk-na-Amure *Town* Russian Federation 79 L6
Konin *Town* Poland 62 E7
Konispol *Town* Albania 65 F13
Konotop *Town* Ukraine 69 J2
Konstanz *Town* Germany 57 D10
Konya *Town* Turkey 76 F6
Kopaonik *Mountain range* Serbia 65 G9
Koper *Town* Slovenia 57 G12
Korat Plateau Thailand 94 F8
Korba *Town* India 87 J5
Korçë *Town* Albania 65 F12
Korea Bay China/North Korea 91 L3
Korea Strait Japan/South Korea 91 M4
Korhogo *Town* Côte d'Ivoire 40 H7
Kórinthos *see* Corinth
Kōriyama *Town* Japan 93 G9
Korla *Town* China 88 F5
Korosten' *Town* Ukraine 68 H2
Kortrijk *Town* Belgium 53 C11
Kos *Town* Greece 67 H13
Kościerzyna *Town* Poland 62 E5
Košice *Town* Slovakia 63 G10
Koson *Town* Uzbekistan 85 I4

L

Myanmar (Burma) *Country* 94 B5
Myanaung *Town* Myanmar 94 B8
Myaungmya *Town* Myanmar 95 B9
Myeik Archipelago *Island chain* Myanmar 95 C11
Myingyan *Town* Myanmar 94 B6
Myitkyina *Town* Myanmar 94 C5
Mykolayiv *Town* Ukraine 69 J5
Myrhorod *Town* Ukraine 69 K3
Mýrina *Town* Greece 67 F9
Myrtle Beach *Town* South Carolina, USA 11 K4
Mysore *Town* India 86 H8
My Tho *Town* Vietnam 95 G11
Mzuzu *Town* Malawi 45 J3

N

Naberezhnyye Chelny *Town* Russian Federation 73 F9
Nablus *Town* Israel 81 D11
Nacala *Town* Mozambique 45 K4
Nadi *Town* Fiji 103 I7
Nadvirna *Town* Ukraine 68 F4
Nadym *Town* Russian Federation 78 G5
Naga *Town* Philippines 97 J2
Nagano *Town* Japan 93 F10
Nagaoka *Town* Japan 93 F9
Nagasaki *Town* Japan 93 B14
Nagato *Town* Japan 93 C12
Nāgercoil *Town* India 86 H9
Nagorno-Karabakh *Region* Azerbaijan 77 M4
Nagoya *Town* Japan 93 F11
Nāgpur *Town* India 87 I5
Nagqu *Town* China 88 G7
Nagykanizsa *Town* Hungary 63 D12
Nagykőrös *Town* Hungary 63 F11
Naha *Town* Ryukyu Islands 93 A16
Nā'īn *Town* Iran 82 F7
Nain *Town* Newfoundland & Labrador, Canada 7 K3
Nairobi *Capital* Kenya 39 F11
Najin *Town* North Korea 91 M2
Najrān *Town* Saudi Arabia 83 C12
Nakagawa *Town* Japan 92 F4
Nakamura *Town* Japan 93 D13
Nakatsugawa *Town* Japan 93 F11
Nakhodka *Town* Russian Federation 79 M7
Nakhon Ratchasima *Town* Thailand 95 E9
Nakhon Sawan *Town* Thailand 95 D9
Nakhon Si Thammarat *Town* Thailand 95 D12
Nakuru *Town* Kenya 39 F11
Nal'chik *Town* Russian Federation 73 C13
Nālūt *Town* Libya 37 J5
Namangan *Town* Uzbekistan 85 K3
Nam Đinh *Town* Vietnam 94 G7
Namib Desert Namibia 44 E5
Namibe *Town* Angola 44 D4
Namibia *Country* 44 E5
Nampa *Town* Idaho, USA 14 H4
Nampula *Town* Mozambique 45 K4
Namur *Town* Belgium 53 E12
Nanaimo *Town* British Colombia, Canada 4 G9
Nancha *Town* China 89 M2
Nanchang *Town* China 91 J6
Nanchong *Town* China 90 H6
Nancy *Town* France 54 H7
Nānded *Town* India 86 H6
Nanfeng *Town* China 91 J7
Nanjing *Town* China 91 K5
Nanning *Town* China 90 H8
Nanping *Town* China 91 K7
Nanterre *Town* France 54 E6
Nantes *Town* France 54 C8
Nantucket *Town* Massachusetts, USA 9 K6
Nantucket Island Massachusetts, USA 9 K6
Nanyang *Town* China 91 I5
Napa *Town* California, USA 14 F6
Napier *Town* New Zealand 106 H7
Naples *Town* Italy 61 F10
Napoli *see* Naples
Napo, Río *River* Peru 26 C8
Narathiwat *Town* Thailand 95 E13
Narita *Town* Japan 93 G10
Närpes *Town* Finland 48 F8
Närpiö *see* Närpes
Narva *Town* Estonia 70 H4
Narvik *Town* Norway 48 E4
Năsăud *Town* Romania 68 F5
Nāshik *Town* India 86 G5
Nashua *Town* New Hampshire, USA 9 J5
Nashville *Town* Tennessee, USA 10 G3
Nassau *Capital* The Bahamas 22 G2
Nasser *Lake* Egypt 38 E6
Nata *Town* Botswana 44 H5
Natal *Town* Brazil 29 N3
Natitingou *Town* Benin 41 J6
Natzrat *see* Nazareth
Nauru *Country* 102 H4
Nauta *Town* Peru 27 C9
Navapolatsk *Town* Belarus 70 G8 *see also* Novopolotsk
Navassa Island *Dependent territory* USA, Atlantic Ocean 22 H5
Navoiy *Town* Uzbekistan 85 I4
Navojoa *Town* Mexico 18 F5
Nawābshāh *Town* Pakistan 86 F3
Nayoro *Town* Japan 92 F4
Nay Pyi Taw *Capital* Myanmar 94 C7
Nazareth *Town* Israel 81 D10
Nazca *Town* Peru 27 C11
Nazilli *Town* Turkey 76 D6
Nazrēt *Town* Ethiopia 39 G9
N'Dalatando *Town* Angola 44 E2
Ndélé *Town* Central African Republic 42 F7
N'Djaména *Capital* Chad 42 D6
Neagh, Lough *Lake* Northern Ireland, UK 50 D8
Neápoli *Town* Greece 67 G14
Neápoli *Town* Greece 67 C9
Near Islands *Island Group* Alaska, USA 4 A3
Nebraska *State* USA 12 F5
Necochea *Town* Argentina 31 G10
Neftekamsk *Town* Russian Federation 73 F9
Negēlē *Town* Ethiopia 39 G10
Negev *Desert* Israel 81 D12
Negombo *Town* Sri Lanka 87 I9
Negotin *Town* Serbia 64 H8
Negro, Rio *River* Brazil 28 G2
Neijiang *Town* China 90 G6
Nei Mongol Zizhiqu *see* Inner Mongolia
Neiva *Town* Colombia 26 B7
Nellore *Town* India 87 I7
Nelson *Town* New Zealand 107 E9
Nemuro *Town* Japan 92 H4
Nepal *Country* 87 J3
Neryungri *Town* Russian Federation 79 K6
Netanya *Town* Israel 81 D11
Netherlands *Country* 52 E7
Neubrandenburg *Town* Germany 56 F5
Neuchâtel *Town* Switzerland 57 C11
Neufchâteau *Town* Belgium 53 F13
Neumünster *Town* Germany 56 D4
Neunkirchen *Town* Germany 57 C9
Neuquén *Town* Argentina 31 D10
Neustadt an der Weinstrasse *Town* Germany 57 C9
Neu-Ulm *Town* Germany 57 E10
Neuwied *Town* Germany 56 C8
Nevada *State* USA 14 H6
Nevinnomyssk *Town* Russian Federation 73 C11
Nevşehir *Town* Turkey 76 G5
New Amsterdam *Town* Guyana 26 G6
Newark *Town* New Jersey, USA 9 I7
Newark *Town* New York, USA 8 G5
New Bedford *Town* Massachusetts, USA 9 K6
Newberg *Town* Oregon, USA 14 F3
New Britain *Island* Papua New Guinea 102 F5
New Caledonia *Island* New Caledonia 102 G8
New Caledonia *Dependent territory* France, Pacific Ocean 102 G7
Newcastle *Town* New South Wales, Australia 105 M7
Newcastle upon Tyne *Town* England, UK 50 F7
New Delhi *Capital* India 86 H3
Newfoundland *Island* Ontario, Canada 7 M5
Newfoundland & Labrador *Province* Canada 7 L4
Newfoundland Basin *Undersea feature* Atlantic Ocean 33 J2
New Glasgow *Town* Nova Scotia, Canada 7 L7
New Guinea *Island* Indonesia/Papua New Guinea 102 D5
New Hampshire *State* USA 9 J4
New Haven *Town* Connecticut, USA 8 I6
New Iberia *Town* Louisiana, USA 10 E6
New Jersey *State* USA 9 I7
Newman *Town* Western Australia, Australia 104 E4
New Mexico *State* USA 17 I4
New Orleans *Town* Louisiana, USA 10 F6
New Plymouth *Town* New Zealand 106 F7
Newport *Town* Vermont, USA 9 I3
Newport *Town* Wales, UK 51 F11
Newport News *Town* Virginia, USA 11 L3
New Providence *Island* The Bahamas 22 G2
Newquay *Town* England, UK 51 E12
Newry *Town* Northern Ireland, UK 50 D8
New Siberian Islands *Island group* Russian Federation 79 K3
New South Wales *State* Australia 105 L7
Newtownabbey *Town* Northern Ireland, UK 50 D7
New York *State* USA 8 G5
New York *Town* New York, USA 9 I7
New Zealand *Country* 107 E9
Ngaoundéré *Town* Cameroon 42 D7
Ngo *Town* Congo 43 D10
Nguigmi *Town* Niger 41 M5
Nha Trang *Town* Vietnam 95 H10
Niagara Falls *Town* Ontario, Canada 6 G8
Niagara Falls *Town* New York, USA 8 E5
Niagara Falls *Waterfall* Canada/USA 8 E6
Niamey *Capital* Niger 41 J5
Nia-Nia *Town* Democratic Republic of the Congo 43 H9
Nicaragua *Country* 20 H5
Nicaragua, Lago de *Lake* Nicaragua 21 I6
Nice *Town* France 55 H11
Nicholls Town *Town* The Bahamas 22 F2
Nicobar Islands *Island group* India 87 M8
Nicosia *Capital* Cyprus 80 B8
Nicoya *Town* Costa Rica 20 H7
Nicoya, Golfo de *Gulf* Costa Rica 21 I7
Nida *Town* Lithuania 70 C6
Nieuw-Bergen *Town* Netherlands 53 F9
Niğde *Town* Turkey 76 G6
Niger *Country* 41 K5
Niger *River* Niger/Nigeria 41 J6
Nigeria *Country* 41 M7
Niger, Mouths of the *Coastal feature* Nigeria 41 K8
Niigata *Town* Japan 93 F9
Niihama *Town* Japan 93 D12
Niitsu *Town* Japan 93 F9
Nijmegen *Town* Netherlands 53 F9
Nikiniki *Town* Indonesia 97 J8
Nikopol' *Town* Ukraine 69 K5
Nikšić *Town* Montenegro 65 E10
Nile *River* East Africa 38 E5
Nile Delta Egypt 38 E4
Nîmes *Town* France 55 F11
Ninetyeast Ridge *Undersea feature* Indian Ocean 99 K4
Ninety Mile Beach *Coastal feature* New Zealand 106 E3
Ningbo *Town* China 91 L6
Ningxia *Administrative region* China 89 J6
Niort *Town* France 54 D8
Nipigon, Lake Québec, Canada 6 E6
Niš *Town* Serbia 65 H9
Nişab *Town* Saudi Arabia 82 D8
Nitra *Town* Slovakia 63 E10
Niue *Dependent territory* New Zealand, Pacific Ocean 103 K7
Nizāmābād *Town* India 87 I6
Nizhnekamsk *Town* Russian Federation 73 F9
Nizhnevartovsk *Town* Russian Federation 78 G5
Nizhniy Novgorod *Town* Russian Federation 73 E9
Nizhniy Odes *Town* Russian Federation 72 G7
Nizhyn *Town* Ukraine 69 J2
Nkayi *Town* Congo 43 D11
Nkongsamba *Town* Cameroon 42 C8
Nobeoka *Town* Japan 93 C14
Noboribetsu *Town* Japan 92 F6
Nogales *Town* Arizona, USA 16 F6
Nogales *Town* Mexico 18 E3
Nokia *Town* Finland 48 G8
Nokou *Town* Chad 42 D5
Nong Khai *Town* Thailand 94 E8
Noordwijk aan Zee *Town* Netherlands 52 D8
Norak *Town* Tajikistan 85 J5
Norderstedt *Town* Germany 56 E5
Nordhorn *Town* Germany 56 C6
Nordkapp *see* North Cape
Norfolk *Town* Nebraska, USA 12 G5
Norfolk *Town* Virginia, USA 11 L3
Norfolk Island *Dependent territory* Australia, Pacific Ocean 109 I7
Noril'sk *Town* Russian Federation 78 H4
Norman *Town* Oklahoma, USA 17 L4
Normandy *Region* France 54 D6
Norrköping *Town* Sweden 49 E10
Norrtälje *Town* Sweden 49 E10
North Albanian Alps *Mountain range* Serbia/Montenegro 65 F10
Northampton *Town* England, UK 51 G10
North Bay *Town* Ontario, Canada 6 G7
North Cape *Coastal feature* New Zealand 106 E3
North Cape *Coastal feature* Norway 48 G2
North Carolina *State* USA 11 K4
North Charleston *Town* South Carolina, USA 11 J5
North Dakota *State* USA 12 F3
Northern Cook Islands *Island group* Cook Islands 103 M6
Northern Dvina *River* Russian Federation 72 E7
Northern Ireland *Political region* UK 50 D7
Northern Mariana Islands *Dependent territory* USA, Pacific Ocean 102 D1
Northern Sporades *Island group* Greece 67 E10
Northern Territory *State* Australia 104 H4
North Island New Zealand 106 G7
North Korea *Country* 91 M3
North Little Rock *Town* Arkansas, USA 10 E4
North Sea Europe 50 G4
North West Highlands *Mountain range* Scotland, UK 50 E4
Northwest Pacific Basin *Undersea feature* Pacific Ocean 109 I3
Northwest Territories *Province* Canada 4 H6
Norway *Country* 48 B8
Norwegian Sea Arctic Ocean 111 M8
Norwich *Town* England, UK 51 H9
Noshiro *Town* Japan 92 F7
Noşratābād *Town* Iran 82 H7
Nottingham *Town* England, UK 51 G9
Nouâdhibou *Town* Mauritania 40 E3
Nouakchott *Capital* Mauritania 40 E4
Nouméa *Capital* New Caledonia 102 H8
Nova Iguaçu *Town* Brazil 29 L7
Novara *Town* Italy 60 C5
Novaya Zemlya *Island* Russian Federation 72 G4
Novi Sad *Town* Serbia 64 F7
Novocheboksarsk *Town* Russian Federation 73 E9
Novocherkassk *Town* Russian Federation 73 C11
Novodvinsk *Town* Russian Federation 72 E6
Novokuznetsk *Town* Russian Federation 78 H7
Novolazarevskaya *Research station* Antarctica 110 E3
Novomoskovs'k *Town* Ukraine 69 K4
Novomoskovsk *Town* Russian Federation 73 C9
Novopolotsk *Town* Belarus 70 G8 *see also* Navapolatsk

Novorossiysk *Town* Russian Federation 73 B12
Novoshakhtinsk *Town* Russian Federation 73 C11
Novosibirsk *Town* Russian Federation 78 H6
Novotroyits'ke *Town* Ukraine 69 K6
Nowy Sącz *Town* Poland 63 F9
Noyon *Town* France 54 F6
Nsawam *Town* Ghana 41 I8
Nubian Desert Sudan 38 E6
Nueva Gerona *Town* Cuba 22 D3
Nueva Rosita *Town* Mexico 19 I4
Nuevitas *Town* Cuba 22 G4
Nuevo Casas Grandes *Town* Mexico 18 G3
Nuevo Laredo *Town* Mexico 19 J4
Nuku' alofa *Capital* Tonga 103 K8
Nukus *Town* Uzbekistan 84 F2
Nullarbor Plain Australia 104 G6
Nunavut *Province* Canada 5 J5
Nuneaton *Town* England, UK 51 G10
Nuremberg *Town* Germany 57 E9
Nürnberg *see* Nuremberg
Nurota *Town* Uzbekistan 85 I4
Nusa Tenggara *see* Lesser Sunda Islands
Nusaybin *Town* Turkey 77 J6
Nuuk *Town* Greenland 111 B8
Nyagan' *Town* Russian Federation 78 G5
Nyainqêntanglha Shan *Mountain range* China 88 G8
Nyala *Town* Sudan 38 C8
Nyamapanda *Town* Mozambique 45 I4
Nyasa, Lake Malawi 45 J3
Nyeri *Town* Kenya 39 F11
Nyíregyháza *Town* Hungary 63 G10
Nykøbing *Town* Denmark 49 C13
Nyköping *Town* Sweden 49 E10
Nzega *Town* Tanzania 39 E12

O

Oakland *Town* California, USA 14 F6
Oakland *Town* Maryland, USA 8 E8
Oamaru *Town* New Zealand 107 D12
Oaxaca *Town* Mexico 19 L8
Ob' *River* Russian Federation 78 G4
Obihiro *Town* Japan 92 G5
Obock *Town* Djibouti 38 G8
Ocala *Town* Florida, USA 11 I7
Ocaña *Town* Spain 59 I6
Occidental, Cordillera *Mountain range* Peru 27 C11
Ocean Falls *Town* British Colombia, Canada 4 F8
Oceanside *Town* California, USA 14 G8
Ochakiv *Town* Ukraine 69 I6
Ochamchire *Town* Georgia 77 J2
Ocozocuautla *Town* Mexico 19 M8
Ōdate *Town* Japan 92 F7
Ödemiş *Town* Turkey 76 C5
Odense *Town* Denmark 49 B12
Oder *River* Poland 62 C6
Odesa *Town* Ukraine 69 I6
Odessa *Town* Texas, USA 17 J6
Odienné *Town* Côte d'Ivoire 40 G7
Offenbach *Town* Germany 56 D8
Offenburg *Town* Germany 57 C10
Ogaden *Plateau* Ethiopia 39 H9
Ōgaki *Town* Japan 93 E11
Ogbomosho *Town* Nigeria 41 K7
Ogden *Town* Utah, USA 15 I5
Ogdensburg *Town* New York, USA 9 H3
Ohio *State* USA 13 L6
Ohio River Central USA, 13 M7
Ohrid *Town* Macedonia 65 F12
Ohrid, Lake Albania 65 F12
Ohura *Town* New Zealand 106 G7
Oirschot *Town* Netherlands 53 F10
Ōita *Town* Japan 93 C13
Ojinaga *Town* Mexico 18 H3
Okāra *Town* India 86 H2
Okavango Delta Botswana 44 G5
Okayama *Town* Japan 93 D12
Okazaki *Town* Japan 93 F11
Okeechobee, Lake Florida, USA 11 J8
Okefenokee Swamp *Wetlands* Georgia, USA 11 I6
Okhotsk *Town* Russian Federation 78 L5
Okhotskoye More *see* Okhotsk, Sea of
Okhotsk, Sea of Pacific Ocean 92 G4
Okhtyrka *Town* Ukraine 69 K3
Okinawa *Island* Ryukyu Islands 93 A16
Oklahoma *State* USA 17 L4
Oklahoma City *Town* Oklahoma, USA 17 L3
Oktyabr'skiy *Town* Russian Federation 73 F10
Öland *Island* Sweden 49 E12
Olavarría *Town* Argentina 31 F9
Oldenburg *Town* Germany 56 D5
Olëkminsk *Town* Russian Federation 78 K5
Oleksandrivka *Town* Ukraine 69 J4
Oleksandriya *Town* Ukraine 69 J4
Olenegorsk *Town* Russian Federation 72 D4
Olenëk *Town* Russian Federation 78 J4
Olifa *Town* Namibia 44 E4
Olivet *Town* France 54 E7
Olmaliq *Town* Uzbekistan 85 J4
Olomouc *Town* Czechia 63 D9
Olovyannaya *Town* Russian Federation 78 K7
Olpe *Town* Germany 56 C7
Olsztyn *Town* Poland 62 F5
Olympia *Town* Washington, USA 14 F2
Ólympos *Mountain* Greece 67 D9
Omagh *Town* Northern Ireland, UK 50 C8
Omaha *Town* Nebraska, USA 12 G6
Oman *Country* 83 G11
Oman, Gulf of Indian Ocean 83 H9
Omdurman *Town* Sudan 38 E7
Omsk *Town* Russian Federation 78 G6
Ōmuta *Town* Japan 93 B13
Öndörhaan *Town* Mongolia 89 J3
Onega *Town* Russian Federation 72 D6
Onega, Lake Russian Federation 72 D6
Oneonta *Town* New York, USA 8 H5
Ongole *Town* India 87 I7
Onitsha *Town* Nigeria 41 L8
Ontario *Province* Canada 6 F5
Ontario, Lake Canada/USA 8 F5
Oostende *see* Ostend
Oosterhout *Town* Netherlands 53 E9
Opava *Town* Czechia 63 E9
Opochka *Town* Russian Federation 72 B7
Opole *Town* Poland 62 E8
Oradea *Town* Romania 68 D5
Oran *Town* Algeria 36 G3
Orange *Town* France 55 F11
Orange River Namibia 44 F7
Oranjestad *Capital* Aruba 23 J8
Oravipa *Town* Romania 68 D6
Orcadas *Research station* Antarctica 110 B3
Ordu *Town* Turkey 76 H4
Orealla *Town* Guyana 26 G6
Örebro *Town* Sweden 49 D10
Oregon *State* USA 14 H4
Orël *Town* Russian Federation 73 C9
Orem *Town* Utah, USA 15 J5
Ore Mountains Germany 56 F7
Orenburg *Town* Russian Federation 73 F11
Orense *see* Ourense
Oreor *Capital* Palau 102 C3
Orestiáda *Town* Greece 66 G7
Orihuela *Town* Spain 59 K7
Orinoco, Río *River* Venezuela 26 F5
Orinoquía-Amazonía *Physical region* Venezuela 26 C7
Oristano *Town* Sardinia, Italy 61 B10
Orkney Islands *Island group* Scotland, UK 50 E3
Orlando *Town* Florida, USA 11 J7
Orléans *Town* France 54 E7
Orleans *Town* Massachusetts, USA 9 L6
Örnsköldsvik *Town* Sweden 48 E7
Orsha *Town* Belarus 71 G9
Orsk *Town* Russian Federation 73 G11
Ortona *Town* Italy 60 F8
Oruro *Town* Bolivia 27 E12
Ōsaka *Town* Japan 93 E12
Osh *Town* Kyrgyzstan 85 K4
Oshawa *Town* Ontario, Canada 6 H8
Oshkosh *Town* Wisconsin, USA 13 J4
Osijek *Town* Croatia 64 E6
Oslo *Capital* Norway 49 C10
Osmaniye *Town* Turkey 76 H6
Osnabrück *Town* Germany 56 C6
Osorno *Town* Chile 31 C10
Oss *Town* Netherlands 53 F9
Ossora *Town* Russian Federation 78 M4
Ostend *Town* Belgium 53 C10
Östersund *Town* Sweden 48 D8
Ostiglia *Town* Italy 60 E5
Ostrava *Town* Czechia 63 E9
Ostrołęka *Town* Poland 62 G6
Ostrov *Town* Russian Federation 72 B7
Ostrowiec Świętokrzyski *Town* Poland 62 G8
Ostrów Wielkopolski *Town* Poland 62 E7
Ōsumi-shotō *Island group* Japan 93 B15
Oswego *Town* New York, USA 8 G5
Otago Peninsula New Zealand 107 C13
Otaru *Town* Japan 92 F5
Otawara *Town* Japan 93 G9
Otranto, Strait of Albania 65 E12
Ōtsu *Town* Japan 93 E11
Ottawa *Capital* Canada 6 H7
Ottumwa *Town* Iowa, USA 13 I6
Ouachita Mountains Arkansas, USA 10 D4
Ouagadougou *Capital* Burkina Faso 41 J6
Ouahigouya *Town* Burkina Faso 41 I5
Ouanary *Town* French Guiana 26 I6
Ouarâne *Desert* Mauritania 40 G3
Ouargla *Town* Algeria 37 I5
Ouarzazate *Town* Morocco 36 E5
Ouésso *Town* Congo 43 E9
Oujda *Town* Morocco 36 G4
Oulu *Town* Finland 48 G6
Oupeye *Town* Belgium 53 F11
Ourense *Town* Spain 58 F3
Outer Hebrides *Island group* Scotland, UK 50 C4
Ovalle *Town* Chile 30 C7
Oviedo *Town* Spain 58 G2
Ovruch *Town* Ukraine 68 H2
Owensboro *Town* Kentucky, USA 10 G2
Owen Stanley Range *Mountain range* Papua New Guinea 102 E5
Owerri *Town* Nigeria 41 L8
Owo *Town* Nigeria 41 K7
Oxford *Town* New Zealand 107 E11
Oxford *Town* England, UK 51 G11
Oxnard *Town* California, USA 14 G8
Oyama *Town* Japan 93 G10
Oyem *Town* Gabon 43 C9
Oyo *Town* Nigeria 41 K7
Ozark *Town* Alabama, USA 10 H6
Ozark Plateau Missouri, USA 12 H8

P

Pabianice *Town* Poland 62 E7
Pabna *Town* Bangladesh 87 L4
Pachuca *Town* Mexico 19 K7
Pacific Ocean 108–109
Padang *Town* Indonesia 96 D6
Paderborn *Town* Germany 56 D7
Padova *Town* Italy 60 E5
Paducah *Town* Kentucky, USA 10 G3
Pago Pago *Capital* American Samoa 103 K6
Paide *Town* Estonia 70 G4
Päijänne *Lake* Finland 48 G8
Painted Desert Arizona, USA 16 F3
Paisley *Town* Scotland, UK 50 E6
País Vasco *see* Basque Country, The
Pakistan *Country* 86 F3
Pakokku *Town* Myanmar 94 B6
Paks *Town* Hungary 63 E12
Pakxan *Town* Laos 94 F8
Pakxé *Town* Laos 95 G9
Pālanpur *Town* India 86 G4
Palau *Country* 102 C3
Palawan Passage South China Sea 96 H4
Palembang *Town* Indonesia 96 E7
Palencia *Town* Spain 58 H4
Palenque *Ancient site* Mexico 19 N8
Palermo *Town* Sicily, Italy 61 E12
Pāli *Town* India 86 G4
Palikir *Capital* Micronesia 102 G3
Palliser, Cape *Coastal feature* New Zealand 107 G9
Palma *Town* Mallorca, Spain 59 M6
Palmas do Tocantis *Town* Brazil 29 K4
Palma Soriano *Town* Cuba 22 G4
Palmer *Research station* Antarctica 110 B4
Palmer Land *Region* Antarctica 110 C5
Palmerston North *Town* New Zealand 106 G8
Palmi *Town* Italy 61 G12
Palmira *Town* Colombia 26 B6
Palm Springs *Town* California, USA 14 H8
Palmyra *see* Tudmur
Palmyra Atoll *Dependent territory* USA, Pacific Ocean 103 M3
Palo Alto *Town* California, USA 14 F6
Palu *Town* Indonesia 97 I6
Pamirs *Mountain range* Tajikistan 85 K5
Pampas *Plain* Argentina 30 E8
Pamplona *Town* Spain 59 J3
Panaji *Town* India 86 G7
Panama *Country* 21 L8
Panama Canal Panama 21 L8
Panama City *Capital* Panama 21 M8
Panama, Gulf of Panama 21 M9
Pančevo *Town* Serbia 64 G7
Panevėžys *Town* Lithuania 70 E7
Pangkalpinang *Town* Indonesia 96 F6
Pantanal *Wetlands* Brazil 29 I6
Panyabungan *Town* Indonesia 96 D6
Panzhihua *Town* China 90 F7
Papantla *Town* Mexico 19 K7
Papeete *Capital* French Polynesia 103 N7
Papua *Province* Indonesia 97 N7
Papua, Gulf of Pacific Ocean 102 E6
Papua New Guinea *Country* 102 F5
Papuk *Mountain range* Croatia 64 D6
Paraguay *Country* 30 G4
Paraguay *River* Argentina/Paraguay 30 G5
Parakou *Town* Benin 41 J7
Paramaribo *Capital* Suriname 26 H6
Paraná *Town* Argentina 30 F7
Paraná *River* Argentina/Paraguay 30 H6
Pardubice *Town* Czechia 63 C9
Parechcha *Town* Belarus 70 D8
Parecis, Chapada dos *Mountain range* Brazil 28 H5
Parepare *Town* Indonesia 97 I7
Paria, Gulf of Trindad & Tobago 23 O9
Paris *Capital* France 54 E6
Parma *Town* Italy 60 D6
Parnaíba *Town* Brazil 29 L2
Pärnu *Town* Estonia 70 F4
Parral *Town* Chile 31 C9
Parramatta *Town* New South Wales, Australia 105 M7
Pasadena *Town* California, USA 14 G8
Pasadena *Town* Texas, USA 17 N7
Pasco *Town* Washington, USA 14 G3
Pasinler *Town* Turkey 77 J4
Pasni *Town* Pakistan 86 E3
Passau *Town* Germany 57 G10
Passo Fundo *Town* Brazil 29 J8
Pasto *Town* Colombia 26 B7
Patagonia *Region* Argentina 31 D12
Paterson *Town* New Jersey, USA 9 I7
Pathein *Town* Myanmar 94 B8
Patna *Town* India 87 J4
Patnos *Town* Turkey 77 K5
Pátra *Town* Greece 67 C11
Pau *Town* France 55 C11
Paulatuk *Town* Northwest Territories, Canada 4 H5
Pavia *Town* Italy 60 C5
Pāvilosta *Town* Latvia 70 D5
Pavlodar *Town* Kazakhstan 78 G7
Pavlohrad *Town* Ukraine 69 L4
Pawtucket *Town* Rhode Island, USA 8 J6
Paysandú *Town* Uruguay 30 H7
Pazar *Town* Turkey 77 J3
Pazardzhik *Town* Bulgaria 66 F7
Pearl River Mississippi, USA 10 F5
Peawanuk *Town* Ontario, Canada 6 F4
Pechora *River* Russian Federation 72 G6
Pechora *Town* Russian Federation 72 G6
Peć *Town* Kosovo 65 F10 *see also* Pejë
Pécs *Town* Hungary 63 E12

Q

Quincy *Town* Missouri, USA 13 I7
Quito *Capital* Ecuador 26 B7
Qŭrghonteppa *Town* Tajikistan 85 J5
Quy Nhơn *Town* Vietnam 95 H10
Quzhou *Town* China 91 K6

R

Rabat *Capital* Morocco 36 E4
Rabinal *Town* Guatemala 20 E4
Rabyānah, Ramlat *Desert* Libya 37 M6
Race, Cape *Coastal feature* Newfoundland & Labrador, Canada 7 N6
Rach Gia *Town* Vietnam 95 F12
Racine *Town* Wisconsin, USA 13 J5
Radom *Town* Poland 62 G7
Rafaela *Town* Argentina 30 F7
Rafah *Town* Israel 81 C12
Ragusa *Town* Sicily, Italy 61 F14
Rahīmyār Khān *Town* Pakistan 86 G3
Rāichūr *Town* India 86 H6
Raipur *Town* India 87 J5
Rājahmundry *Town* India 87 J6
Rājkot *Town* India 86 G4
Rajshahi *Town* Bangladesh 87 K4
Raleigh *Town* North Carolina, USA 11 K3
Ralik Chain *Island chain* Marshall Islands 102 H2
Râmnicu Vâlcea *Town* Romania 68 E7
Rancagua *Town* Chile 30 D8
Rānchi *Town* India 87 J4
Randers Denmark 49 B12
Rangoon *see* Yangon
Rangpur *Town* Pakistan 87 L3
Rankin Inlet *Town* Nunavut, Canada 5 J6
Rapid City *Town* South Dakota, USA 12 E4
Ra's al 'Ayn *Town* Syria 80 G4
Rasht *Town* Iran 82 E5
Ratak Chain *Island chain* Marshall Islands 102 H2
Rathkeale *Town* Ireland 51 B10
Rat Islands *Island Group* Alaska, USA 4 A4
Ratlām *Town* India 86 H4
Raton *Town* New Mexico, USA 17 I3
Rättvik *Town* Sweden 49 D9
Raukumara Range *Mountain range* New Zealand 106 I7
Rauma *Town* Finland 49 F9
Rāurkela *Town* India 87 J5
Ravenna *Town* Italy 60 E6
Rāwalpindi *Town* Pakistan 86 G1
Rawicz *Town* Poland 62 D7
Rawlins *Town* Wyoming, USA 15 K5
Rawson *Town* Argentina 31 F11
Razgrad *Town* Bulgaria 66 G5
Reading *Town* Pennsylvania, USA 9 H7
Reading *Town* England, UK 51 G11
Realicó *Town* Argentina 30 E8
Rechytsa *Town* Belarus 71 F11
Recife *Town* Brazil 29 N4
Recklinghausen *Town* Germany 56 C7
Recogne *Town* Belgium 53 E13
Reconquista *Town* Argentina 30 G6
Red Deer *Town* Alberta, Canada 4 H8
Redding *Town* California, USA 14 F5
Red River USA 17 K4
Red Sea Africa/Asia 83 B9
Reefton *Town* New Zealand 107 D10
Regensburg *Town* Germany 57 F9
Reggane *Town* Algeria 36 G6
Reggio di Calabria *Town* Italy 61 G13
Reggio nell' Emilia *Town* Italy 60 D6
Regina *Town* Saskatchewan, Canada 5 I9
Rehovot *Town* Israel 81 D11
Reims *Town* France 54 F6
Rengat *Town* Indonesia 96 E6
Rennes *Town* France 54 C7
Reno *Town* Nevada, USA 14 G5
Renqiu *Town* Hebei, China 91 J3
Republika Srpska *Administrative region* Bosnia & Herzegovina 64 D7
Repulse Bay *Town* Nunavut, Canada 5 K5
Resistencia *Town* Argentina 30 G6
Reșipa *Town* Romania 68 D6
Resolute *Town* Nunavut, Canada 5 J3
Réunion *Dependent territory* France, Indian Ocean 45 O6
Reus *Town* Spain 59 L4
Reutlingen *Town* Germany 57 D10
Reyes *Town* Bolivia 27 E11
Reykjavík *Capital* Iceland 111 D9
Reynosa *Town* Mexico 19 K5
Rēzekne *Town* Latvia 70 G7
Rheine *Town* Germany 56 C6
Rhine *River* Europe 56 C8
Rho *Town* Italy 60 C5
Rhode Island *State* USA 9 J6
Rhodes *Town* Greece 67 I13
Rhodope Mountains *Mountain range* Bulgaria 66 G7
Rhône *River* France 55 F11
Ribeirão Preto *Town* Brazil 29 K7
Rîbnipa *Town* Moldova 68 H5
Richmond *Town* Kentucky, USA 10 H2
Richmond *Town* Virginia, USA 11 K2
Ridder *Town* Kazakhstan 78 H7
Ried im Innkreis *Town* Austria 57 G10
Rīga *Capital* Latvia 70 E5
Riga, Gulf of Latvia 70 E5
Rijeka *Town* Croatia 64 B6
Rimini *Town* Italy 60 E7
Rimouski *Town* Québec, Canada 7 J6
Riobamba *Town* Ecuador 26 A8
Río Bravo *Town* Mexico 19 K5
Río Cuarto *Town* Argentina 30 E8
Rio de Janeiro *Town* Brazil 29 L7
Río Gallegos *Town* Argentina 31 E14
Rio Grande *Town* Brazil 29 J9
Ríohacha *Town* Colombia 26 C4
Rio Lagartos *Town* Mexico 19 O6
Río Verde *Town* Mexico 19 J7
Rivera *Town* Uruguay 30 H7
River Falls *Town* Wisconsin, USA 13 I4
Riverside *Town* California, USA 14 G8
Riverton *Town* Wyoming, USA 15 K4
Rivne *Town* Ukraine 68 G2
Rivoli *Town* Italy 60 B5
Riyadh *Capital* Saudi Arabia 83 D9
Road Town *Capital* British Virgin Islands 23 M5
Rize *Town* Turkey 77 J3
Roanoke *Town* Virginia, USA 11 J3
Roatán *Town* Honduras 20 G3
Robinson Range *Mountain range* Western Australia, Australia 104 F5
Robstown *Town* Texas, USA 17 L8
Rochefort *Town* Belgium 53 E12
Rochefort *Town* France 55 D9
Rochester *Town* New York, USA 8 F5
Rochester *Town* Minnesota, USA 13 I4
Rockford *Town* Illinois, USA 13 J5
Rockhampton *Town* Queensland, Australia 105 M4
Rock Hill *Town* South Carolina, USA 11 J4
Rock Sound *Town* The Bahamas 22 G2
Rocky Mountains Canada/USA 4, 14
Ródos *see* Rhodes
Roeselare *Town* Belgium 53 C11
Rogatica *Town* Bosnia & Herzegovina 64 E8
Rogers *Town* Arkansas, USA 10 D3
Roi Et *Town* Thailand 95 F9
Rokycany *Town* Czechia 63 B9
Roma *Town* Queensland, Australia 105 M5
Roma *see* Rome
Roman *Town* Romania 68 G5
Romania *Country* 68 E6
Rome *Capital* Italy 61 E9
Romny *Town* Ukraine 69 J2
Rondonópolis *Town* Brazil 29 I6
Ronne Ice Shelf *Ice feature* Antarctica 110 C5
Roosendaal *Town* Netherlands 53 D10
Røros *Town* Norway 48 C8
Rosario *Town* Argentina 30 F8
Rosario *Town* Paraguay 30 H5
Rosarito *Town* Mexico 18 C2
Roseau *Capital* Dominica 23 O6
Rosenheim *Town* Germany 57 F10
Roslavl' *Town* Russian Federation 73 B9
Ross *Town* New Zealand 107 D10
Ross Ice Shelf *Ice feature* Antarctica 110 D7
Rosso *Town* Mauritania 40 E4
Rossosh' *Town* Russian Federation 73 C10
Ross Sea Antarctica 110 D7
Rostock *Town* Germany 56 F4
Rostov-na-Donu *Town* Russian Federation 73 C11
Roswell *Town* New Mexico, USA 17 I5
Rothera *Research station* Antarctica 110 B5
Rotorua *Town* New Zealand 106 G6
Rotorua, Lake New Zealand 106 G6
Rotterdam *Town* Netherlands 53 E9
Roubaix *Town* France 54 F5
Rouen *Town* France 54 E6
Round Rock *Town* Texas, USA 17 L6
Rovigo *Town* Italy 60 E6
Roxas City *Town* Philippines 97 J3
Rozdol'ne *Town* Ukraine 69 J6
Rožňava *Town* Slovakia 63 F10
Ruatoria *Town* New Zealand 106 I6
Rubizhne *Town* Ukraine 69 M4
Rudnyy *Town* Kazakhstan 78 E6
Rudzyensk *Town* Belarus 71 E10
Rufino *Town* Argentina 30 F8
Rukwa, Lake Tanzania 39 E13
Ruoqiang *Town* China 88 F5
Ruse *Town* Bulgaria 66 G5
Rushmore, Mount *Mountain* South Dakota, USA 12 E4
Russellville *Town* Arkansas, USA 10 E3
Russian Federation *Country* 78 G6
Rustavi *Town* Georgia 77 L3
Ruston *Town* Louisiana, USA 10 E5
Rutland *Town* Vermont, USA 9 I4
Rwanda *Country* 39 D12
Ryazan' *Town* Russian Federation 73 D9
Rybinsk *Town* Russian Federation 72 D8
Rybnik *Town* Poland 62 E8
Ryki *Town* Poland 62 G7
Ryukyu Islands *Island chain* Japan 93 A16
Rzeszów *Town* Poland 63 G9
Rzhev *Town* Russian Federation 72 C8

S

Saalfeld *Town* Germany 56 E8
Saarbrücken *Town* Germany 57 C9
Sab' Ābār *Town* Syria 80 F8
Šabac *Town* Serbia 64 F7
Sabadell *Town* Spain 59 M4
Sabah *Cultural region* Malaysia 96 H5
Sabaya *Town* Bolivia 27 D12
Sabhā *Town* Libya 37 K6
Sabinas *Town* Mexico 19 I4
Sabinas Hidalgo *Town* Mexico 19 J4
Sable Island Québec, Canada 7 M7
Sabzevār *Town* Iran 82 G5
Sacramento *Town* California, USA 14 F6
Sacramento Mountains New Mexico/ Texas, USA 16 H5
Sacramento Valley California, USA 14 F5
Şa'dah *Town* Yemen 83 C12
Şafāshahr *Town* Iran 82 F7
Safi *Town* Morocco 36 E4
Sagaing *Town* Myanmar 94 B6
Sāgar *Town* India 87 I4
Saginaw *Town* Michigan, USA 13 L5
Sagua la Grande *Town* Cuba 22 E3
Sagunto *Town* Spain 59 K6
Sahara *Desert* North Africa 36–37, 40–41
Sahel *Desert* North Africa 41 K5
Saïda *Town* Lebanon 81 D9
Saiki *Town* Japan 93 C13
Saimaa *Lake* Finland 48 H8
St Albans *Town* England, UK 51 H10
Saint Albans *Town* West Virginia, USA 11 I2
St Andrews *Town* Scotland, UK 50 F6
St. Anthony *Town* Newfoundland & Labrador, Canada 7 M4
Saint Augustine *Town* Florida, USA 11 J6
St-Brieuc *Town* France 54 B6
St. Catharines *Town* Ontario, Canada 6 G8
St-Chamond *Town* France 55 F10
St-Claude *Town* France 55 G9
St Croix *Island* Virgin Islands 23 M5
St-Denis *Capital* Réunion 45 O6
St-Étienne *Town* France 55 F10
St-Gaudens *Town* France 55 D11
St-Georges *Town* French Guiana 26 I6
St. George's *Capital* Grenada 23 O8
St George's Channel Europe 51 D10
St Helena *Dependent Territory* UK, Atlantic Ocean 33 L6
St Helier *Capital* Jersey, Channel Islands 51 G13
St-Jean, Lac *Lake* Canada 7 I6
Saint John *Town* New Brunswick, Canada 7 K7
St John's *Capital* Antigua & Barbuda 23 N5
St. John's *Town* Newfoundland & Labrador, Canada 7 N5
Saint Joseph *Town* Missouri, USA 12 H7
Saint Kitts & Nevis *Country* 23 N6
St-Laurent-du-Maroni *Town* French Guiana 26 H6
St. Lawrence *River* Canada/USA 7 J6
St. Lawrence, Gulf of Canada 7 L6
Saint Lawrence Island Alaska, USA 4 D4
Saint Louis *Town* Senegal 40 E5
Saint Louis *Town* Illinois, USA 13 J7
St. Lucia *Country* 23 O7
St Lucia Channel Martinique 23 O7
St-Malo *Town* France 54 C6
St. Moritz *Town* Switzerland 57 D12
St-Nazaire *Town* France 54 B8
St-Omer *Town* France 54 E5
Saint Paul *Town* Minnesota, USA 13 I4
St Peter Port *Capital* Guernsey, Channel Islands 51 F13
Saint Petersburg *Town* Russian Federation 72 C7
Saint Petersburg *Town* Florida, USA 11 I8
St Pierre & Miquelon *Dependent Territory* France, Atlantic Ocean 7 M6
St-Quentin *Town* France 54 F6
Saint Vincent *Island* St Vincent and the Grenadines 23 O7
Saint Vincent & The Grenadines *Country* 23 O7
Saint Vincent Passage *Strait* St. Lucia 23 O7
Sakai *Town* Japan 93 E12
Sakata *Town* Japan 92 F8
Sakhalin, Ostrov *Island* Russian Federation 79 M6
Şäki *Town* Azerbaijan 77 M3
Salado, Río *River* Argentina 30 F6
Salamanca *Town* Chile 30 C7
Salamanca *Town* Spain 58 G5
Salamīyah *Town* Syria 80 E7
Salavat *Town* Russian Federation 73 G10
Saldus *Town* Latvia 70 D5
Salé *Town* Morocco 36 F4
Salem *Town* Nepal 87 I8
Salem *Town* Oregon, USA 14 F3
Salerno *Town* Italy 61 F10
Salihorsk *Town* Belarus 71 E10
Salima *Town* Malawi 45 J3
Salina *Town* Kansas, USA 12 G7
Salina Cruz *Town* Mexico 19 M9
Salinas *Town* California, USA 14 F7
Salisbury *Town* Maryland, USA 9 H9
Salonica *Town* Greece 66 E8
Salonta *Town* Romania 68 D5
Sal'sk *Town* Russian Federation 73 C11
Salta *Town* Argentina 30 E5
Saltillo *Town* Mexico 19 J5
Salt Lake City *Town* Utah, USA 15 I5
Salto *Town* Uruguay 30 G7
Salvador *Town* Brazil 29 M5
Salween *River* Myanmar 94 C7
Salyān *Town* Nepal 87 J3
Salzburg *Town* Austria 57 F10
Salzgitter *Town* Germany 56 E6
Samalayuca *Town* Mexico 18 G3
Samar *Island* Philippines 97 K3
Samara *Town* Russian Federation 73 E10
Samarinda *Town* Indonesia 97 I6
Samarqand *Town* Uzbekistan 85 I4
Şamaxi *Town* Azerbaijan 77 N3
Sambalpur *Town* India 87 J5
Samoa *Country* 103 K6
Sampit *Town* Indonesia 96 G7

T

Turkana, Lake Kenya 39 F10
Turkistan *Town* Kazakhstan 78 F7
Turkey *Country* 76 F5
Türkmenabat *Town* Turkmenistan 84 H4
Turkmenbaşy *Town* Turkmenistan 84 D3
Turkmenistan *Country* 84 F4
Turks & Caicos Islands *Dependent Territory* UK, Atlantic Ocean 23 I3
Turku *Town* Finland 49 F9
Turnov *Town* Czechia 63 C9
Tuscaloosa *Town* Mississippi, USA 10 G5
Tuscany *Region* Italy 60 D7
Tuticorin *Town* India 87 I9
Tutuala *Town* East Timor 97 K8
Tuvalu *Country* 103 I6
Tuxpán *Town* Mexico 19 K7
Tuxpan *Town* Mexico 19 I8
Tuxtepec *Town* Mexico 19 L8
Tuxtla *Town* Mexico 19 N8
Tuy Hoa *Town* Vietnam 95 H10
Tuz Gölü *see* Tuz, Lake
Tuzla *Town* Bosnia & Herzegovina 64 E7
Tuz, Lake Turkey 76 F5
Tver' *Town* Russian Federation 72 C8
Twin Falls *Town* Idaho, USA 15 I4
Tychy *Town* Poland 63 E9
Tyler *Town* Texas, USA 17 M5
Tynda *Town* Russian Federation 79 K6
Tyrrhenian Sea Mediterranean Sea 61 F11
Tyumen' *Town* Russian Federation 78 F5

U

Ubangi *River* Central Africa 42 F8
Ube *Town* Japan 93 C13
Uberaba *Town* Brazil 29 K6
Uberlândia *Town* Brazil 29 K6
Ubon Ratchathani *Town* Thailand 95 F9
Ubrique *Town* Spain 58 G8
Uchiura-wan *Bay* Japan 92 G6
Uchquduq *Town* Uzbekistan 84 H3
Udaipur *Town* India 86 G4
Udine *Town* Italy 60 F5
Udon Thani *Town* Thailand 94 E8
Udupi *Town* India 86 G7
Uele *River* Democratic Republic of the Congo 42 H8
Uelzen *Town* Germany 56 E5
Ufa *Town* Russian Federation 73 G10
Uganda *Country* 39 D11
Uitenhage *Town* South Africa 44 G9
Ukhta *Town* Russian Federation 72 G7
Ukmergė *Town* Lithuania 70 E7
Ukraine *Country* 68 G3
Ulaanbaatar *see* Ulan Bator
Ulaangom *Town* Mongolia 88 G3
Ulan Bator *Capital* Mongolia 89 J3
Ulan Qab *Town* China 91 J4
Ulan-Ude *Town* Russian Federation 79 J7
Ulft *Town* Netherlands 53 G9
Ullapool *Town* Scotland, UK 50 E4
Ulm *Town* Germany 57 D10
Ulsan *Town* South Korea 91 M4
Ulster *Cultural region* Northern Ireland, UK 50 C8
Uluru *Peak* Northern Territory, Australia 104 H5
Ulyanivka *Town* Ukraine 69 I4
Ul'yanovsk *Town* Russian Federation 73 E9
Uman' *Town* Ukraine 69 I4
Umeå *Town* Sweden 48 F7
Umm Ruwaba *Town* Sudan 38 E8
Uncía *Town* Bolivia 27 E12
Ungava Bay Québec, Canada 7 I2
Ungava Peninsula Québec, Canada 6 H2
Uniontown *Town* Pennsylvania, USA 8 E8
United Arab Emirates *Country* 83 F10
United Kingdom *Country* 50 E8
United States of America *Country* 8 I7
Ünye *Town* Turkey 76 H3
Upington *Town* South Africa 44 F7
Uppsala *Town* Sweden 49 E10
Ural Mountains *Mountain range* Russian Federation 73 H9
Ural'sk *Town* Kazakhstan 78 E5
Ural'skiye Gory *see* Ural Mountains
Uraricoera *Town* Brazil 28 H1
Uren' *Town* Russian Federation 72 E8
Urganch *Town* Uzbekistan 84 G3
Uroševac *Town* Kosovo 65 G10 *see also* Ferizaj
Ŭroteppa *Town* Tajikistan 85 J4
Uruapan *Town* Mexico 19 J8
Uruguay *Country* 30 G8
Ürümqi *Town* China 88 F4
Uşak *Town* Turkey 76 D5
Ushuaia *Town* Argentina 31 D15
Usinsk *Town* Russian Federation 72 G6
Usol'ye-Sibirskoye *Town* Russian Federation 79 I7
Ussel *Town* France 55 E9
Ussuriysk *Town* Russian Federation 79 M7
Ust'-Ilimsk *Town* Russian Federation 79 I6
Ústí nad Labem *Town* Czechia 62 B8
Ustka *Town* Poland 62 D4
Ust'-Kamchatsk *Town* Russian Federation 79 M4
Ust'-Kamenogorsk *Town* Kazakhstan 78 G7
Ust'-Kut *Town* Russian Federation 79 J6
Ust'-Olenëk *Town* Russian Federation 79 J4
Ustyurt Plateau Uzbekistan 84 F1
Usulután *Town* El Salvador 20 F5
Utah *State* USA 15 I6
Utica *Town* New York, USA 8 H5
Utrecht *Town* Netherlands 52 E8
Utsunomiya *Town* Japan 93 G10
Uulu *Town* Estonia 70 F5
Uvalde *Town* Texas, USA 17 K7
Uvaravichy *Town* Belarus 71 G11
Uwajima *Town* Japan 93 D13
Uxmal *Ancient site* Mexico 19 O6
Uyo *Town* Nigeria 41 L8
Uyuni *Town* Bolivia 27 E13
Uzbekistan *Country* 84 H3
Uzhhorod *Town* Ukraine 68 E4

V

Vaal *River* South Africa 44 H7
Vaasa *Town* Finland 48 F8
Vaassen *Town* Netherlands 52 F8
Vác *Town* Hungary 63 E11
Valdés, Peninsula Argentina 31 F11
Val-d'Or *Town* Québec, Canada 6 H6
Vadodara *Town* India 86 G5
Vaduz *Capital* Liechtenstein 57 D11
Valday *Town* Russian Federation 72 C7
Valdez *Town* Alaska, USA 4 E5
Valdivia *Town* Chile 31 C10
Valdosta *Town* Georgia, USA 11 I6
Valence *Town* France 55 F10
Valencia *Town* Spain 59 K6
Valencia *Town* Venezuela 26 D5
Valencia, Golfo de *Gulf* Spain 59 L6
Valera *Town* Venezuela 26 D5
Valga *Town* Estonia 70 G5
Valladolid *Town* Mexico 19 O6
Valladolid *Town* Spain 58 H4
Valledupar *Town* Colombia 26 C5
Vallenar *Town* Chile 30 C6
Valletta *Capital* Malta 61 E15
Valley, The *Capital* Anguilla 23 N5
Valls *Town* Spain 59 L4
Valmiera *Town* Latvia 70 F5
Valozhyn *Town* Belarus 71 E9
Valparaíso *Town* Chile 30 C8
Van *Town* Turkey 77 K5
Vanadzor *Town* Armenia 77 L3
Vancouver *Town* British Colombia, Canada 4 G5
Vancouver Island British Colombia, Canada 4 F9
Van Diemen Gulf Australia 104 H1
Vänern *Lakes* Sweden 49 D10
Van Gölü *see* Van, Lake
Van, Lake Turkey 77 K5
Vantaa *Town* Finland 49 G9
Vanua Levu *Island* Fiji 103 I7
Vanuatu *Country* 102 G7
Vārānasi *Town* India 87 J4
Varberg *Town* Sweden 49 C11
Vardar *River* Macedonia 65 H12
Varde *Town* Denmark 49 B12
Varese *Town* Italy 60 C4
Varna *Town* Bulgaria 66 H5
Vasa *see* Vaasa
Vaslui *Town* Romania 68 G6
Västerås *Town* Sweden 49 E10
Vatican City *Country* 61 E9
Vättern *Lake* Sweden 49 D10
Vaughn *Town* New Mexico, USA 17 I4
Vawkavysk *Town* Belarus 71 C9
Växjö *Town* Sweden 49 D11
Velebit *Mountain range* Croatia 64 B7
Veles *Town* Macedonia 65 G11
Velikiye Luki *Town* Russian Federation 72 B8
Velikiy Novgorod *Town* Russian Federation 72 C7
Veliko Tŭrnovo *Town* Bulgaria 66 G6
Vellore *Town* India 87 I7
Velsen-Noord *Town* Netherlands 52 E8
Vel'sk *Town* Russian Federation 72 E7
Vendôme *Town* France 54 D7
Venezia *see* Venice
Venezuela *Country* 26 E5
Venice *Town* Louisiana, USA 10 F7
Venice *Town* Italy 60 E5
Venice, Gulf of Italy 60 F6
Venlo *Town* Netherlands 53 G10
Ventimiglia *Town* Italy 60 B6
Ventspils *Town* Latvia 70 D4
Veracruz *Town* Mexico 19 L7
Vercelli *Town* Italy 60 C5
Verkhoyanskiy Khrebet *Mountain range* Russian Federation 79 K4
Vermont *State* USA 9 I4
Verona *Town* Italy 60 D5
Versailles *Town* France 54 E7
Verviers *Town* Belgium 53 F11
Vesterålen *Island group* Norway 48 D4
Vesuvius *Volcano* Italy 61 F10
Veszprém *Town* Hungary 63 E11
Veurne *Town* Belgium 53 B10
Viangchan *see* Vientiane
Viareggio *Town* Italy 60 D6
Vicenza *Town* Italy 60 E5
Vichy *Town* France 55 F9
Victoria *Capital* Seychelles 99 I5
Victoria *Town* British Colombia, Canada 4 G9
Victoria *Town* Texas, USA 17 M7
Victoria *State* Australia 105 K8
Victoria Falls *Waterfall* Zambia 44 G4
Victoria Island Northern Canada 5 I5
Victoria, Lake East Africa 39 E11
Victoria Land *Region* Antarctica 110 E7
Vidin *Town* Bulgaria 66 D5
Vienna *Capital* Austria 57 H10
Vientiane *Capital* Laos 94 E8
Vierzon *Town* France 54 E8
Vietnam *Country* 94 G8
Vieux Fort *Town* St. Lucia 23 O7
Vigo *Town* Spain 58 E3
Vijayawāda *Town* India 87 I6
Vila Nova de Gaia *Town* Portugal 58 E4
Vila Real *Town* Portugal 58 F4
Villa Acuña *Town* Mexico 19 I3
Villach *Town* Austria 57 G11
Villahermosa *Town* Mexico 19 N8
Villa María *Town* Argentina 30 F7
Villa Martin *Town* Bolivia 27 D13
Villa Mercedes *Town* Argentina 30 E8
Villarrica *Town* Paraguay 30 H5
Villavicencio *Town* Colombia 26 C6
Villeurbanne *Town* France 55 G9
Villingen-Schwenningen *Town* Germany 57 D10
Vilnius *Capital* Lithuania 70 E8
Viña del Mar *Town* Chile 30 C8
Vinaròs *Town* Spain 59 L5
Vindhya Range *Mountain range* India 86 H4
Vineland *Town* New Jersey, USA 8 H8
Vinh *Town* Vietnam 94 G8
Vinnytsya *Town* Ukraine 68 H4
Vinson Massif *Mountain* Antarctica 110 C5
Viranşehir *Town* Turkey 76 H6
Virginia *State* USA 11 K2
Virginia Beach *Town* Virginia, USA 11 L3
Virgin Islands *Dependent territory* USA, Atlantic Ocean 23 M5
Virôchey *Town* Cambodia 95 G10
Virovitica *Town* Croatia 64 D6
Virton *Town* Belgium 53 F14
Virtsu *Town* Estonia 70 F4
Visaginas *Town* Lithuania 70 F7
Visākhapatnam *Town* India 87 J6
Viscount Melville Sound *Bay* Canada 5 I4
Viseu *Town* Portugal 58 F5
Vitebsk *Town* Belarus 71 H9 *see also* Vitsyebsk
Viterbo *Town* Italy 60 E8
Viti Levu *Island* Fiji 103 I7
Vitória *Town* Brazil 29 M6
Vitória da Conquista *Town* Brazil 29 L5
Vitoria-Gasteiz *Town* Spain 59 I3
Vitsyebsk *Town* Belarus 71 H9 *see also* Vitebsk
Vittoria *Town* Sicily, Italy 61 F13
Vizianagaram *Town* India 87 J6
Vlaardingen *Town* Netherlands 53 D9
Vladikavkaz *Town* Russian Federation 73 C13
Vladimir *Town* Russian Federation 72 D8
Vladivostok *Town* Russian Federation 79 M7
Vlagtwedde *Town* Netherlands 52 G6
Vlijmen *Town* Netherlands 53 E9
Vlissingen *Town* Netherlands 53 C10
Vlorë *Town* Albania 65 E12
Vojvodina *Region* Serbia 64 F6
Volga *River* Russian Federation 73 D11
Volgodonsk *Town* Russian Federation 73 C11
Volgograd *Town* Russian Federation 73 D11
Volkhov *Town* Russian Federation 72 C7
Volnovakha *Town* Ukraine 69 L5
Vologda *Town* Russian Federation 72 D7
Vólos *Town* Greece 67 E10
Vol'sk *Town* Russian Federation 73 E10
Volta *River* Ghana 41 J8
Volta, Lake Ghana 41 I7
Volturno *River* Italy 61 F9
Volzhskiy *Town* Russian Federation 73 D11
Vóreioi Sporádes *see* Northern Sporades
Vorkuta *Town* Russian Federation 72 H5
Voronezh *Town* Russian Federation 73 C10
Vostok *Research station* Antarctica 110 F6
Voznesens'k *Town* Ukraine 69 I5
Vratsa *Town* Bulgaria 66 E6
Vrbas *Town* Serbia 64 F6
Vršac *Town* Serbia 64 G7
Vung Tau *Town* Vietnam 95 G11
Vyborg *Town* Russian Federation 72 C6

W

Waal *River* Netherlands 53 F9
Waco *Town* Texas, USA 17 M6
Wadayama *Town* Japan 93 D11
Waddān *Town* Libya 37 L5
Waddeneilanden *see* West Frisian Islands
Waddenzee *Sea* Netherlands 52 E6
Waddington, Mount *Mountain* British Colombia, Canada 4 G8
Wadi Halfa *Town* Sudan 38 E6
Wad Medani *Town* Sudan 38 E8
Wagga Wagga *Town* New South Wales, Australia 105 L8
Wāh *Town* Pakistan 86 G1
Wahai *Town* Indonesia 97 L7
Waiouru *Town* New Zealand 106 G7
Wairoa *Town* New Zealand 106 H7
Wakayama *Town* Japan 93 E12
Wake Island *Dependent Territory* US, Pacific Ocean 109 I4
Wakkanai *Town* Japan 92 F4
Wałbrzych *Town* Poland 62 D8
Wales *Political Region* UK 51 F10
Wallachia *Cultural region* Romania 68 E7
Wallis & Futuna *Dependent Territory* France, Pacific Ocean 103 J6
Walvis Bay *Town* Namibia 44 E6

Wanaka *Town* New Zealand 107 C12
Wandel Sea Arctic Ocean 111 M7
Wanyuan *Town* China 90 H5
Wanzhou *Town* China 90 H6
Warangal *Town* India 87 I6
Warren *Town* Michigan, USA 13 L5
Warren *Town* Ohio, USA 13 L6
Warren *Town* Pennsylvania, USA 8 E6
Warri *Town* Nigeria 41 K8
Warsaw *Capital* Poland 62 F6
Warszawa *see* Warsaw
Warwick *Town* Rhode Island, USA 8 J6
Washington *State* USA 14 H2
Washington, D.C. *Capital* USA 8 G9
Waspam *Town* Nicaragua 21 I4
Waterbury *Town* Connecticut, USA 8 I6
Waterford *Town* Ireland 51 C10
Waterloo *Town* Iowa, USA 13 I5
Watertown *Town* New York, USA 8 G4
Watford *Town* England, UK 51 H11
Wau *Town* Southern Sudan 39 D9
Waukegan *Town* Illinois, USA 13 J5
Waukesha *Town* Wisconsin, USA 13 J5
Wavre *Town* Belgium 53 E11
Weddell Sea Antarctica 110 C4
Weifang *Town* China 91 K4
Weimar *Town* Germany 56 E7
Welkom *Town* South Africa 44 H7
Wellington *Capital* New Zealand 107 F9
Wells *Town* Nevada, USA 14 H5
Wellsford *Town* New Zealand 106 F5
Wels *Town* Austria 57 G10
Wenchi *Town* Ghana 41 I7
Wenshan *Town* China 90 G8
Wenxian *Town* China 89 J7
Wenzhou *Town* China 91 K6
Weser *River* Germany 56 D6
West Antarctica *Region* Antarctica 110 D6
West Bank *Disputed region* Near East 81 D11
West Cape *Coastal feature* New Zealand 107 A13
Westerland *Town* Germany 56 D4
Western Australia *State* Australia 104 G5
Western Dvina *River* W Europe 70 F7
West Frisian Islands *Island group* Netherlands 52 B5
Western Ghats *Mountain range* India 86 H6
Western Sahara *Disputed territory* 36 C6
Weston-super-Mare *Town* England, UK 51 F11
West Palm Beach *Town* Florida, USA 11 J8
West Siberian Plain Russian Federation 78 H5
West Virginia *State* USA 11 J2
Wetzlar *Town* Germany 56 D8
Wevok *Town* Alaska, USA 4 E3
Wexford *Town* Ireland 51 D10
Whakatane *Town* New Zealand 106 H6
Wheeler Peak *Mountain* New Mexico, USA 16 H3
Whitby *Town* England, UK 50 G8
Whitehorse *Town* Northwest Territories, Canada 4 F6
White Nile *River* Sudan/S Sudan 38 E8
White Sea Russian Federation 72 E5
White Volta *River* Ghana 41 I7
Whitney, Mount *Mountain* California, USA 14 G7
Wichita *Town* Kansas, USA 12 G8
Wichita Falls *Town* Texas, USA 17 L5
Wick *Town* Scotland, UK 50 F4
Wieliczka *Town* Poland 63 F9
Wien *see* Vienna
Wiener Neustadt *Town* Austria 57 H10
Wiesbaden *Town* Germany 56 C8
Wight, Isle of *Island* England, UK 51 G12
Wilcox *Town* Pennsylvania, USA 8 F6
Wilhelm, Mount *Mountain* Papua New Guinea 102 E5
Wilhelmshaven *Town* Germany 56 C5
Wilkes Barre *Town* Pennsylvania, USA 8 H6
Willard *Town* New Mexico, USA 16 H4
Willemstad *Capital* Curaçao 23 K8
Williston *Town* North Dakota, USA 12 E2
Wilmington *Town* Delaware, USA 8 H8
Wilmington *Town* North Carolina, USA 11 K4
Winchester *Town* England, UK 51 G11
Windhoek *Capital* Namibia 44 E6
Windsor *Town* Ontario, Canada 6 F8
Windward Islands *Island group* Caribbean Sea 23 P8
Windward Passage *Strait* Cuba/Haiti 22 H5
Winnipeg *Town* Manitoba, Canada 5 K9
Winnipeg, Lake Manitoba, Canada 5 J8
Winona *Town* Wisconsin, USA 13 I4
Winston Salem *Town* North Carolina, USA 11 J3
Winterthur *Town* Switzerland 57 D11
Wisconsin *State* USA 13 I4
Wismar *Town* Germany 56 E5
Wittstock *Town* Germany 56 F5
Włocławek *Town* Poland 62 F6
Wodzisław Śląski *Town* Poland 63 E9
Woking *Town* England, UK 51 H11
Wolfsberg *Town* Austria 57 H11
Wolfsburg *Town* Germany 56 E6
Wollongong *Town* New South Wales, Australia 105 M7
Wolverhampton *Town* England, UK 51 F10
Wŏnsan *Town* North Korea 91 M3
Woodburn *Town* Oregon, USA 14 F3
Woodruff *Town* Wisconsin, USA 13 J3
Woods, Lake of the Ontario, Canada 6 D6
Woodville *Town* New Zealand 106 G8
Worcester *Town* Massachusetts, USA 9 J5
Worcester *Town* England, UK 51 F10
Worms *Town* Germany 57 C9
Worthington *Town* South Dakota, USA 12 H5
Wrocław *Town* Poland 62 D8
Wuday'ah *Town* Saudi Arabia 83 D12
Wuhai *Town* China 89 J5
Wuhan *Town* China 91 J6
Wuhu *Town* China 91 K5
Wuliang Shan *Mountain range* China 90 F8
Wuppertal *Town* Germany 56 C7
Würzburg *Town* Germany 56 D8
Wuxi *Town* China 91 K5
Wyoming *State* USA 15 L4

X

Xaignabouli *Town* Laos 94 E7
Xai-Xai *Town* Mozambique 45 I6
Xalapa *Town* Mexico 19 L7
Xankändi *Town* Azerbaijan 77 M4
Xiamen *Town* China 91 K8
Xi'an *Town* China 90 H5
Xiangfang *Town* China 91 I5
Xiangtan *Town* China 91 I7
Xianyang *Town* China 90 H4
Xichang *Town* China 90 F6
Xilinhot *Town* China 89 K4
Xingu, Rio *River* Brazil 29 J3
Xingxi *Town* China 90 G7
Xingxingxia *Town* China 88 G5
Xining *Town* China 89 I6
Xinjiang *Administrative region* China 88 F5
Xinxiang *Town* China 91 J4
Xinyang *Town* China 91 J5
Xi Ujimqin Qi *Town* China 89 K3
Xixon *see* Gijon
Xuzhou *Town* China 91 J5

Y

Ya'an *Town* China 90 G6
Yablis *Town* Nicaragua 21 J4
Yafran *Town* Libya 37 K4
Yakeshi *Town* China 89 L2
Yakima *Town* Washington, USA 14 G2
Yakutsk *Town* Russian Federation 79 K5
Yalova *Town* Turkey 76 D4
Yalta *Town* Ukraine 69 K7
Yamaguchi *Town* Japan 93 C12
Yambol *Town* Bulgaria 66 G6
Yamoussoukro *Capital* Côte d'Ivoire 40 H7
Yan'an *Town* China 90 H4
Yanbu'al Baḥr *Town* Saudi Arabia 83 A9
Yangiyo'l *Town* Uzbekistan 85 J3
Yangon *Town* Myanmar 94 B8
Yangtze *River* China 90 G7
Yangzhou *Town* China 91 K5
Yanji *Town* China 89 N3
Yankton *Town* Iowa, USA 12 G5
Yantai *Town* China 91 K3
Yaoundé *Capital* Cameroon 42 C8
Yaroslavl' *Town* Russian Federation 72 D8
Yatsushiro *Town* Japan 93 B14
Yaviza *Town* Panama 21 O8
Yazd *Town* Iran 82 F7
Ye *Town* Myanmar 95 C9
Yecheng *Town* China 88 D5
Yefremov *Town* Russian Federation 73 C9
Yekaterinburg *Town* Russian Federation 78 F5
Yelets *Town* Russian Federation 73 C9
Yellowknife *Town* Northwest Territories, Canada 4 H6
Yellow River *River* China 91 I4
Yellow Sea Pacifc Ocean 91 L4
Yellowstone River Montana, USA 15 K3
Yel'sk *Town* Belarus 71 E12
Yemen *Country* 83 D12
Yemva *Town* Russian Federation 72 F7
Yenakiyeve *Town* Ukraine 69 M5
Yenierenköy *see* Agialoúsa
Yenisey *River* Russian Federation 78 H5
Yeosu *Town* South Korea 91 M4
Yerevan *Capital* Armenia 77 L4
Yevlax *Town* Azerbaijan 77 M3
Yevpatoriya *Town* Ukraine 69 J7
Yichang *Town* China 91 I6
Yichun *Town* China 89 M2
Yildizeli *Town* Turkey 76 H4
Yinchuan *Town* China 89 J5
Yining *Town* China 88 E4
Yogyakarta *Town* Indonesia 96 G8
Yokohama *Town* Japan 93 G10
Yokote *Town* Japan 92 G8
Yonago *Town* Japan 93 D11
Yong'an *Town* China 91 K7
Yongzhou *Town* China 91 I7
Yonkers *Town* New York, USA 9 I6
York *Town* England, UK 51 G8
York *Town* Pennsylvania, USA 9 G8
York, Cape *Coastal feature* Australia 105 K1
Yoro *Town* Honduras 20 G4
Yosemite National Park California, USA 14 G6
Yoshkar-Ola *Town* Russian Federation 73 E9
Youngstown *Town* Ohio, USA 13 M6
Yreka *Town* California, USA 14 F4
Yucatán Channel Mexico 19 O6
Yucatán Peninsula Mexico 19 O7
Yuci *Town* China 91 I4
Yueyang *Town* China 91 I6
Yukhavichy *Town* Belarus 70 G8
Yukon River Alaska/Yukon Territory 4 E4
Yukon *Province* Canada 4 F5
Yulin *Town* China 90 H8
Yuma *Town* Arizona, USA 16 D5
Yunnan *Administrative region* China 90 F7
Yushu *Town* Qinghai, China 88 H7
Yuxi *Town* China 90 F7
Yuzhno-Sakhalinsk *Town* Russian Federation 79 M6

Z

Zaanstad *Town* Netherlands 52 E8
Zabaykal'sk *Town* Russian Federation 78 K7
Zacapa *Town* Guatemala 20 E4
Zacatecas *Town* Mexico 19 I6
Zacatepec *Town* Mexico 19 K8
Zadar *Town* Croatia 64 B7
Zafra *Town* Spain 58 G7
Zagreb *Capital* Croatia 64 C6
Zagros Mountains *Mountain range* Iran 82 E7
Zāhedān *Town* Iran 82 H7
Záhony *Town* Hungary 63 H10
Zaječar *Town* Serbia 65 H9
Zalaegerszeg *Town* Hungary 63 D12
Zalău *Town* Romania 68 E5
Ẓalim *Town* Saudi Arabia 83 C10
Zambezi *River* Southern Africa 45 J4
Zambia *Country* 44 G4
Zamboanga *Town* Philippines 97 J4
Zamora *Town* Spain 58 G4
Zamość *Town* Poland 62 H8
Zanjān *Town* Iran 82 E5
Zanzibar *Town* Tanzania 39 G12
Zanzibar *Island* Tanzania 39 G13
Zaozhuang *Town* China 91 K4
Zapadnaya Dvina *Town* Russian Federation 2 B8
Zapala *Town* Argentina 31 D10
Zapolyarnyy *Town* Russian Federation 72 D4
Zaporizhzhya *Town* Ukraine 69 K5
Zaqatala *Town* Azerbaijan 77 M3
Zaragoza *Town* Spain 59 K4
Zaranj *Town* Afghanistan 84 G8
Zárate *Town* Argentina 30 G8
Zaria *Town* Nigeria 41 L6
Zavidovići *Town* Bosnia & Herzegovina 64 E8
Zawiercie *Town* Poland 62 F8
Zawīlah *Town* Libya 37 L6
Zeebrugge *Town* Belgium 53 C10
Zeist *Town* Netherlands 52 E8
Zelenoborskiy *Town* Russian Federation 72 D5
Zelenograd *Town* Russian Federation 72 C8
Zemun *Town* Serbia 64 G7
Zenica *Town* Bosnia & Herzegovina 64 D8
Zgierz *Town* Poland 62 E7
Zhanaozen *Town* Kazakhstan 78 D6
Zhangjiakou *Town* China 91 J3
Zhangzhou *Town* China 91 K8
Zhanjiang *Town* China 91 I9
Zhaoqing *Town* China 91 I8
Zhejiang *Administrative region* China 91 K6
Zheleznogorsk *Town* Russian Federation 73 B9
Zhengzhou *Town* China 91 I4
Zhezkazgan *Town* Kazakhstan 78 F7
Zhlobin *Town* Belarus 71 F11
Zhoatong *Town* China 90 G7
Zhodzina *Town* Belarus 71 F9
Zhongdian *Town* China 90 F6
Zhosaly *Town* Kazakhstan 78 E7
Zhovti Vody *Town* Ukraine 69 J4
Zhytomyr *Town* Ukraine 68 H3
Zibo *Town* China 91 K4
Zielona Góra *Town* Poland 62 C7
Zigong *Town* China 90 G6
Ziguinchor *Town* Senegal 40 E6
Žilina *Town* Slovakia 63 E9
Zimbabwe *Country* 44 H5
Zimovniki *Town* Russian Federation 73 C11
Zinder *Town* Niger 41 L5
Zipaquira *Town* Colombia 26 C6
Zlín *Town* Czechia 63 D9
Zoetermeer *Town* Netherlands 52 E8
Zolochiv *Town* Ukraine 68 F3
Zomba *Town* Malawi 45 J4
Zonguldak *Town* Turkey 76 E3
Żory *Town* Poland 63 E9
Zouar *Town* Chad 42 E4
Zrenjanin *Town* Serbia 64 G7
Zug *Town* Switzerland 57 D11
Zuidhorn *Town* Netherlands 52 G6
Zula *Town* Eritrea 38 G7
Zunyi *Town* China 90 H7
Županja *Town* Croatia 64 E7
Zürich *Town* Switzerland 57 D11
Zutphen *Town* Netherlands 52 G8
Zuwārah *Town* Libya 37 J4
Zvishavane *Town* Zimbabwe 45 I5
Zwedru *Town* Liberia 40 G8
Zwettl *Town* Austria 57 H10
Zwickau *Town* Germany 56 F8
Zwolle *Town* Netherlands 52 F7
Zyryanovsk *Town* Kazakhstan 78 H7

Index

Acknowledgments

For the 2017 edition, Dorling Kindersley would like to thank:

Bharti Bedi, Priyanka Kharbanda, and Antara Raghavan for editorial assistance; Heena Sharma for design assistance; Shanker Prasad for CTS assistance; Deepak Negi for picture research assistance; and Simon Mumford for the Earth globe images.

Internet usage data has been sourced from Internet World Stats, www.internetworldstats.com

The publisher would like to thank the following for their kind permission to reproduce their photographs: (Key: a-above; b-below/bottom; c-centre; f-far; l-left; r-right; t-top)

i Corbis: B.S.P.I. (bl); Steve Rayner (fbr). **Photoshot:** World Pictures (fbl, br). **ii Corbis:** Stephanie Maze (br). **Getty Images:** Jim Cummins / Stone (cra). **Science Photo Library:** 1995 Worldsat International, and J. Knighton (l). **iii Corbis:** Sergio Pitamitz (br). **Robert Harding Picture Library:** Robert Frerck (cl); Frans Lemmens (cra). **v Corbis:** Frans Lanting (clb); Ludovic Maisant (bl); Werner H. Mueller (cla/dunes). **vi Corbis:** Howard Davies (br). **viii Corbis:** Jacky Naegelen / Reuters (cra). **2 Corbis:** Alan Schein Photography (bl). **Robert Harding Picture Library:** John Miller (cra). **3 Corbis:** Peter M. Wilson (clb). **Science Photo Library:** 1995 Worldsat International, and J. Knighton (globe). **4 Alaska Stock:** (clb). **Corbis:** Gunter Marx Photography (bl); Charles O'Rear (tr). **Photoshot:** World Pictures (bc). **5 Corbis:** Staffan Widstrand (tc); Peter M. Wilson (br/mountain background). **NHPA / Photoshot:** T. Kitchin and V. Hurst (cra); Andy Rouse (fbr/bear). **6 Cephas Picture Library:** Fred R. Palmer (tr). **Corbis:** Benjamin Rondel (bl/Toronto). Press Association Images: Tony Marshall / EMPICS Sport; (bc). **7 Corbis:** William A. Bake (br); Richard J. Nowitz (cra). **Photoshot:** Egmont Strigl / imagebroker; (tr); World Pictures (tl). **8 Pictures Colour Library:** (ca). **Robert Harding Picture Library:** Stuart Pearce / Age Fotostock (bl). **9 Corbis:** Alan Schein Photography (br); Paul Barton (crb); Ralf-Finn Hestoft (tl); Farrell Grehan (c). **Robert Harding Picture Library:** Andy Caulfield / Panoramic Images (tr). **10 Corbis:** Owen Franken (crb). **Getty Images:** Andy Sacks (cla). **Redferns:** (bc). **Robert Harding Picture Library:** Peter Lilja / Age Fotostock (br). **11 Corbis:** Tony Arruza (br); Flip Schulke (cb). **Getty Images:** Matthew Stockman (tc). **12 Corbis:** Blaine Harrington III (cl/buffalo). **Dorling Kindersley:** American Museum of Natural History, London (fcl). **Rex Features:** Sipa Press (bc). **Robert Harding Picture Library:** Sergio Pitamitz (bl). **13 Corbis:** Philip Gould (br); Julie Habel (tl). **Getty Images:** Jim Cummins / Stone (crb). **14 Robert Harding Picture Library:** Liane Cary / age fotostock (bl); Melissa Farlow / National Geographic (tc). **15 Corbis:** Dean Conger (ca); Jong Beom Kim / TongRo (clb); Lester Lefkowitz (br). **Rex Features:** Sipa Press (bc). **Robert Harding Picture Library:** Louise Murray (tr). **Science Photo Library:** George Bernard (bl). **16 Corbis:** B.S.P.I. (br); Richard Ransier (ftr). **Dorling Kindersley:** Hopi Learning Centre (br/doll). **Getty Images:** Eric Schnakenberg / Photographer's Choice (tr). **Robert Harding Picture Library:** Tony Gervis (bl). **17 NASA:** (tr). **Robert Harding Picture Library:** Walter Rawlings (bl). **18 Corbis:** Keith Dannemiller (tr); Danny Lehman (br). **Robert Harding Picture Library:** Robert Frerck / Odyssey / Chicago (cl). **Still Pictures:** Julio Etchart (bl). **19 Corbis:** Macduff Everton (tr); Tim Thompson (tc). **Getty Images:** Bruce Stoddard / Stone (ftl). 20 Corbis: Stephen Frink (cl); Sergio Pitamitz (crb). **Eye Ubiquitous / Hutchison:** Robert Francis (br). Photoshot: World Pictures (bl). **21 Corbis:** Poisson d'avril / Photocuisine (ca); Arvind Garg (tl). **Eye Ubiquitous / Hutchison:** Robert Francis (clb). **Photoshot:** World Pictures / Intervision (tr). **Robert Harding Picture Library:** Jose Enrique Molina / age fotostock (crb). **22 Corbis:** Bill Gentile (cl). **Photoshot:** Martin Engelmann (bl). **23 Corbis:** Wolfgang Kaehler (cb); Peter Turnley (clb). **Eye Ubiquitous / Hutchison:** John Fuller (tl). **Photoshot:** World Pictures (ca). **Robert Harding Picture Library:** John Miller (tr). **24 Robert Harding Picture Library:** P. Narayan / Age Fotostock (cra). **South American Pictures:** Jason Howe (b). **25 Photoshot:** World Pictures (clb). **Science Photo Library:** 1995, Worldsat International and J. Knighton (globe). **26 Corbis:** Pablo Corral V (cla). **Photoshot:** World Pictures (cr). **South American Pictures:** (tl). **27 Dorling Kindersley:** British Museum (br). **Eye Ubiquitous / Hutchison:** H. Jelliffee (tr); Paul Seheult (tl); Eric Lawrie (cra). **Photoshot:** World Pictures (bl). **Robert Harding Picture Library:** Gavin Hellier (cr). **28 Corbis:** Yann Arthus-Bertrand (crb). **Eye Ubiquitous / Hutchison:** Dr Nigel Smith (br). **Robert Harding Picture Library:** (clb). **South American Pictures:** Jason Howe (bl). **29 Corbis:** Stephanie Maze (cra). **Photoshot:** (br). **Tomek Sierek:** (tr). **30 Corbis:** Tony Arruza (br). **Photoshot:** World Pictures (bc). **Robert Harding Picture Library:** Bildagentur Schuster / Gluske (ca); Ken Welsh / Age Fotostock (tl). **31 Corbis:** Fulvio Roiter (tr). **Photoshot:** World Pictures (cla). **Robert Harding Picture Library:** Victor Englebert (bl); P. Narayan / Age Fotostock (tl). **South American Pictures:** (br). **32 Corbis:** Carlos Dominguez (crb); Wolfgang Kaehler (br). **NHPA / Photoshot:** B. & C. Alexander (bl). **Robert Harding Picture Library:** (tr); Roy Rainford (cra); Adam Woolfitt (clb). **33 Corbis:** George D. Lepp (br); Hans Strand (tr). **35 Science Photo Library:** Tom Van Sant, Geosphere Project / Planetary Visions (t). **36 Eye Ubiquitous / Hutchison:** Mary Jelliffee (br). **Photoshot:** World Pictures (tr, cl). **37 Corbis:** Benjamin Lowy (b). **Dorling Kindersley:** British Museum (tc). **Getty Images:** Frans Lemmens / The Image Bank (crb). **Photoshot:** World Pictures (tr). **Robert Harding Picture Library:** T.D. Winter (tl). **38 Corbis:** Michael Hanson / National Geographic Society (tr). **Photoshot:** World Pictures (br). **Robert Harding Picture Library:** Nakamura (ca). **39 Corbis:** Karl Ammann (br). **Eye Ubiquitous / Hutchison:** (tr); Jeremy Horner (bl); Sarah Errington (bc). **40 Dorling Kindersley:** Barnabas Kindersley (bl). **Panos Pictures:** Teun Voeten; (br/diamond). **Robert Harding Picture Library:** J. Lightfoot (cla). **41 Corbis:** Charles & Josette Lenars (bl). **Eye Ubiquitous / Hutchison:** Crispin Hughes (cr, br). **Panos Pictures:** Clive Shirley (tl). **42 Corbis:** Skip Brown / National Geographic Society (tl). **Dorling Kindersley:** Powell Cotton Museum (bc). **Eye Ubiquitous / Hutchison:** Sarah Errington (br). **Photoshot:** World Pictures (tc). **43 Dorling Kindersley:** Natural History Museum, London (cra/copper). **Eye Ubiquitous / Hutchison:** (c); Trevor Page (br). **Getty Images:** Nicolas Cotto / AFP (tr); Per-Anders Pettersson / The Image Bank (bl). **44 Corbis:** Anthony Bannister (cla). **Photoshot:** (bl). **Robert Harding Picture Library:** Alain Evrard (bc). **45 Alamy Images:** AfriPics.com (br/buffalo background). **Corbis:** Peter Turnley (bl). **Dreamstime.com:** Eric Isselée (fbr/lion). **Eye Ubiquitous / Hutchison:** Sarah Errington (tl); Liba Taylor (tr); Crispin Hughes (tc). **Robert Harding Picture Library:** Chris Mattison / age fotostock (crb/lemur). **47 Photoshot:** World Pictures (cr). **Science Photo Library:** Tom Van Sant, Geosphere Project / Planetary Visions (t). **48 Corbis:** Charles & Josette Lenars (bl). **Photoshot:** Paul Thompson / World Pictures (br). **Robert Harding Picture Library:** Kim Hart (ftl). **49 Corbis:** Jean-Pierre Amet / Sygma (tl); Dave Bartruff (tr); Stephanie Maze (cla). **TopFoto.co.uk:** Francis Dean / Imageworks (crb). **50 Corbis:** David Paterson / WildCountry (tr); Michael St. Maur Sheil (br). **Pictures Colour Library:** (bc). **Robert Harding Picture Library:** Eye Ubiquitous (tc). **51 Corbis:** Tommy Hindley / NewSport (bc). **Eye Ubiquitous / Hutchison:** Philp Wolmouth (br). **Pictures Colour Library:** Charles Bowman (cr). **Robert Harding Picture Library:** Mark Mawson / Robert Harding World Imagery (tr). **52 Corbis:** Owen Franken (br). **Photoshot:** World Pictures (bc). **Robert Harding Picture Library:** Adam Woolfitt (tl). **53 Corbis:** Dave Bartruff (br); Ray Juno (br); Owen Franken (tr, tl). **54 Corbis:** G. Bowater (cb); Roger Ressmeyer (ftl). **Photoshot:** (tl). **55 Corbis:** Pierre Perrin / Sygma (bl); Kim Sayer (br); Mike Powell (cra). **Photoshot:** Carol Pucci / Seattle Times / MCT (tl). **56 Corbis:** Arnd Wiegmann / akw / Reuters (tl). **Getty Images:** Michael Rosenfeld (bc). **Masterfile:** Didier Dorval (tr). **Rex Features:** Sipa Press (br). **57 Corbis:** Dominic Ebenbichler / Reuters (cr). **Getty Images:** Sylvain Grandadam (tr); Jess Stock (br). **58 Corbis:** Morton Beebe (bl). **Dreamstime.com:** Photooiasson (Álvaro Germán Vilela) (clb). **Robert Harding Picture Library:** Jesus Nicolas Sanchez / age fotostock (cla). **59 Corbis:** Patrick Ward (br). **Getty Images:** AFP (tr). **Panos Pictures:** David Constantine (cr). **Pictures Colour Library:** © FMGB Guggenheim Bilbao Museoa. Photo by Charles Bowman. All rights reserved. Total or partial reproduction is prohibited. (tl). **Robert Harding Picture Library:** Robert Frerck (bl). **60 Corbis:** Jörg Carstensen / DPA (cl). **Rex Features:** Enrica Scalfari (tr). **Robert Harding Picture Library:** R. Richardson (br). **61 Art Directors & TRIP:** (cra). **Eye Ubiquitous / Hutchison:** Trevor Page (bc). **Photoshot:** World Pictures (r). **Pictures Colour Library:** (clb). **62 Dreamstime.com:** Taratorki (Ewa Rejmer) (tr). **Panos Pictures:** David Constantine (cla). **Robert Harding Picture Library:** (tl). **63 Eye Ubiquitous / Hutchison:** Liba Taylor (cb). **Photoshot:** Rick Strange / World Pictures (tl); World Pictures (tr, br). **64 Eye Ubiquitous / Hutchison:** (ca). **Press Association Images:** Tony Marshall (bc). **Photoshot:** World Pictures (tl). **65 Corbis:** John Heseltine (cb). **Eye Ubiquitous / Hutchison:** David Watson (br). **Robert Harding Picture Library:** G. R. Richardson (tr); Phil Robinson (bl). **66 Corbis:** Marco Cristofori / Robert Harding World Imagery (tl). **Eye Ubiquitous / Hutchison:** Melanie Friend (crb, br). **Robert Harding Picture Library:** (tr). **67 Corbis:** Dallas & John Heaton / Free Agents Limited (cb); Clay Perry (tl). **Photoshot:** Lorraine Nicol / World Pictures (bl); World Pictures (tr); World Pictures / Mauritius Images (br). **68 Art Directors & TRIP:** P. Mercea (br). **Eye Ubiquitous / Hutchison:** Nick Haslam (clb). **Photoshot:** World Pictures (bl). **Pictures Colour Library:** (cla). **69 Art Directors & TRIP:** D. Mossienko (tr); N.& J. Wiseman (cr). **Corbis:** Barry Lewis (bl). **Eye Ubiquitous / Hutchison:** Liba Taylor (br). **70 Art Directors & TRIP:** T. Noorits (tl). **Robert Harding Picture Library:** Angelo Cavalli (bc). **71 Corbis:** Serge Attal / Sygma (bl); Dimitri Iundt / TempSport (tr); Niall Benvie (fcra); Nik Wheeler (tl); Staffan Widstrand (bc). **Photoshot:** Paul Thompson / World Pictures (br). **72 Corbis:** Robbie Jack (bc); Steve Rayner (tr). **Photoshot:** World Pictures (cla). **73 Art Directors & TRIP:** D. Iusupov (ca). **Corbis:** Gavin Hellier / Robert Harding World Imagery (br). **Dorling Kindersley:** Pitt Rivers Museum (tc). **Eye Ubiquitous / Hutchison:** Victoria Ivleva-Yorke (tr); Liba Taylor (bl, tl). **75 Science Photo Library:** Tom Van Sant / Geosphere Project / Planetary Visions (t). **76 Corbis:** Dave G. Houser (br); Lawrence Manning (cl); Adam Woolfitt (tr). **Photoshot:** Adina Amsel / World Pictures (bl). **77 Corbis:** Arne Hodalic (bl); David Turnley (tr); Nik Wheeler (br). **78 Corbis:** Peter Turnley (bc). **Eye Ubiquitous / Hutchison:** Sarah Errington (bl). **79 Alamy Images:** Arcticphoto (tr). **Corbis:** Wolfgang Kaehler (bl); Gregor Schmid (crb). **Pictures Colour Library:** (cr). **Robert Harding Picture Library:** Morales (br). **80 Corbis:** David Turnley (cla). **Photoshot:** José Nicolas / Hemis.fr / World Pictures (cb); Rick Strange / World Pictures (br); World Pictures (fcla). **81 Corbis:** Christine Osborne (fcrb/police officer). **Eye Ubiquitous / Hutchison:** Bernard Gerard (bl); James Henderson (tr). **Photoshot:** Jonathan Carlile / Imagebrokers (tl). **Robert Harding Picture Library:** Michael Short (br/landscape). **82 Dorling Kindersley:** British Library (c). **Eye Ubiquitous / Hutchison:** Bernard Gerard (b). **Getty Images:** Bruno Morandi (tc). **Rex Features:** Stuart Clarke (tl). **83 Dorling Kindersley:** Barnabas Kindersley (br). **Eye Ubiquitous / Hutchison:** John Nowell (crb). **Robert Harding Picture Library:** Mohamed Amin (bl); Walter Bibikow (tl). **84 Corbis:** S. Sabawoon (bl). **Getty Images:** Shah Marai / AFP (cb). **85 Corbis:** David Turnley (cr); Nevada Wier (cb, tr/mountains, tr). **Robert Harding Picture Library:** Ivan Vdovin (br). **86 Corbis:** Keren Su (br). **Eye Ubiquitous / Hutchison:** Sarah Errington (clb). **Getty Images:** Martin Puddy (cl). **87 Alamy Images:** Tibor Bognar (tr). **Eye Ubiquitous / Hutchison:** Horner (bl). **Getty Images:** Indranil Mukherjee / AFP (crb). **Robert Harding Picture Library:** David Beatty (tl); Frans Lemmens (clb). **88 Eye Ubiquitous / Hutchison:** Sarah Murray (b); Stephen Pem (cla). **88-89 Robert Harding Picture Library:** Philippe Michel (tc). **89 Eye Ubiquitous / Hutchison:** Melanie Friend (bl); Stephen Pern (tr). **Photoshot:** Rudi Pigneter (clb). **Robert Harding Picture Library:** G. Hellier (br); Doug Traverso (cr). **90 Corbis:** Douglas Peebles (tr). **Eye Ubiquitous / Hutchison:** Melanie Friend (cb); Jeremy Horner (bl). **Photoshot:** World Pictures (cla). **91 Corbis:** Michael S. Yamashita (bc). **Eye Ubiquitous / Hutchison:** Trevor Page (tl); Christine Pemberton (br). **Getty Images:** Kim Jae-Hwan / AFP (cra). **Photoshot:** World Pictures (crb). **92 Corbis:** Robert Holmes (tl). **Getty Images:** Paul Chesley / Stone (cl). **Photoshot:** World Pictures (br). **Pictures Colour Library:** (tr). **93 Corbis:** Michael S. Yamashita (bl). **Eye Ubiquitous / Hutchison:** Jon Burbank (tl); N. Haslam (clb). **Getty Images:** Panoramic Images (tr). **Robert Harding Picture Library:** Gavin Hellier (ca). **94 Corbis:** (cla). **Eye Ubiquitous / Hutchison:** Rene Giudicelli (tl). **Photoshot:** (tc); World Pictures (tr). **95 Eye Ubiquitous / Hutchison:** Norman Froggatt (cr). **Photoshot:** Stuart Pearce / World Pictures (br). **Robert Harding Picture Library:** (clb); Alain Evrard (tr). **96 Corbis:** (cl); Tom Brakefield (tr). **Eye Ubiquitous / Hutchison:** John Halt (br); Juliet Highet (bl). **Rex Features:** Tim Rooke (cra). **97 Corbis:** Dean Conger (br). **Eye Ubiquitous / Hutchison:** Michael Macintyre (ca); Dr Nigel Smith (cr). **Rex Features:** Sipa Press (tr). **98 Eye Ubiquitous / Hutchison:** Isabella Tree (tr). **Photoshot:** Josef Beck (cla); Hartmut Röder (cr); World Pictures (bl). **Still Pictures:** Roland Seitre (cb). **99 Corbis:** Theo Allofs (cra). **Photoshot:** Eye Ubiquitous / Hutchison (tr). **Rex Features:** Wilhemsen (br). **100 Corbis:** Sergio Pitamitz (bl); Keren Su (cra). **101 Corbis:** Wolfgang Kaehler (cl). **Getty Images:** Travel Pix (br). **Science Photo Library:** 1995, Worldsat International and J. Knighton (globe). **102 Corbis:** B.S.P.I. (tr). **Dorling Kindersley:** Mark O'Shea (bl). **Eye Ubiquitous / Hutchison:** Michael Macintyre (bc). **103 Corbis:** Wolfgang Kaehler (bl). Eye Ubiquitous / Hutchison: Nick Haslam (cra); Michael MacIntyre (tr). **Robert Harding Picture Library:** Upperhall Ltd (tl). **104 Corbis:** Penny Tweedie (cla). **Eye Ubiquitous / Hutchison:** N. Durrell McKenna (clb). **Getty Images:** Panoramic Images (cla/landscape background). **Press Association Images:** Phil Walter / EMPICS Sport (bc). **Robert Harding Picture Library:** Ken Gillham (tr). **105 Corbis:** Sergio Pitamitz (br). **Eye Ubiquitous / Hutchison:** Robert Francis (bl). **Getty Images:** Jeff Hunter / Photographer's Choice (cra). **Robert Harding Picture Library:** Neale Clark (crb). **106 Photoshot:** Rick Strange / World Pictures (crb); Paul Thompson / World Pictures (tl); World Pictures (br). **107 Photoshot:** Jeny McMillan (tr). **Rex Features:** Simon Runting (bl). **Robert Harding Picture Library:** Jeremy Bright (cb); Julia Thorne (tl). **108 Getty Images:** Andy Hall / Australian Defense Force (clb); Jeremy Woodhouse / Photodisc (cra). **Photolibrary:** Seiden Allan / Pacific Stock; ; (tr). **Robert Harding Picture Library:** Andoni Canela (bl). **Verena Tunnicliffe:** (crb). **109 Corbis:** Wolfgang Kaehler (tr); Stephanie Maze (br). **Robert Harding Picture Library:** Warren Finlay / International Stock (cra). **110 Eye Ubiquitous / Hutchison:** Isabella Tree (bl). **NASA:** (cla). **Robert Harding Picture Library:** Thorsten Milse (br); Geoff Renner (tr). **Still Pictures:** Marc Steinmetz / VISUM; (clb). **111 Corbis:** Composite Image / Alaska Stock LLC (tr); Tim Davis (br); Vince Streano (cla); Torleif Svensson (crb).

All other images © Dorling Kindersley

For further information see: www.dkimages.com